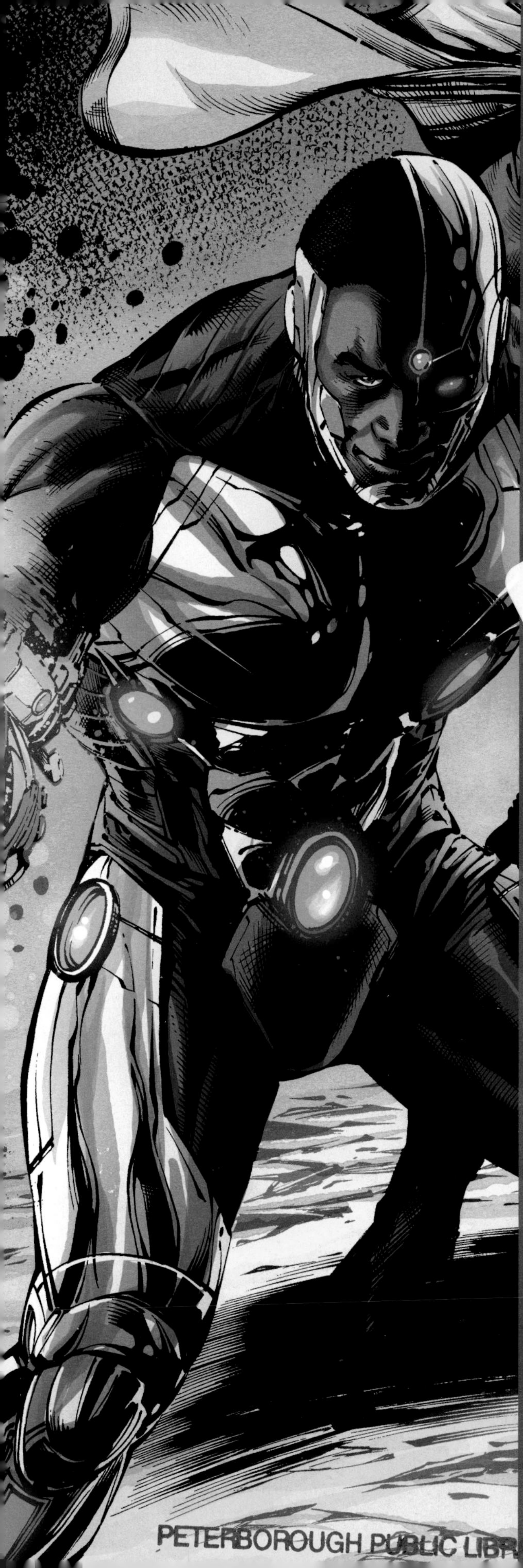

CYBORG

VOLUME 2

ENEMY OF THE STATE

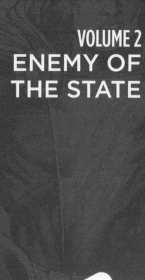

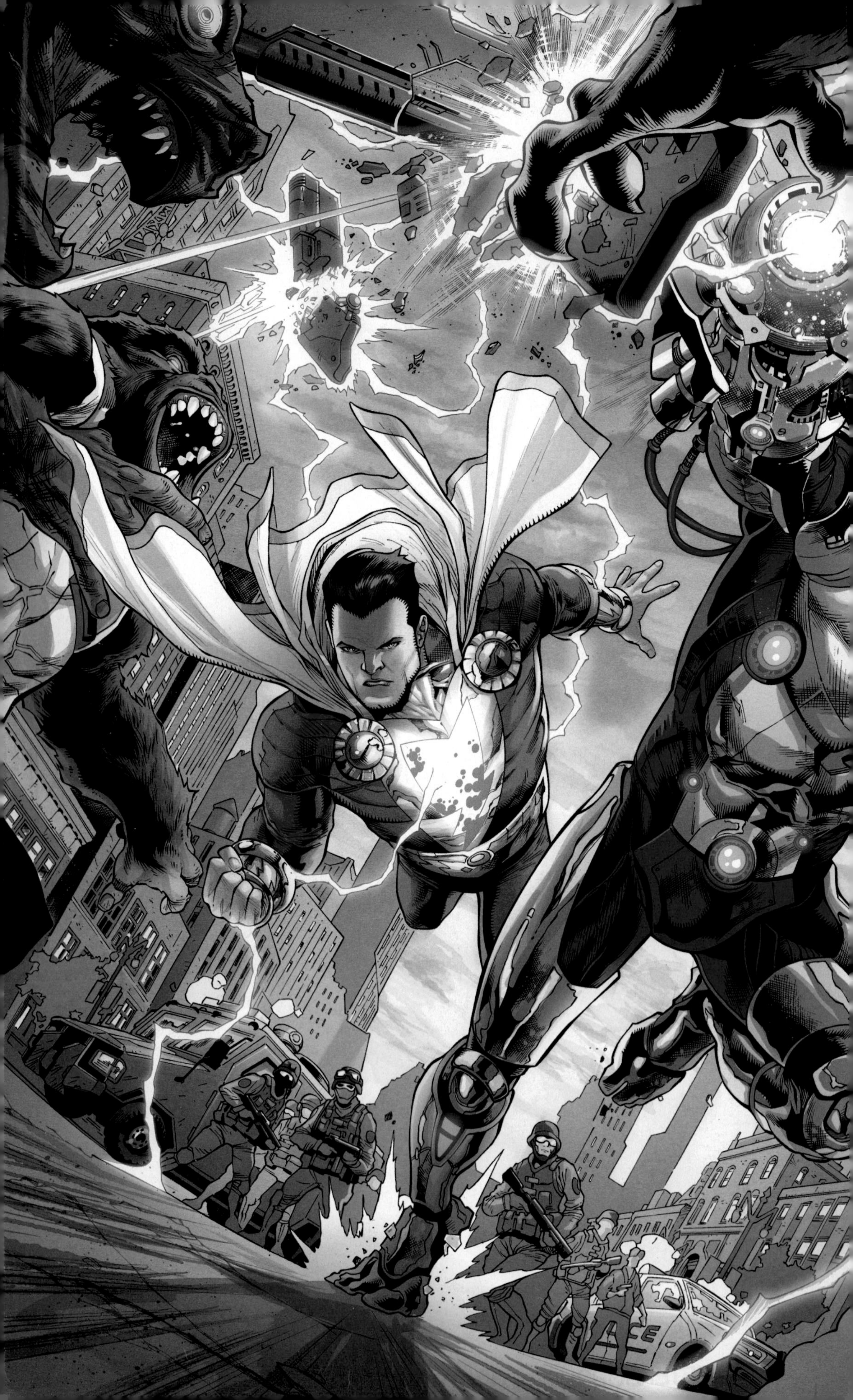

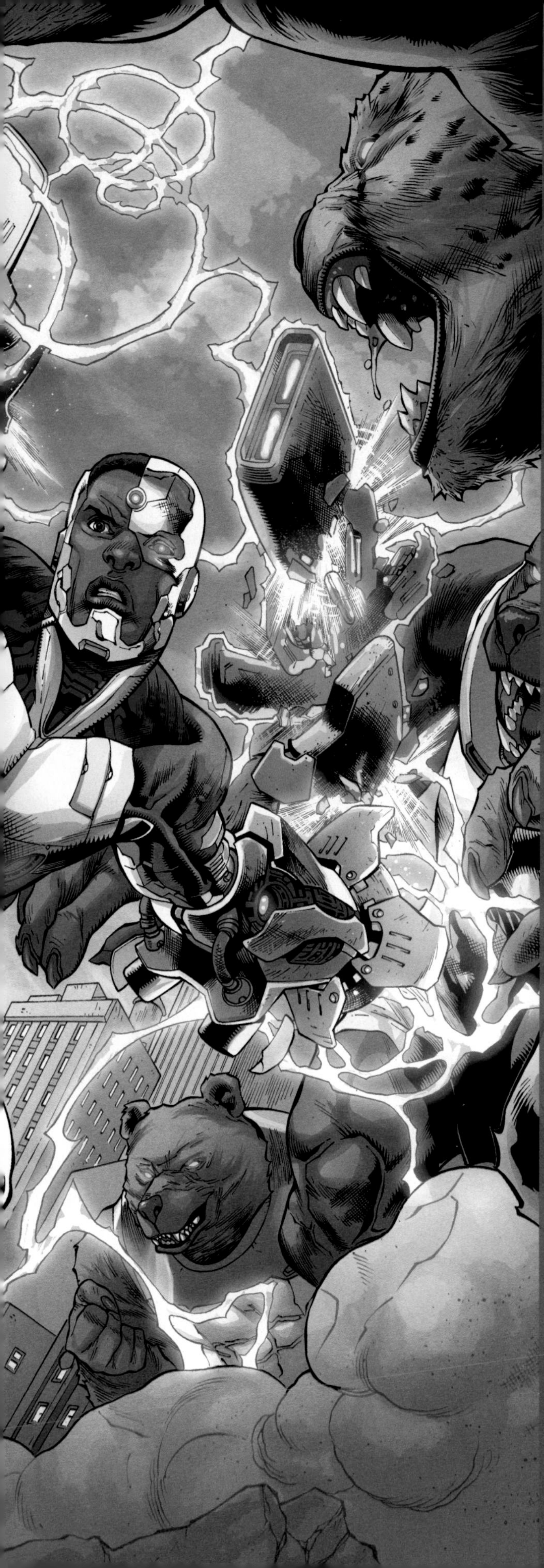

CYBORG

VOLUME 2
ENEMY OF THE STATE

WRITTEN BY
DAVID F. WALKER
MARV WOLFMAN

PENCILS BY
CLAUDE ST. AUBIN
FELIPE WATANABE
DANIEL HDR
JÚLIO FERREIRA

LAYOUTS BY
IVAN REIS

INKS BY
ANDY OWENS
OCLAIR ALBERT
JÚLIO FERREIRA

COLOR BY
ADRIANO LUCAS

LETTERS BY
ROB LEIGH
COREY BREEN

COLLECTION COVER ART BY
JOHN ROMITA JR.
with DANNY MIKI
& ALEX SINCLAIR

CYBORG CREATED BY
GEORGE PÉREZ and
MARV WOLFMAN

HARVEY RICHARDS Editor - Original Series
JEB WOODARD Group Editor - Collected Editions
PAUL SANTOS Editor - Collected Edition
STEVE COOK Design Director - Books
DAMIAN RYLAND Publication Design

BOB HARRAS Senior VP - Editor-in-Chief, DC Comics

DIANE NELSON President
DAN DiDIO Publisher
JIM LEE Publisher
GEOFF JOHNS President & Chief Creative Officer
AMIT DESAI Executive VP - Business & Marketing Strategy, Direct to Consumer & Global Franchise Management
SAM ADES Senior VP - Direct to Consumer
BOBBIE CHASE VP - Talent Development
MARK CHIARELLO Senior VP - Art, Design & Collected Editions
JOHN CUNNINGHAM Senior VP - Sales & Trade Marketing
ANNE DePIES Senior VP - Business Strategy, Finance & Administration
DON FALLETTI VP - Manufacturing Operations
LAWRENCE GANEM VP - Editorial Administration & Talent Relations
ALISON GILL Senior VP - Manufacturing & Operations
HANK KANALZ Senior VP - Editorial Strategy & Administration
JAY KOGAN VP - Legal Affairs
THOMAS LOFTUS VP - Business Affairs
JACK MAHAN VP - Business Affairs
NICK J. NAPOLITANO VP - Manufacturing Administration
EDDIE SCANNELL VP - Consumer Marketing
COURTNEY SIMMONS Senior VP - Publicity & Communications
JIM (SKI) SOKOLOWSKI VP - Comic Book Specialty Sales & Trade Marketing
NANCY SPEARS VP - Mass, Book, Digital Sales & Trade Marketing

CYBORG VOLUME 2: ENEMY OF THE STATE

DC Comics, 2900 West Alameda Ave., Burbank, CA 91505
Printed by LSC Communications, Salem, VA, USA. 10/28/16. First Printing.
ISBN: 978-1-4012-6531-1

Library of Congress Cataloging-in-Publication Data is available.

PEFC
PEFC/29-31-337
PEFC Certified
Printed on paper from sustainably managed forests, controlled sources
www.pefc.org

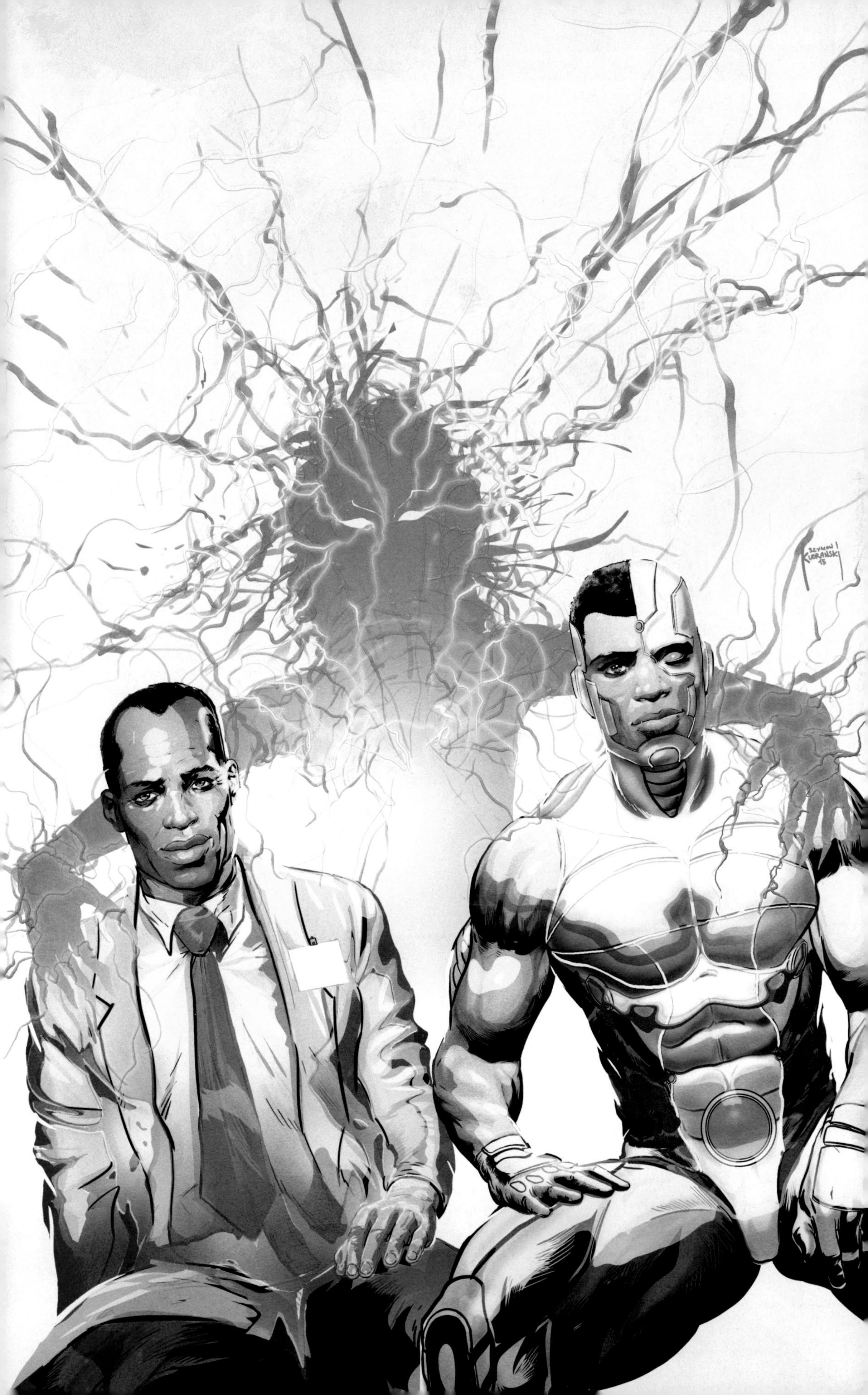

REUNION

DAVID F. WALKER writer **CLAUDE ST. AUBIN** penciller **ANDY OWENS** inker **SZYMON KUDRANSKI** cover

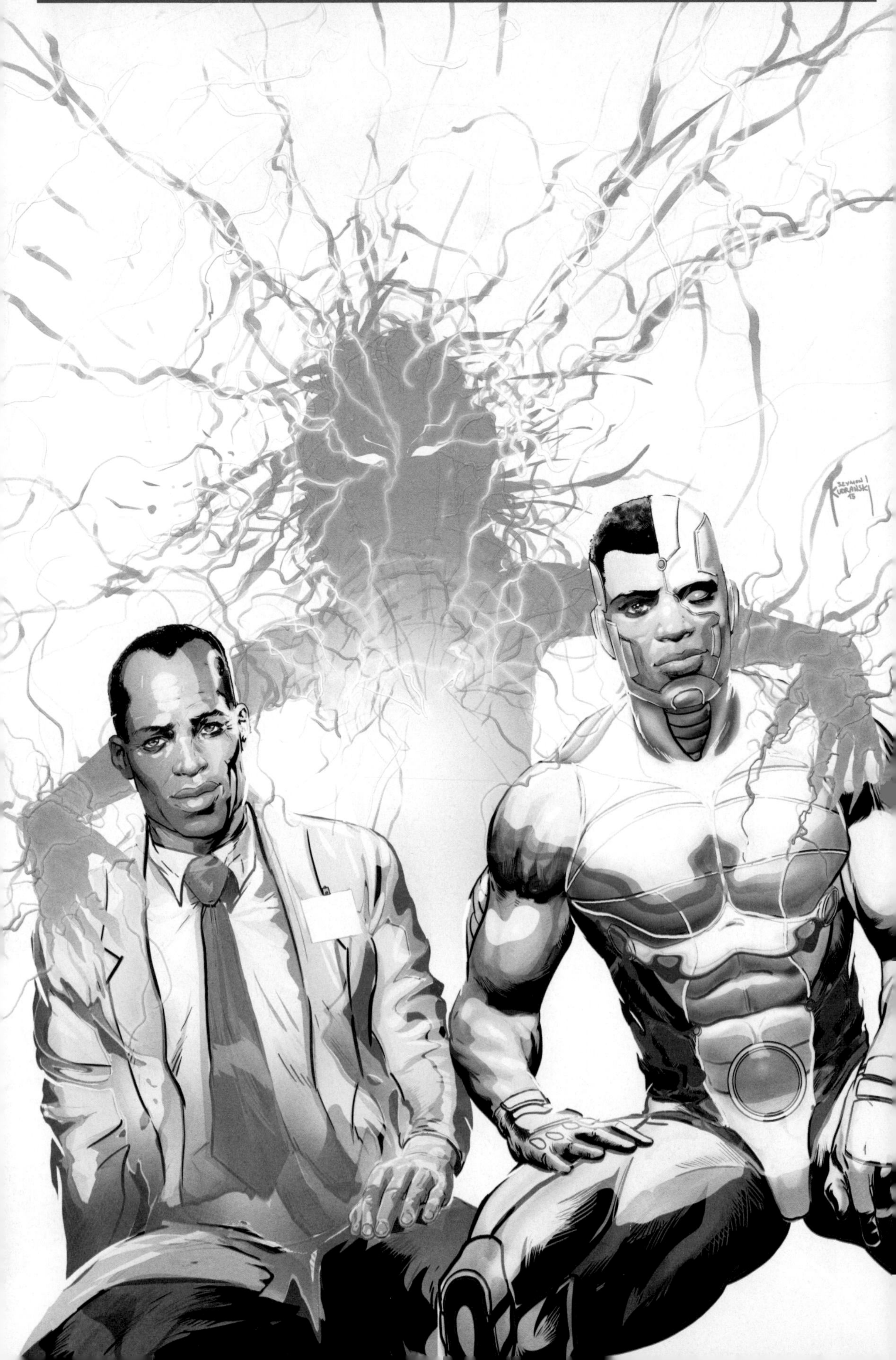

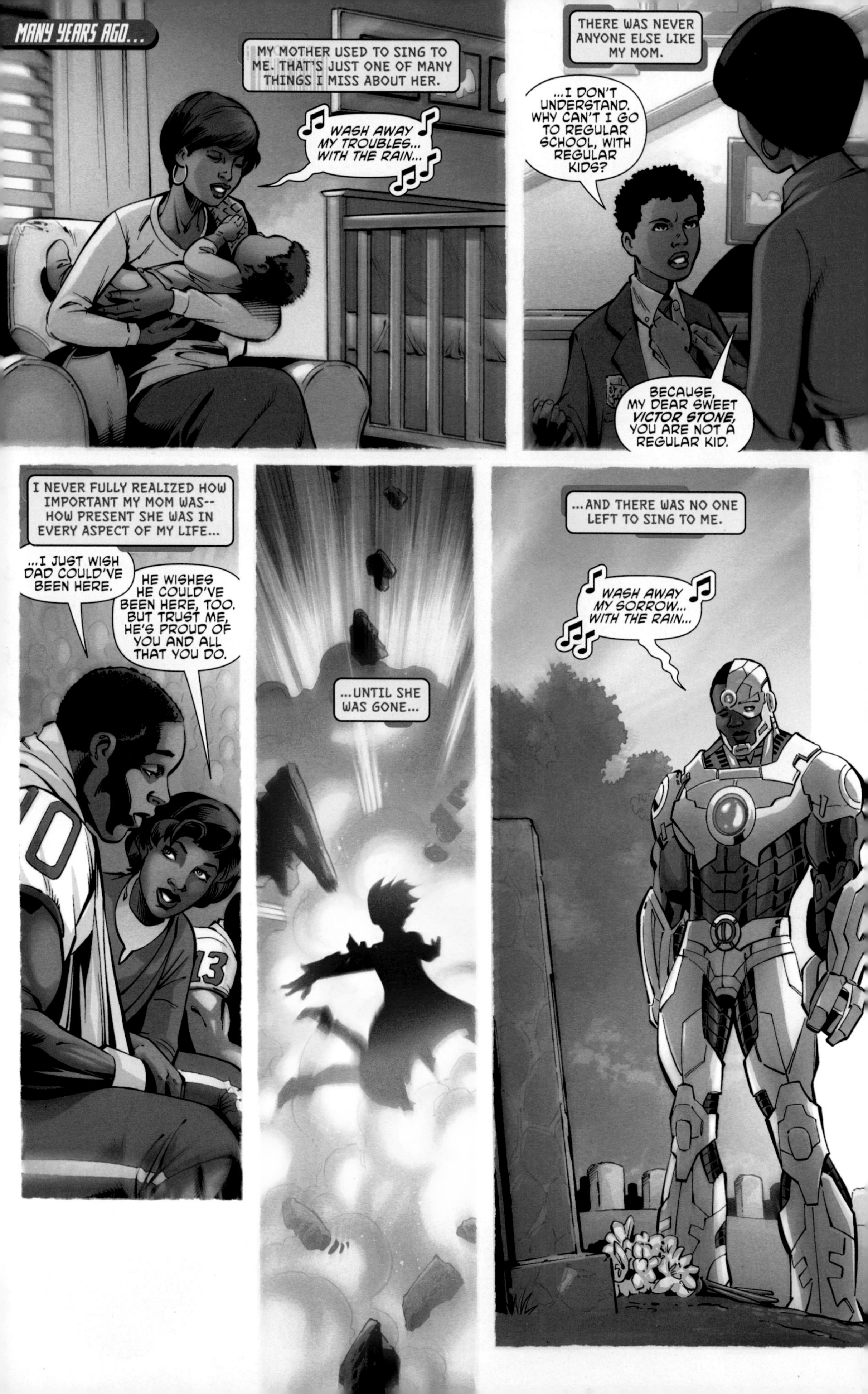
MANY YEARS AGO...
MY MOTHER USED TO SING TO ME. THAT'S JUST ONE OF MANY THINGS I MISS ABOUT HER.
WASH AWAY MY TROUBLES... WITH THE RAIN...
THERE WAS NEVER ANYONE ELSE LIKE MY MOM.
...I DON'T UNDERSTAND. WHY CAN'T I GO TO REGULAR SCHOOL, WITH REGULAR KIDS?
BECAUSE, MY DEAR SWEET VICTOR STONE, YOU ARE NOT A REGULAR KID.
I NEVER FULLY REALIZED HOW IMPORTANT MY MOM WAS-- HOW PRESENT SHE WAS IN EVERY ASPECT OF MY LIFE...
...I JUST WISH DAD COULD'VE BEEN HERE.
HE WISHES HE COULD'VE BEEN HERE, TOO. BUT TRUST ME, HE'S PROUD OF YOU AND ALL THAT YOU DO.
...UNTIL SHE WAS GONE...
...AND THERE WAS NO ONE LEFT TO SING TO ME.
WASH AWAY MY SORROW... WITH THE RAIN...

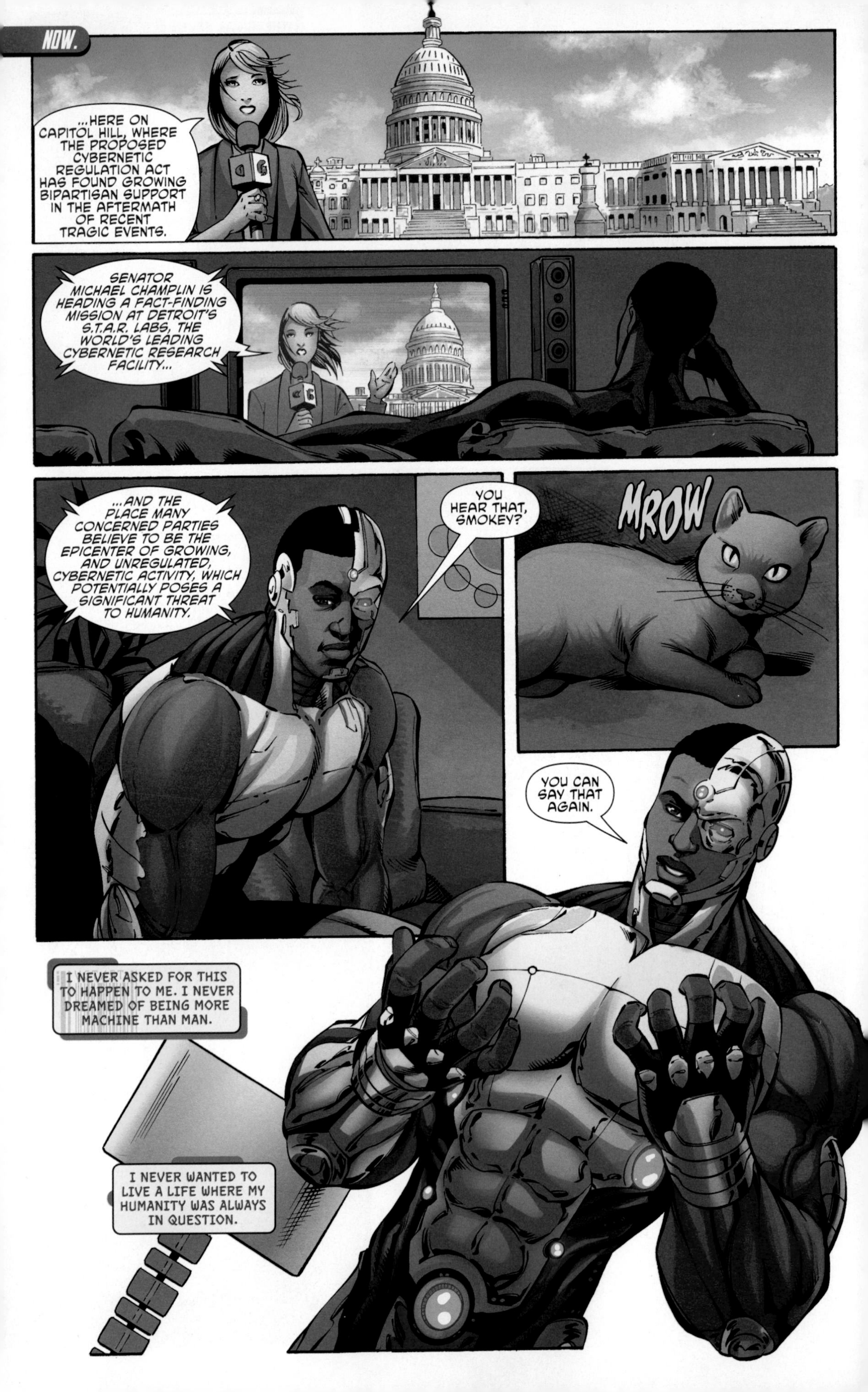
NOW.
...HERE ON CAPITOL HILL, WHERE THE PROPOSED CYBERNETIC REGULATION ACT HAS FOUND GROWING BIPARTISAN SUPPORT IN THE AFTERMATH OF RECENT TRAGIC EVENTS.
SENATOR MICHAEL CHAMPLIN IS HEADING A FACT-FINDING MISSION AT DETROIT'S S.T.A.R. LABS, THE WORLD'S LEADING CYBERNETIC RESEARCH FACILITY...
...AND THE PLACE MANY CONCERNED PARTIES BELIEVE TO BE THE EPICENTER OF GROWING, AND UNREGULATED, CYBERNETIC ACTIVITY, WHICH POTENTIALLY POSES A SIGNIFICANT THREAT TO HUMANITY.
YOU HEAR THAT, SMOKEY?
MROW
YOU CAN SAY THAT AGAIN.
I NEVER ASKED FOR THIS TO HAPPEN TO ME. I NEVER DREAMED OF BEING MORE MACHINE THAN MAN.
I NEVER WANTED TO LIVE A LIFE WHERE MY HUMANITY WAS ALWAYS IN QUESTION.

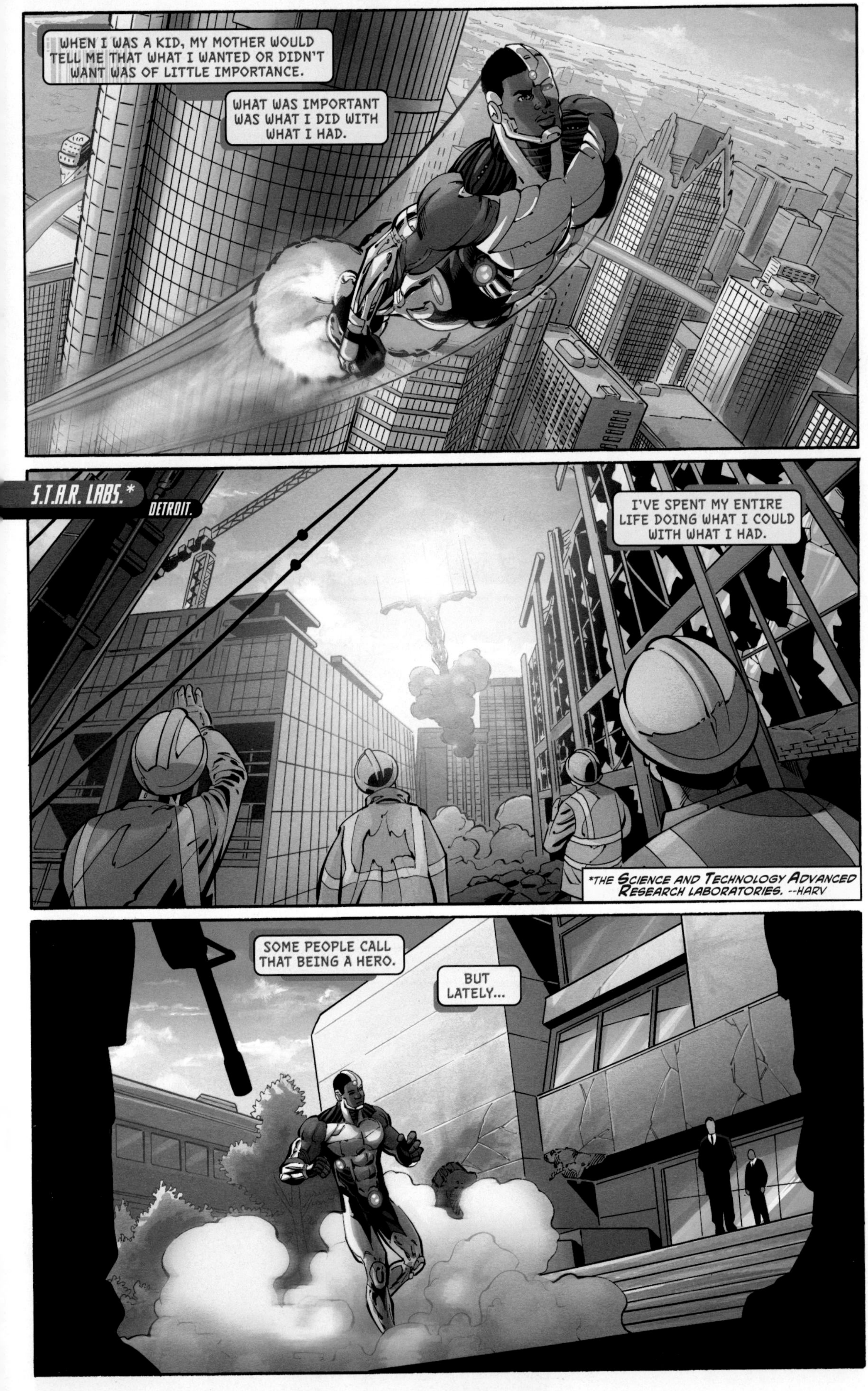
WHEN I WAS A KID, MY MOTHER WOULD TELL ME THAT WHAT I WANTED OR DIDN'T WANT WAS OF LITTLE IMPORTANCE.
WHAT WAS IMPORTANT WAS WHAT I DID WITH WHAT I HAD.
S.T.A.R. LABS.*
DETROIT.
I'VE SPENT MY ENTIRE LIFE DOING WHAT I COULD WITH WHAT I HAD.
*THE SCIENCE AND TECHNOLOGY ADVANCED RESEARCH LABORATORIES. --HARV
SOME PEOPLE CALL THAT BEING A HERO.
BUT LATELY...

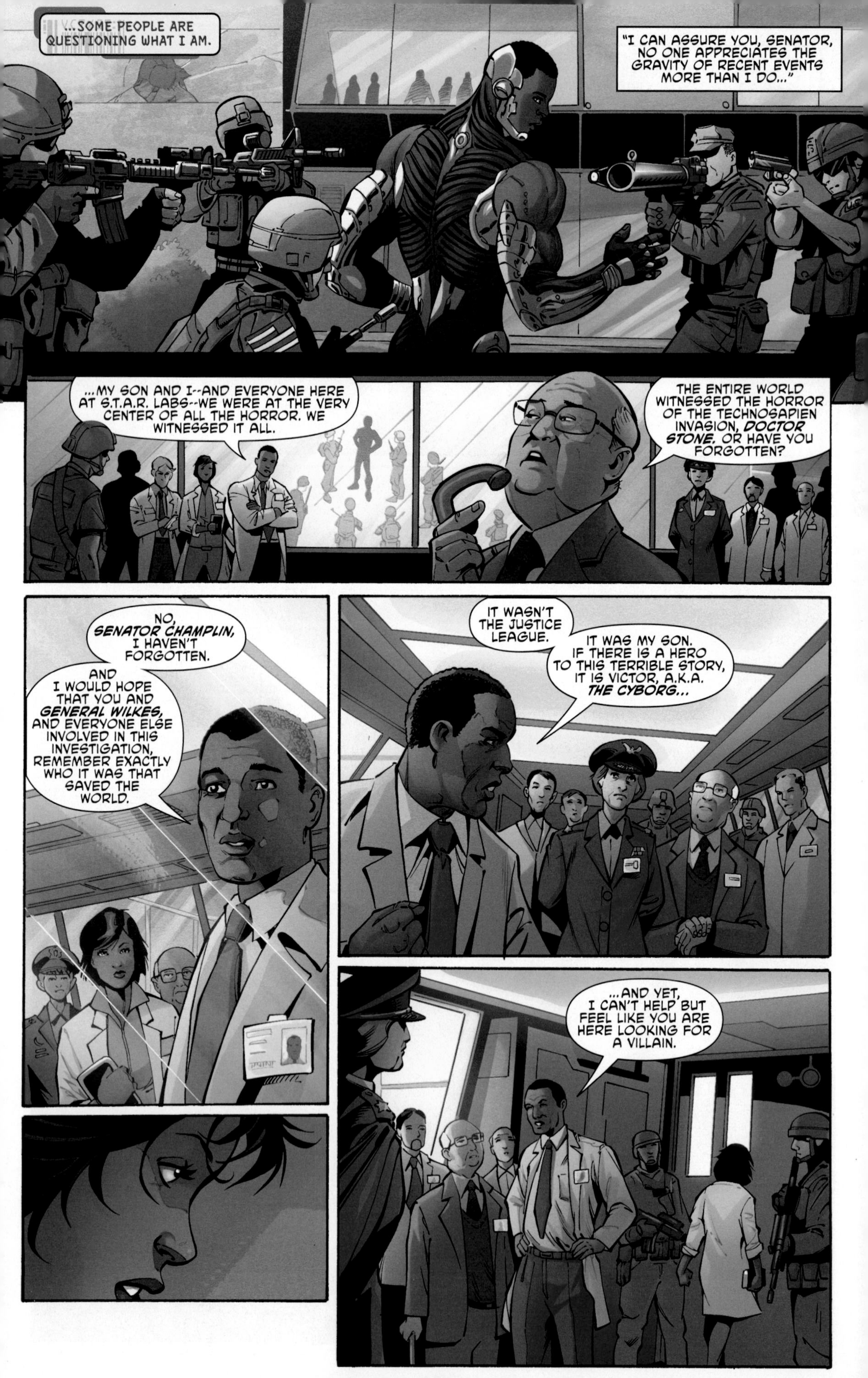
...SOME PEOPLE ARE QUESTIONING WHAT I AM.
"I CAN ASSURE YOU, SENATOR, NO ONE APPRECIATES THE GRAVITY OF RECENT EVENTS MORE THAN I DO..."
...MY SON AND I--AND EVERYONE HERE AT S.T.A.R. LABS--WE WERE AT THE VERY CENTER OF ALL THE HORROR. WE WITNESSED IT ALL.
THE ENTIRE WORLD WITNESSED THE HORROR OF THE TECHNOSAPIEN INVASION, DOCTOR STONE. OR HAVE YOU FORGOTTEN?
NO, SENATOR CHAMPLIN, I HAVEN'T FORGOTTEN.
AND I WOULD HOPE THAT YOU AND GENERAL WILKES, AND EVERYONE ELSE INVOLVED IN THIS INVESTIGATION, REMEMBER EXACTLY WHO IT WAS THAT SAVED THE WORLD.
IT WASN'T THE JUSTICE LEAGUE.
IT WAS MY SON. IF THERE IS A HERO TO THIS TERRIBLE STORY, IT IS VICTOR, A.K.A. THE CYBORG...
...AND YET, I CAN'T HELP BUT FEEL LIKE YOU ARE HERE LOOKING FOR A VILLAIN.

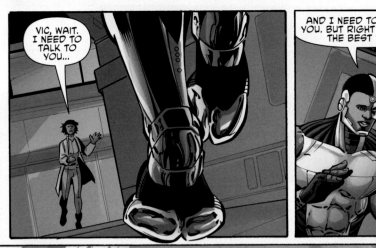

VIC, WAIT. I NEED TO TALK TO YOU...

AND I NEED TO TALK TO YOU. BUT RIGHT NOW ISN'T THE BEST TIME.

YOU SHOULDN'T BE HERE. THAT SENATOR CHAMPLIN IS LOOKING TO TAKE THIS PLACE OVER. HE WANTS ACCESS TO EVERYTHING WE'VE BEEN WORKING ON-- INCLUDING YOUR CYBERNETICS.

IT ISN'T SAFE FOR YOU HERE.

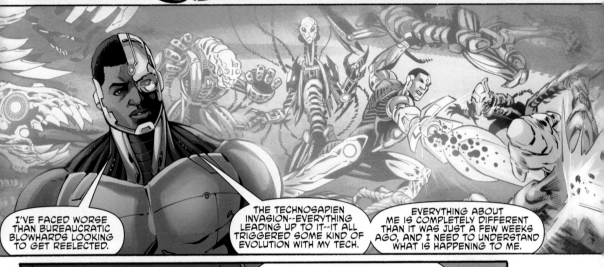

I'VE FACED WORSE THAN BUREAUCRATIC BLOWHARDS LOOKING TO GET REELECTED.

THE TECHNOSAPIEN INVASION--EVERYTHING LEADING UP TO IT--IT ALL TRIGGERED SOME KIND OF EVOLUTION WITH MY TECH.

EVERYTHING ABOUT ME IS COMPLETELY DIFFERENT THAN IT WAS JUST A FEW WEEKS AGO, AND I NEED TO UNDERSTAND WHAT IS HAPPENING TO ME.

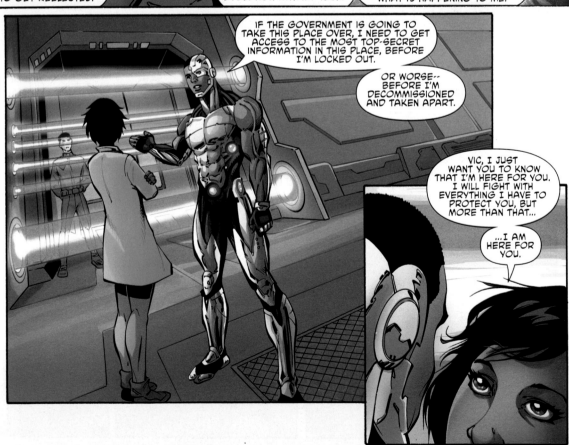

IF THE GOVERNMENT IS GOING TO TAKE THIS PLACE OVER, I NEED TO GET ACCESS TO THE MOST TOP-SECRET INFORMATION IN THIS PLACE, BEFORE I'M LOCKED OUT.

OR WORSE-- BEFORE I'M DECOMMISSIONED AND TAKEN APART.

VIC, I JUST WANT YOU TO KNOW THAT I'M HERE FOR YOU. I WILL FIGHT WITH EVERYTHING I HAVE TO PROTECT YOU, BUT MORE THAN THAT...

...I AM HERE FOR YOU.

I KNOW. IT MEANS MORE TO ME THAN YOU CAN EVER KNOW.

I PROMISE, WE WILL TALK SOON.

BUT FIRST...

"...I NEED TO FIND SOME ANSWERS. I NEED TO BETTER UNDERSTAND THE HISTORY OF MY TECH."

THE RED ROOM.

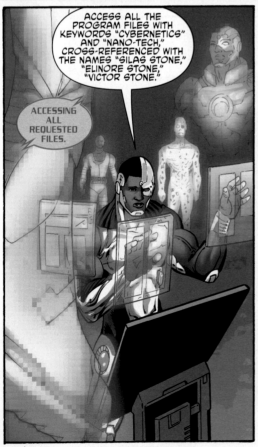

ACCESS ALL THE PROGRAM FILES WITH KEYWORDS "CYBERNETICS" AND "NANO-TECH," CROSS-REFERENCED WITH THE NAMES "SILAS STONE," "ELINORE STONE," "VICTOR STONE."

ACCESSING ALL REQUESTED FILES.

WHO'S THERE?

VIC? VIC, IS THAT YOU?

WHA... WHO...?

THIS CAN'T BE...

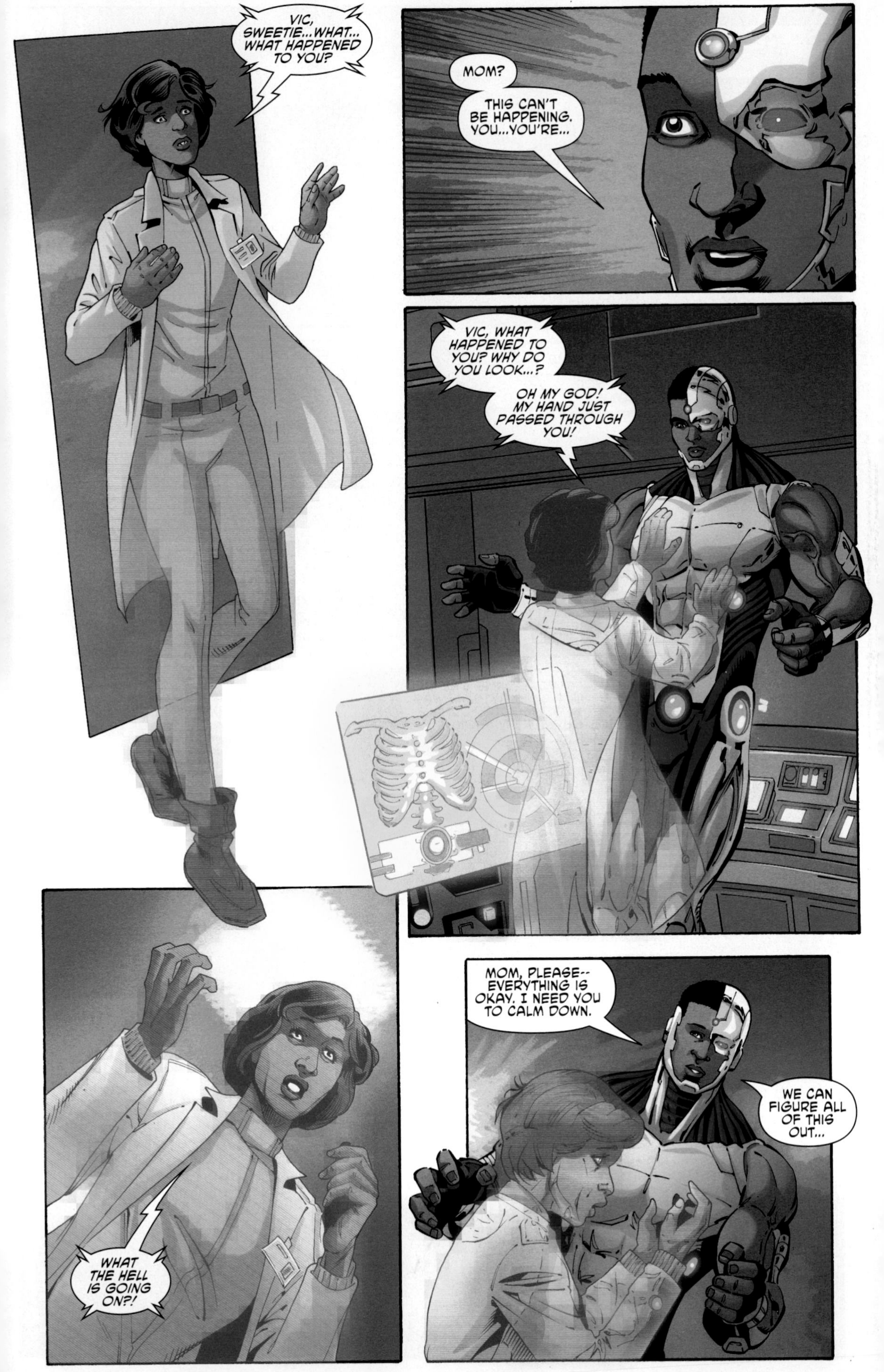
VIC, SWEETIE...WHAT... WHAT HAPPENED TO YOU?
MOM?
THIS CAN'T BE HAPPENING. YOU...YOU'RE...
VIC, WHAT HAPPENED TO YOU? WHY DO YOU LOOK...?
OH MY GOD! MY HAND JUST PASSED THROUGH YOU!
WHAT THE HELL IS GOING ON?!
MOM, PLEASE-- EVERYTHING IS OKAY. I NEED YOU TO CALM DOWN.
WE CAN FIGURE ALL OF THIS OUT...

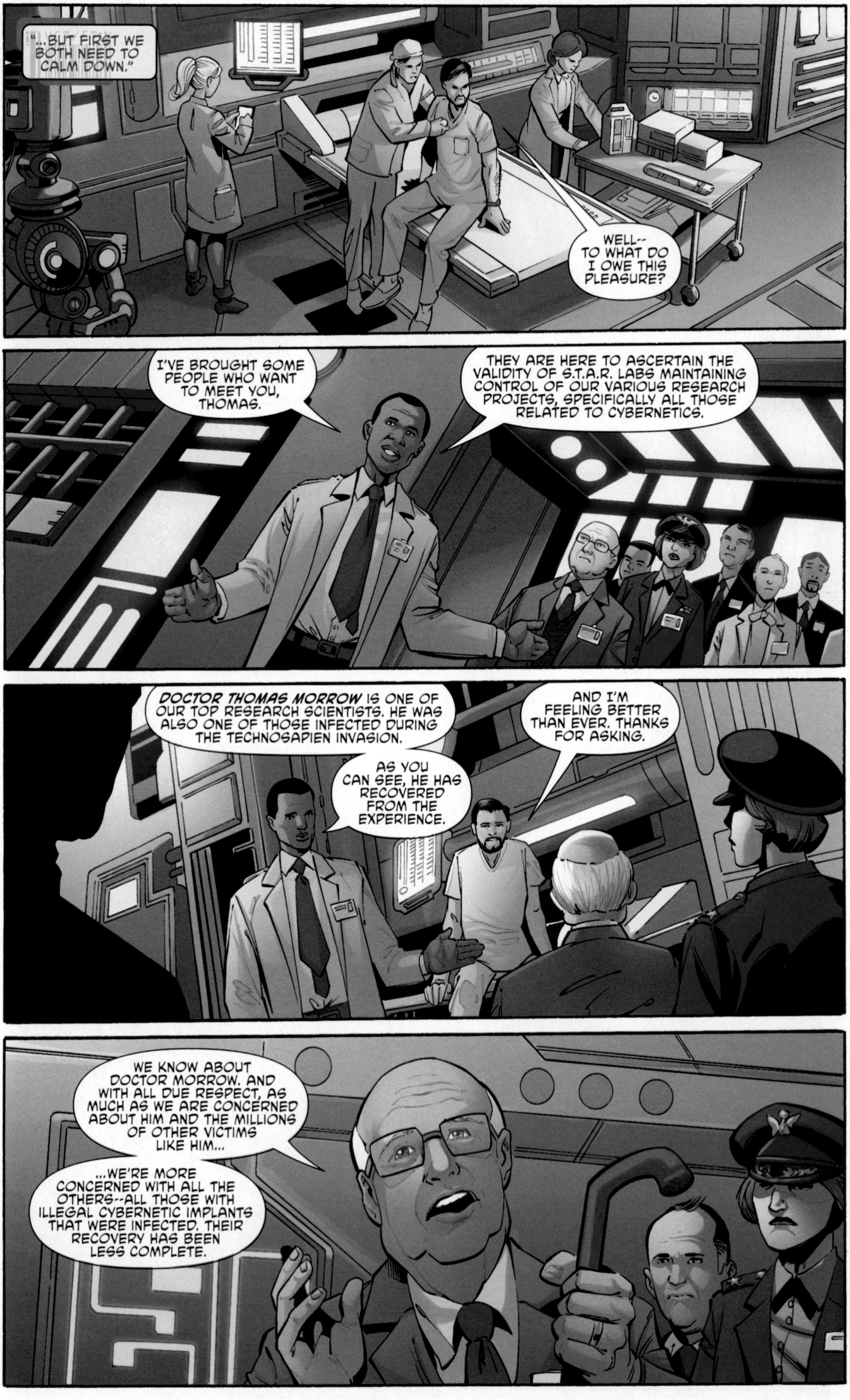
"...BUT FIRST WE BOTH NEED TO CALM DOWN."
WELL-- TO WHAT DO I OWE THIS PLEASURE?
I'VE BROUGHT SOME PEOPLE WHO WANT TO MEET YOU, THOMAS.
THEY ARE HERE TO ASCERTAIN THE VALIDITY OF S.T.A.R. LABS MAINTAINING CONTROL OF OUR VARIOUS RESEARCH PROJECTS, SPECIFICALLY ALL THOSE RELATED TO CYBERNETICS.
DOCTOR THOMAS MORROW IS ONE OF OUR TOP RESEARCH SCIENTISTS. HE WAS ALSO ONE OF THOSE INFECTED DURING THE TECHNOSAPIEN INVASION.
AS YOU CAN SEE, HE HAS RECOVERED FROM THE EXPERIENCE.
AND I'M FEELING BETTER THAN EVER. THANKS FOR ASKING.
WE KNOW ABOUT DOCTOR MORROW. AND WITH ALL DUE RESPECT, AS MUCH AS WE ARE CONCERNED ABOUT HIM AND THE MILLIONS OF OTHER VICTIMS LIKE HIM...
...WE'RE MORE CONCERNED WITH ALL THE OTHERS--ALL THOSE WITH ILLEGAL CYBERNETIC IMPLANTS THAT WERE INFECTED. THEIR RECOVERY HAS BEEN LESS COMPLETE.

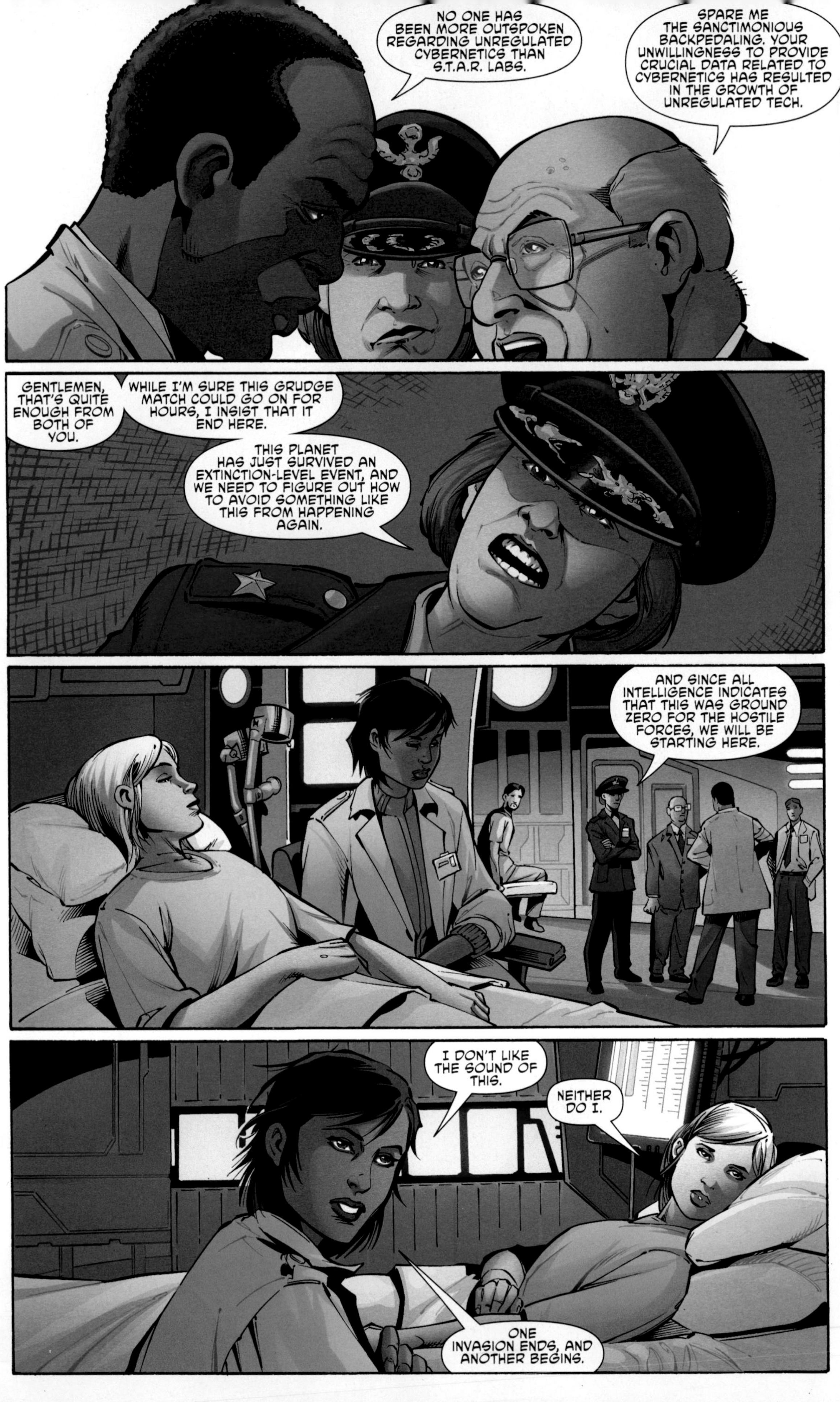
NO ONE HAS BEEN MORE OUTSPOKEN REGARDING UNREGULATED CYBERNETICS THAN S.T.A.R. LABS.
SPARE ME THE SANCTIMONIOUS BACKPEDALING. YOUR UNWILLINGNESS TO PROVIDE CRUCIAL DATA RELATED TO CYBERNETICS HAS RESULTED IN THE GROWTH OF UNREGULATED TECH.
GENTLEMEN, THAT'S QUITE ENOUGH FROM BOTH OF YOU.
WHILE I'M SURE THIS GRUDGE MATCH COULD GO ON FOR HOURS, I INSIST THAT IT END HERE.
THIS PLANET HAS JUST SURVIVED AN EXTINCTION-LEVEL EVENT, AND WE NEED TO FIGURE OUT HOW TO AVOID SOMETHING LIKE THIS FROM HAPPENING AGAIN.
AND SINCE ALL INTELLIGENCE INDICATES THAT THIS WAS GROUND ZERO FOR THE HOSTILE FORCES, WE WILL BE STARTING HERE.
I DON'T LIKE THE SOUND OF THIS.
NEITHER DO I.
ONE INVASION ENDS, AND ANOTHER BEGINS.

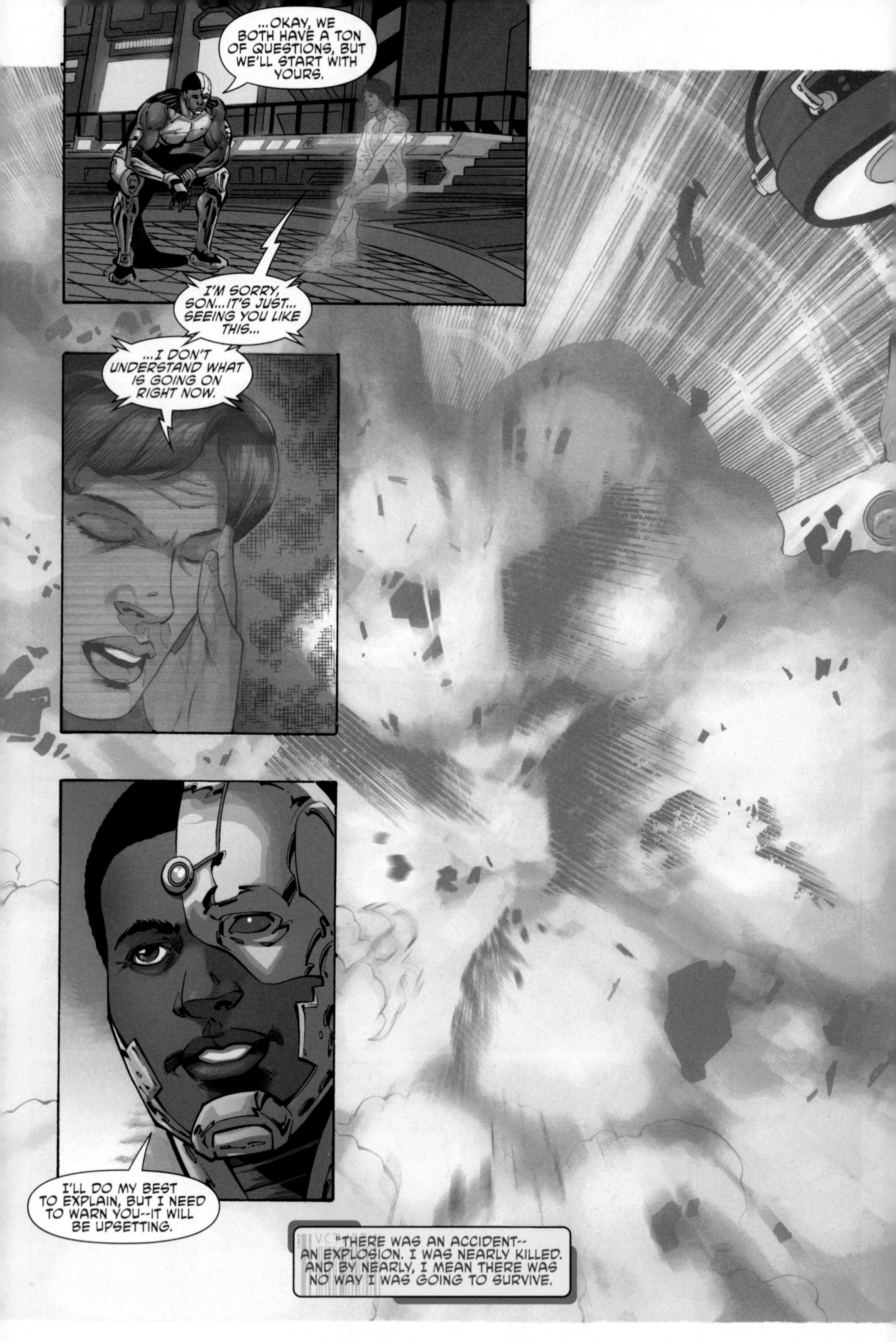
...OKAY, WE BOTH HAVE A TON OF QUESTIONS, BUT WE'LL START WITH YOURS.
I'M SORRY, SON...IT'S JUST... SEEING YOU LIKE THIS...
...I DON'T UNDERSTAND WHAT IS GOING ON RIGHT NOW.
I'LL DO MY BEST TO EXPLAIN, BUT I NEED TO WARN YOU--IT WILL BE UPSETTING.
"THERE WAS AN ACCIDENT-- AN EXPLOSION. I WAS NEARLY KILLED. AND BY NEARLY, I MEAN THERE WAS NO WAY I WAS GOING TO SURVIVE.

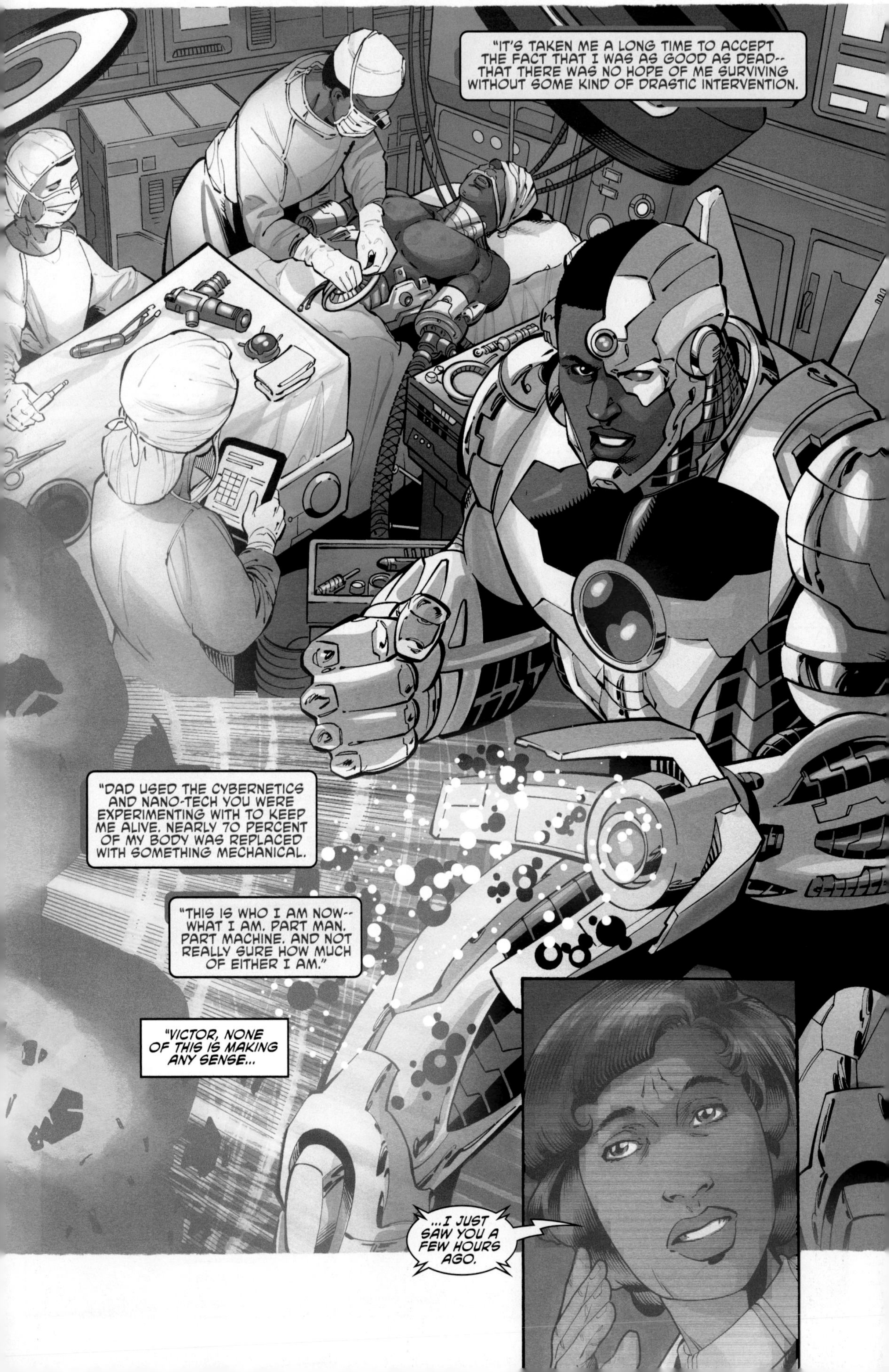
"IT'S TAKEN ME A LONG TIME TO ACCEPT THE FACT THAT I WAS AS GOOD AS DEAD--THAT THERE WAS NO HOPE OF ME SURVIVING WITHOUT SOME KIND OF DRASTIC INTERVENTION.
"DAD USED THE CYBERNETICS AND NANO-TECH YOU WERE EXPERIMENTING WITH TO KEEP ME ALIVE. NEARLY 70 PERCENT OF MY BODY WAS REPLACED WITH SOMETHING MECHANICAL.
"THIS IS WHO I AM NOW--WHAT I AM. PART MAN. PART MACHINE. AND NOT REALLY SURE HOW MUCH OF EITHER I AM."
"VICTOR, NONE OF THIS IS MAKING ANY SENSE...
...I JUST SAW YOU A FEW HOURS AGO.

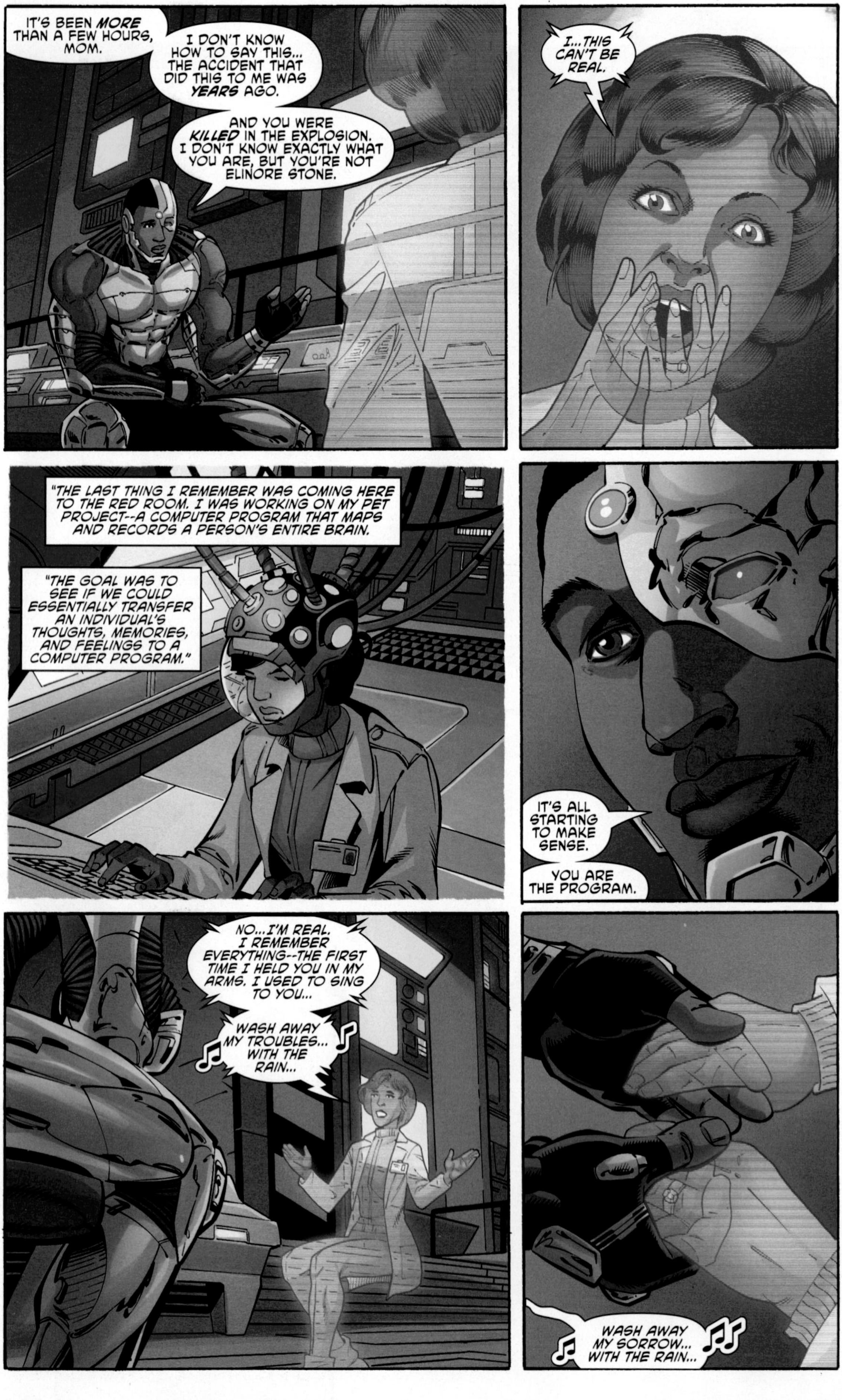
IT'S BEEN MORE THAN A FEW HOURS, MOM.
I DON'T KNOW HOW TO SAY THIS... THE ACCIDENT THAT DID THIS TO ME WAS YEARS AGO.
AND YOU WERE KILLED IN THE EXPLOSION. I DON'T KNOW EXACTLY WHAT YOU ARE, BUT YOU'RE NOT ELINORE STONE.
I...THIS CAN'T BE REAL.
"THE LAST THING I REMEMBER WAS COMING HERE TO THE RED ROOM. I WAS WORKING ON MY PET PROJECT--A COMPUTER PROGRAM THAT MAPS AND RECORDS A PERSON'S ENTIRE BRAIN.
"THE GOAL WAS TO SEE IF WE COULD ESSENTIALLY TRANSFER AN INDIVIDUAL'S THOUGHTS, MEMORIES, AND FEELINGS TO A COMPUTER PROGRAM."
IT'S ALL STARTING TO MAKE SENSE.
YOU ARE THE PROGRAM.
NO...I'M REAL. I REMEMBER EVERYTHING--THE FIRST TIME I HELD YOU IN MY ARMS. I USED TO SING TO YOU...
WASH AWAY MY TROUBLES... WITH THE RAIN...
WASH AWAY MY SORROW... WITH THE RAIN...

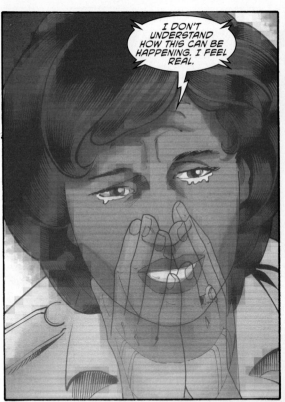

I DON'T UNDERSTAND HOW THIS CAN BE HAPPENING. I FEEL REAL.

THERE'S SO MUCH I DON'T UNDERSTAND RIGHT NOW.

AND IT FEELS REAL TO ME.

BUT YOU...

...YOU'RE A GHOST.

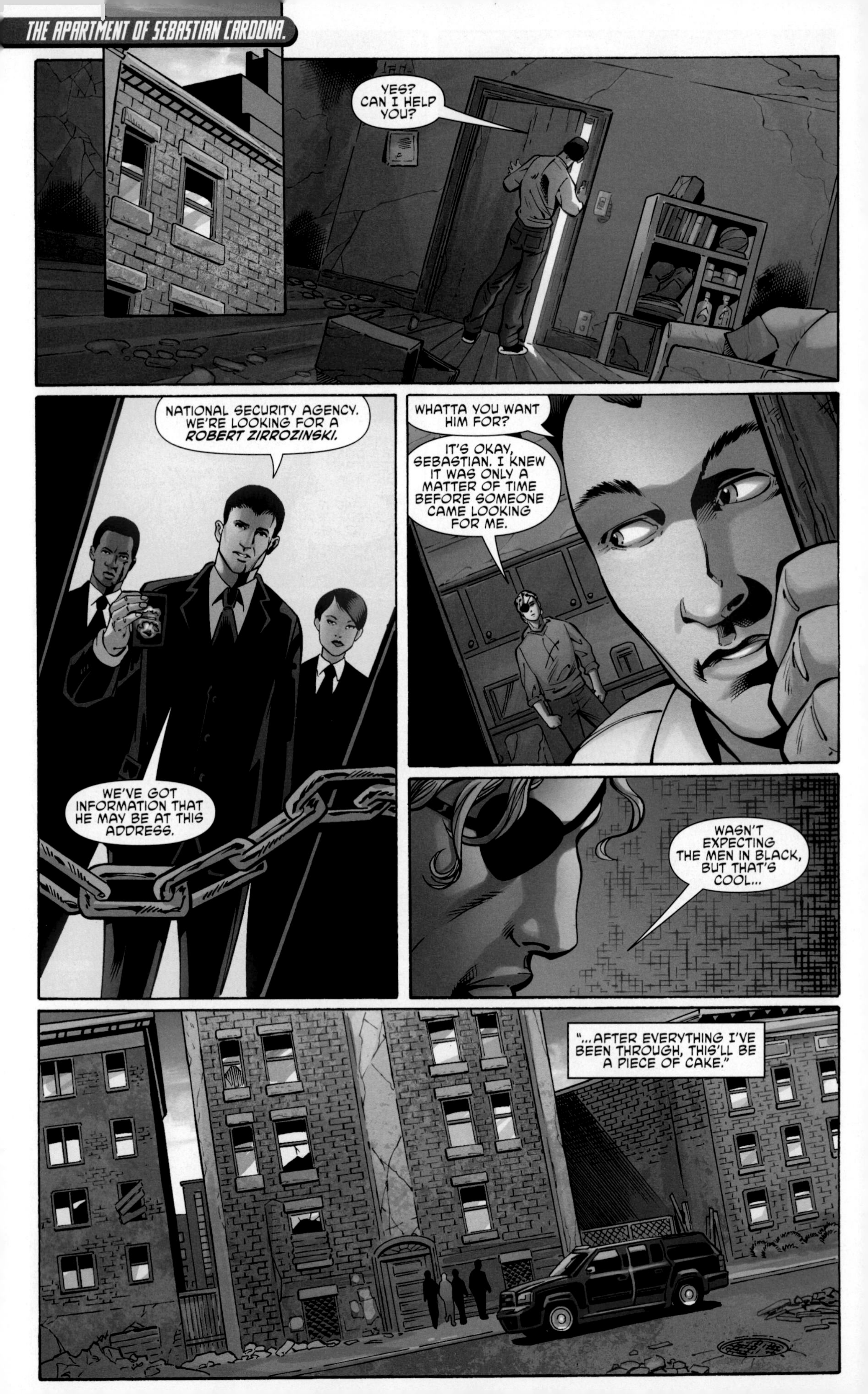
THE APARTMENT OF SEBASTIAN CARDONA.
YES? CAN I HELP YOU?
NATIONAL SECURITY AGENCY. WE'RE LOOKING FOR A *ROBERT ZIRROZINSKI.*
WE'VE GOT INFORMATION THAT HE MAY BE AT THIS ADDRESS.
WHATTA YOU WANT HIM FOR?
IT'S OKAY, SEBASTIAN. I KNEW IT WAS ONLY A MATTER OF TIME BEFORE SOMEONE CAME LOOKING FOR ME.
WASN'T EXPECTING THE MEN IN BLACK, BUT THAT'S COOL...
"...AFTER EVERYTHING I'VE BEEN THROUGH, THIS'LL BE A PIECE OF CAKE."

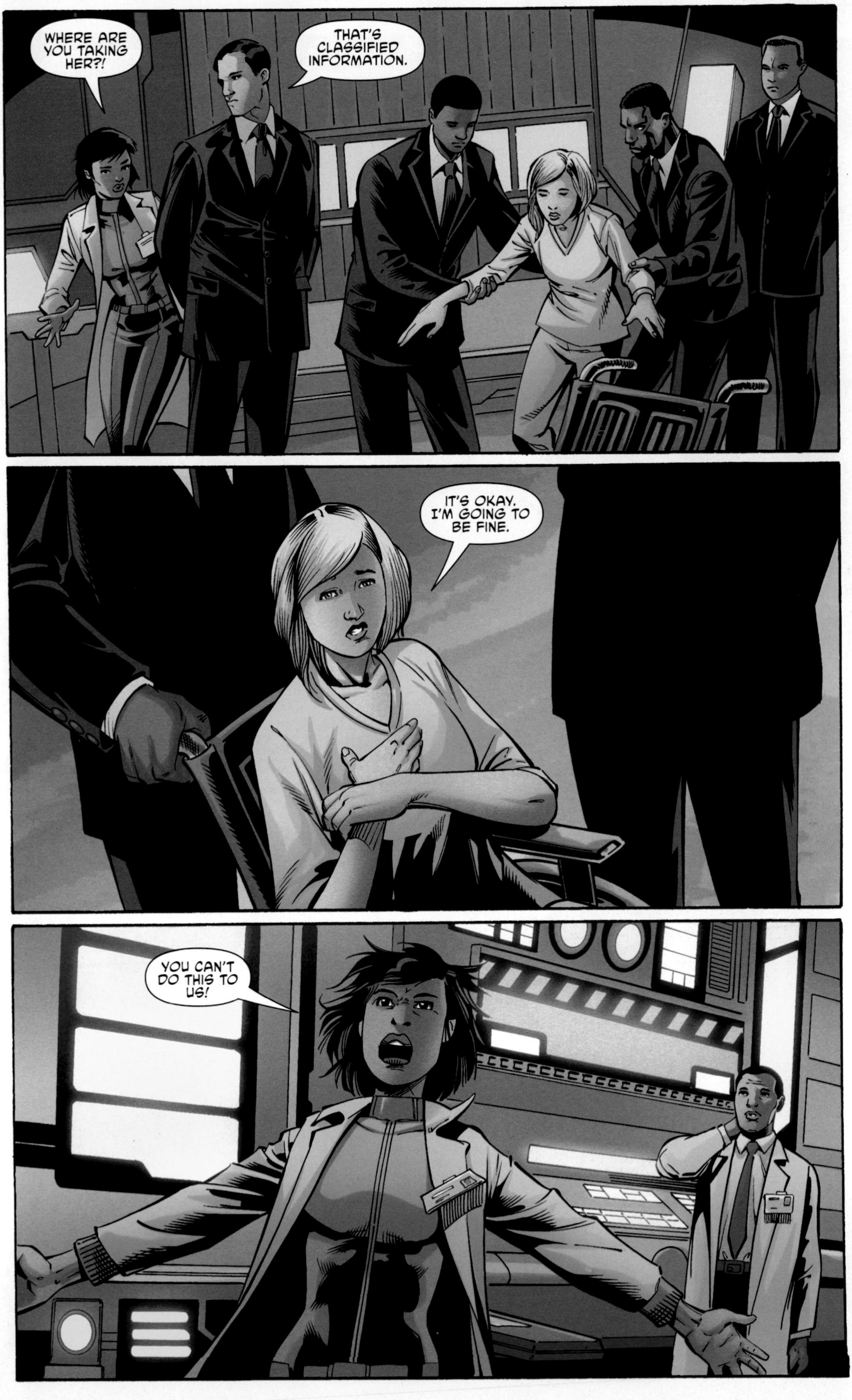
WHERE ARE YOU TAKING HER?!
THAT'S CLASSIFIED INFORMATION.
IT'S OKAY. I'M GOING TO BE FINE.
YOU CAN'T DO THIS TO US!

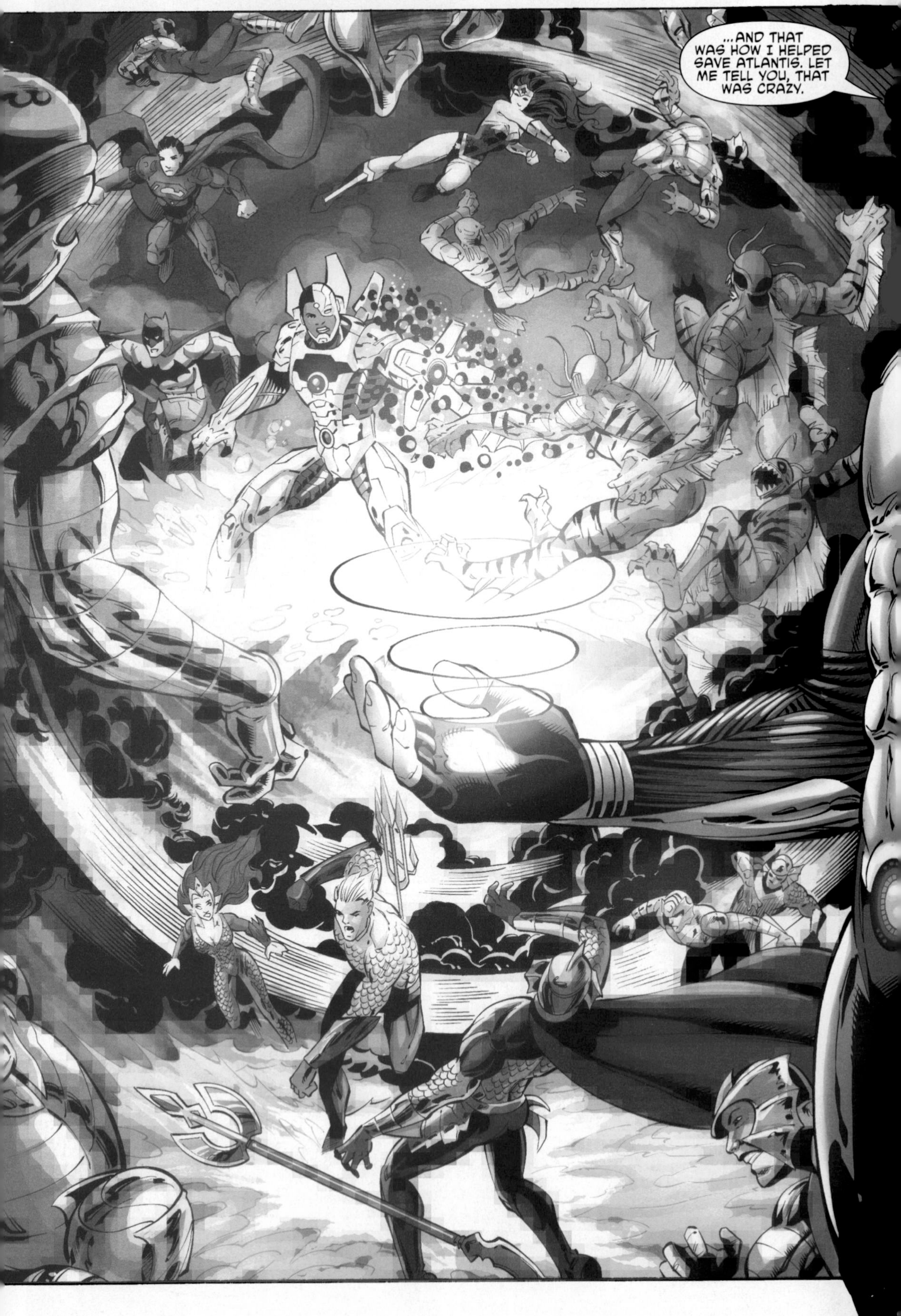
...AND THAT WAS HOW I HELPED SAVE ATLANTIS. LET ME TELL YOU, THAT WAS CRAZY.

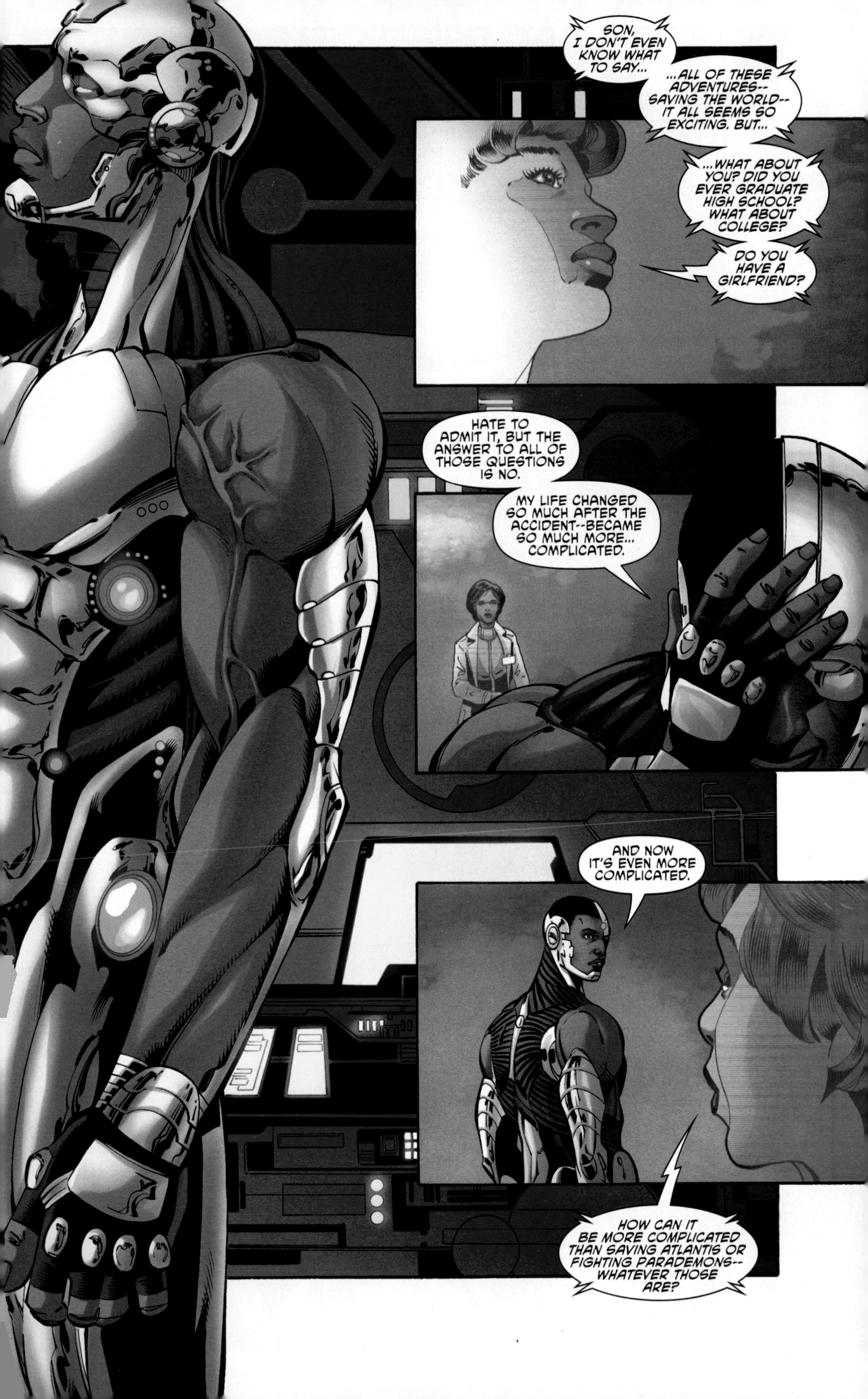
SON, I DON'T EVEN KNOW WHAT TO SAY...
...ALL OF THESE ADVENTURES-- SAVING THE WORLD-- IT ALL SEEMS SO EXCITING. BUT...
...WHAT ABOUT YOU? DID YOU EVER GRADUATE HIGH SCHOOL? WHAT ABOUT COLLEGE?
DO YOU HAVE A GIRLFRIEND?
HATE TO ADMIT IT, BUT THE ANSWER TO ALL OF THOSE QUESTIONS IS NO.
MY LIFE CHANGED SO MUCH AFTER THE ACCIDENT--BECAME SO MUCH MORE... COMPLICATED.
AND NOW IT'S EVEN MORE COMPLICATED.
HOW CAN IT BE MORE COMPLICATED THAN SAVING ATLANTIS OR FIGHTING PARADEMONS-- WHATEVER THOSE ARE?

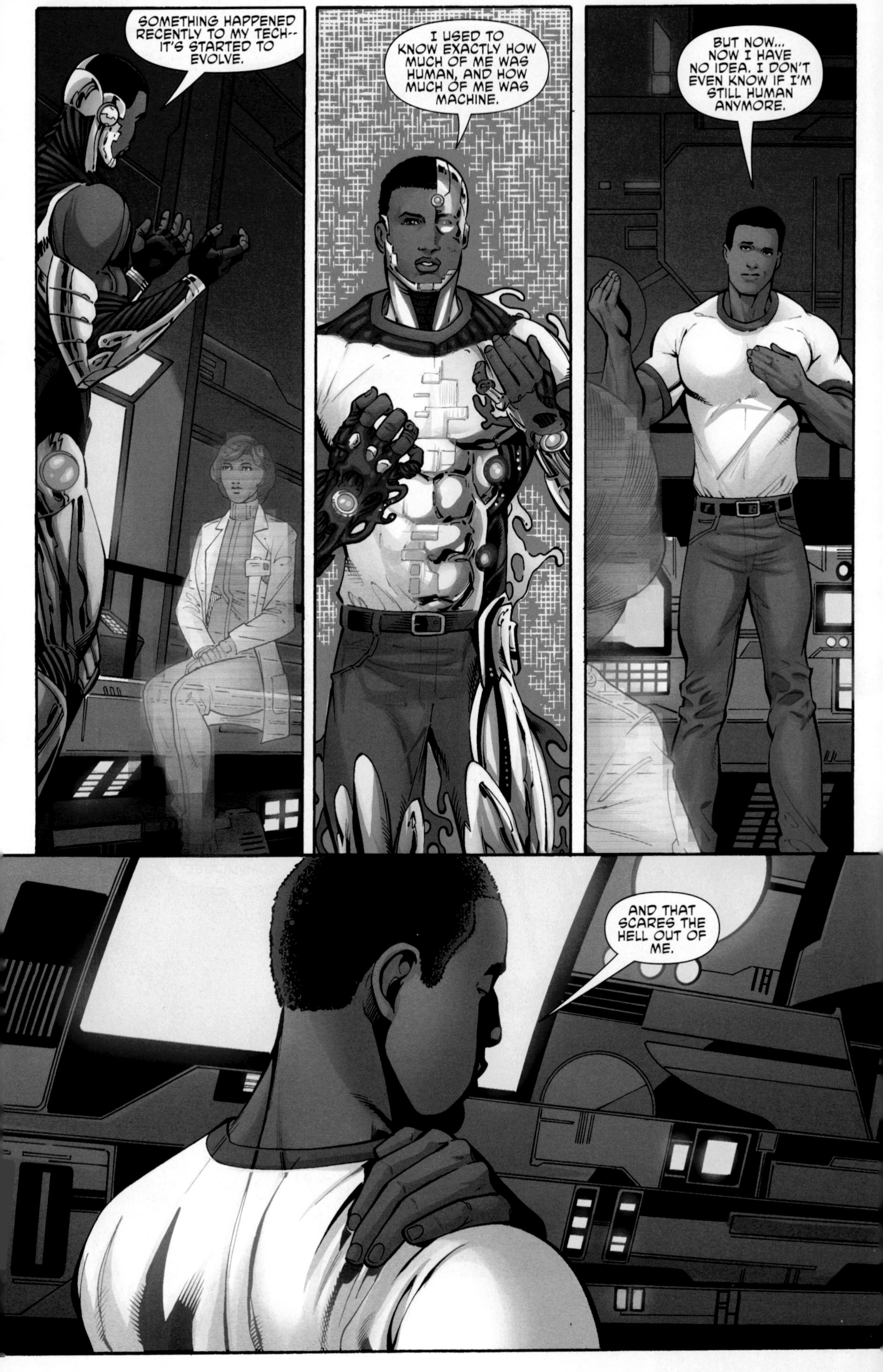
SOMETHING HAPPENED RECENTLY TO MY TECH-- IT'S STARTED TO EVOLVE.
I USED TO KNOW EXACTLY HOW MUCH OF ME WAS HUMAN, AND HOW MUCH OF ME WAS MACHINE.
BUT NOW... NOW I HAVE NO IDEA. I DON'T EVEN KNOW IF I'M STILL HUMAN ANYMORE.
AND THAT SCARES THE HELL OUT OF ME.

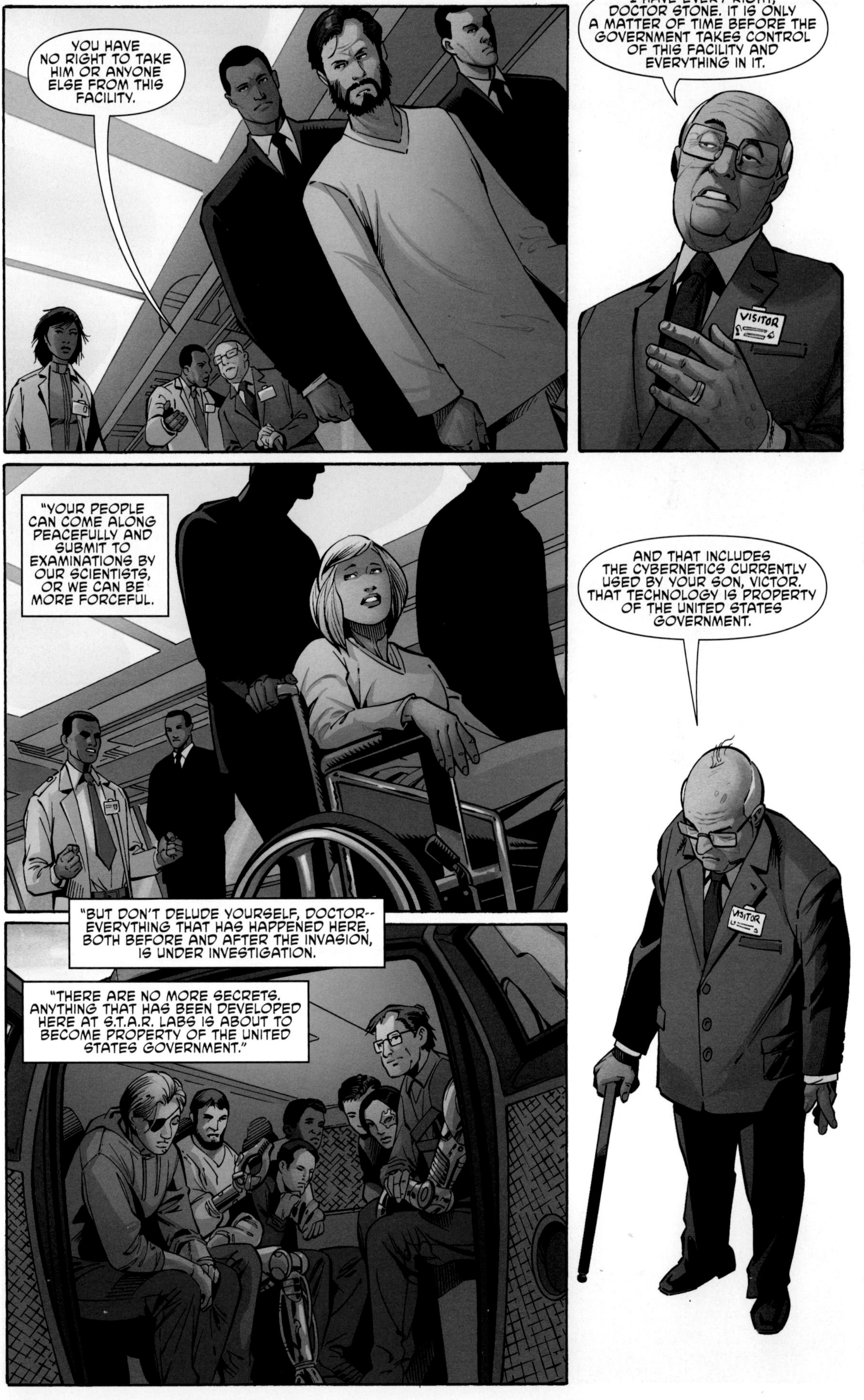

YOU HAVE NO RIGHT TO TAKE HIM OR ANYONE ELSE FROM THIS FACILITY.
I HAVE EVERY RIGHT, DOCTOR STONE. IT IS ONLY A MATTER OF TIME BEFORE THE GOVERNMENT TAKES CONTROL OF THIS FACILITY AND EVERYTHING IN IT.
VISITOR
"YOUR PEOPLE CAN COME ALONG PEACEFULLY AND SUBMIT TO EXAMINATIONS BY OUR SCIENTISTS, OR WE CAN BE MORE FORCEFUL.
AND THAT INCLUDES THE CYBERNETICS CURRENTLY USED BY YOUR SON, VICTOR. THAT TECHNOLOGY IS PROPERTY OF THE UNITED STATES GOVERNMENT.
VISITOR
"BUT DON'T DELUDE YOURSELF, DOCTOR-- EVERYTHING THAT HAS HAPPENED HERE, BOTH BEFORE AND AFTER THE INVASION, IS UNDER INVESTIGATION.
"THERE ARE NO MORE SECRETS. ANYTHING THAT HAS BEEN DEVELOPED HERE AT S.T.A.R. LABS IS ABOUT TO BECOME PROPERTY OF THE UNITED STATES GOVERNMENT."

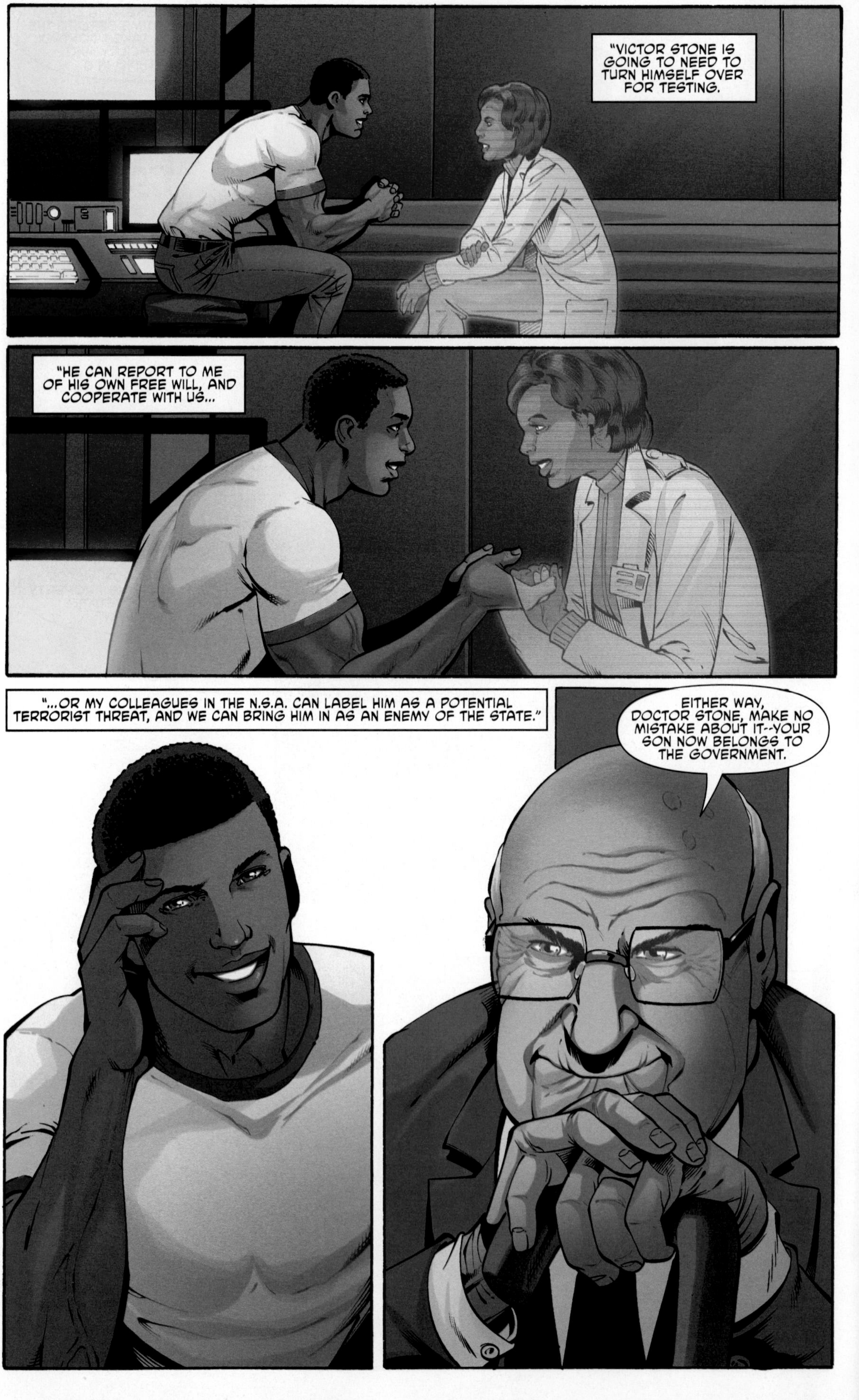
"VICTOR STONE IS GOING TO NEED TO TURN HIMSELF OVER FOR TESTING.
"HE CAN REPORT TO ME OF HIS OWN FREE WILL, AND COOPERATE WITH US...
"...OR MY COLLEAGUES IN THE N.S.A. CAN LABEL HIM AS A POTENTIAL TERRORIST THREAT, AND WE CAN BRING HIM IN AS AN ENEMY OF THE STATE."
EITHER WAY, DOCTOR STONE, MAKE NO MISTAKE ABOUT IT--YOUR SON NOW BELONGS TO THE GOVERNMENT.

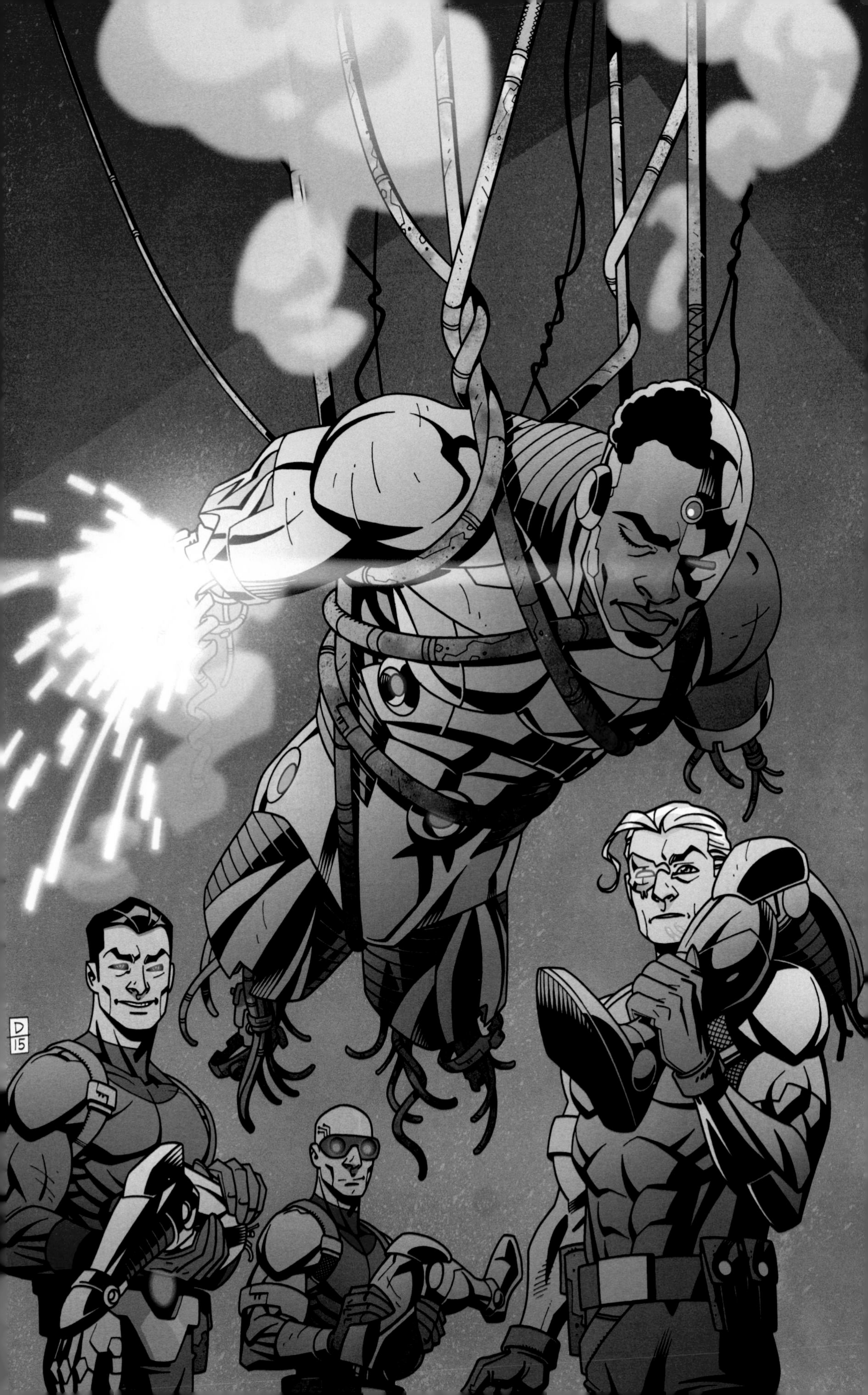
D
15

TARGET: CYBORG

DAVID F. WALKER writer **FELIPE WATANABE, DANIEL HDR & JÚLIO FERREIRA** pencillers **OCLAIR ALBERT & JÚLIO FERREIRA** inkers **DEREC DONOVAN** cover

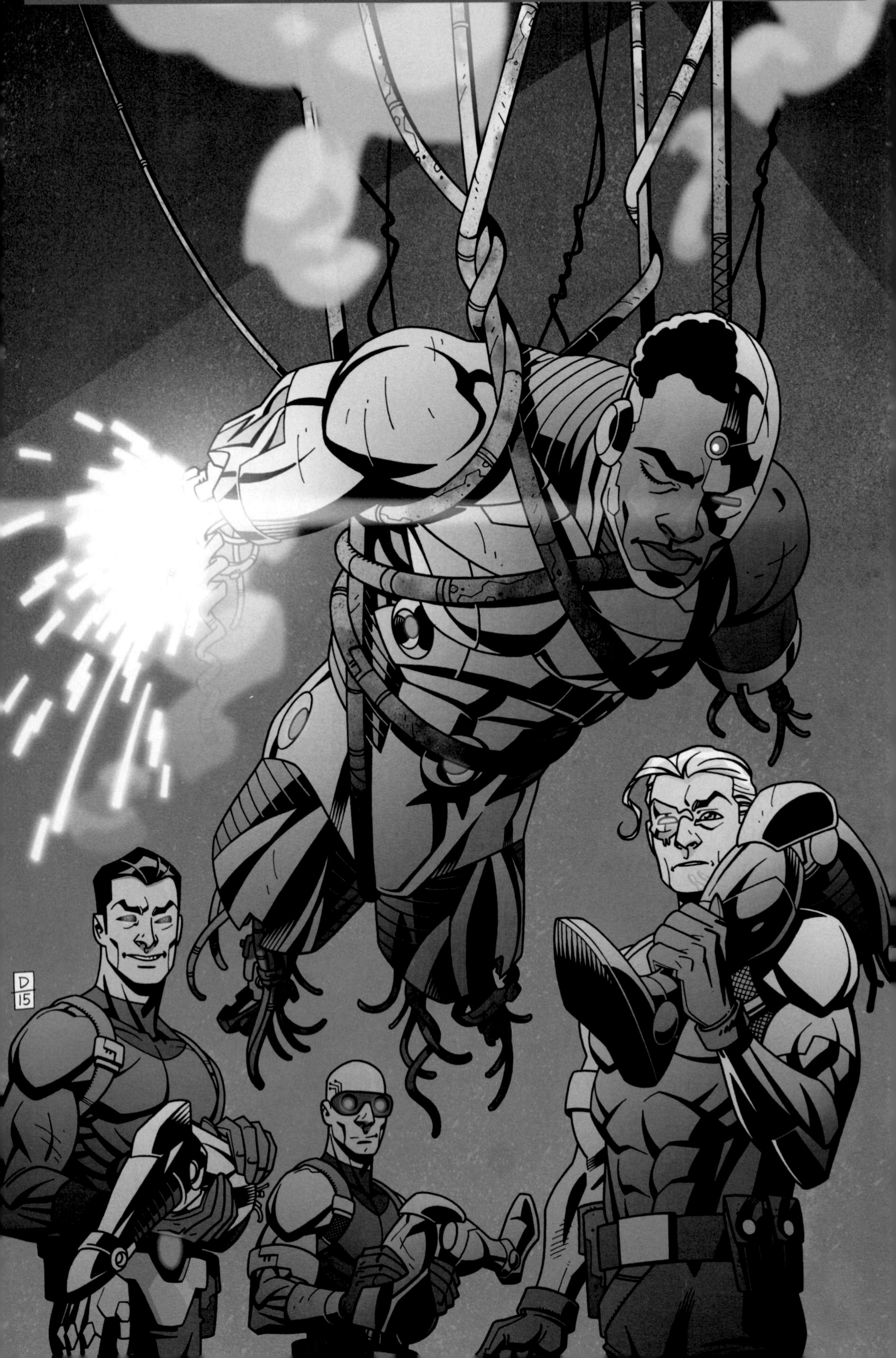
D
15

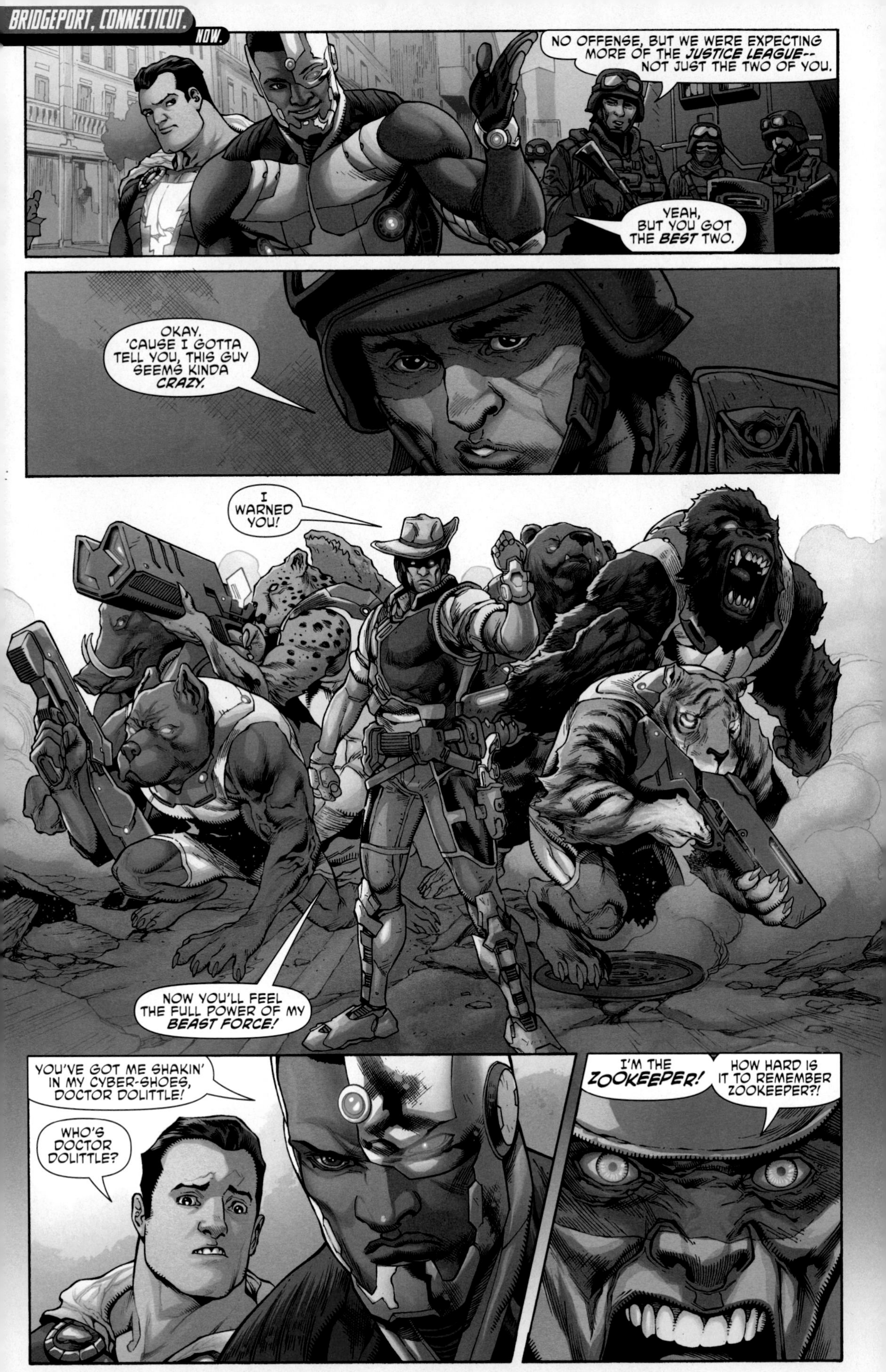
BRIDGEPORT, CONNECTICUT.
NOW.
NO OFFENSE, BUT WE WERE EXPECTING MORE OF THE JUSTICE LEAGUE-- NOT JUST THE TWO OF YOU.
YEAH, BUT YOU GOT THE BEST TWO.
OKAY. 'CAUSE I GOTTA TELL YOU, THIS GUY SEEMS KINDA CRAZY.
I WARNED YOU!
NOW YOU'LL FEEL THE FULL POWER OF MY BEAST FORCE!
YOU'VE GOT ME SHAKIN' IN MY CYBER-SHOES, DOCTOR DOLITTLE!
WHO'S DOCTOR DOLITTLE?
I'M THE ZOOKEEPER!
HOW HARD IS IT TO REMEMBER ZOOKEEPER?!

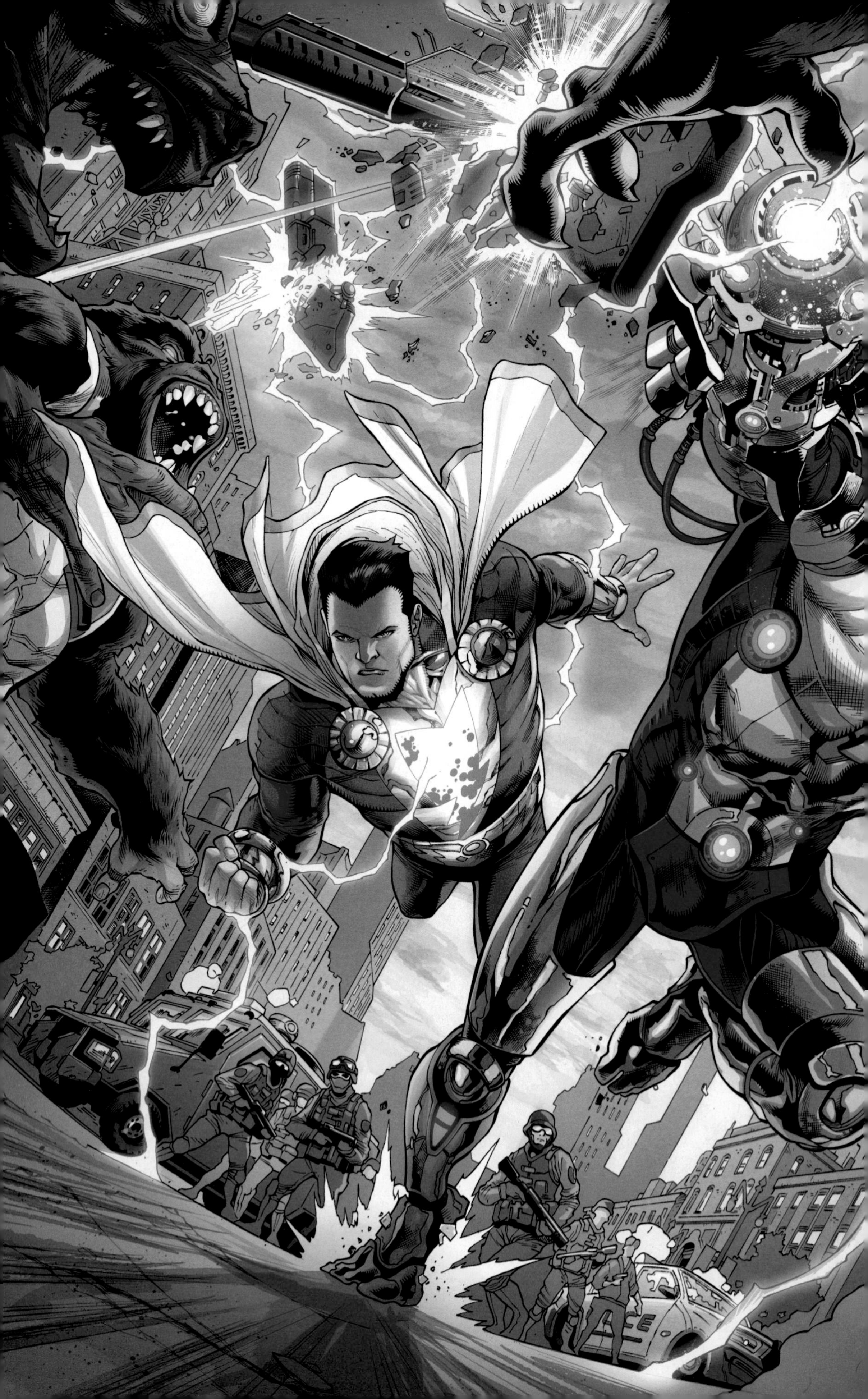

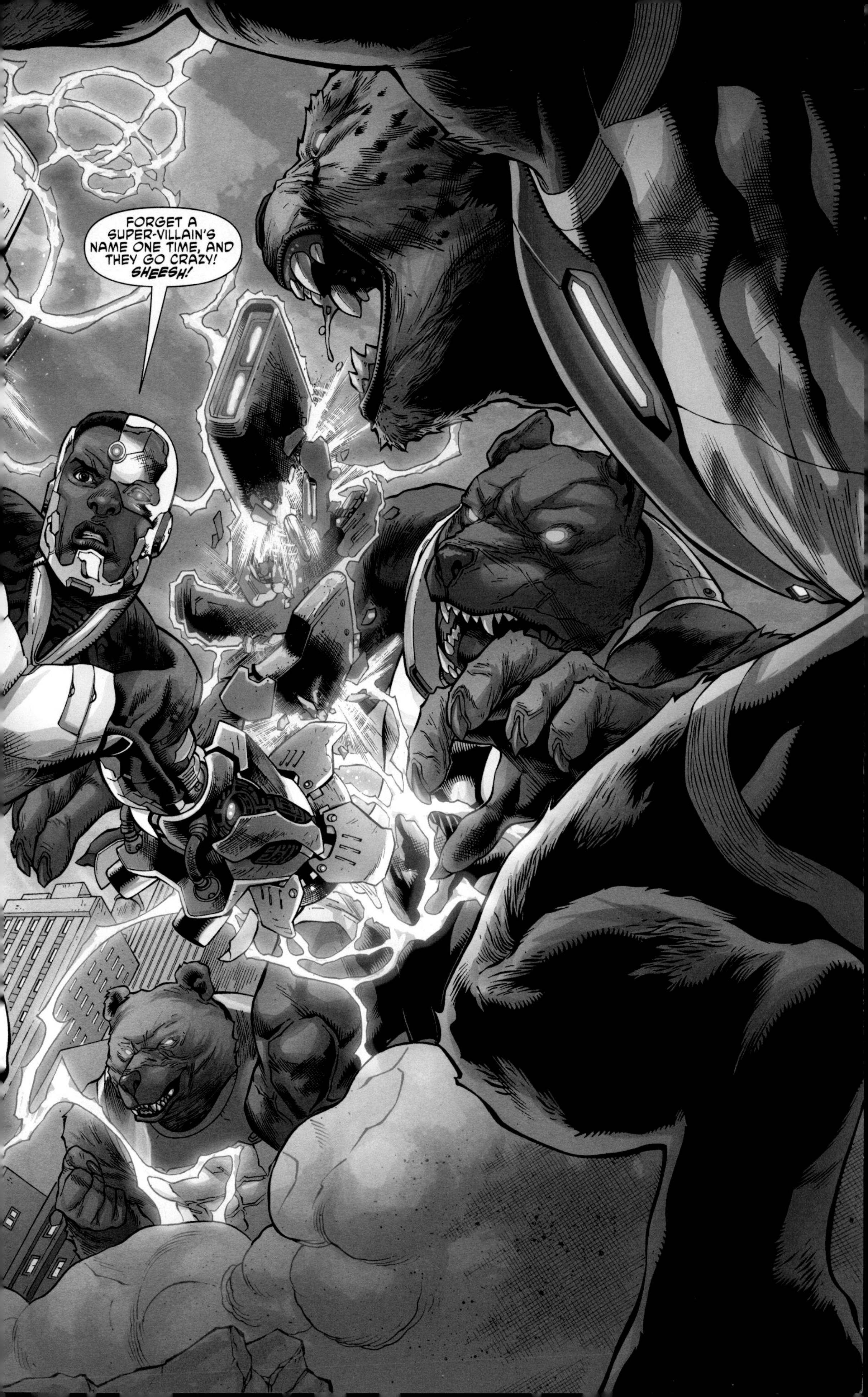
FORGET A SUPER-VILLAIN'S NAME ONE TIME, AND THEY GO CRAZY! SHEESH!

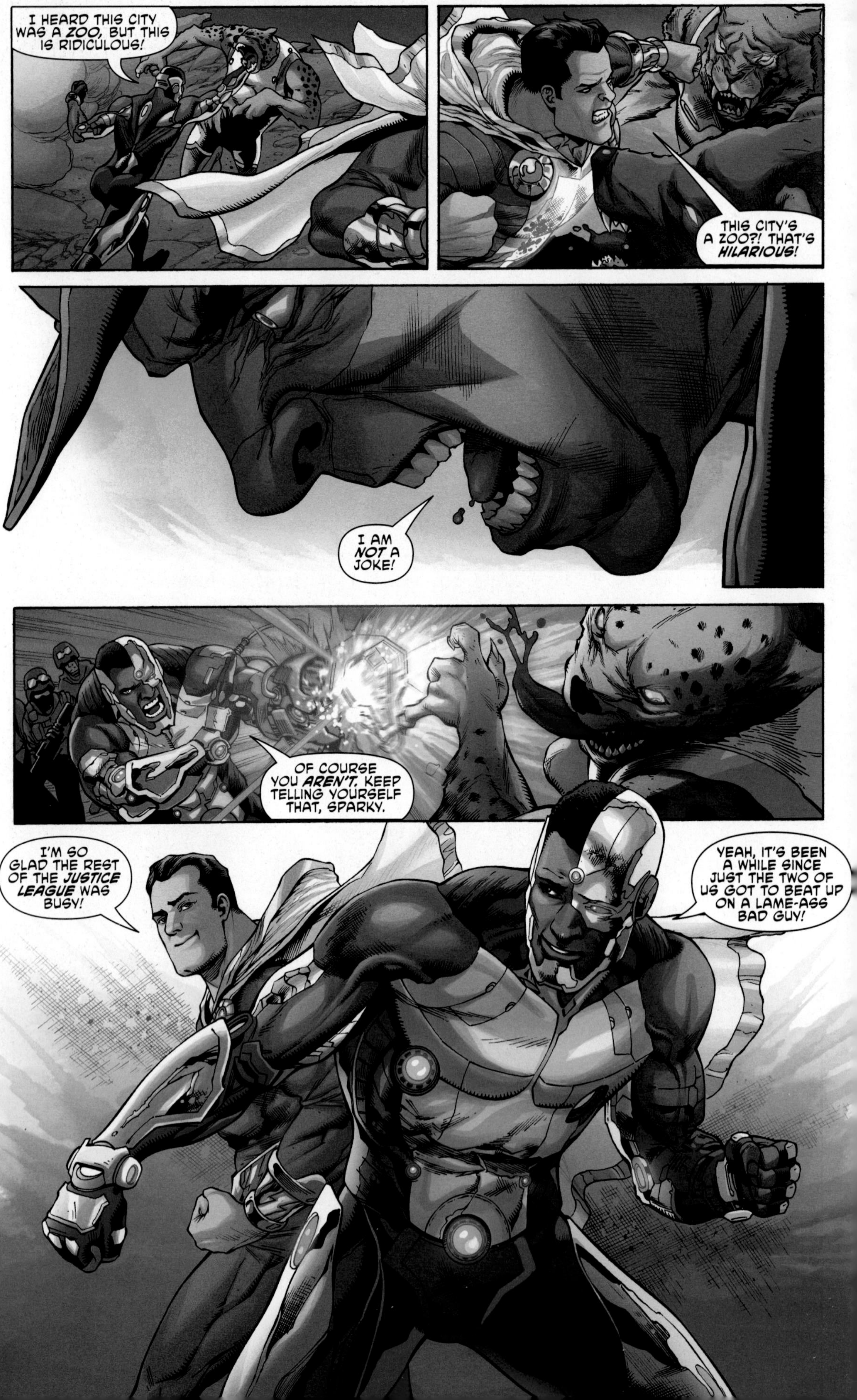
I HEARD THIS CITY WAS A *ZOO*, BUT THIS IS RIDICULOUS!
THIS CITY'S A ZOO?! THAT'S *HILARIOUS!*
I AM *NOT* A JOKE!
OF COURSE YOU *AREN'T.* KEEP TELLING YOURSELF THAT, SPARKY.
I'M SO GLAD THE REST OF THE *JUSTICE LEAGUE* WAS BUSY!
YEAH, IT'S BEEN A WHILE SINCE JUST THE TWO OF US GOT TO BEAT UP ON A LAME-ASS BAD GUY!

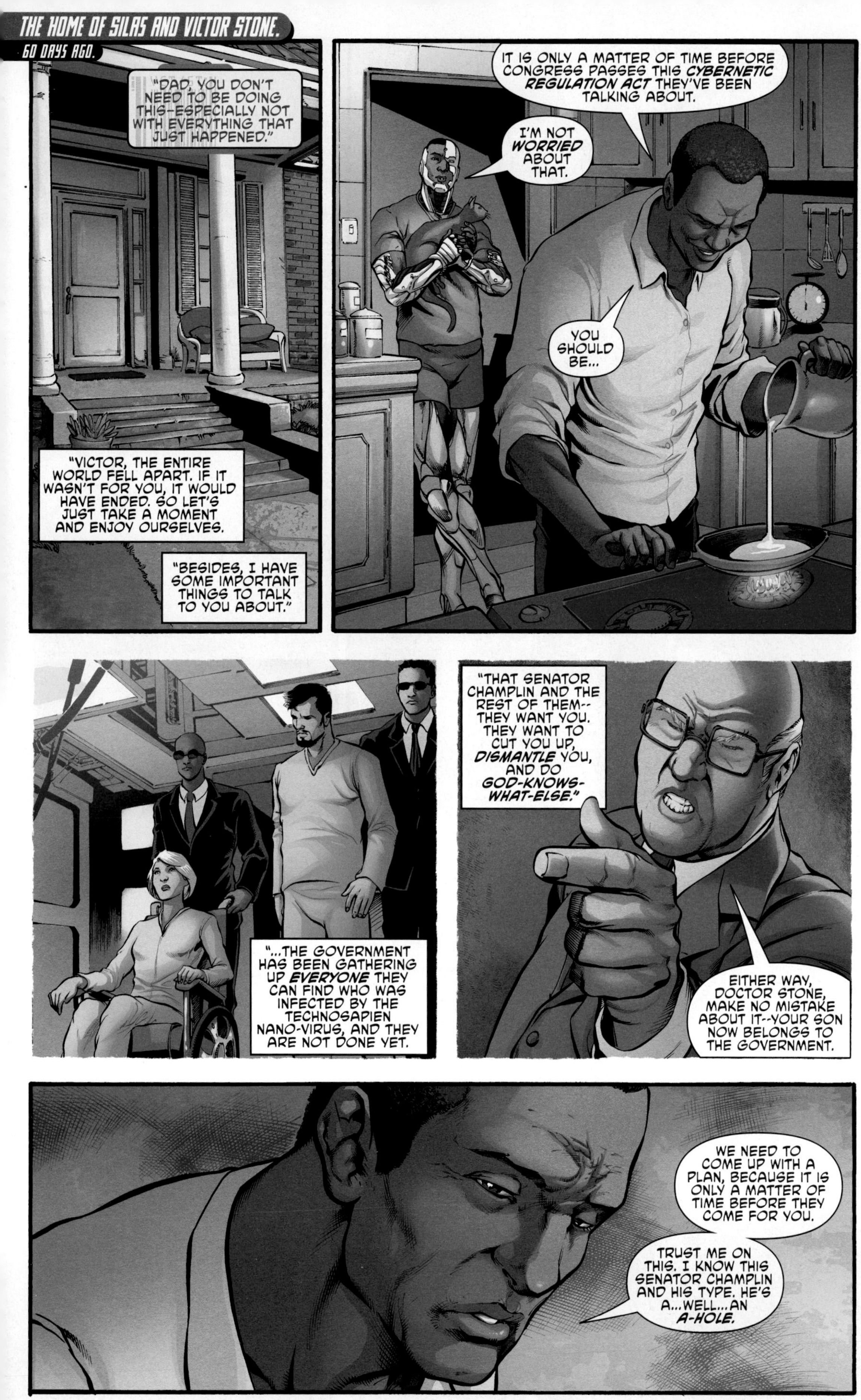
THE HOME OF SILAS AND VICTOR STONE.
60 DAYS AGO.
"DAD, YOU DON'T NEED TO BE DOING THIS--ESPECIALLY NOT WITH EVERYTHING THAT JUST HAPPENED."
"VICTOR, THE ENTIRE WORLD FELL APART. IF IT WASN'T FOR YOU, IT WOULD HAVE ENDED. SO LET'S JUST TAKE A MOMENT AND ENJOY OURSELVES.
"BESIDES, I HAVE SOME IMPORTANT THINGS TO TALK TO YOU ABOUT."
IT IS ONLY A MATTER OF TIME BEFORE CONGRESS PASSES THIS CYBERNETIC REGULATION ACT THEY'VE BEEN TALKING ABOUT.
I'M NOT WORRIED ABOUT THAT.
YOU SHOULD BE...
"...THE GOVERNMENT HAS BEEN GATHERING UP EVERYONE THEY CAN FIND WHO WAS INFECTED BY THE TECHNOSAPIEN NANO-VIRUS, AND THEY ARE NOT DONE YET.
"THAT SENATOR CHAMPLIN AND THE REST OF THEM-- THEY WANT YOU. THEY WANT TO CUT YOU UP, DISMANTLE YOU, AND DO GOD-KNOWS-WHAT-ELSE."
EITHER WAY, DOCTOR STONE, MAKE NO MISTAKE ABOUT IT--YOUR SON NOW BELONGS TO THE GOVERNMENT.
WE NEED TO COME UP WITH A PLAN, BECAUSE IT IS ONLY A MATTER OF TIME BEFORE THEY COME FOR YOU.
TRUST ME ON THIS. I KNOW THIS SENATOR CHAMPLIN AND HIS TYPE. HE'S A...WELL...AN A-HOLE.

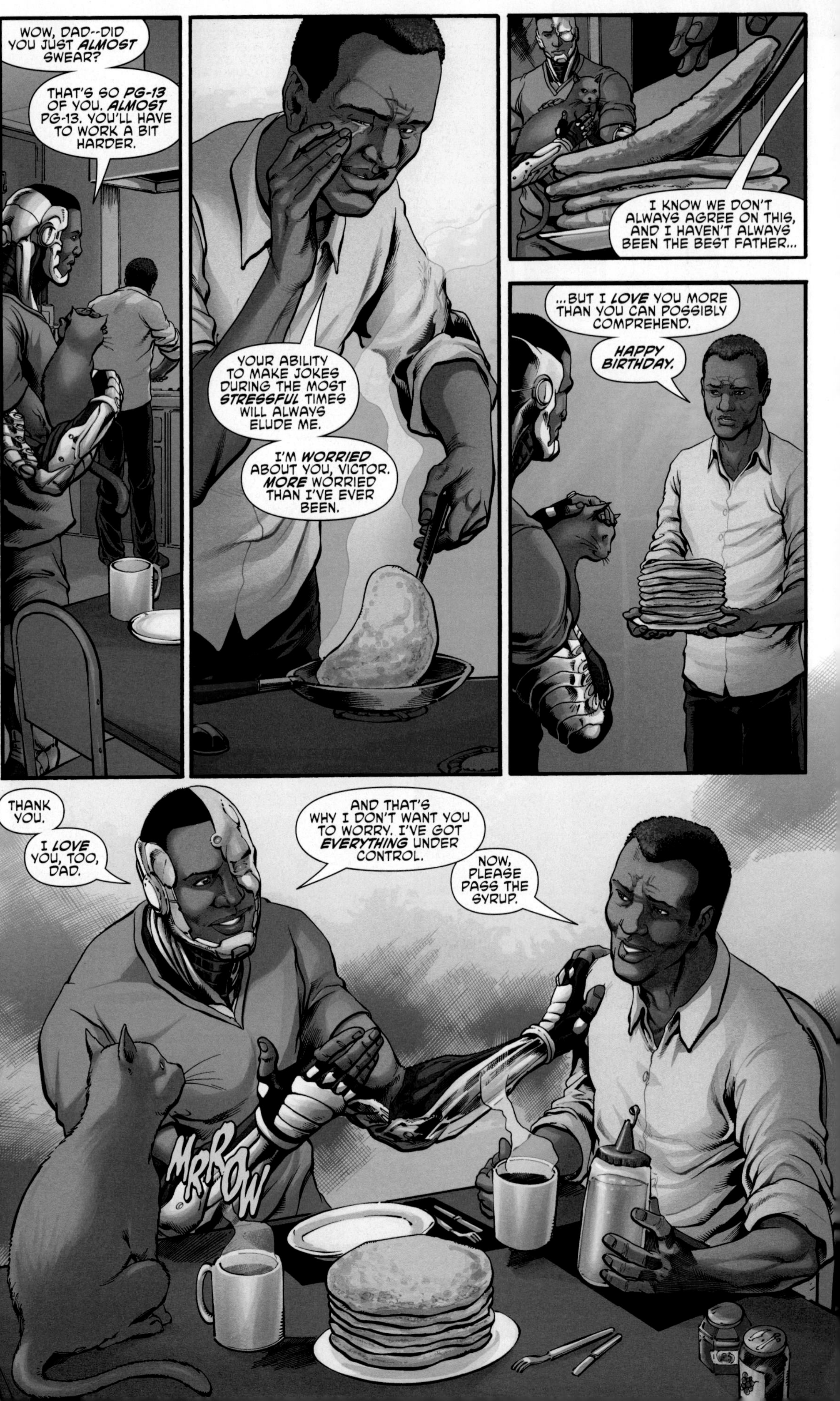
WOW, DAD--DID YOU JUST ALMOST SWEAR?
THAT'S SO PG-13 OF YOU. ALMOST PG-13. YOU'LL HAVE TO WORK A BIT HARDER.
YOUR ABILITY TO MAKE JOKES DURING THE MOST STRESSFUL TIMES WILL ALWAYS ELUDE ME.
I'M WORRIED ABOUT YOU, VICTOR. MORE WORRIED THAN I'VE EVER BEEN.
I KNOW WE DON'T ALWAYS AGREE ON THIS, AND I HAVEN'T ALWAYS BEEN THE BEST FATHER...
...BUT I LOVE YOU MORE THAN YOU CAN POSSIBLY COMPREHEND.
HAPPY BIRTHDAY.
THANK YOU.
I LOVE YOU, TOO, DAD.
AND THAT'S WHY I DON'T WANT YOU TO WORRY. I'VE GOT EVERYTHING UNDER CONTROL.
NOW, PLEASE PASS THE SYRUP.
MRROW

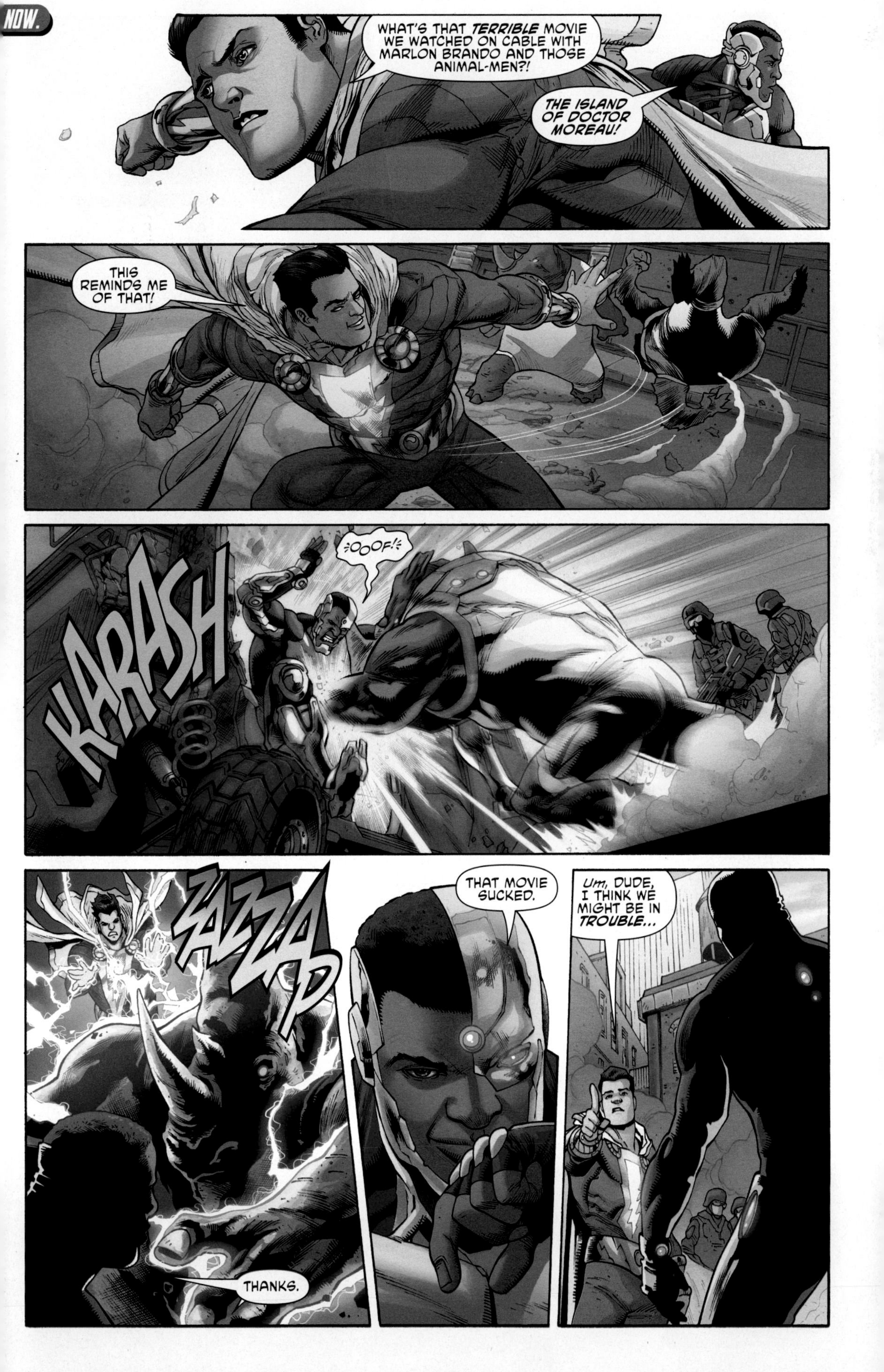
NOW.
WHAT'S THAT TERRIBLE MOVIE WE WATCHED ON CABLE WITH MARLON BRANDO AND THOSE ANIMAL-MEN?!
THE ISLAND OF DOCTOR MOREAU!
THIS REMINDS ME OF THAT!
OOOF!
KARASH
ZAZZAP
THANKS.
THAT MOVIE SUCKED.
Um, DUDE, I THINK WE MIGHT BE IN TROUBLE...

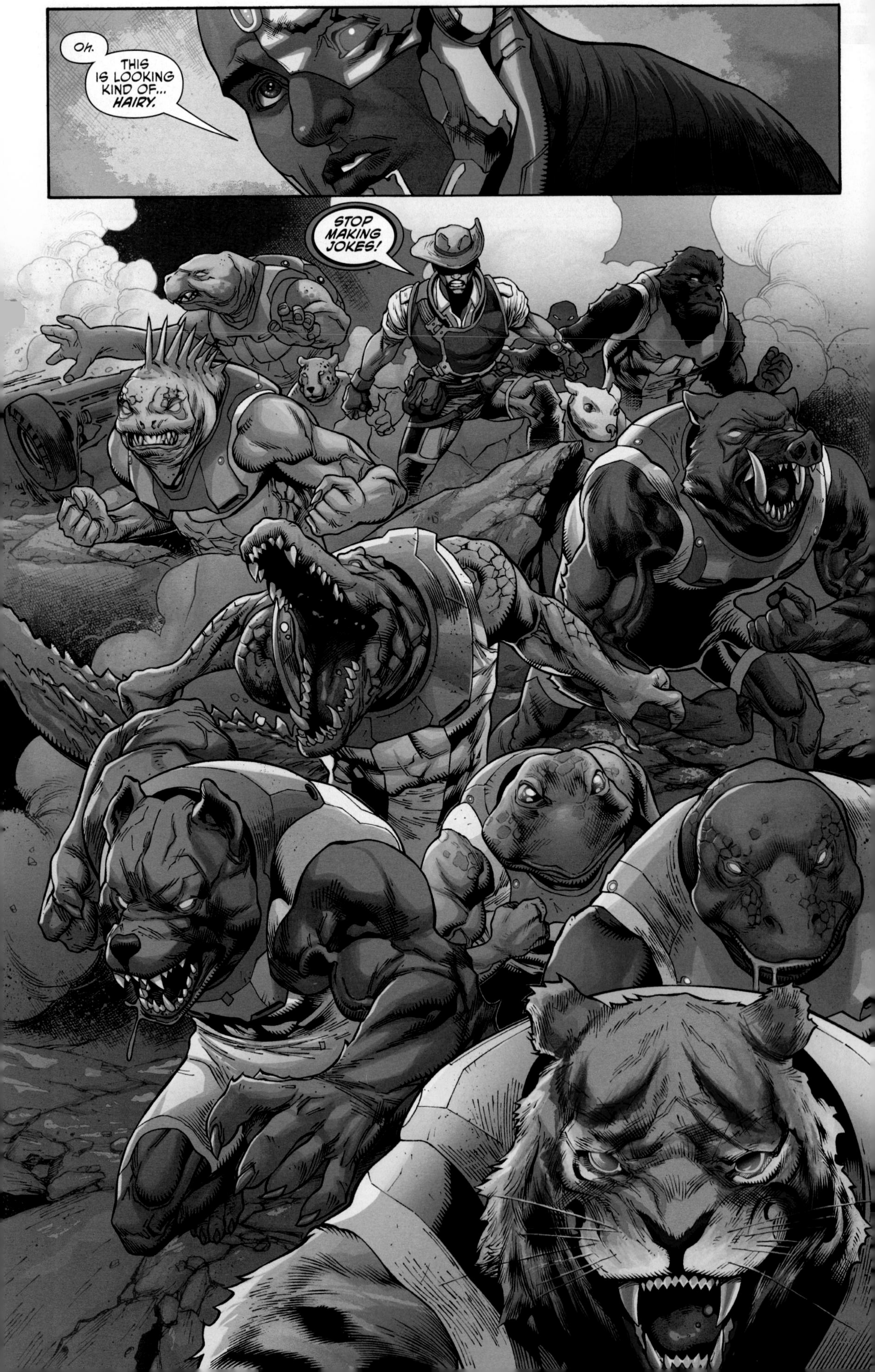

Oh.
THIS IS LOOKING KIND OF... HAIRY.
STOP MAKING JOKES!

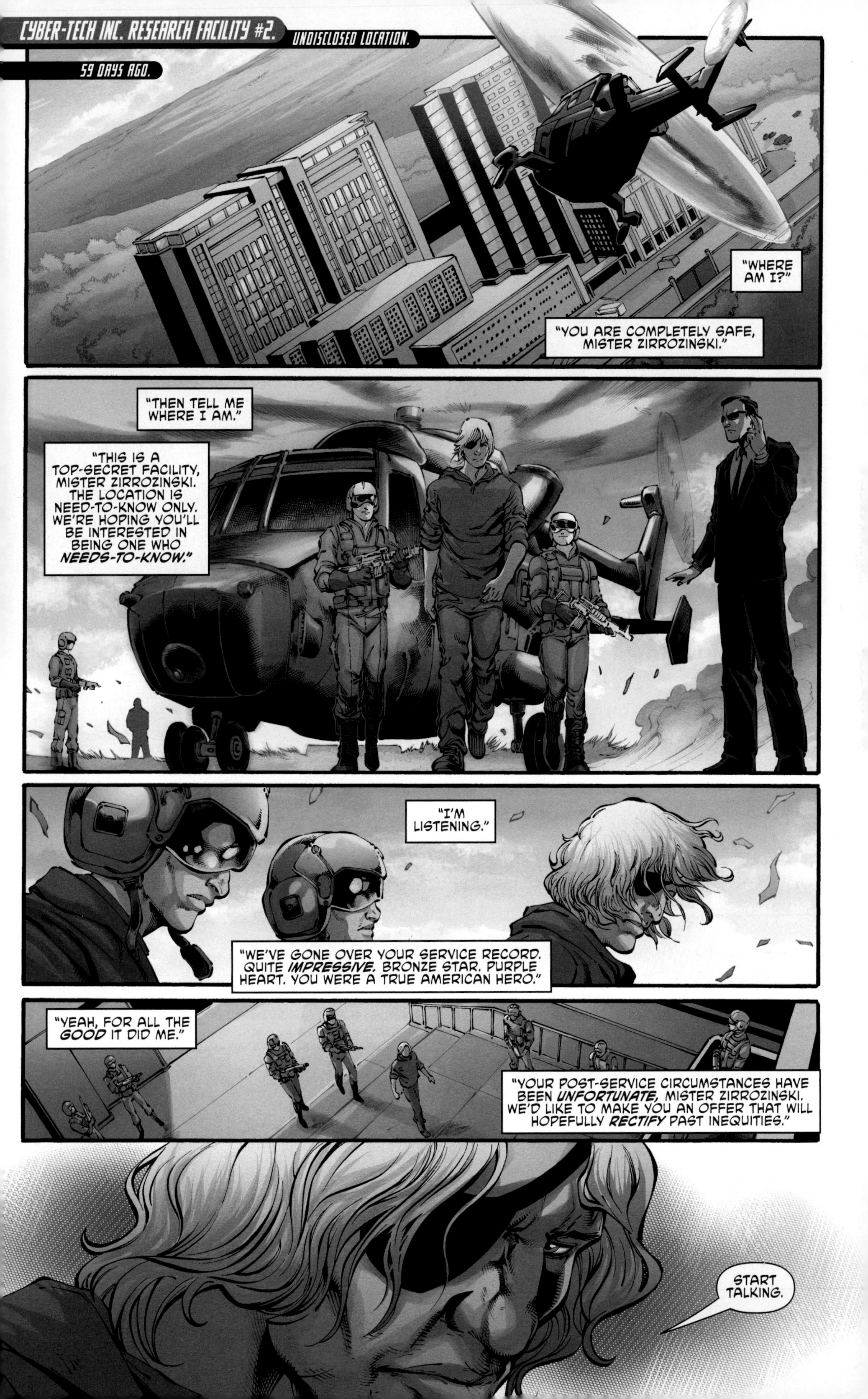
CYBER-TECH INC. RESEARCH FACILITY #2.
UNDISCLOSED LOCATION.
59 DAYS AGO.
"WHERE AM I?"
"YOU ARE COMPLETELY SAFE, MISTER ZIRROZINSKI."
"THEN TELL ME WHERE I AM."
"THIS IS A TOP-SECRET FACILITY, MISTER ZIRROZINSKI. THE LOCATION IS NEED-TO-KNOW ONLY. WE'RE HOPING YOU'LL BE INTERESTED IN BEING ONE WHO NEEDS-TO-KNOW."
"I'M LISTENING."
"WE'VE GONE OVER YOUR SERVICE RECORD. QUITE IMPRESSIVE. BRONZE STAR. PURPLE HEART. YOU WERE A TRUE AMERICAN HERO."
"YEAH, FOR ALL THE GOOD IT DID ME."
"YOUR POST-SERVICE CIRCUMSTANCES HAVE BEEN UNFORTUNATE, MISTER ZIRROZINSKI. WE'D LIKE TO MAKE YOU AN OFFER THAT WILL HOPEFULLY RECTIFY PAST INEQUITIES."
START TALKING.

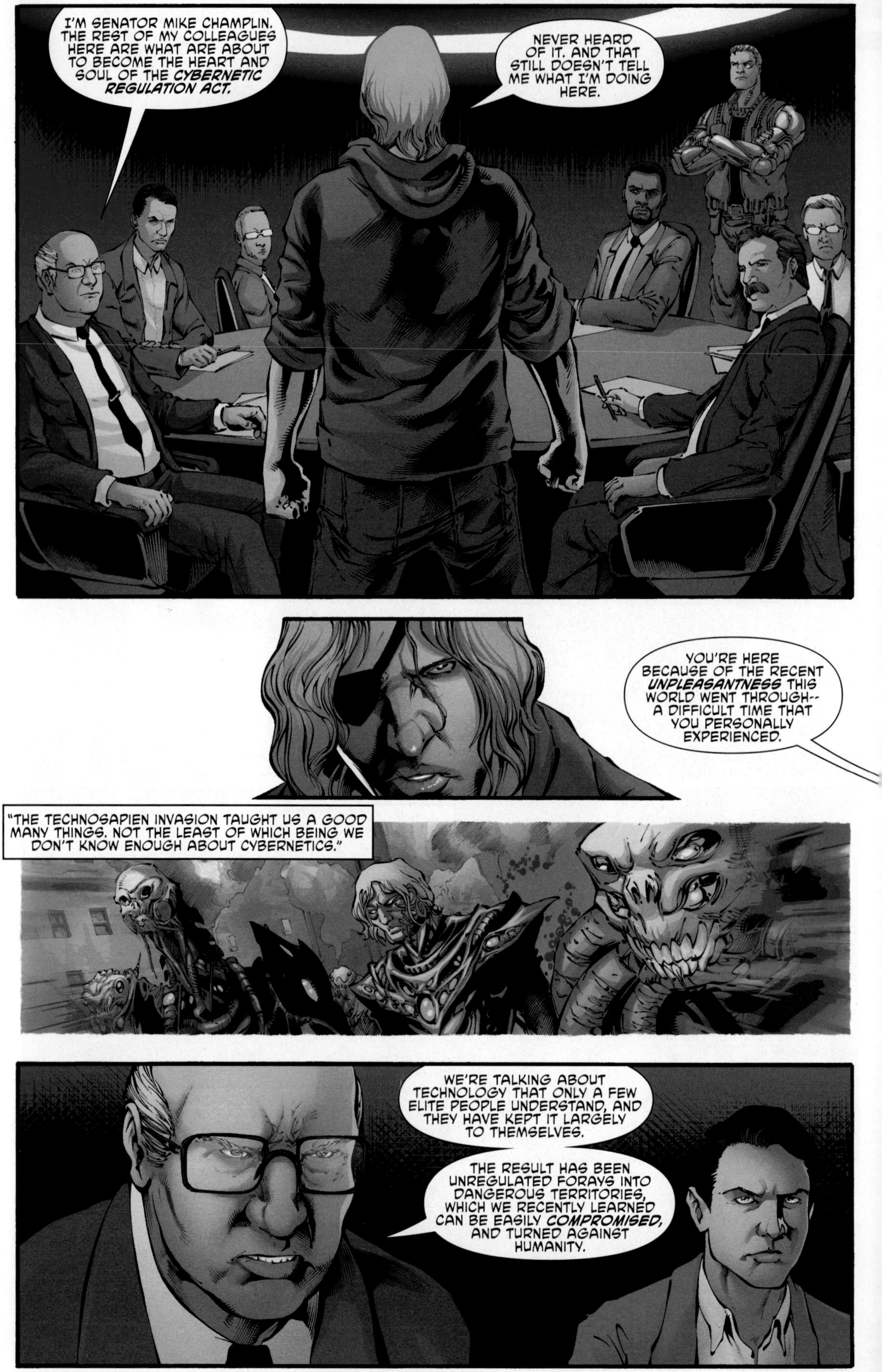
I'M SENATOR MIKE CHAMPLIN. THE REST OF MY COLLEAGUES HERE ARE WHAT ARE ABOUT TO BECOME THE HEART AND SOUL OF THE *CYBERNETIC REGULATION ACT.*
NEVER HEARD OF IT. AND THAT STILL DOESN'T TELL ME WHAT I'M DOING HERE.
YOU'RE HERE BECAUSE OF THE RECENT *UNPLEASANTNESS* THIS WORLD WENT THROUGH-- A DIFFICULT TIME THAT YOU PERSONALLY EXPERIENCED.
"THE TECHNOSAPIEN INVASION TAUGHT US A GOOD MANY THINGS. NOT THE LEAST OF WHICH BEING WE DON'T KNOW ENOUGH ABOUT CYBERNETICS."
WE'RE TALKING ABOUT TECHNOLOGY THAT ONLY A FEW ELITE PEOPLE UNDERSTAND, AND THEY HAVE KEPT IT LARGELY TO THEMSELVES.
THE RESULT HAS BEEN UNREGULATED FORAYS INTO DANGEROUS TERRITORIES, WHICH WE RECENTLY LEARNED CAN BE EASILY *COMPROMISED,* AND TURNED AGAINST HUMANITY.

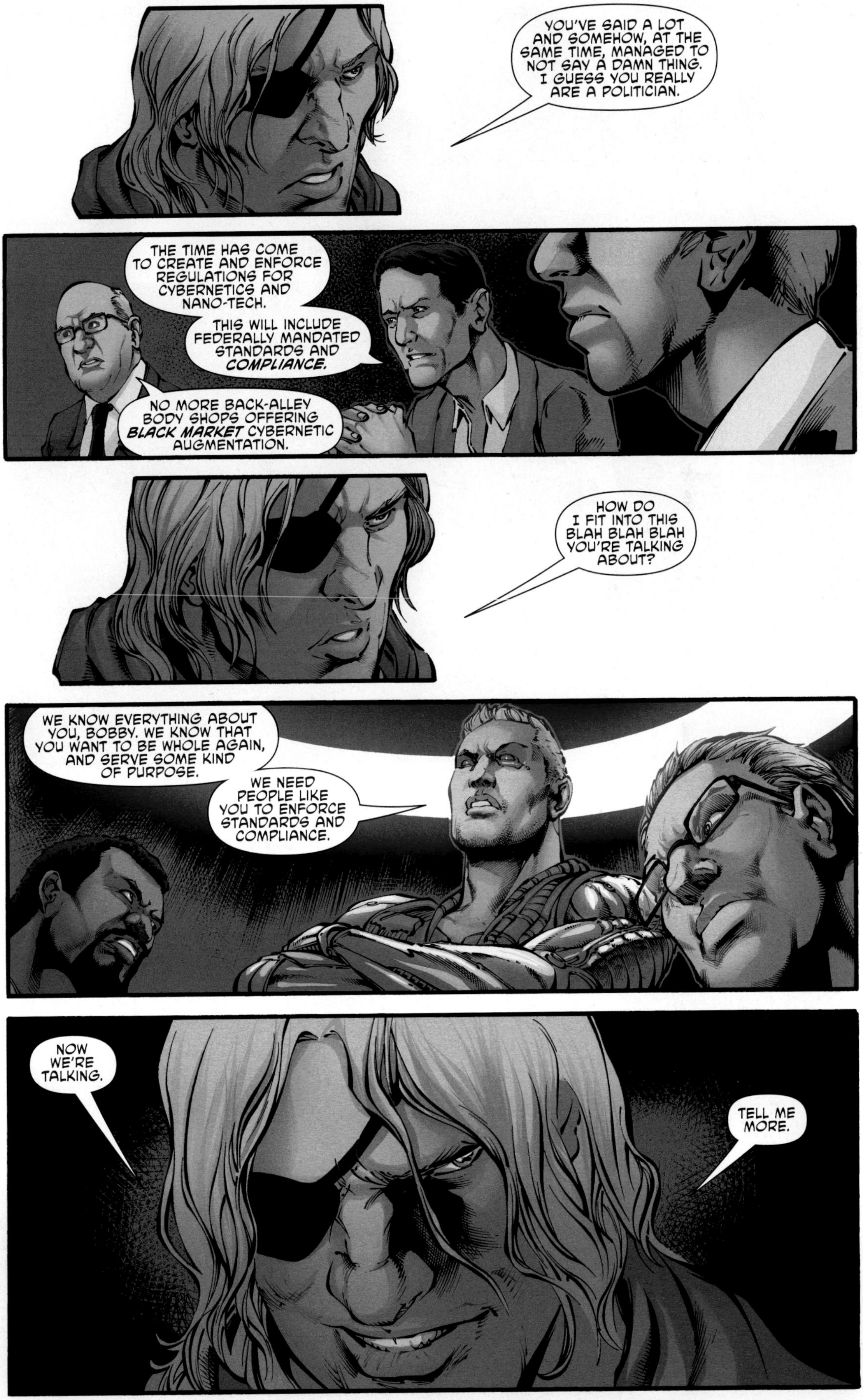
YOU'VE SAID A LOT AND SOMEHOW, AT THE SAME TIME, MANAGED TO NOT SAY A DAMN THING. I GUESS YOU REALLY ARE A POLITICIAN.
THE TIME HAS COME TO CREATE AND ENFORCE REGULATIONS FOR CYBERNETICS AND NANO-TECH.
THIS WILL INCLUDE FEDERALLY MANDATED STANDARDS AND *COMPLIANCE.*
NO MORE BACK-ALLEY BODY SHOPS OFFERING *BLACK MARKET* CYBERNETIC AUGMENTATION.
HOW DO I FIT INTO THIS BLAH BLAH BLAH YOU'RE TALKING ABOUT?
WE KNOW EVERYTHING ABOUT YOU, BOBBY. WE KNOW THAT YOU WANT TO BE WHOLE AGAIN, AND SERVE SOME KIND OF PURPOSE.
WE NEED PEOPLE LIKE YOU TO ENFORCE STANDARDS AND COMPLIANCE.
NOW WE'RE TALKING.
TELL ME MORE.

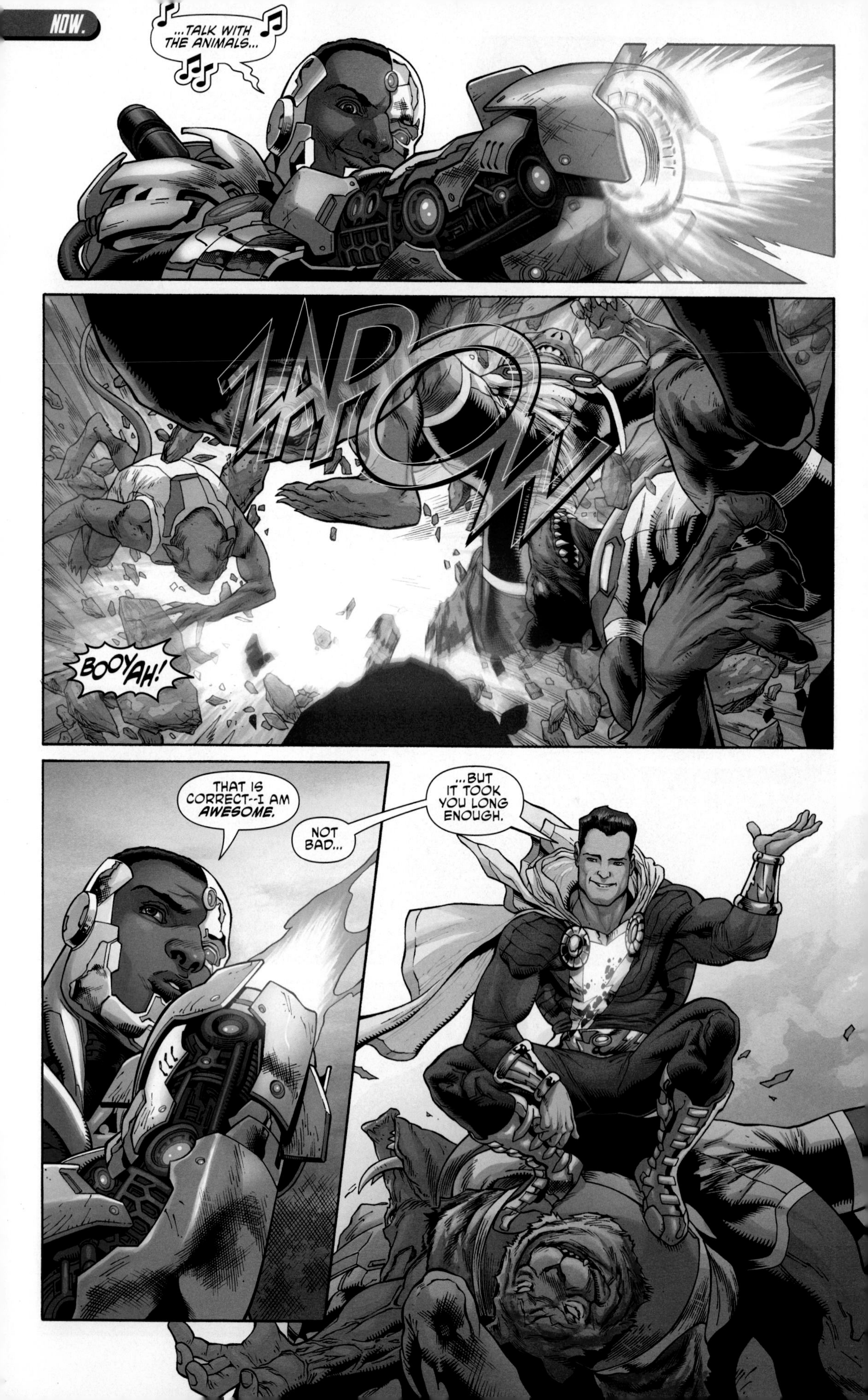
NOW.
...TALK WITH THE ANIMALS...
ZAP
BOOYAH!
THAT IS CORRECT--I AM AWESOME.
NOT BAD...
...BUT IT TOOK YOU LONG ENOUGH.

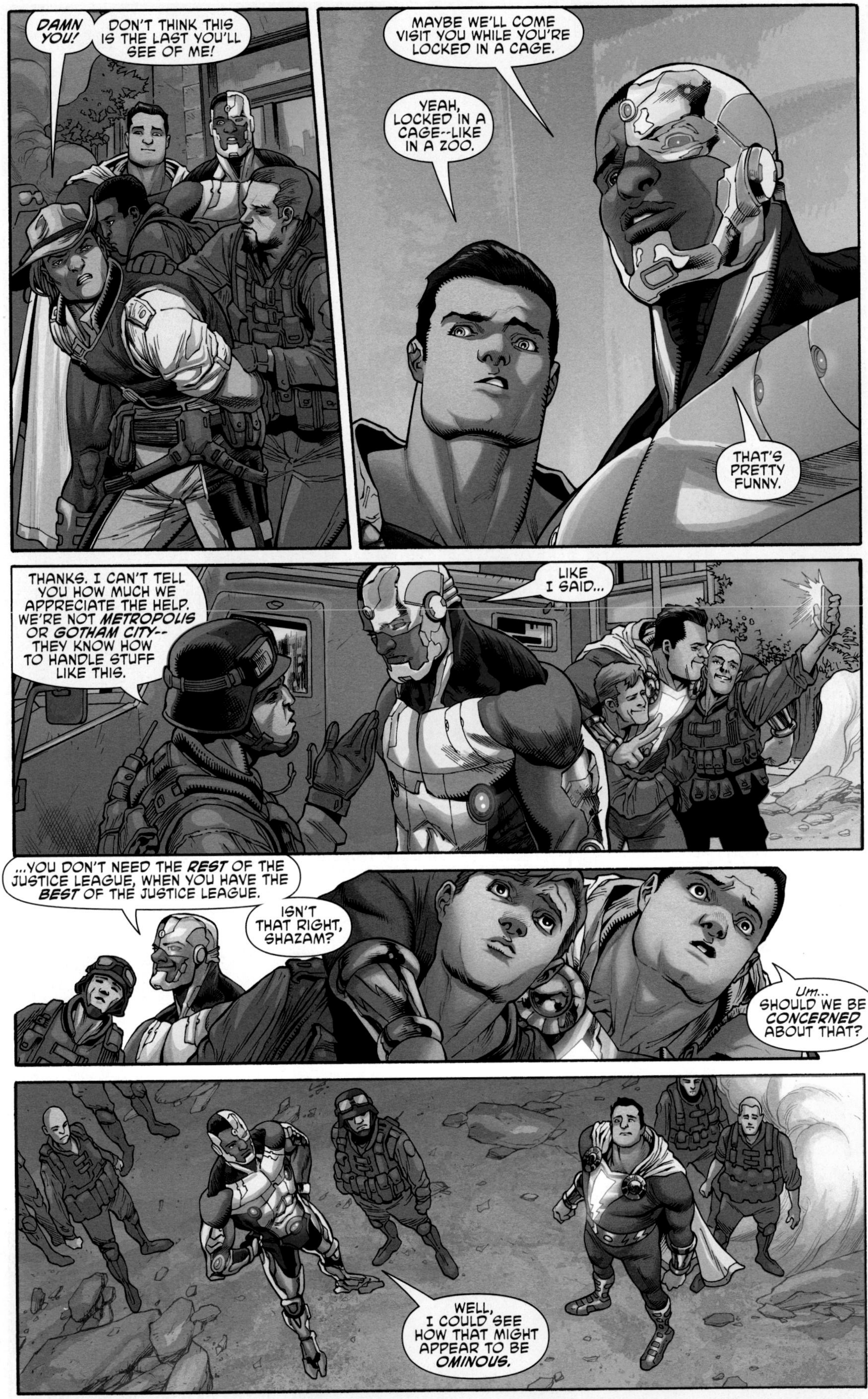
DAMN YOU!
DON'T THINK THIS IS THE LAST YOU'LL SEE OF ME!
MAYBE WE'LL COME VISIT YOU WHILE YOU'RE LOCKED IN A CAGE.
YEAH, LOCKED IN A CAGE--LIKE IN A ZOO.
THAT'S PRETTY FUNNY.
THANKS. I CAN'T TELL YOU HOW MUCH WE APPRECIATE THE HELP. WE'RE NOT METROPOLIS OR GOTHAM CITY-- THEY KNOW HOW TO HANDLE STUFF LIKE THIS.
LIKE I SAID...
...YOU DON'T NEED THE REST OF THE JUSTICE LEAGUE, WHEN YOU HAVE THE BEST OF THE JUSTICE LEAGUE.
ISN'T THAT RIGHT, SHAZAM?
Um... SHOULD WE BE CONCERNED ABOUT THAT?
WELL, I COULD SEE HOW THAT MIGHT APPEAR TO BE OMINOUS.

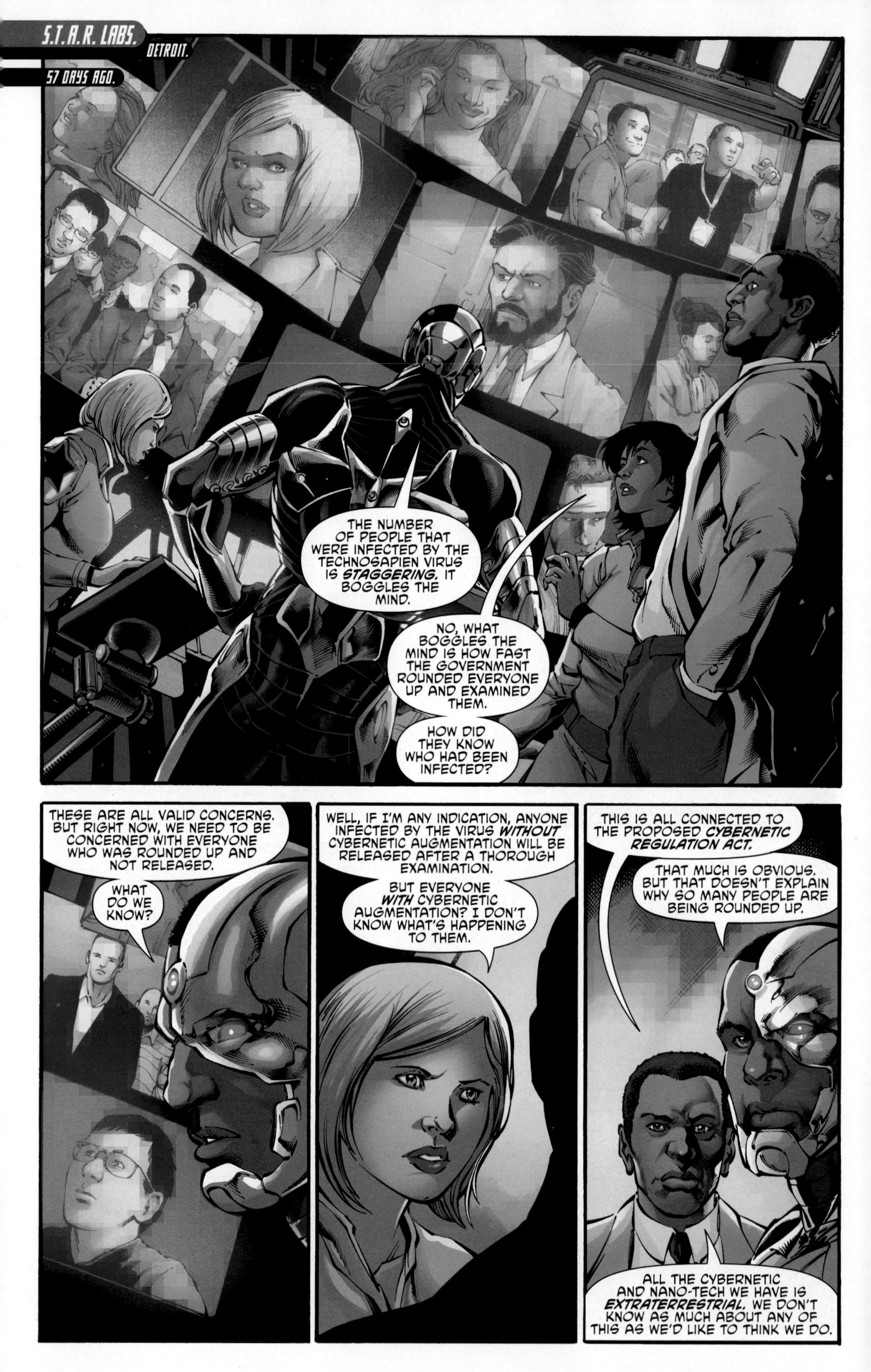
S.T.A.R. LABS.
DETROIT.
57 DAYS AGO.
THE NUMBER OF PEOPLE THAT WERE INFECTED BY THE TECHNOSAPIEN VIRUS IS STAGGERING. IT BOGGLES THE MIND.
NO, WHAT BOGGLES THE MIND IS HOW FAST THE GOVERNMENT ROUNDED EVERYONE UP AND EXAMINED THEM.
HOW DID THEY KNOW WHO HAD BEEN INFECTED?
THESE ARE ALL VALID CONCERNS. BUT RIGHT NOW, WE NEED TO BE CONCERNED WITH EVERYONE WHO WAS ROUNDED UP AND NOT RELEASED.
WHAT DO WE KNOW?
WELL, IF I'M ANY INDICATION, ANYONE INFECTED BY THE VIRUS WITHOUT CYBERNETIC AUGMENTATION WILL BE RELEASED AFTER A THOROUGH EXAMINATION.
BUT EVERYONE WITH CYBERNETIC AUGMENTATION? I DON'T KNOW WHAT'S HAPPENING TO THEM.
THIS IS ALL CONNECTED TO THE PROPOSED CYBERNETIC REGULATION ACT.
THAT MUCH IS OBVIOUS. BUT THAT DOESN'T EXPLAIN WHY SO MANY PEOPLE ARE BEING ROUNDED UP.
ALL THE CYBERNETIC AND NANO-TECH WE HAVE IS EXTRATERRESTRIAL. WE DON'T KNOW AS MUCH ABOUT ANY OF THIS AS WE'D LIKE TO THINK WE DO.

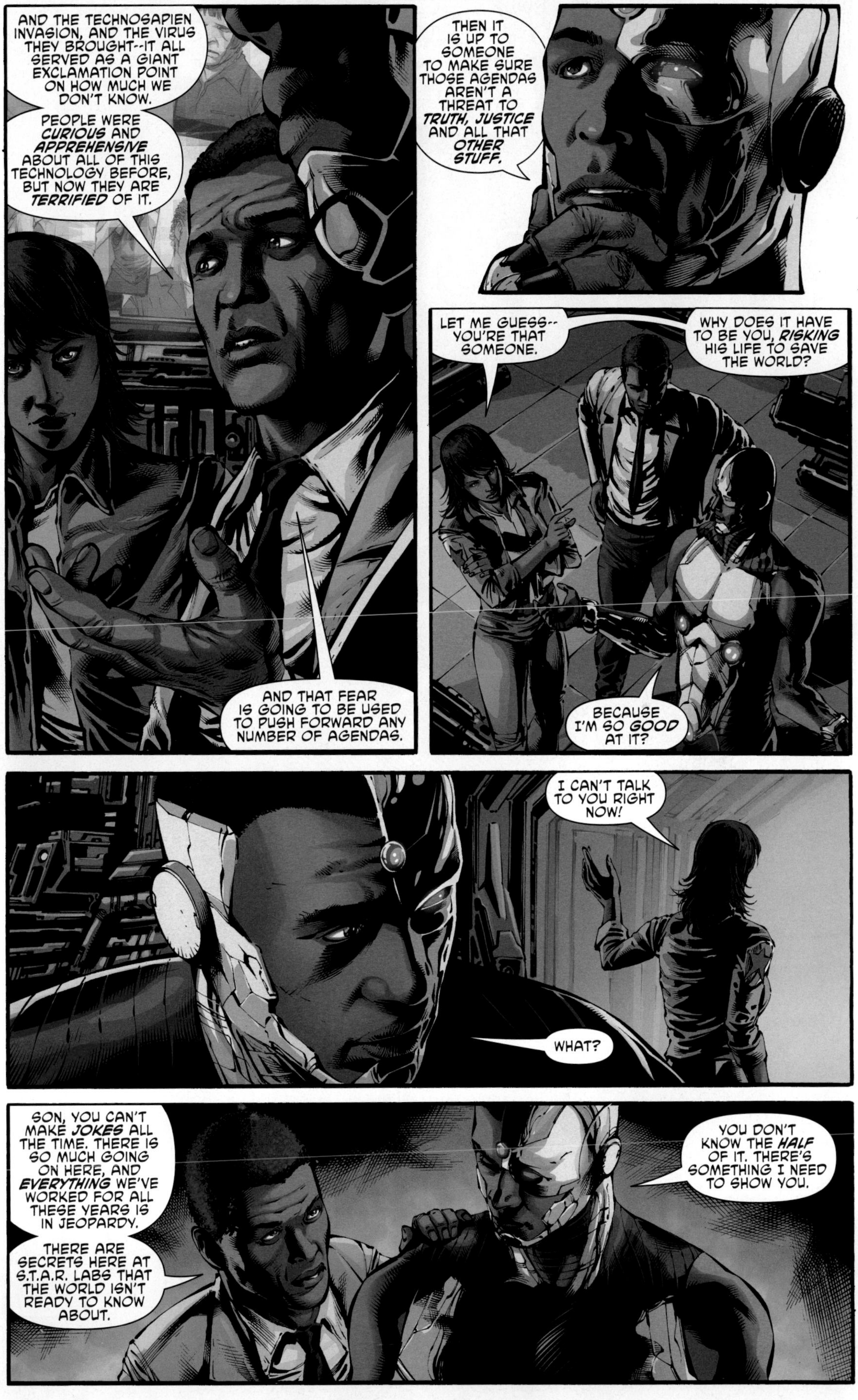
AND THE TECHNOSAPIEN INVASION, AND THE VIRUS THEY BROUGHT--IT ALL SERVED AS A GIANT EXCLAMATION POINT ON HOW MUCH WE DON'T KNOW.
PEOPLE WERE CURIOUS AND APPREHENSIVE ABOUT ALL OF THIS TECHNOLOGY BEFORE, BUT NOW THEY ARE TERRIFIED OF IT.
AND THAT FEAR IS GOING TO BE USED TO PUSH FORWARD ANY NUMBER OF AGENDAS.
THEN IT IS UP TO SOMEONE TO MAKE SURE THOSE AGENDAS AREN'T A THREAT TO TRUTH, JUSTICE AND ALL THAT OTHER STUFF.
LET ME GUESS-- YOU'RE THAT SOMEONE.
WHY DOES IT HAVE TO BE YOU, RISKING HIS LIFE TO SAVE THE WORLD?
BECAUSE I'M SO GOOD AT IT?
I CAN'T TALK TO YOU RIGHT NOW!
WHAT?
SON, YOU CAN'T MAKE JOKES ALL THE TIME. THERE IS SO MUCH GOING ON HERE, AND EVERYTHING WE'VE WORKED FOR ALL THESE YEARS IS IN JEOPARDY.
THERE ARE SECRETS HERE AT S.T.A.R. LABS THAT THE WORLD ISN'T READY TO KNOW ABOUT.
YOU DON'T KNOW THE HALF OF IT. THERE'S SOMETHING I NEED TO SHOW YOU.

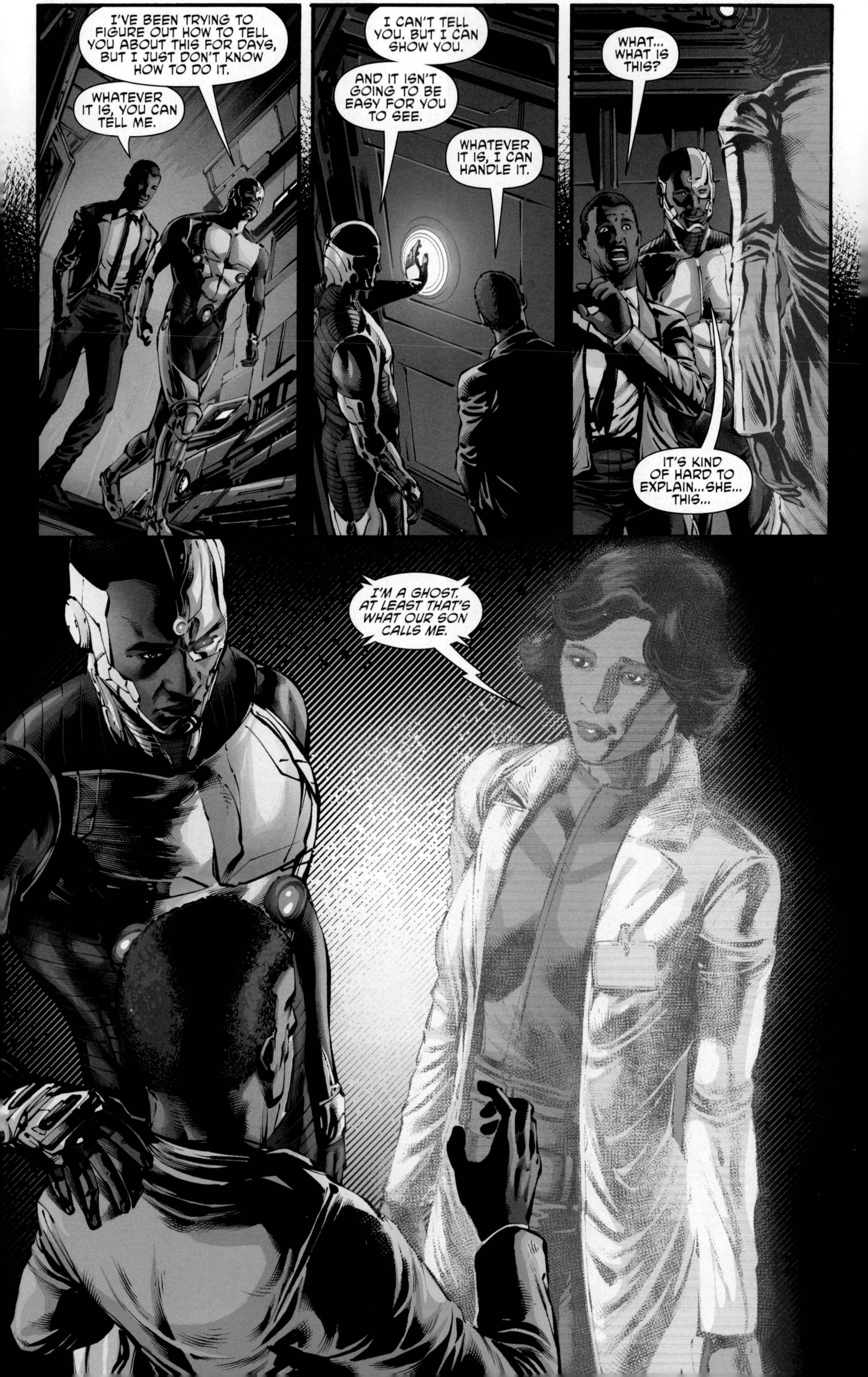
I'VE BEEN TRYING TO FIGURE OUT HOW TO TELL YOU ABOUT THIS FOR DAYS, BUT I JUST DON'T KNOW HOW TO DO IT.
WHATEVER IT IS, YOU CAN TELL ME.
I CAN'T TELL YOU, BUT I CAN SHOW YOU.
AND IT ISN'T GOING TO BE EASY FOR YOU TO SEE.
WHATEVER IT IS, I CAN HANDLE IT.
WHAT... WHAT IS THIS?
IT'S KIND OF HARD TO EXPLAIN...SHE... THIS...
I'M A GHOST. AT LEAST THAT'S WHAT OUR SON CALLS ME.

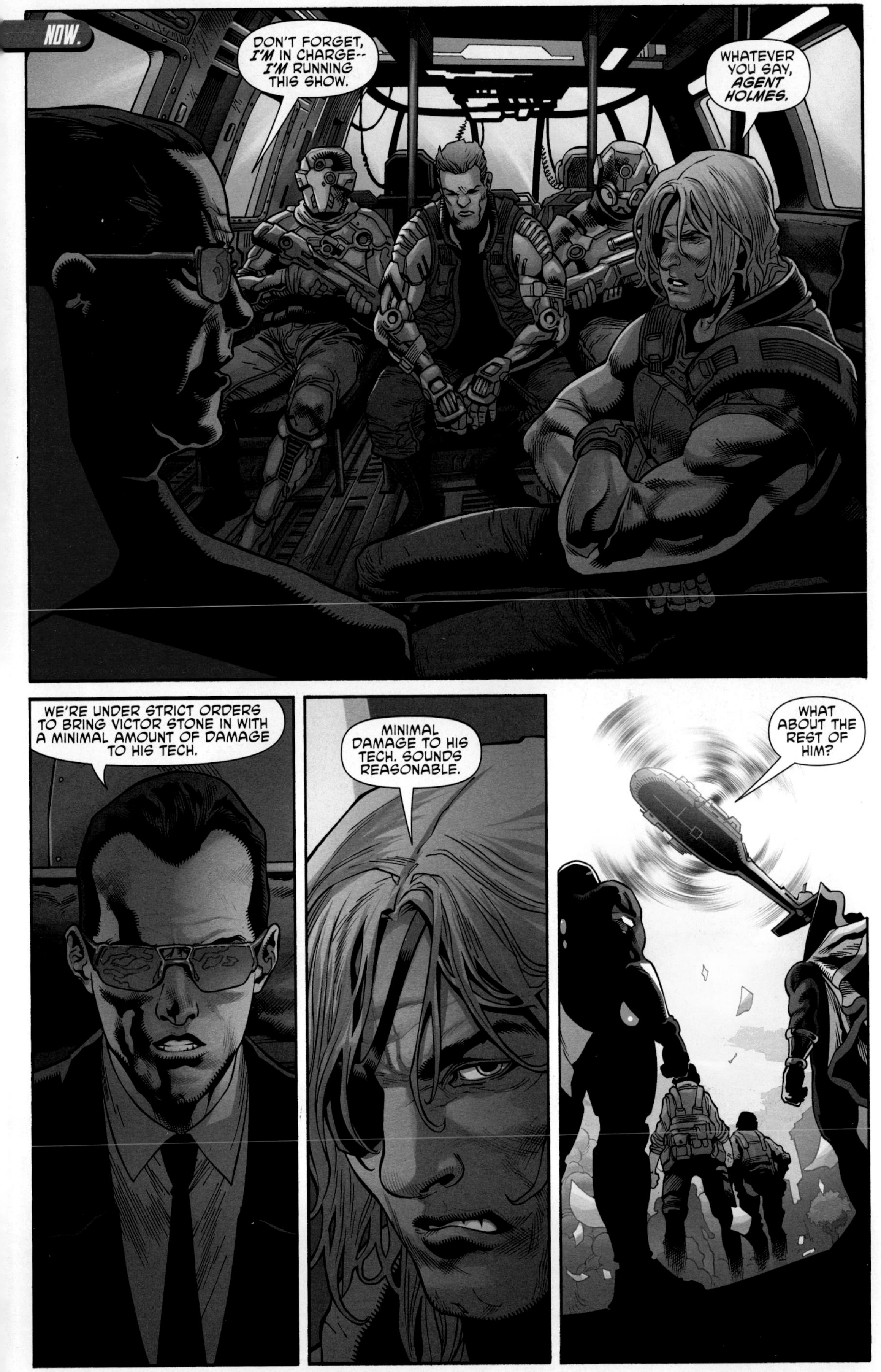
NOW.
DON'T FORGET, I'M IN CHARGE-- I'M RUNNING THIS SHOW.
WHATEVER YOU SAY, AGENT HOLMES.
WE'RE UNDER STRICT ORDERS TO BRING VICTOR STONE IN WITH A MINIMAL AMOUNT OF DAMAGE TO HIS TECH.
MINIMAL DAMAGE TO HIS TECH. SOUNDS REASONABLE.
WHAT ABOUT THE REST OF HIM?

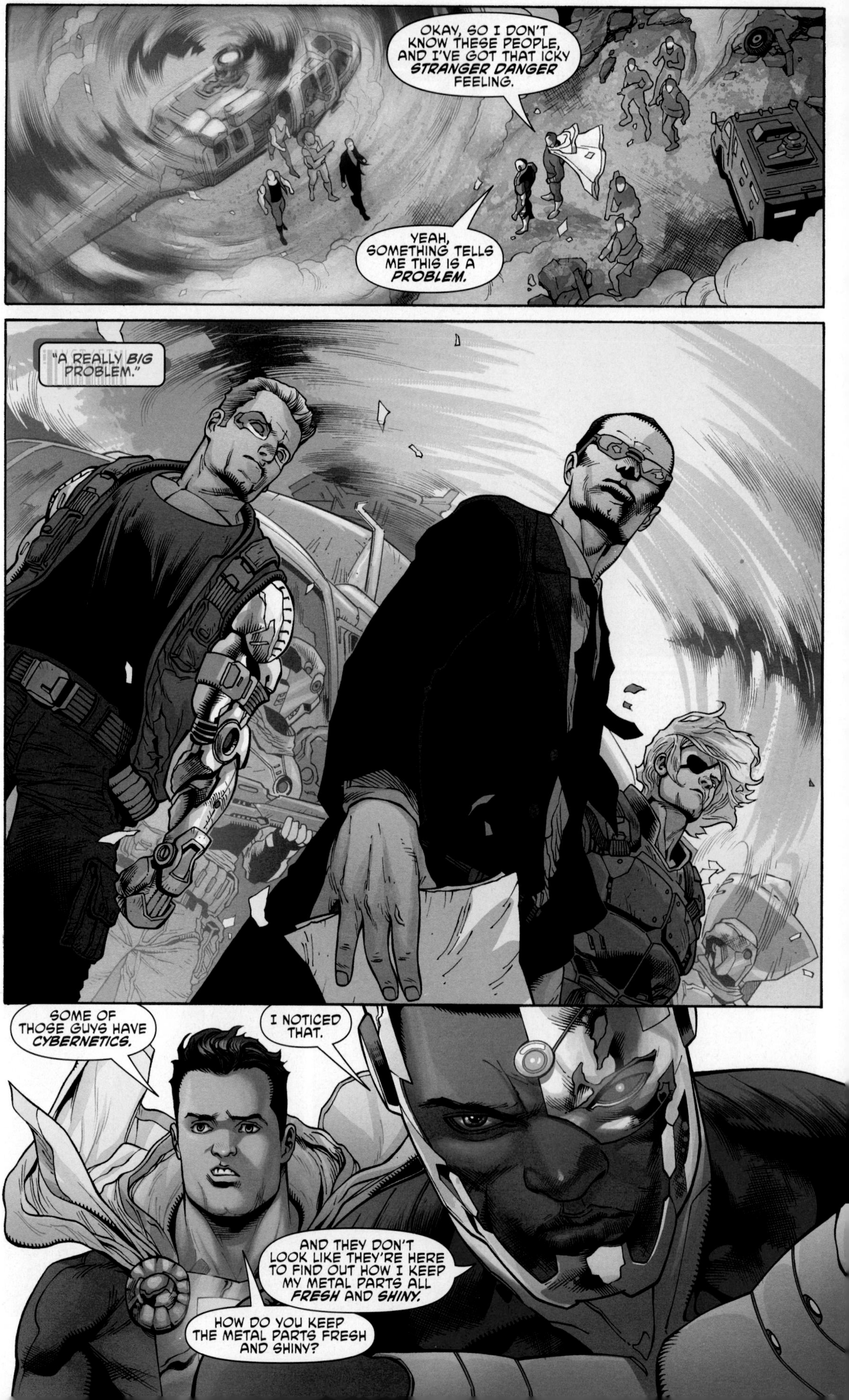
OKAY, SO I DON'T KNOW THESE PEOPLE, AND I'VE GOT THAT ICKY STRANGER DANGER FEELING.
YEAH, SOMETHING TELLS ME THIS IS A PROBLEM.
"A REALLY BIG PROBLEM."
SOME OF THOSE GUYS HAVE CYBERNETICS.
I NOTICED THAT.
AND THEY DON'T LOOK LIKE THEY'RE HERE TO FIND OUT HOW I KEEP MY METAL PARTS ALL FRESH AND SHINY.
HOW DO YOU KEEP THE METAL PARTS FRESH AND SHINY?

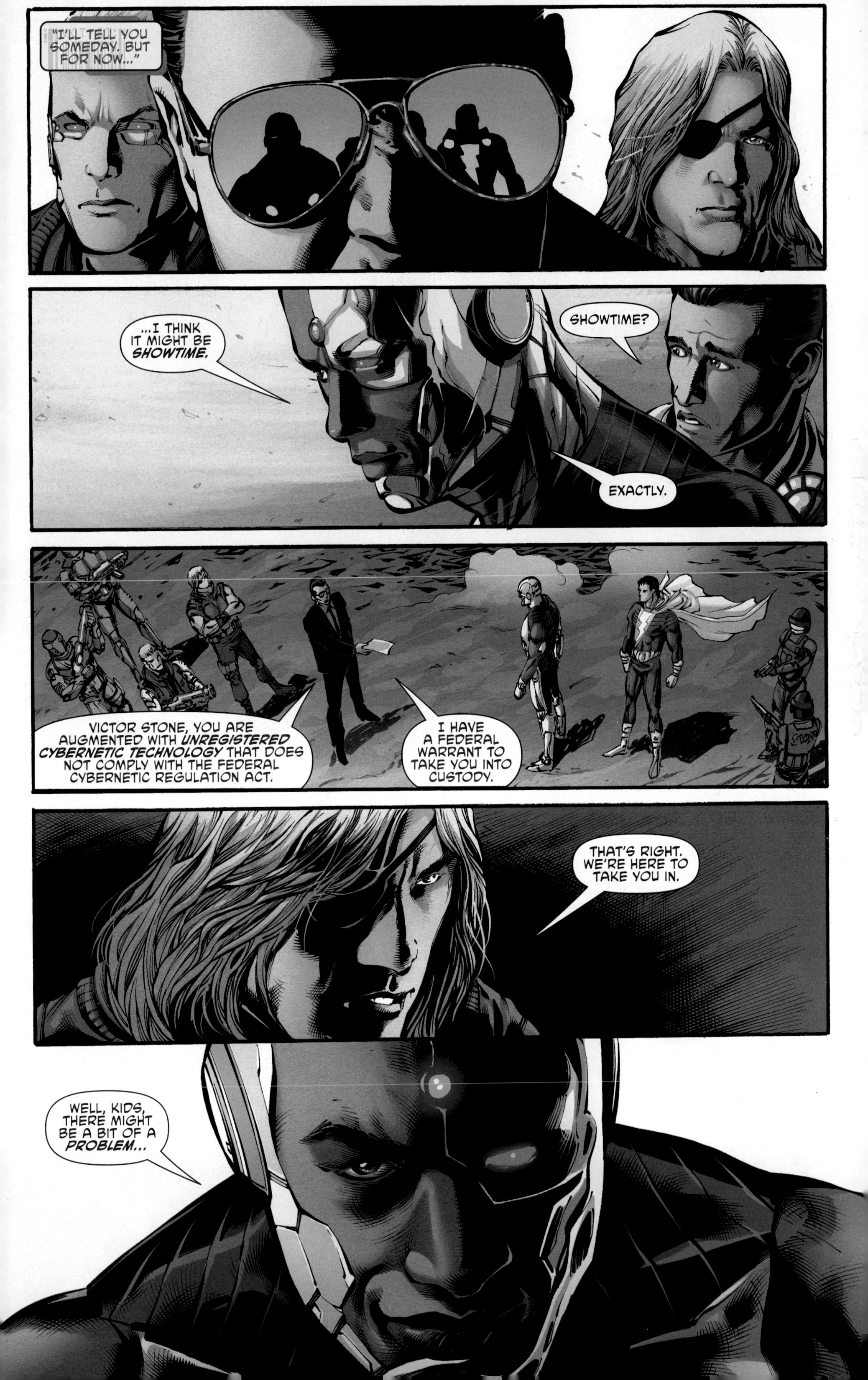
"I'LL TELL YOU SOMEDAY. BUT FOR NOW..."
...I THINK IT MIGHT BE *SHOWTIME.*
SHOWTIME?
EXACTLY.
VICTOR STONE, YOU ARE AUGMENTED WITH *UNREGISTERED CYBERNETIC TECHNOLOGY* THAT DOES NOT COMPLY WITH THE FEDERAL CYBERNETIC REGULATION ACT.
I HAVE A FEDERAL WARRANT TO TAKE YOU INTO CUSTODY.
THAT'S RIGHT. WE'RE HERE TO TAKE YOU IN.
WELL, KIDS, THERE MIGHT BE A BIT OF A *PROBLEM...*

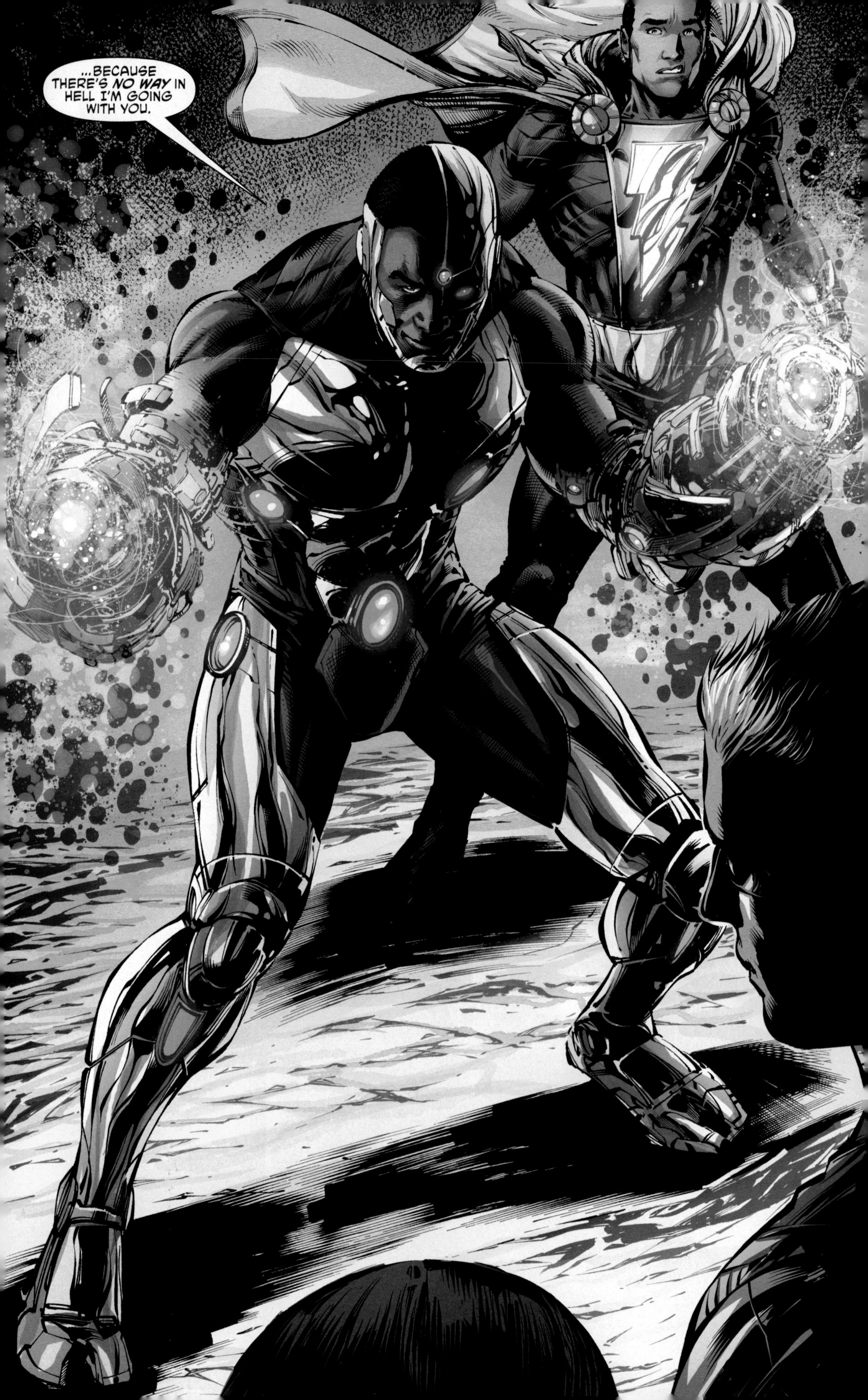
...BECAUSE THERE'S *NO WAY* IN HELL I'M GOING WITH YOU.

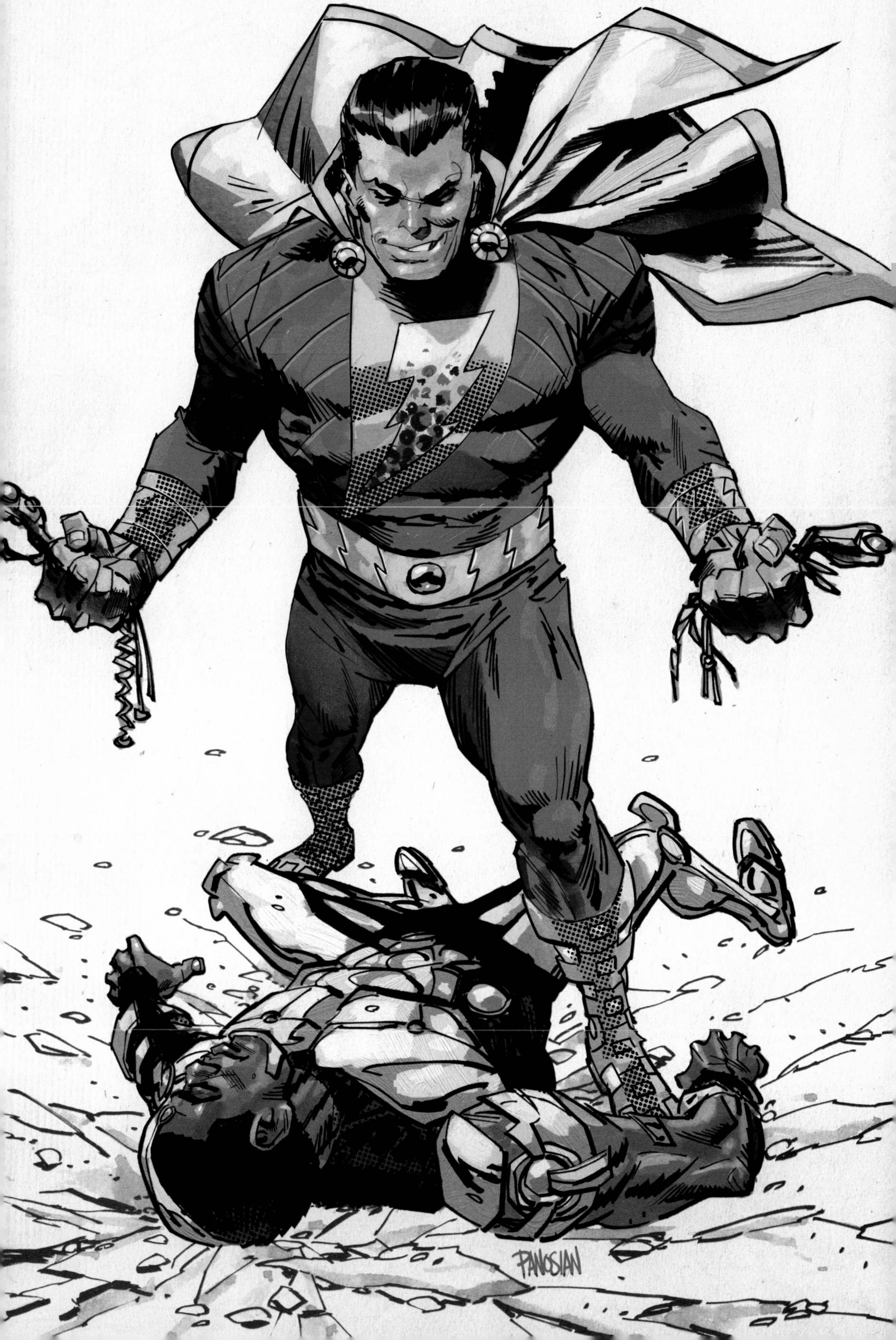
PANOSIAN

PUBLIC ENEMY #1

DAVID F. WALKER writer **FELIPE WATANABE & JÚLIO FERREIRA** pencillers **OCLAIR ALBERT & JÚLIO FERREIRA** inkers **DAN PANOSIAN** cover

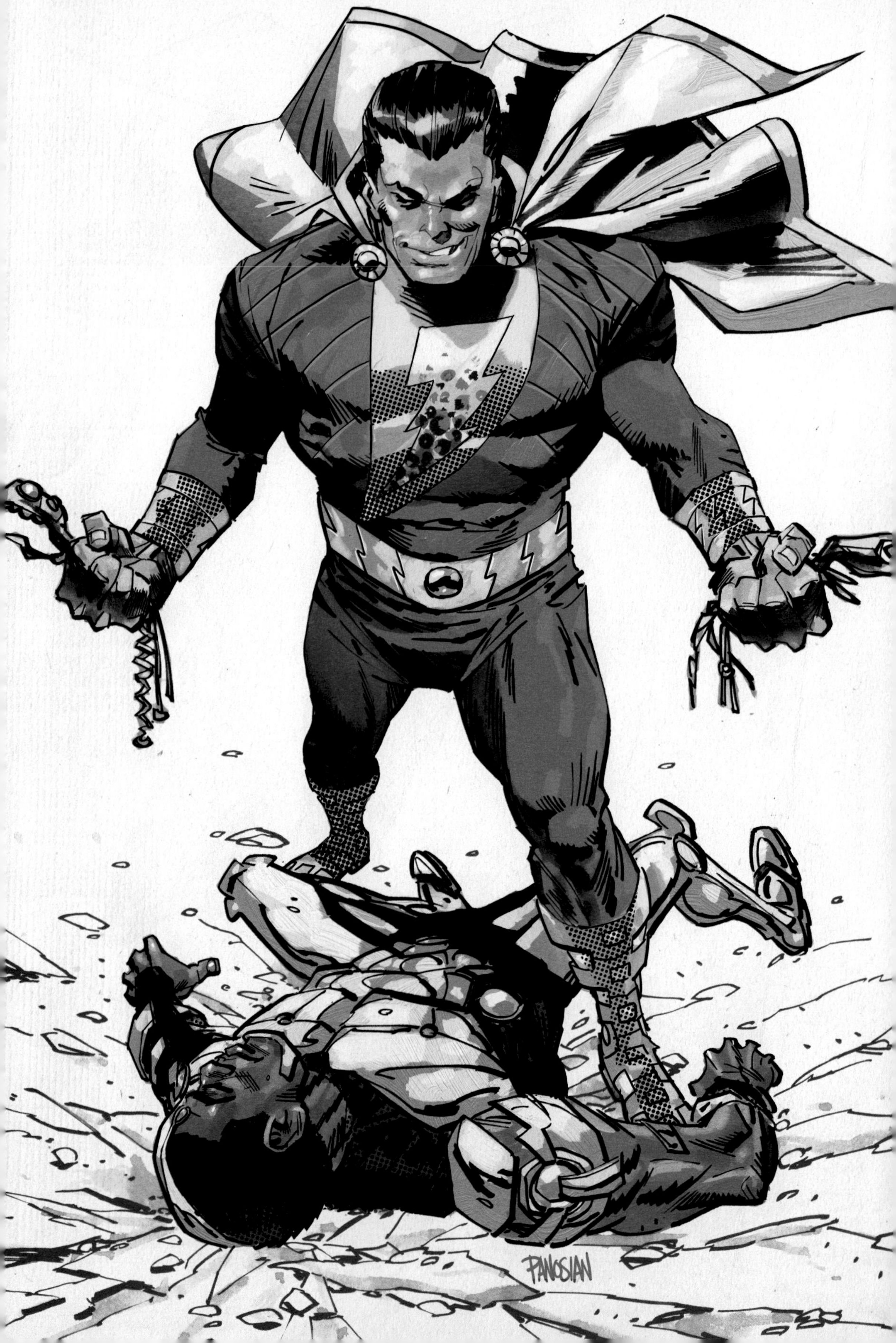
PANOSIAN

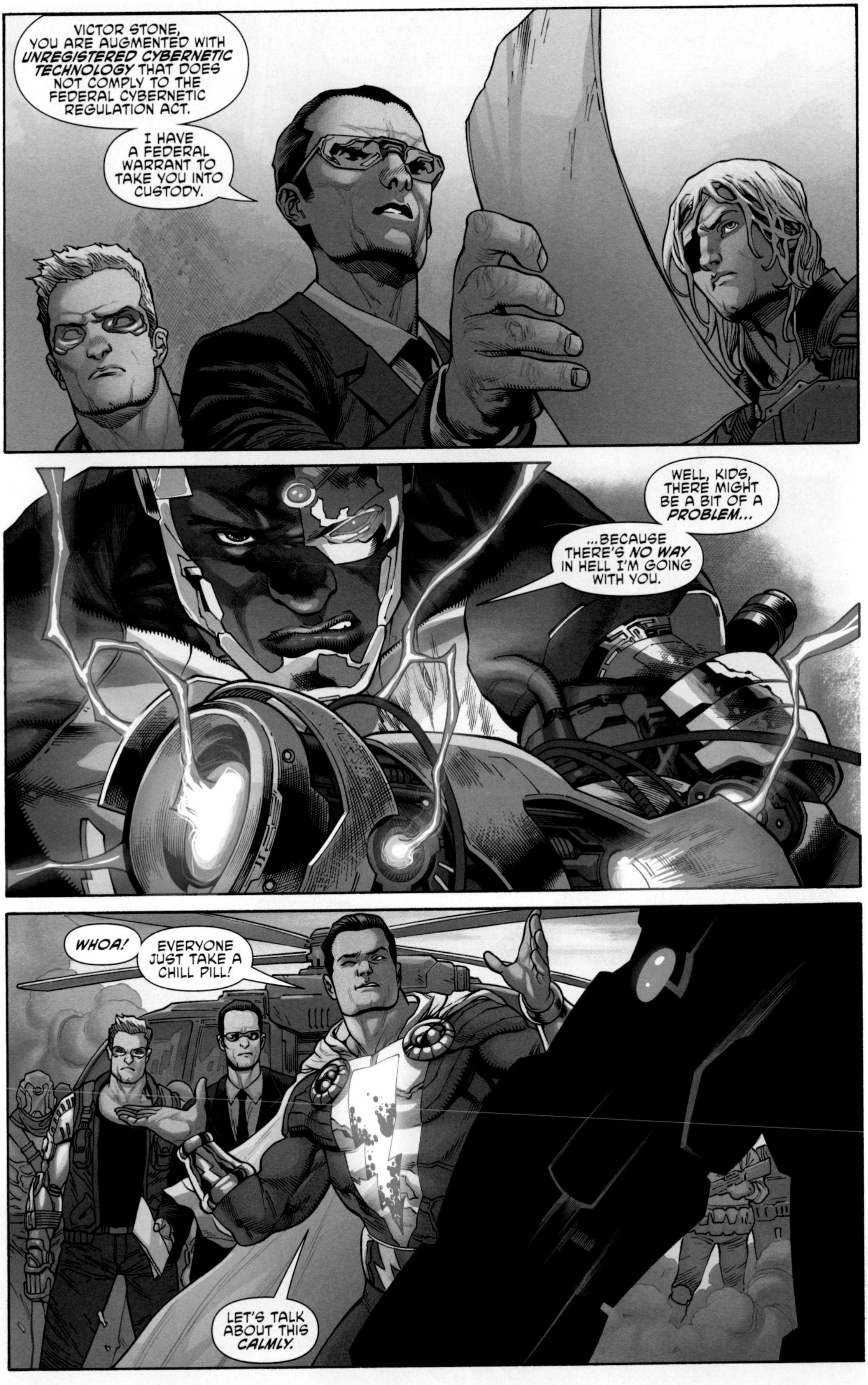
VICTOR STONE, YOU ARE AUGMENTED WITH UNREGISTERED CYBERNETIC TECHNOLOGY THAT DOES NOT COMPLY TO THE FEDERAL CYBERNETIC REGULATION ACT.
I HAVE A FEDERAL WARRANT TO TAKE YOU INTO CUSTODY.
WELL, KIDS, THERE MIGHT BE A BIT OF A PROBLEM...
...BECAUSE THERE'S NO WAY IN HELL I'M GOING WITH YOU.
WHOA!
EVERYONE JUST TAKE A CHILL PILL!
LET'S TALK ABOUT THIS CALMLY.

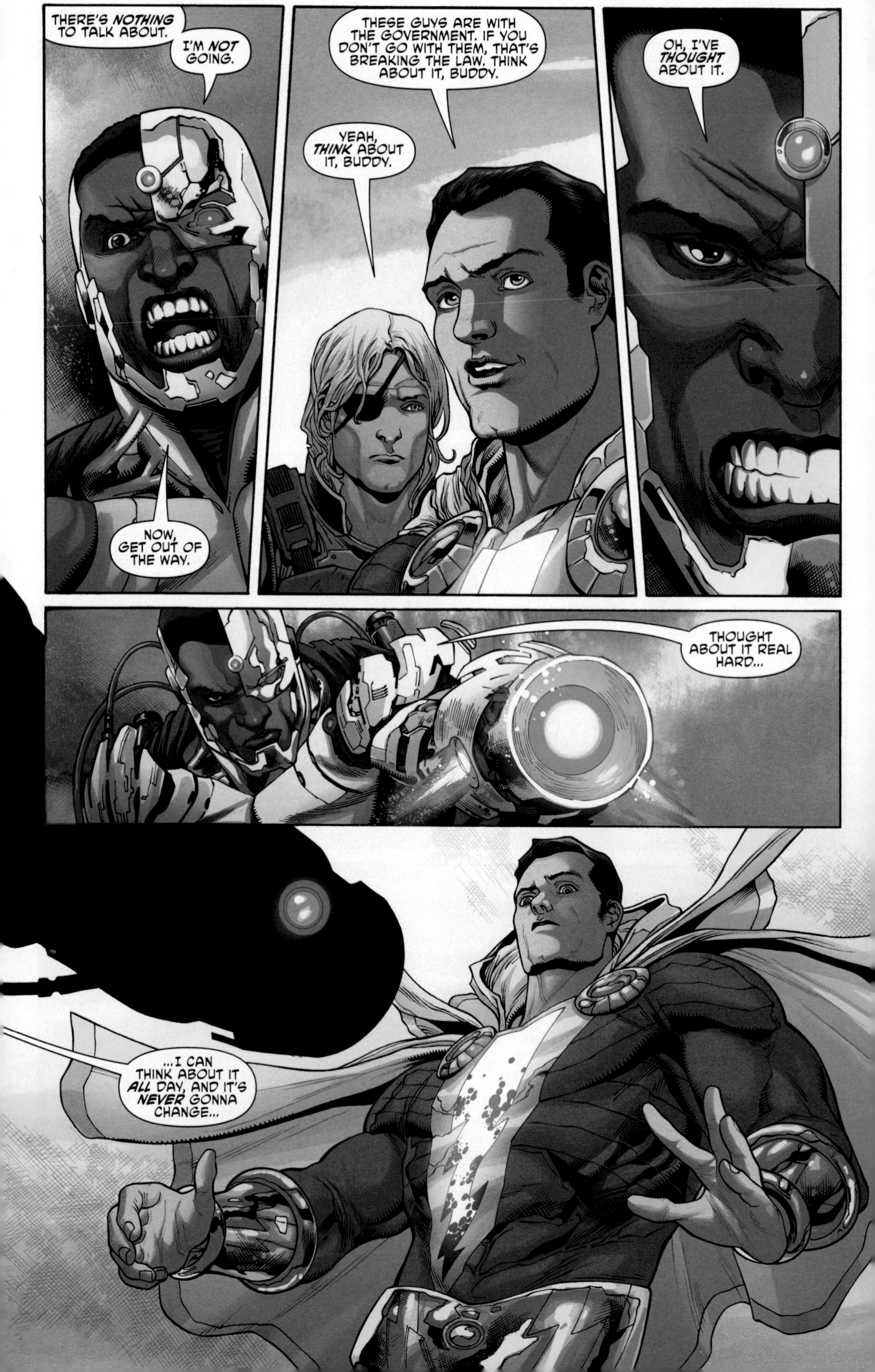

THERE'S *NOTHING* TO TALK ABOUT.
I'M *NOT* GOING.
NOW, GET OUT OF THE WAY.
THESE GUYS ARE WITH THE GOVERNMENT. IF YOU DON'T GO WITH THEM, THAT'S BREAKING THE LAW. THINK ABOUT IT, BUDDY.
YEAH, *THINK* ABOUT IT, BUDDY.
OH, I'VE *THOUGHT* ABOUT IT.
THOUGHT ABOUT IT REAL HARD...
...I CAN THINK ABOUT IT *ALL* DAY, AND IT'S *NEVER* GONNA CHANGE...

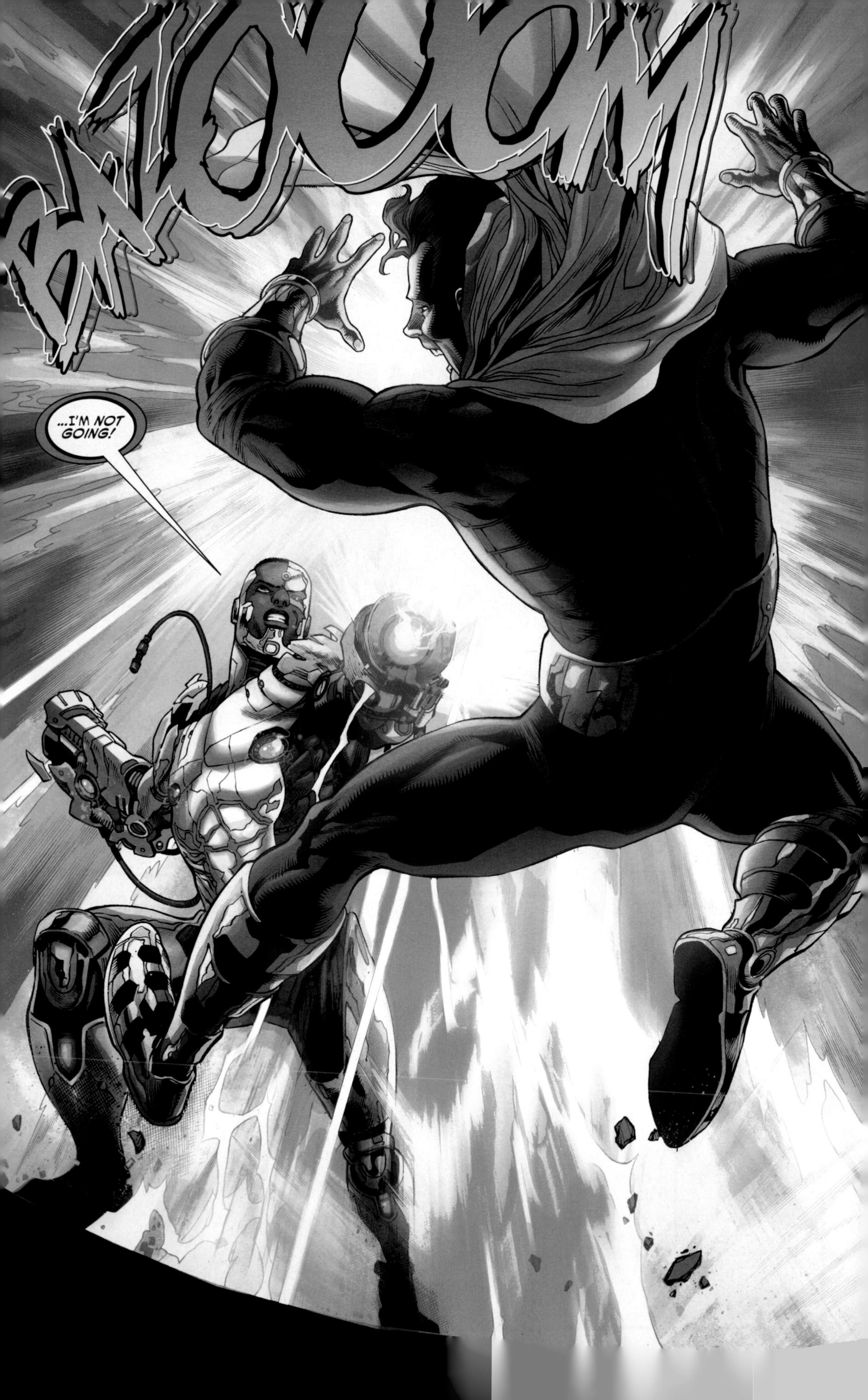
BAZOOOM
...I'M NOT GOING!

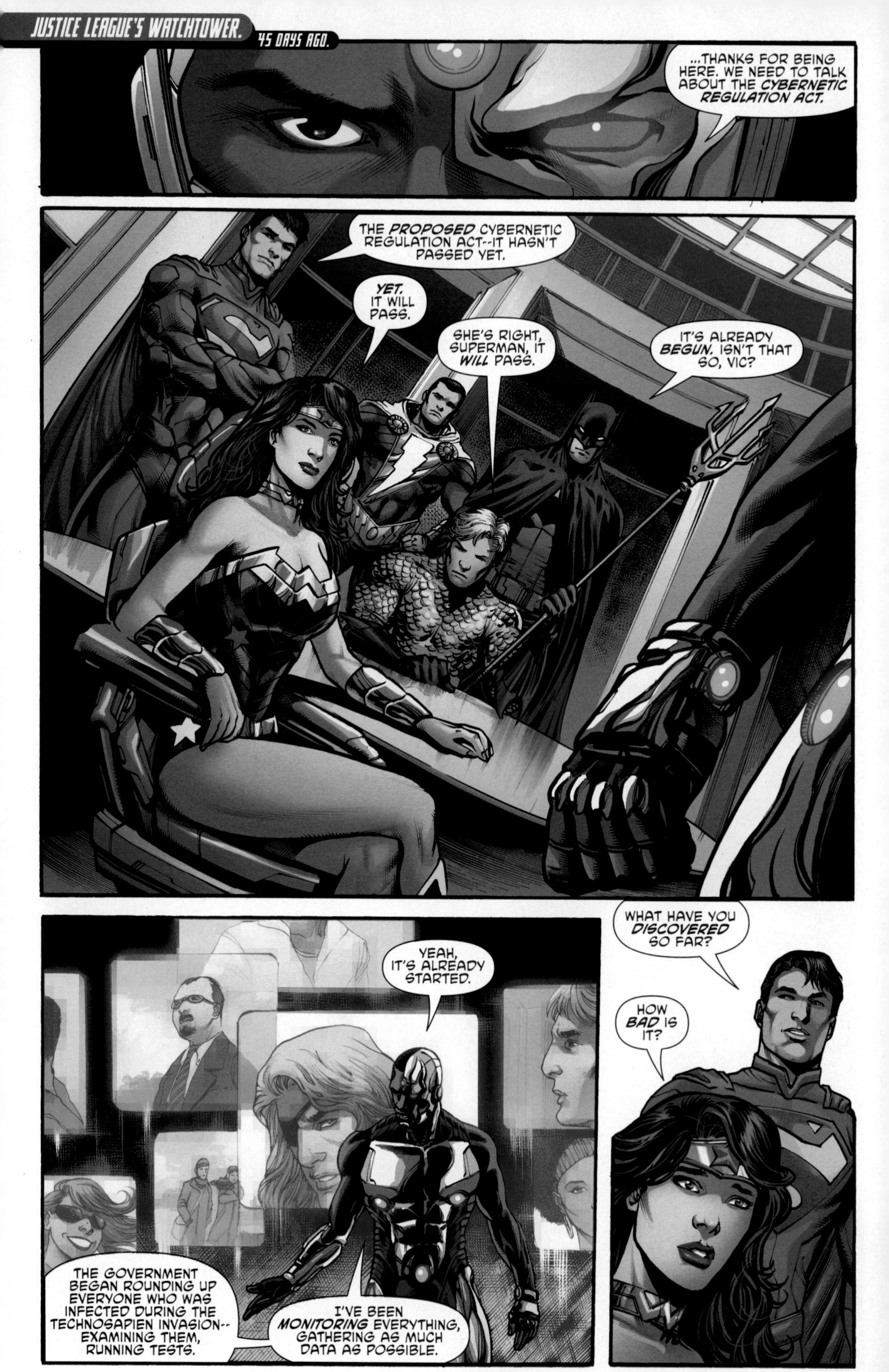
JUSTICE LEAGUE'S WATCHTOWER.
45 DAYS AGO.
...THANKS FOR BEING HERE. WE NEED TO TALK ABOUT THE CYBERNETIC REGULATION ACT.
THE PROPOSED CYBERNETIC REGULATION ACT--IT HASN'T PASSED YET.
YET. IT WILL PASS.
SHE'S RIGHT, SUPERMAN, IT WILL PASS.
IT'S ALREADY BEGUN. ISN'T THAT SO, VIC?
YEAH, IT'S ALREADY STARTED.
WHAT HAVE YOU DISCOVERED SO FAR?
HOW BAD IS IT?
THE GOVERNMENT BEGAN ROUNDING UP EVERYONE WHO WAS INFECTED DURING THE TECHNOSAPIEN INVASION--EXAMINING THEM, RUNNING TESTS.
I'VE BEEN MONITORING EVERYTHING, GATHERING AS MUCH DATA AS POSSIBLE.

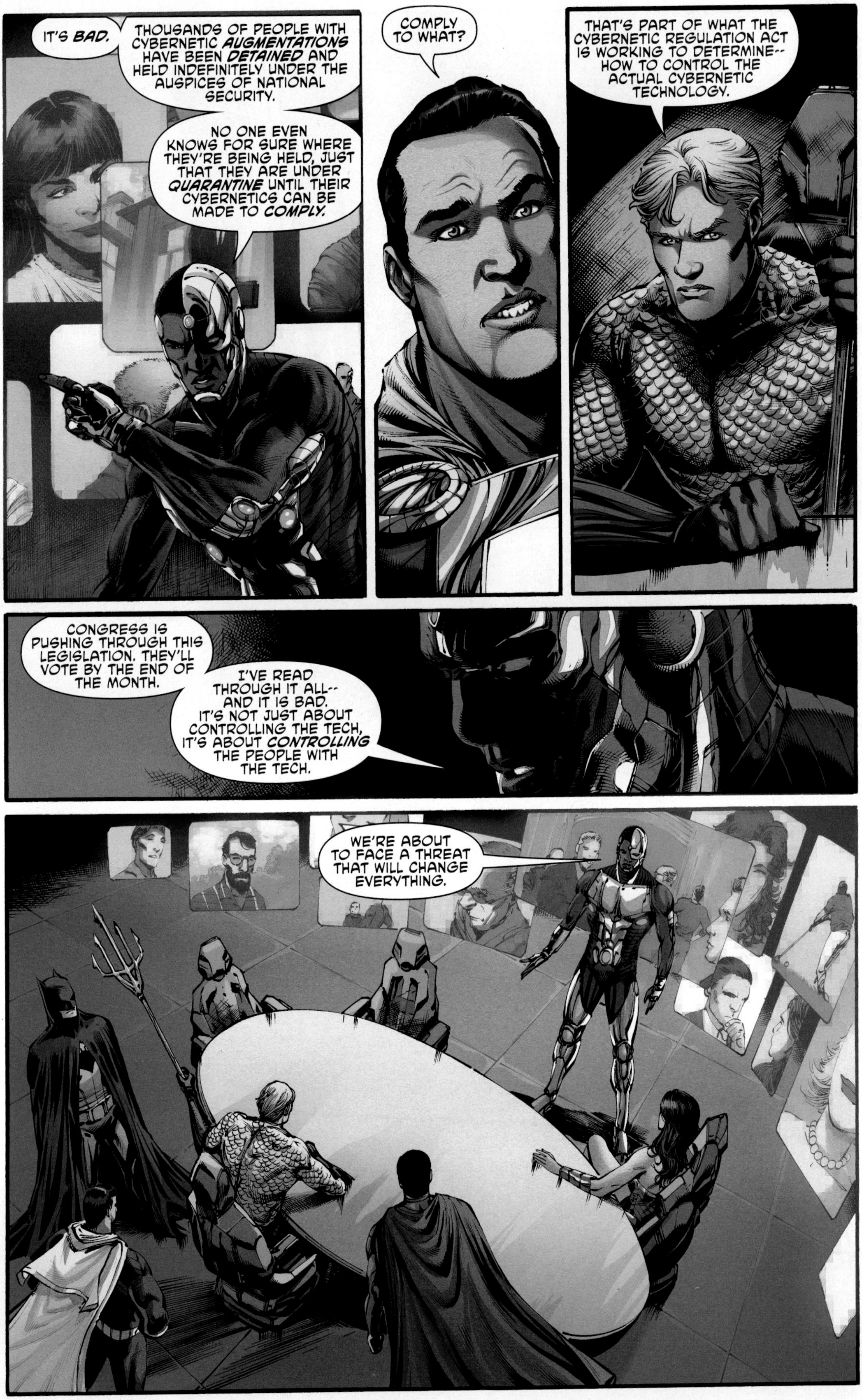
IT'S BAD.
THOUSANDS OF PEOPLE WITH CYBERNETIC AUGMENTATIONS HAVE BEEN DETAINED AND HELD INDEFINITELY UNDER THE AUSPICES OF NATIONAL SECURITY.
NO ONE EVEN KNOWS FOR SURE WHERE THEY'RE BEING HELD, JUST THAT THEY ARE UNDER QUARANTINE UNTIL THEIR CYBERNETICS CAN BE MADE TO COMPLY.
COMPLY TO WHAT?
THAT'S PART OF WHAT THE CYBERNETIC REGULATION ACT IS WORKING TO DETERMINE-- HOW TO CONTROL THE ACTUAL CYBERNETIC TECHNOLOGY.
CONGRESS IS PUSHING THROUGH THIS LEGISLATION. THEY'LL VOTE BY THE END OF THE MONTH.
I'VE READ THROUGH IT ALL-- AND IT IS BAD. IT'S NOT JUST ABOUT CONTROLLING THE TECH, IT'S ABOUT CONTROLLING THE PEOPLE WITH THE TECH.
WE'RE ABOUT TO FACE A THREAT THAT WILL CHANGE EVERYTHING.

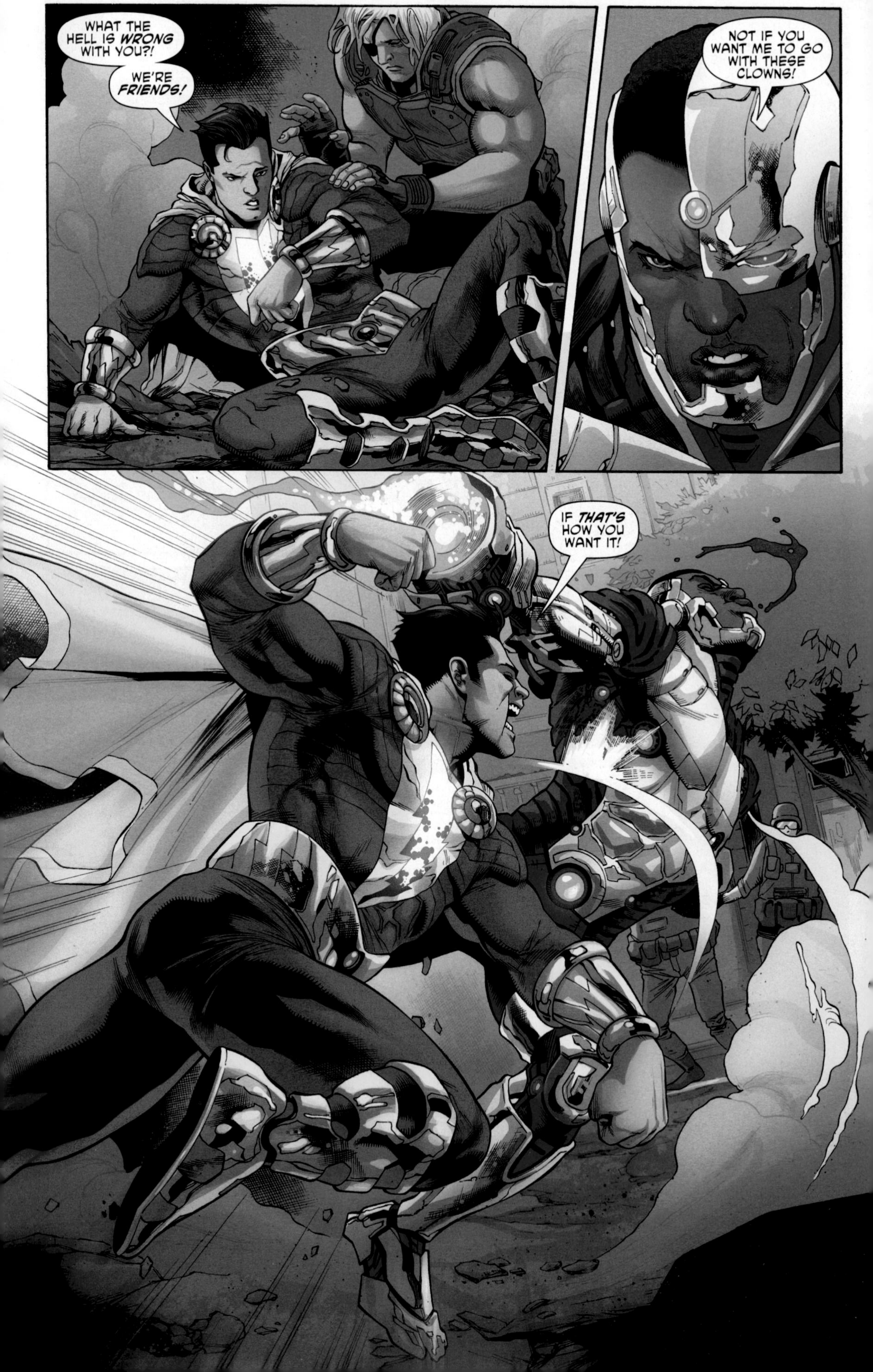
WHAT THE HELL IS WRONG WITH YOU?!
WE'RE FRIENDS!
NOT IF YOU WANT ME TO GO WITH THESE CLOWNS!
IF THAT'S HOW YOU WANT IT!

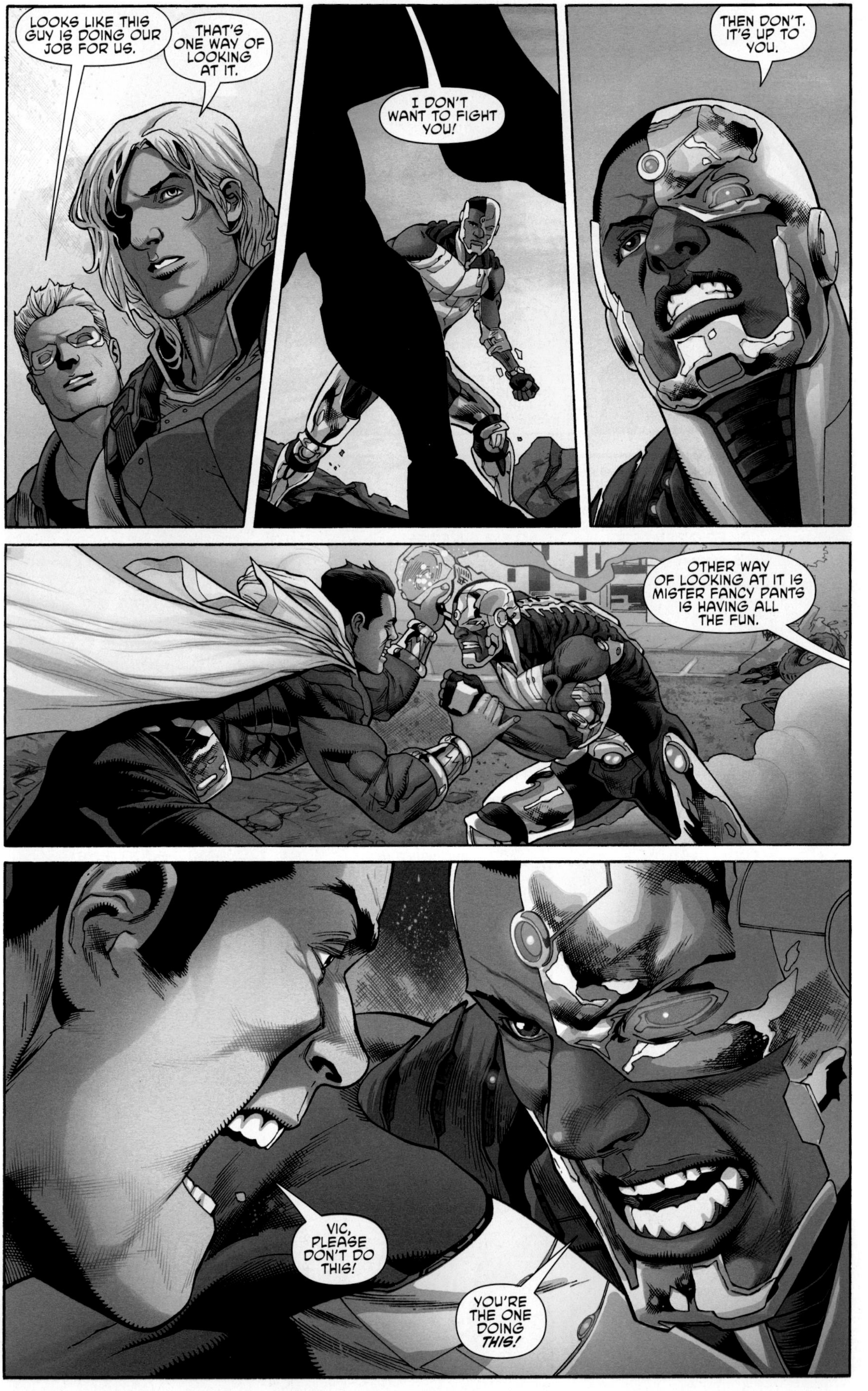
LOOKS LIKE THIS GUY IS DOING OUR JOB FOR US.
THAT'S ONE WAY OF LOOKING AT IT.
I DON'T WANT TO FIGHT YOU!
THEN DON'T. IT'S UP TO YOU.
OTHER WAY OF LOOKING AT IT IS MISTER FANCY PANTS IS HAVING ALL THE FUN.
VIC, PLEASE DON'T DO THIS!
YOU'RE THE ONE DOING *THIS!*

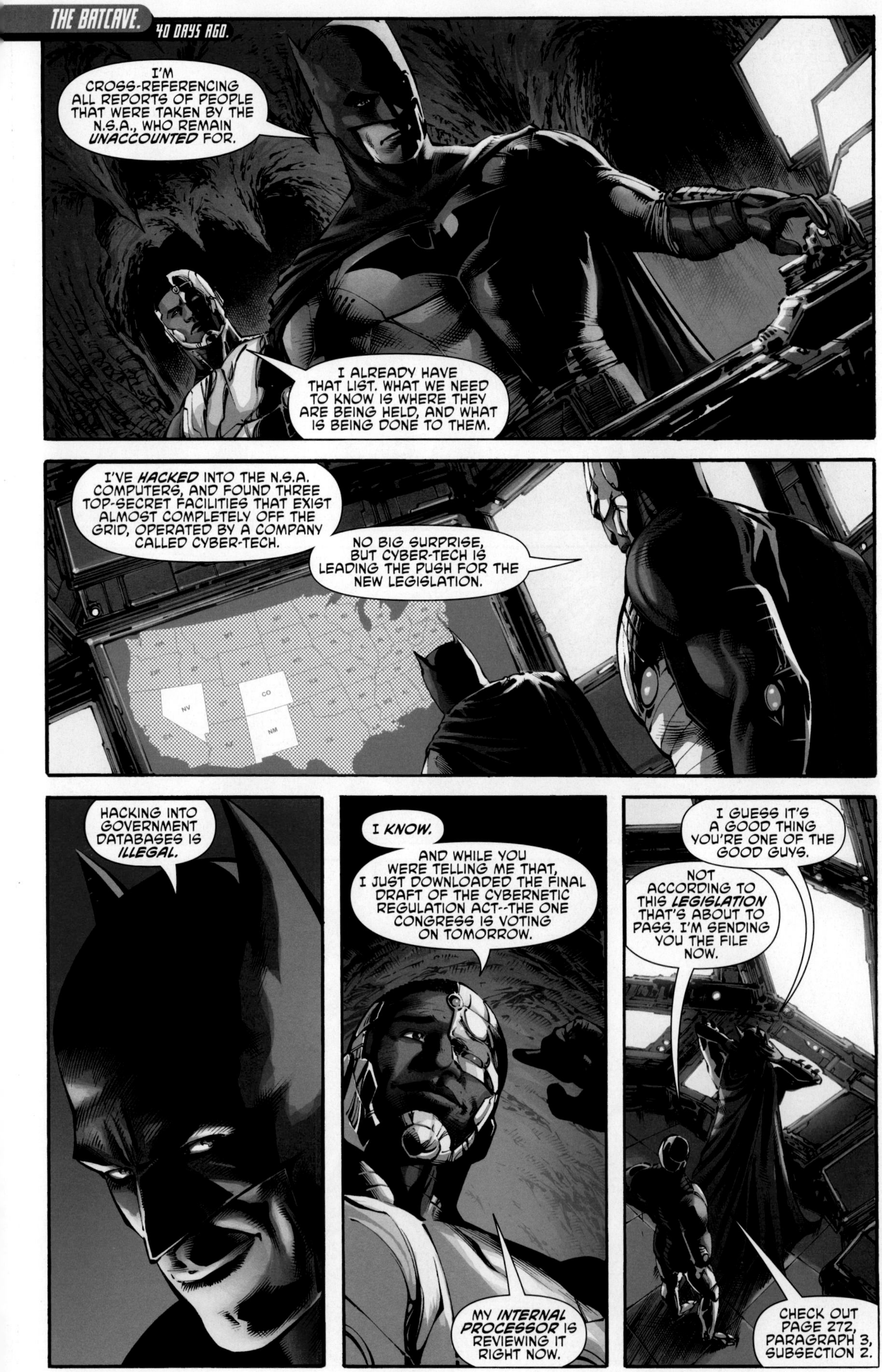
THE BATCAVE.
40 DAYS AGO.
I'M CROSS-REFERENCING ALL REPORTS OF PEOPLE THAT WERE TAKEN BY THE N.S.A., WHO REMAIN *UNACCOUNTED* FOR.
I ALREADY HAVE THAT LIST. WHAT WE NEED TO KNOW IS WHERE THEY ARE BEING HELD, AND WHAT IS BEING DONE TO THEM.
I'VE *HACKED* INTO THE N.S.A. COMPUTERS, AND FOUND THREE TOP-SECRET FACILITIES THAT EXIST ALMOST COMPLETELY OFF THE GRID, OPERATED BY A COMPANY CALLED CYBER-TECH.
NO BIG SURPRISE, BUT CYBER-TECH IS LEADING THE PUSH FOR THE NEW LEGISLATION.
NV
CO
NM
HACKING INTO GOVERNMENT DATABASES IS *ILLEGAL.*
I *KNOW.*
AND WHILE YOU WERE TELLING ME THAT, I JUST DOWNLOADED THE FINAL DRAFT OF THE CYBERNETIC REGULATION ACT--THE ONE CONGRESS IS VOTING ON TOMORROW.
MY *INTERNAL PROCESSOR* IS REVIEWING IT RIGHT NOW.
I GUESS IT'S A GOOD THING YOU'RE ONE OF THE GOOD GUYS.
NOT ACCORDING TO THIS *LEGISLATION* THAT'S ABOUT TO PASS. I'M SENDING YOU THE FILE NOW.
CHECK OUT PAGE 272, PARAGRAPH 3, SUBSECTION 2.

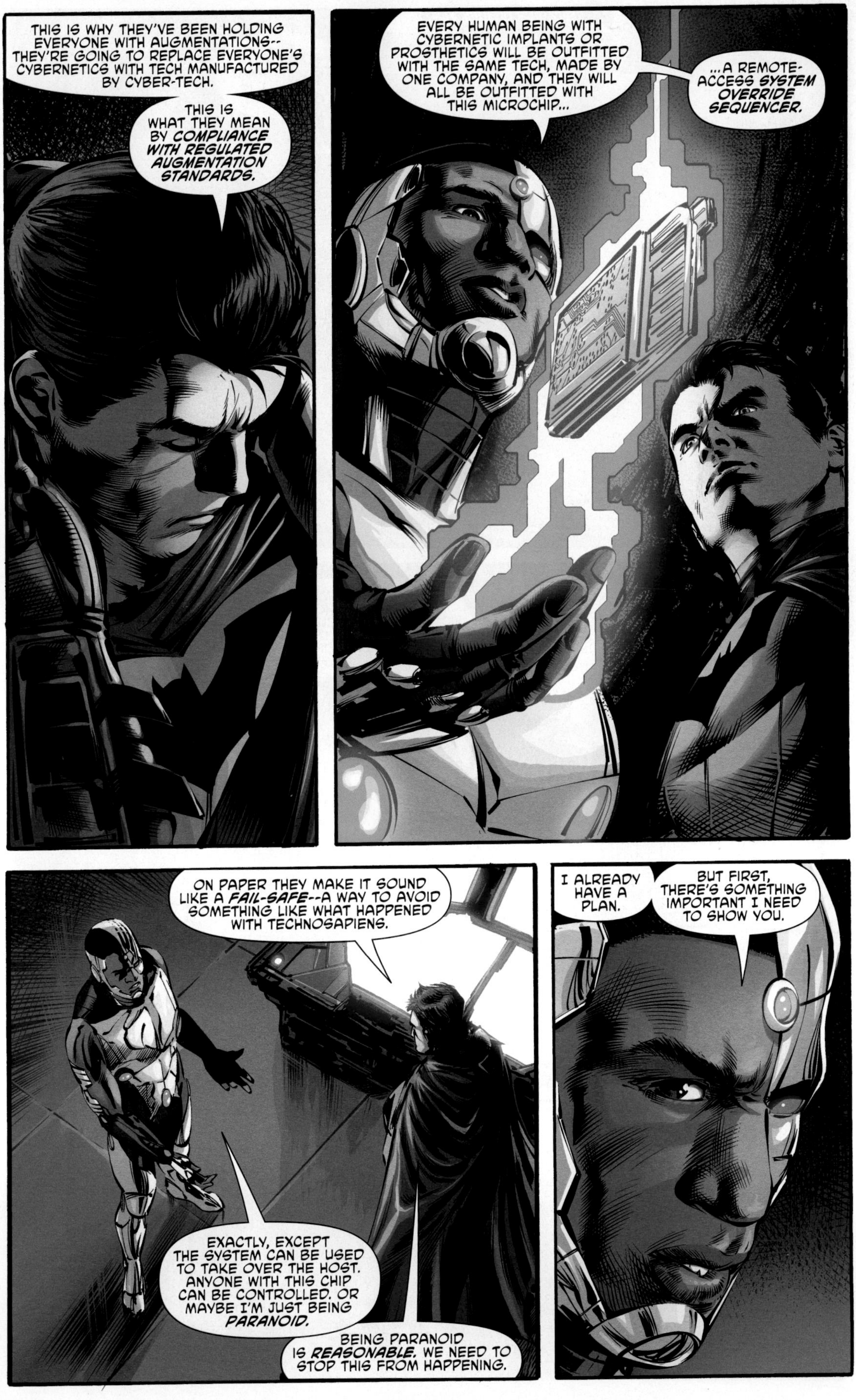
THIS IS WHY THEY'VE BEEN HOLDING EVERYONE WITH AUGMENTATIONS-- THEY'RE GOING TO REPLACE EVERYONE'S CYBERNETICS WITH TECH MANUFACTURED BY CYBER-TECH.
THIS IS WHAT THEY MEAN BY COMPLIANCE WITH REGULATED AUGMENTATION STANDARDS.
EVERY HUMAN BEING WITH CYBERNETIC IMPLANTS OR PROSTHETICS WILL BE OUTFITTED WITH THE SAME TECH, MADE BY ONE COMPANY, AND THEY WILL ALL BE OUTFITTED WITH THIS MICROCHIP...
...A REMOTE-ACCESS SYSTEM OVERRIDE SEQUENCER.
ON PAPER THEY MAKE IT SOUND LIKE A FAIL-SAFE--A WAY TO AVOID SOMETHING LIKE WHAT HAPPENED WITH TECHNOSAPIENS.
EXACTLY, EXCEPT THE SYSTEM CAN BE USED TO TAKE OVER THE HOST. ANYONE WITH THIS CHIP CAN BE CONTROLLED. OR MAYBE I'M JUST BEING PARANOID.
BEING PARANOID IS REASONABLE. WE NEED TO STOP THIS FROM HAPPENING.
I ALREADY HAVE A PLAN.
BUT FIRST, THERE'S SOMETHING IMPORTANT I NEED TO SHOW YOU.

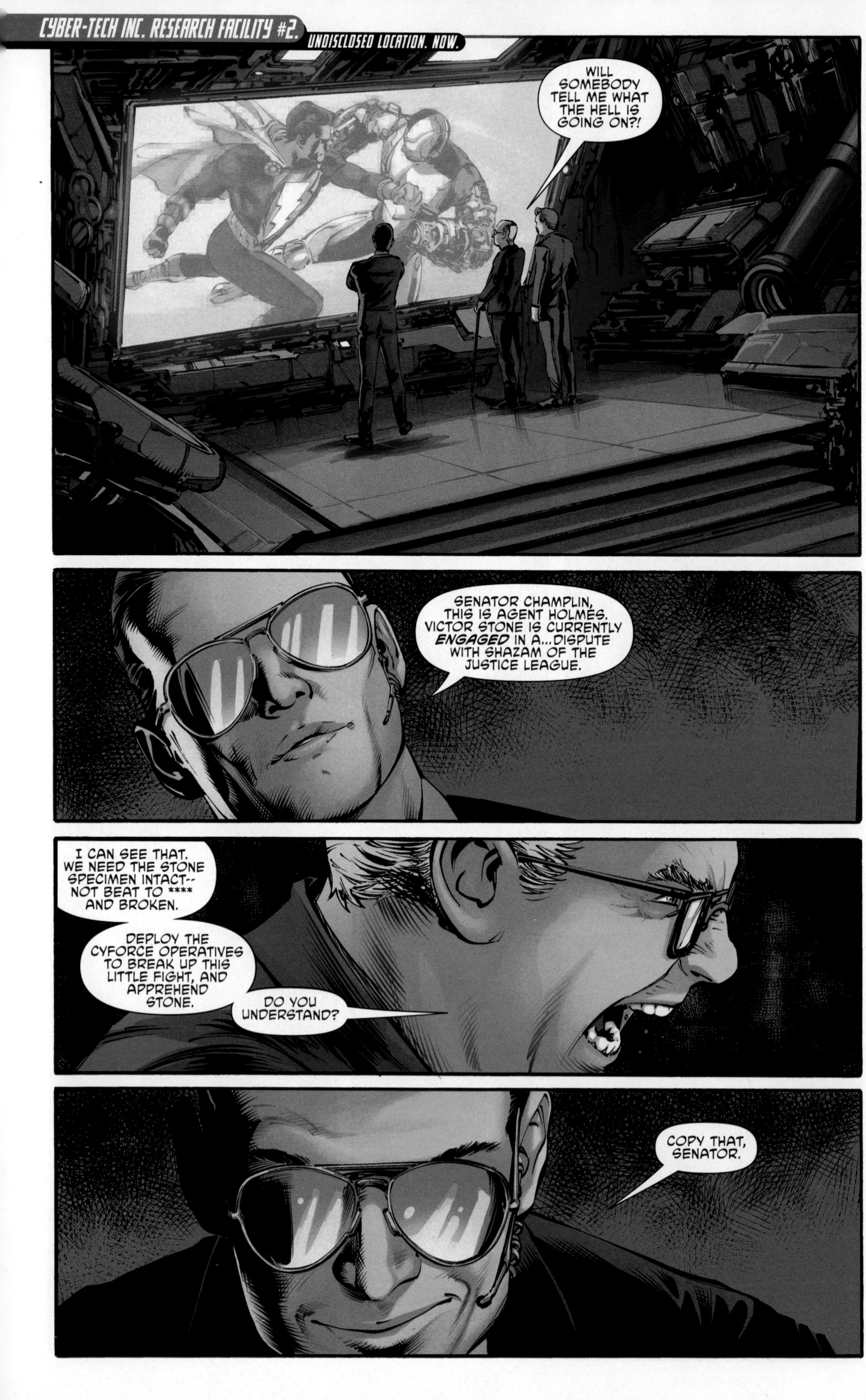
CYBER-TECH INC. RESEARCH FACILITY #2.
UNDISCLOSED LOCATION. NOW.
WILL SOMEBODY TELL ME WHAT THE HELL IS GOING ON?!
SENATOR CHAMPLIN, THIS IS AGENT HOLMES. VICTOR STONE IS CURRENTLY ENGAGED IN A...DISPUTE WITH SHAZAM OF THE JUSTICE LEAGUE.
I CAN SEE THAT. WE NEED THE STONE SPECIMEN INTACT-- NOT BEAT TO **** AND BROKEN.
DEPLOY THE CYFORCE OPERATIVES TO BREAK UP THIS LITTLE FIGHT, AND APPREHEND STONE.
DO YOU UNDERSTAND?
COPY THAT, SENATOR.

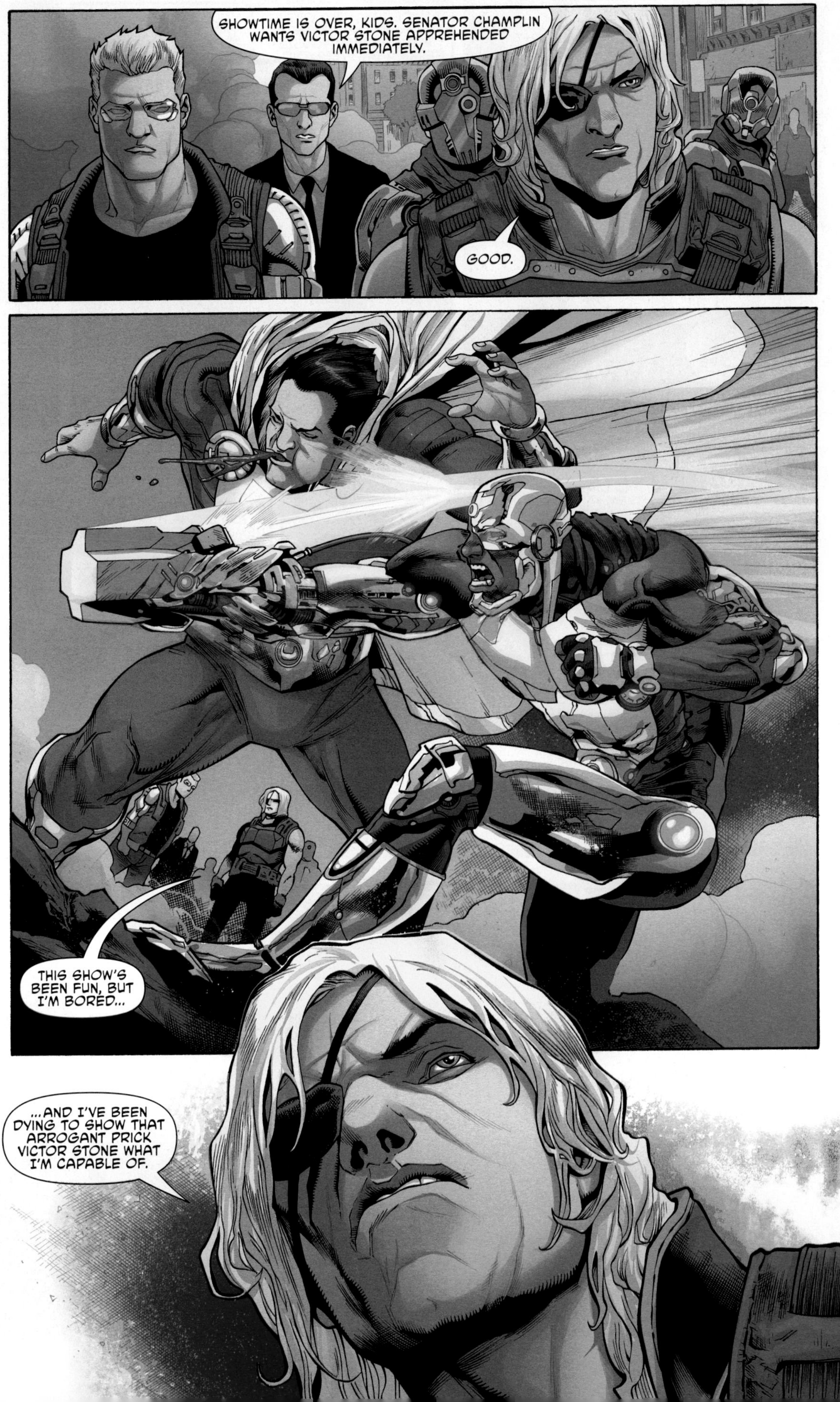
SHOWTIME IS OVER, KIDS. SENATOR CHAMPLIN WANTS VICTOR STONE APPREHENDED IMMEDIATELY.
GOOD.
THIS SHOW'S BEEN FUN, BUT I'M BORED...
...AND I'VE BEEN DYING TO SHOW THAT ARROGANT PRICK VICTOR STONE WHAT I'M CAPABLE OF.

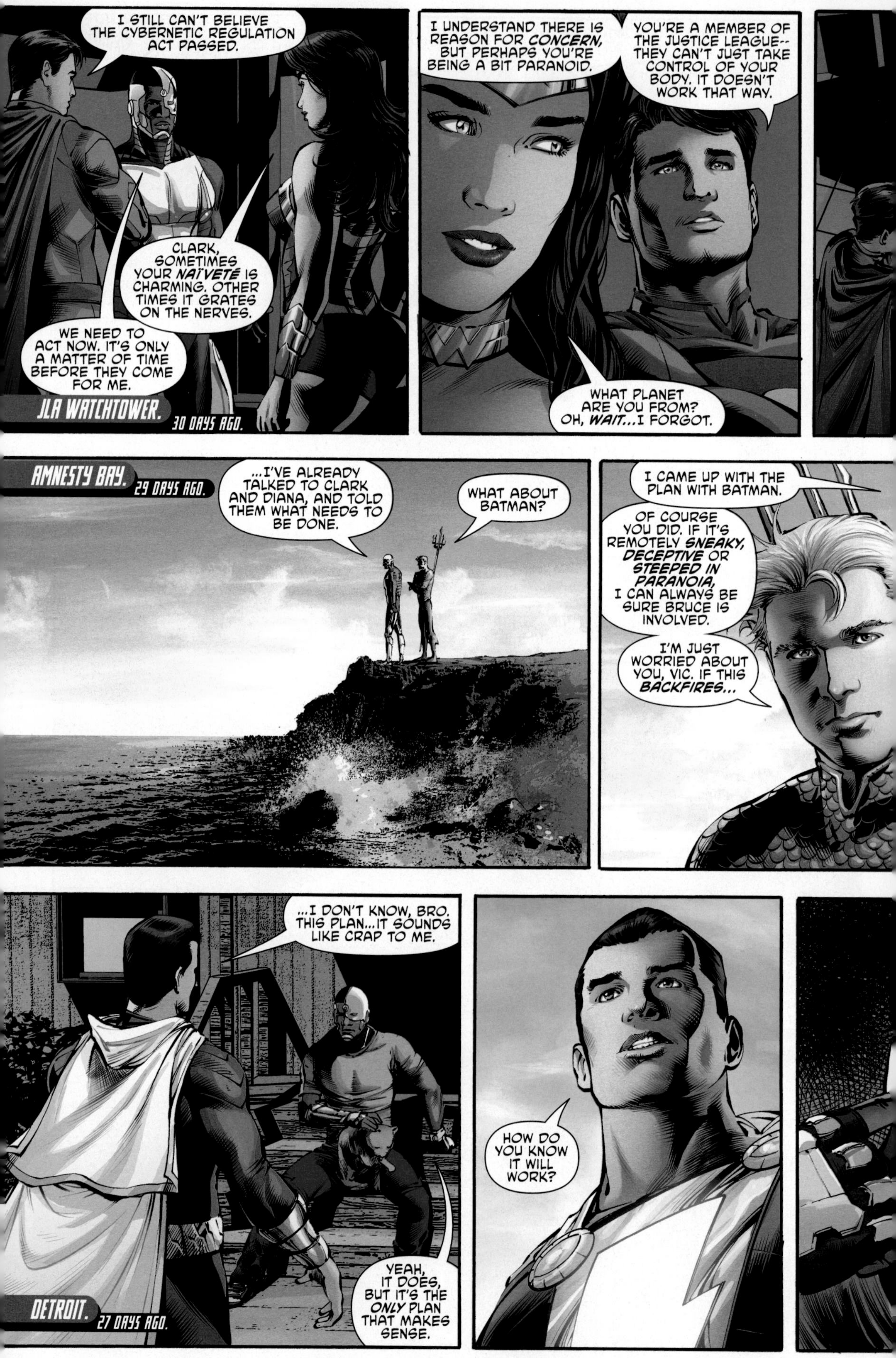
I STILL CAN'T BELIEVE THE CYBERNETIC REGULATION ACT PASSED.
CLARK, SOMETIMES YOUR NAÏVETÉ IS CHARMING. OTHER TIMES IT GRATES ON THE NERVES.
WE NEED TO ACT NOW. IT'S ONLY A MATTER OF TIME BEFORE THEY COME FOR ME.
JLA WATCHTOWER.
30 DAYS AGO.
I UNDERSTAND THERE IS REASON FOR CONCERN, BUT PERHAPS YOU'RE BEING A BIT PARANOID.
YOU'RE A MEMBER OF THE JUSTICE LEAGUE-- THEY CAN'T JUST TAKE CONTROL OF YOUR BODY. IT DOESN'T WORK THAT WAY.
WHAT PLANET ARE YOU FROM? OH, WAIT...I FORGOT.
AMNESTY BAY.
29 DAYS AGO.
...I'VE ALREADY TALKED TO CLARK AND DIANA, AND TOLD THEM WHAT NEEDS TO BE DONE.
WHAT ABOUT BATMAN?
I CAME UP WITH THE PLAN WITH BATMAN.
OF COURSE YOU DID. IF IT'S REMOTELY SNEAKY, DECEPTIVE OR STEEPED IN PARANOIA, I CAN ALWAYS BE SURE BRUCE IS INVOLVED.
I'M JUST WORRIED ABOUT YOU, VIC. IF THIS BACKFIRES...
DETROIT.
27 DAYS AGO.
...I DON'T KNOW, BRO. THIS PLAN...IT SOUNDS LIKE CRAP TO ME.
HOW DO YOU KNOW IT WILL WORK?
YEAH, IT DOES, BUT IT'S THE ONLY PLAN THAT MAKES SENSE.

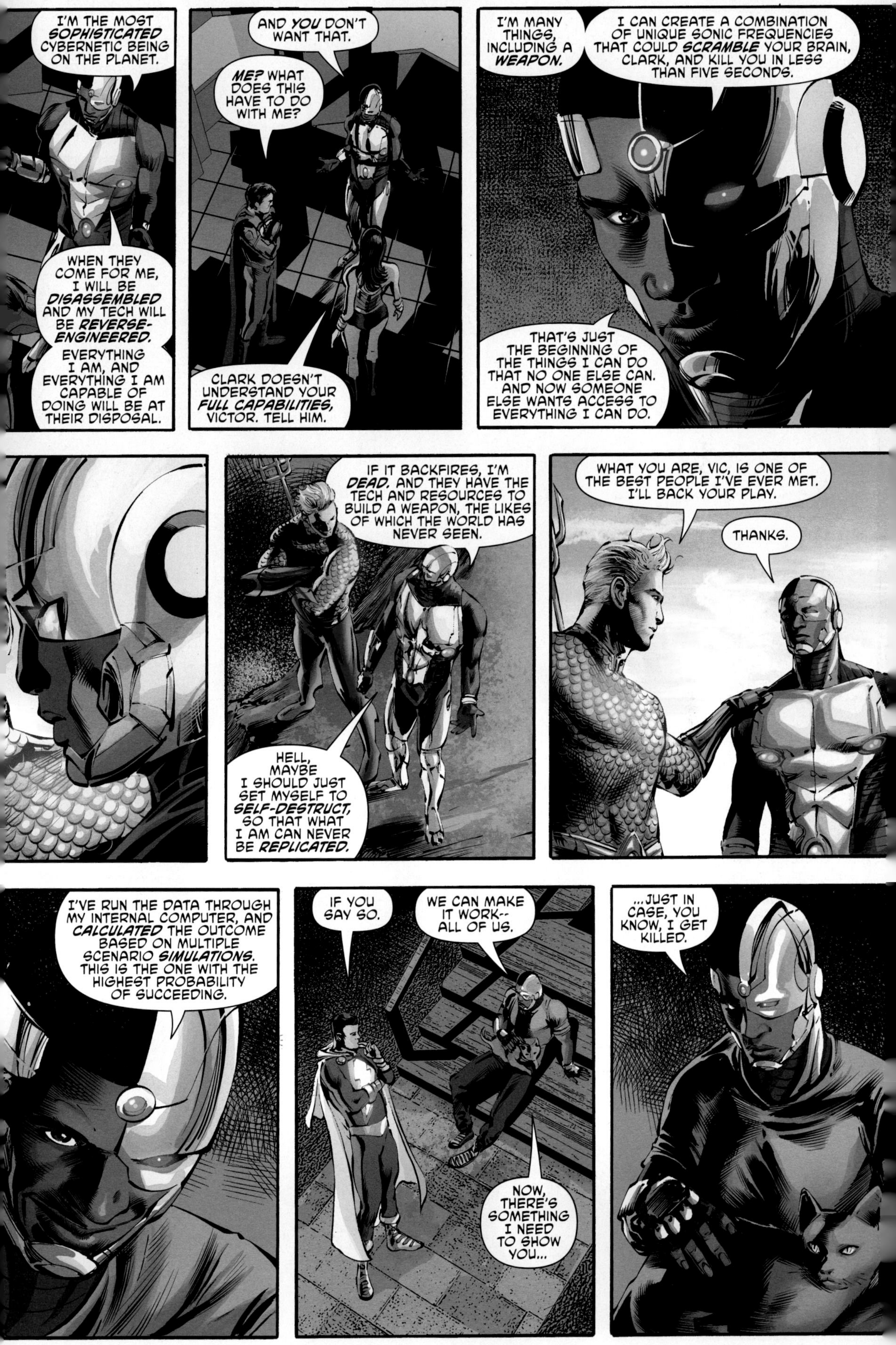
I'M THE MOST SOPHISTICATED CYBERNETIC BEING ON THE PLANET.
WHEN THEY COME FOR ME, I WILL BE DISASSEMBLED AND MY TECH WILL BE REVERSE-ENGINEERED.
EVERYTHING I AM, AND EVERYTHING I AM CAPABLE OF DOING WILL BE AT THEIR DISPOSAL.
AND YOU DON'T WANT THAT.
ME? WHAT DOES THIS HAVE TO DO WITH ME?
CLARK DOESN'T UNDERSTAND YOUR FULL CAPABILITIES, VICTOR. TELL HIM.
I'M MANY THINGS, INCLUDING A WEAPON.
I CAN CREATE A COMBINATION OF UNIQUE SONIC FREQUENCIES THAT COULD SCRAMBLE YOUR BRAIN, CLARK, AND KILL YOU IN LESS THAN FIVE SECONDS.
THAT'S JUST THE BEGINNING OF THE THINGS I CAN DO THAT NO ONE ELSE CAN. AND NOW SOMEONE ELSE WANTS ACCESS TO EVERYTHING I CAN DO.
IF IT BACKFIRES, I'M DEAD. AND THEY HAVE THE TECH AND RESOURCES TO BUILD A WEAPON, THE LIKES OF WHICH THE WORLD HAS NEVER SEEN.
HELL, MAYBE I SHOULD JUST SET MYSELF TO SELF-DESTRUCT, SO THAT WHAT I AM CAN NEVER BE REPLICATED.
WHAT YOU ARE, VIC, IS ONE OF THE BEST PEOPLE I'VE EVER MET. I'LL BACK YOUR PLAY.
THANKS.
I'VE RUN THE DATA THROUGH MY INTERNAL COMPUTER, AND CALCULATED THE OUTCOME BASED ON MULTIPLE SCENARIO SIMULATIONS. THIS IS THE ONE WITH THE HIGHEST PROBABILITY OF SUCCEEDING.
IF YOU SAY SO.
WE CAN MAKE IT WORK-- ALL OF US.
NOW, THERE'S SOMETHING I NEED TO SHOW YOU...
...JUST IN CASE, YOU KNOW, I GET KILLED.

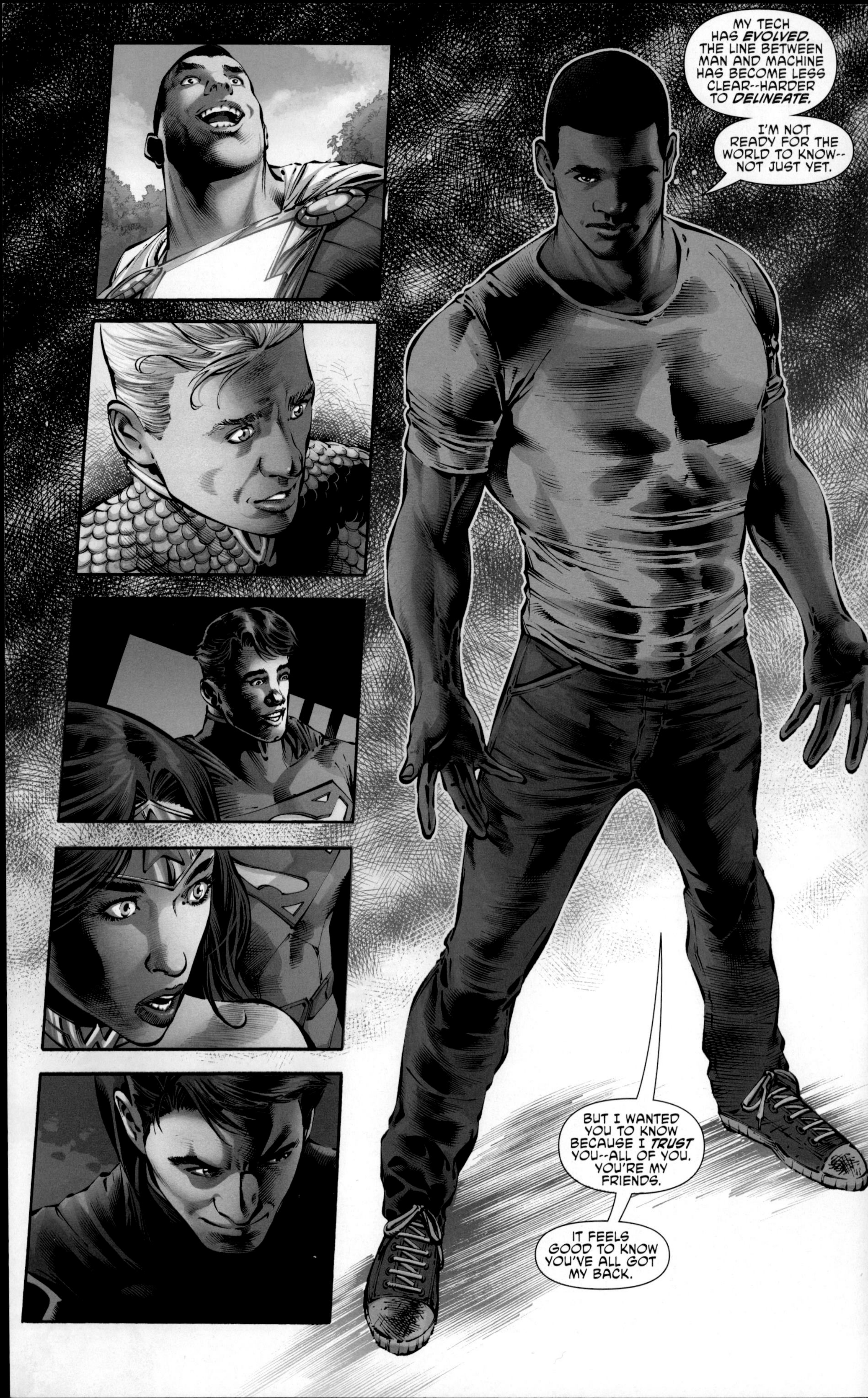
MY TECH HAS EVOLVED. THE LINE BETWEEN MAN AND MACHINE HAS BECOME LESS CLEAR--HARDER TO DELINEATE.
I'M NOT READY FOR THE WORLD TO KNOW--NOT JUST YET.
BUT I WANTED YOU TO KNOW BECAUSE I TRUST YOU--ALL OF YOU. YOU'RE MY FRIENDS.
IT FEELS GOOD TO KNOW YOU'VE ALL GOT MY BACK.

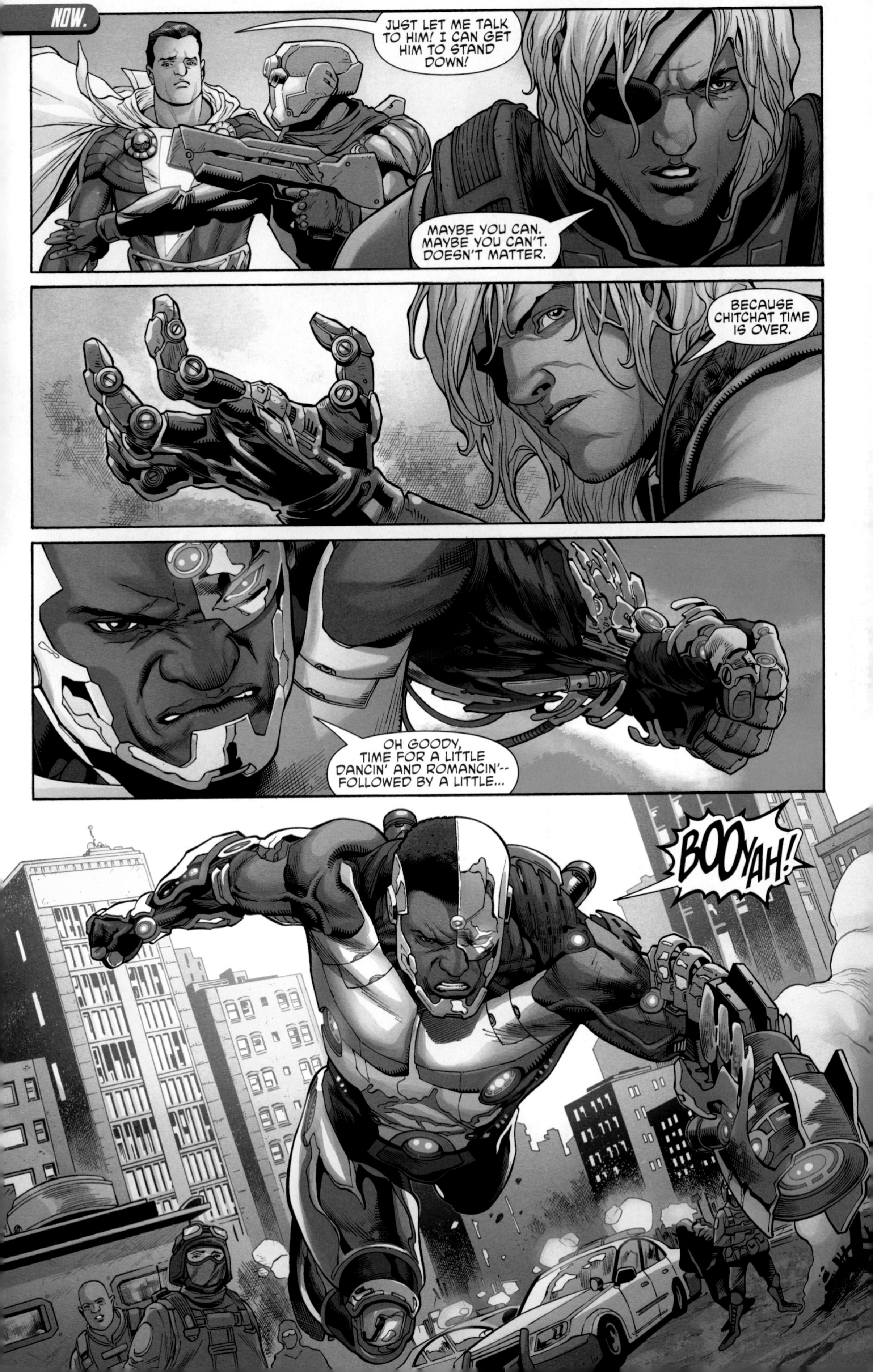
NOW.
JUST LET ME TALK TO HIM! I CAN GET HIM TO STAND DOWN!
MAYBE YOU CAN. MAYBE YOU CAN'T. DOESN'T MATTER.
BECAUSE CHITCHAT TIME IS OVER.
OH GOODY, TIME FOR A LITTLE DANCIN' AND ROMANCIN'-- FOLLOWED BY A LITTLE...
BOOYAH!

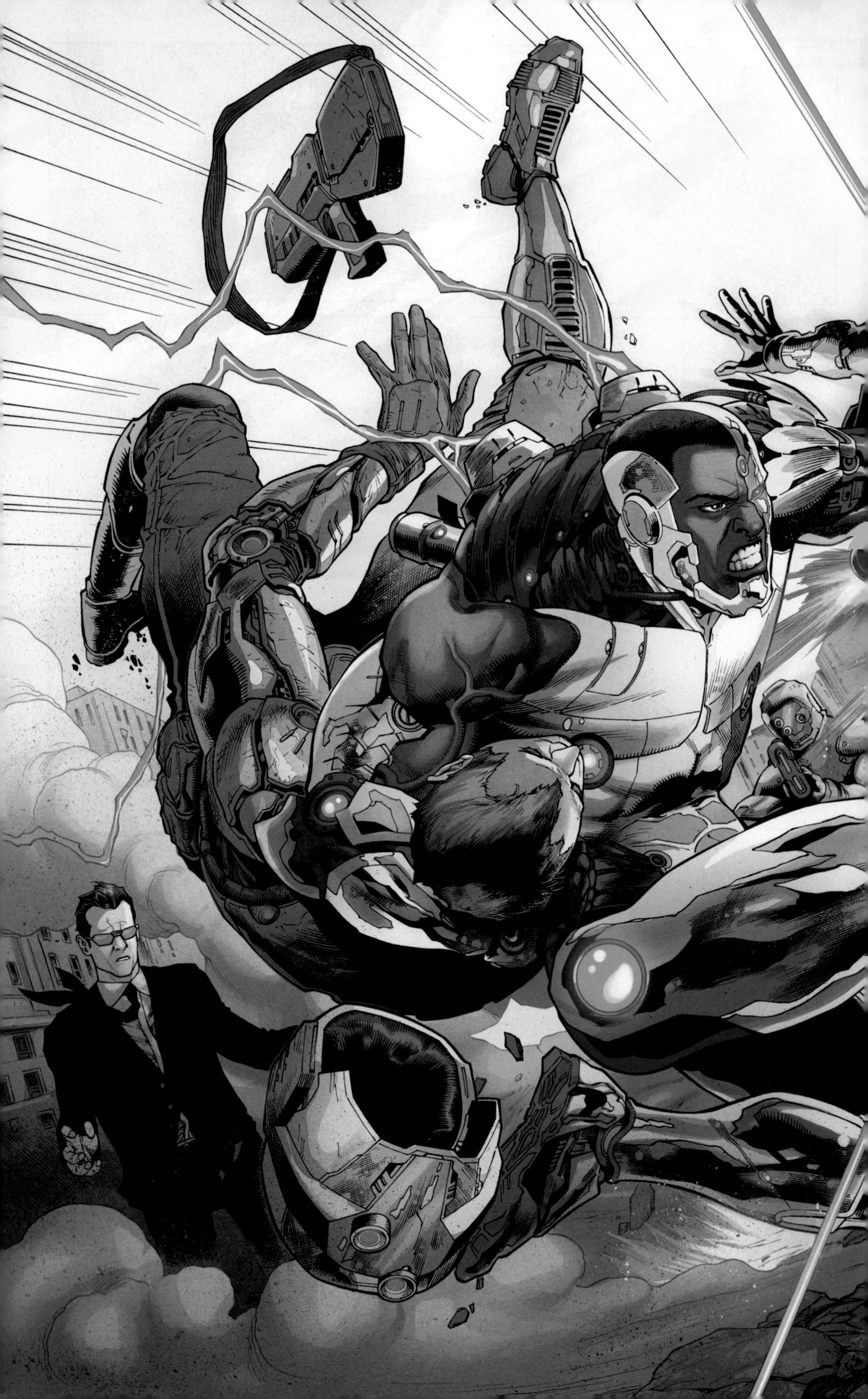

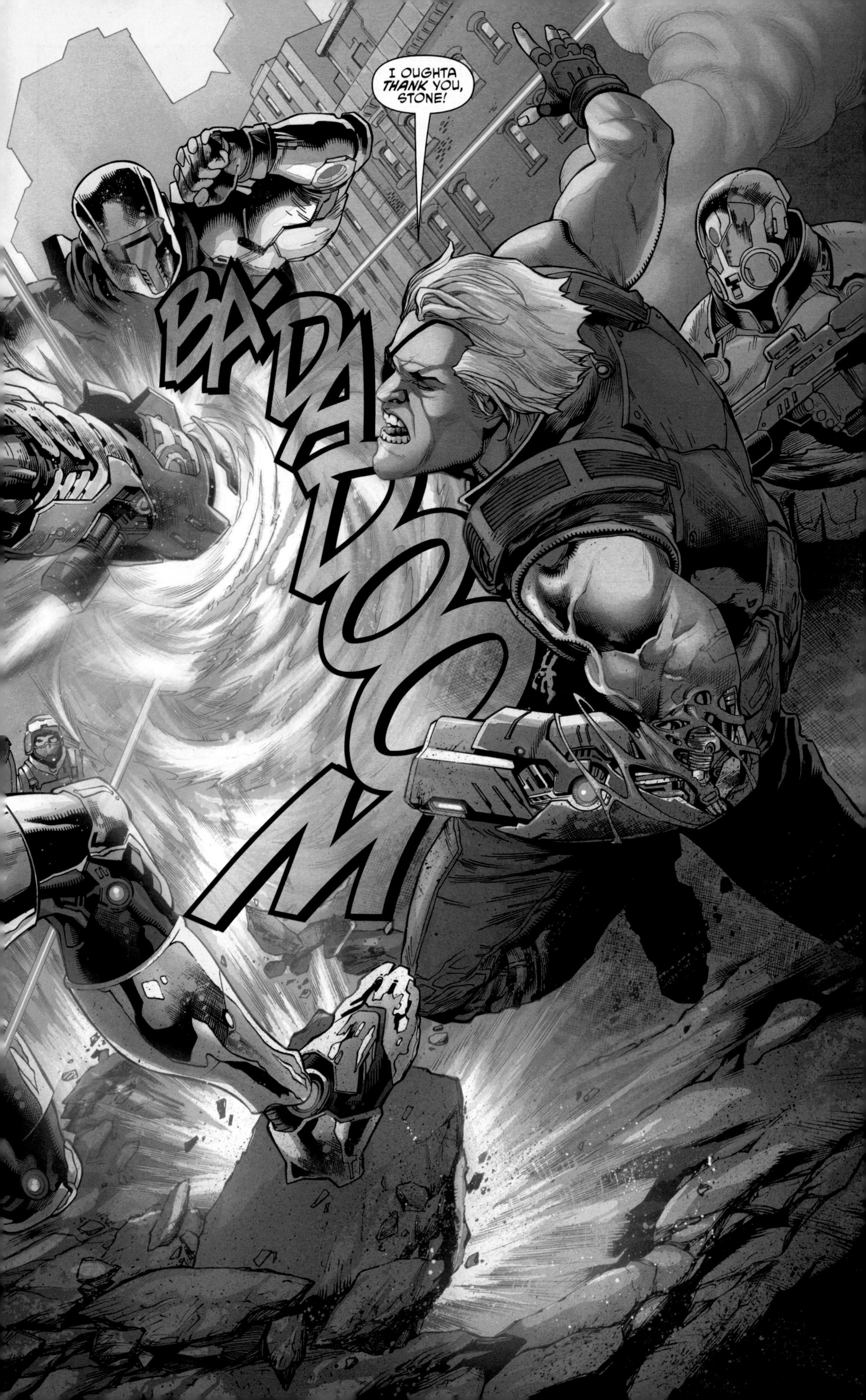
I OUGHTA THANK YOU, STONE!
BA-DA-DOOM

WHEN YOU DESTROYED THE TECHNOSAPIENS, I THOUGHT YOU *DESTROYED* MY LAST CHANCE TO BE WHOLE AGAIN!

ZZAWWAPOW

BUT SOMEHOW YOUR TECH BECAME PART OF ME--MADE ME *BETTER* THAN EVER!

ZZZRAAAK

NO!

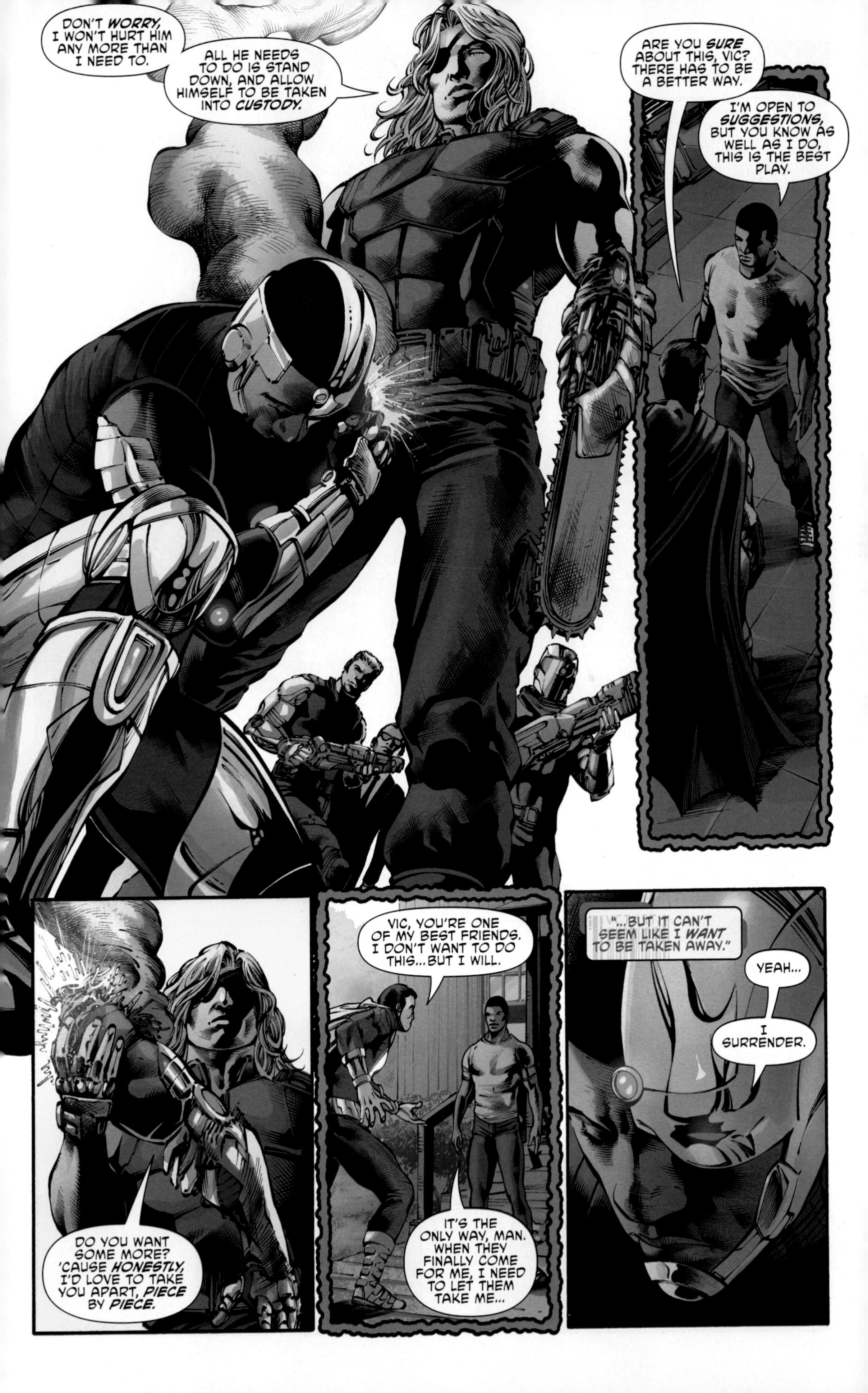
DON'T WORRY, I WON'T HURT HIM ANY MORE THAN I NEED TO.
ALL HE NEEDS TO DO IS STAND DOWN, AND ALLOW HIMSELF TO BE TAKEN INTO CUSTODY.
ARE YOU SURE ABOUT THIS, VIC? THERE HAS TO BE A BETTER WAY.
I'M OPEN TO SUGGESTIONS, BUT YOU KNOW AS WELL AS I DO, THIS IS THE BEST PLAY.
DO YOU WANT SOME MORE? 'CAUSE HONESTLY, I'D LOVE TO TAKE YOU APART, PIECE BY PIECE.
VIC, YOU'RE ONE OF MY BEST FRIENDS. I DON'T WANT TO DO THIS...BUT I WILL.
IT'S THE ONLY WAY, MAN. WHEN THEY FINALLY COME FOR ME, I NEED TO LET THEM TAKE ME...
"...BUT IT CAN'T SEEM LIKE I WANT TO BE TAKEN AWAY."
YEAH...
I SURRENDER.

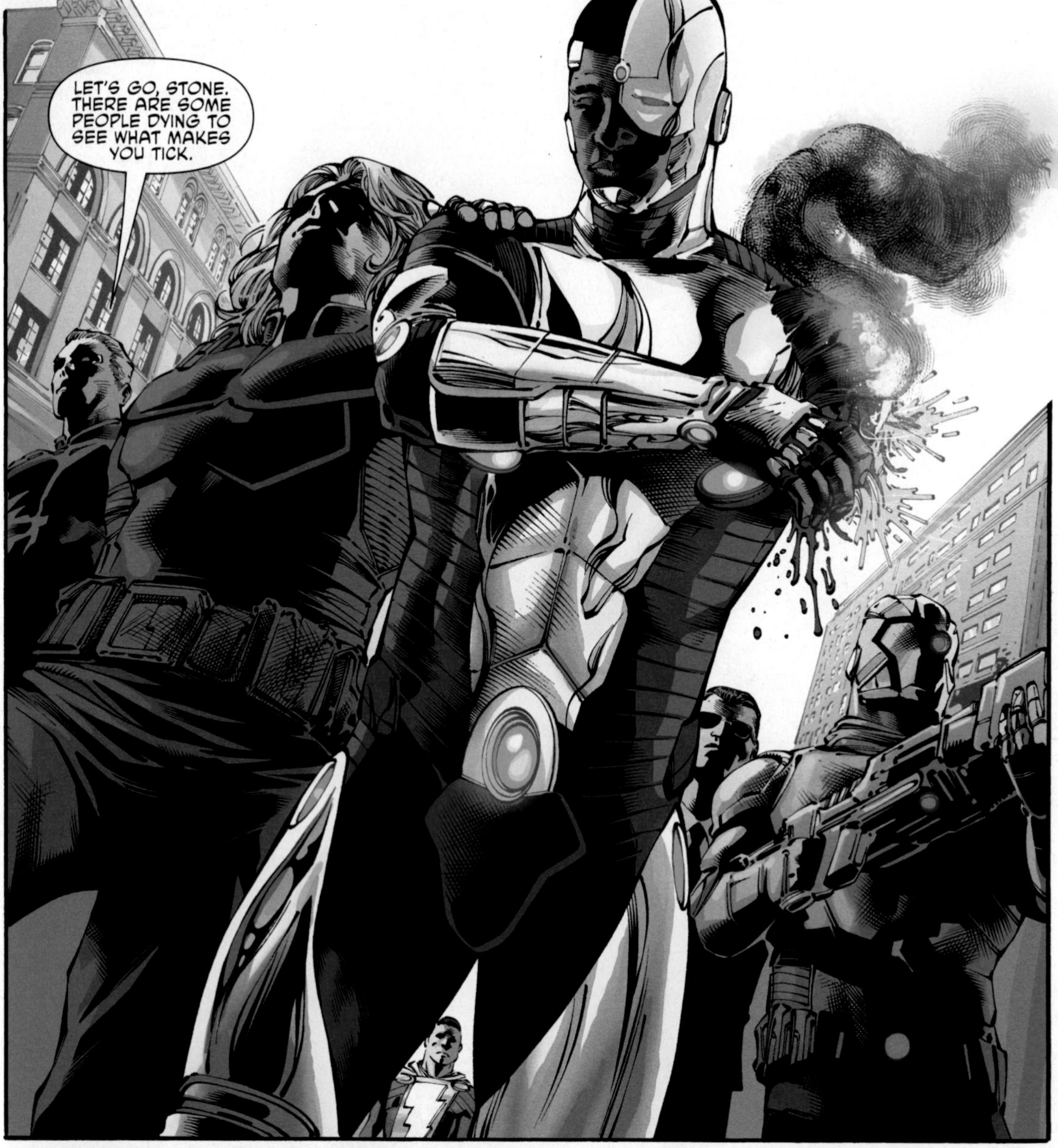
LET'S GO, STONE. THERE ARE SOME PEOPLE DYING TO SEE WHAT MAKES YOU TICK.

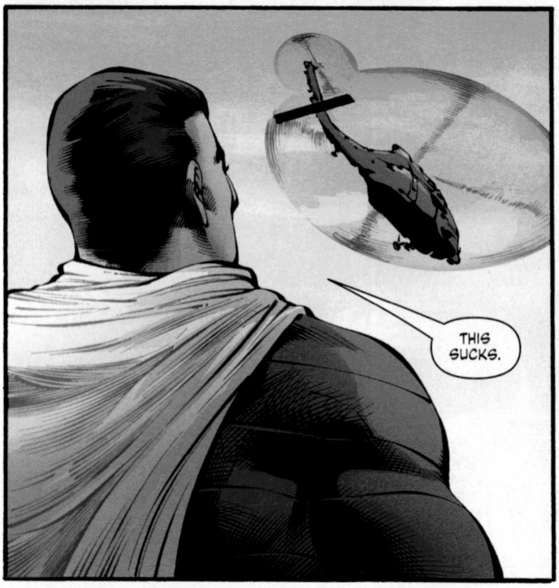
THIS SUCKS.

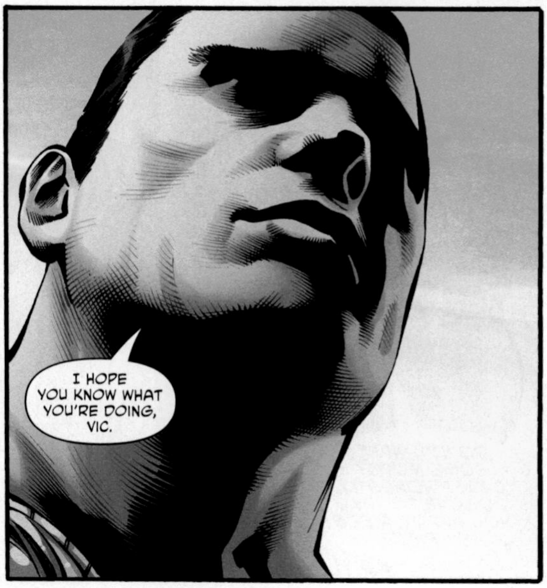
I HOPE YOU KNOW WHAT YOU'RE DOING, VIC.

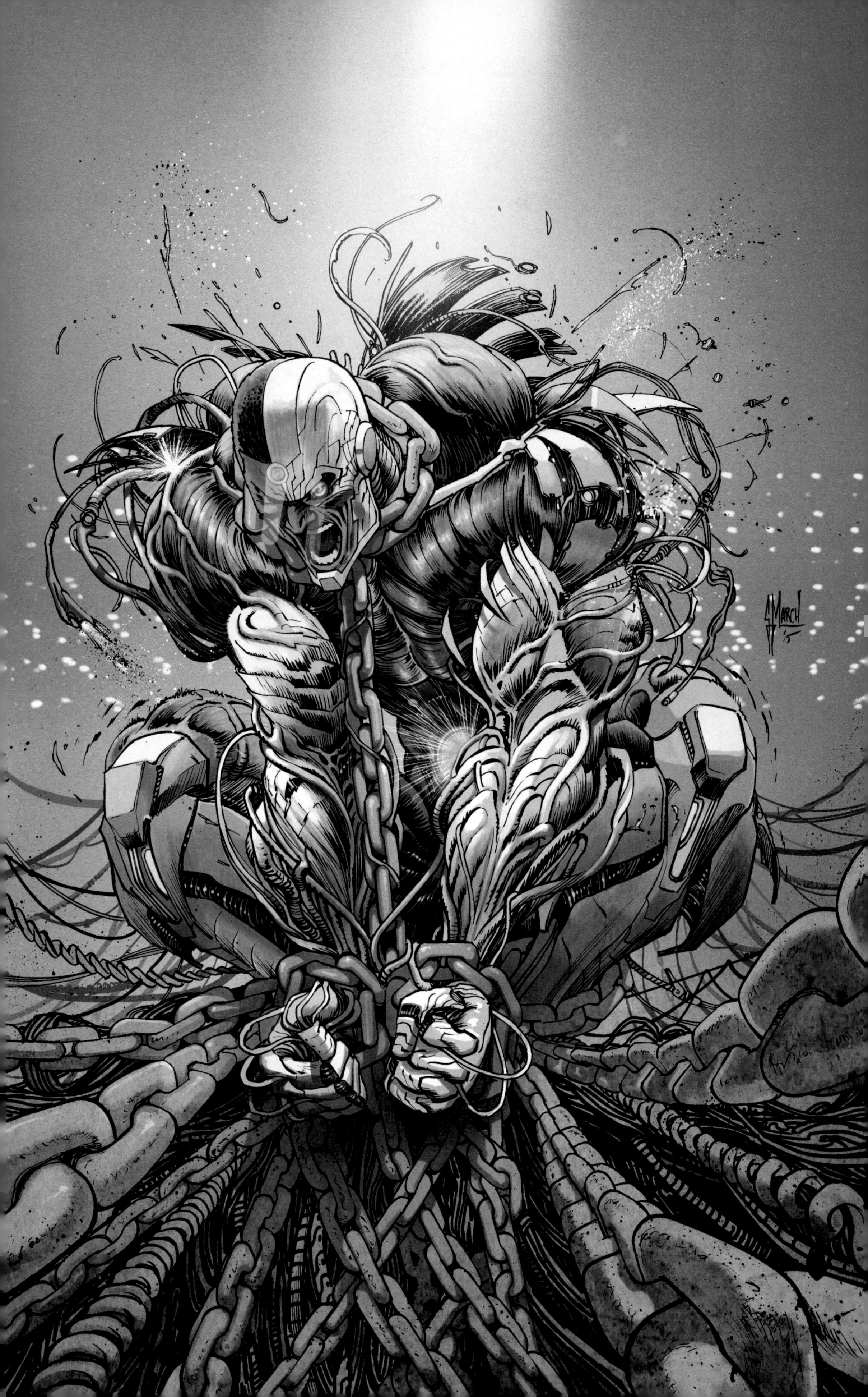

END GAME

MARV WOLFMAN writer **IVAN REIS** layouts **FELIPE WATANABE, DANIEL HDR & JÚLIO FERREIRA** pencillers **OCLAIR ALBERT & JÚLIO FERREIRA** inkers **GUILLEM MARCH** cover

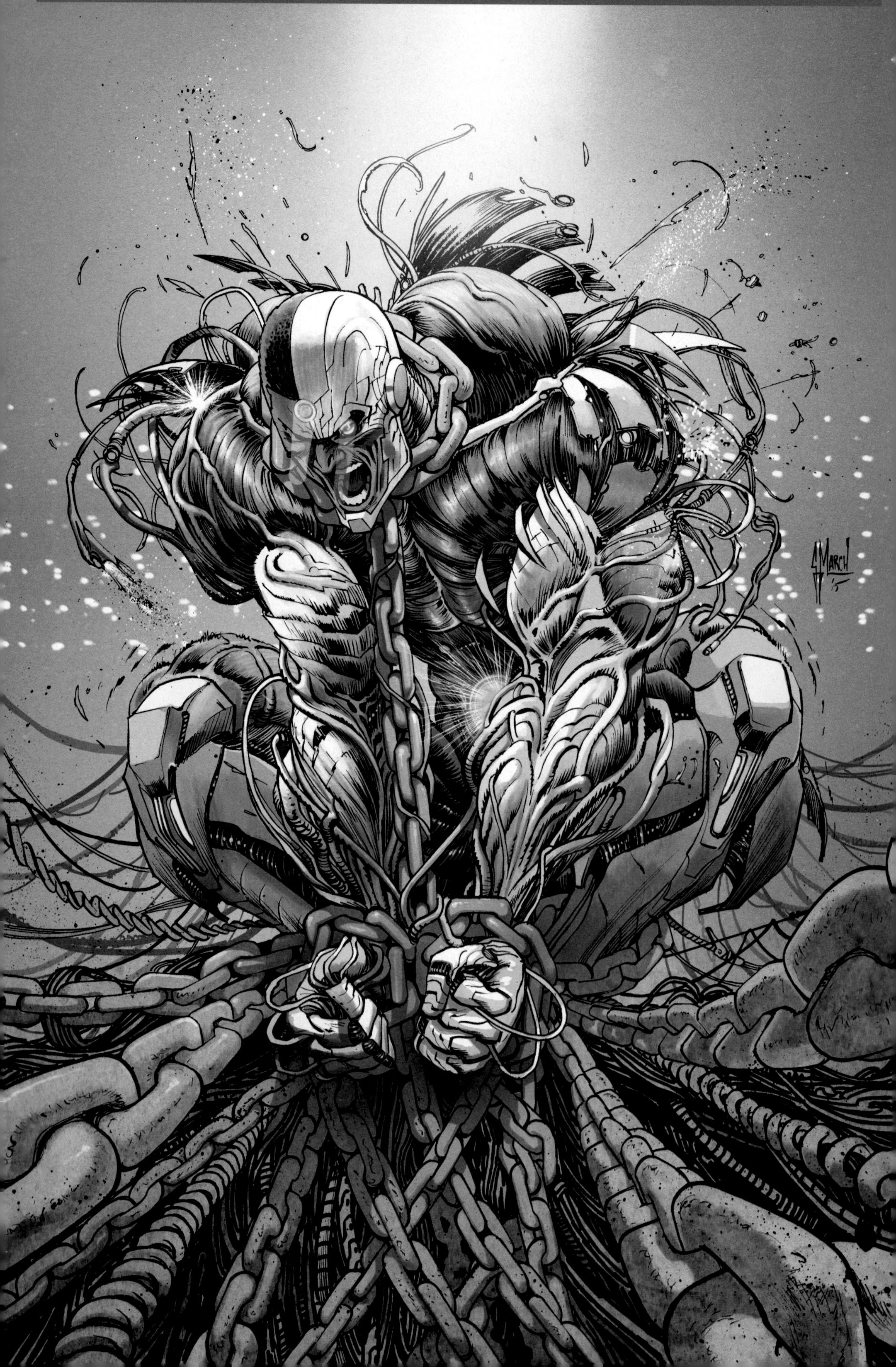

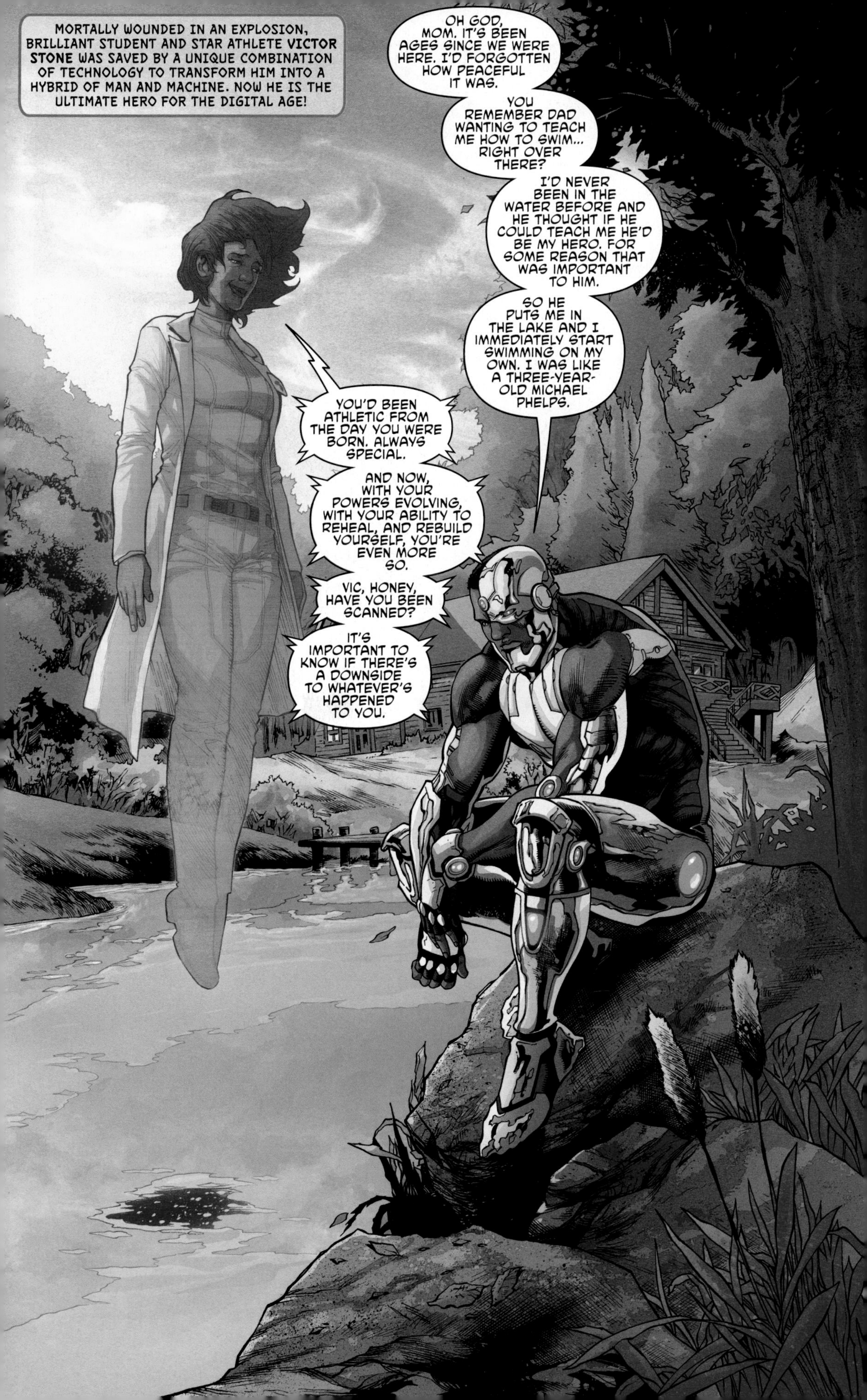
MORTALLY WOUNDED IN AN EXPLOSION, BRILLIANT STUDENT AND STAR ATHLETE VICTOR STONE WAS SAVED BY A UNIQUE COMBINATION OF TECHNOLOGY TO TRANSFORM HIM INTO A HYBRID OF MAN AND MACHINE. NOW HE IS THE ULTIMATE HERO FOR THE DIGITAL AGE!
OH GOD, MOM. IT'S BEEN AGES SINCE WE WERE HERE. I'D FORGOTTEN HOW PEACEFUL IT WAS.
YOU REMEMBER DAD WANTING TO TEACH ME HOW TO SWIM... RIGHT OVER THERE?
I'D NEVER BEEN IN THE WATER BEFORE AND HE THOUGHT IF HE COULD TEACH ME HE'D BE MY HERO. FOR SOME REASON THAT WAS IMPORTANT TO HIM.
SO HE PUTS ME IN THE LAKE AND I IMMEDIATELY START SWIMMING ON MY OWN. I WAS LIKE A THREE-YEAR-OLD MICHAEL PHELPS.
YOU'D BEEN ATHLETIC FROM THE DAY YOU WERE BORN. ALWAYS SPECIAL.
AND NOW, WITH YOUR POWERS EVOLVING, WITH YOUR ABILITY TO REHEAL, AND REBUILD YOURSELF, YOU'RE EVEN MORE SO.
VIC, HONEY, HAVE YOU BEEN SCANNED?
IT'S IMPORTANT TO KNOW IF THERE'S A DOWNSIDE TO WHATEVER'S HAPPENED TO YOU.

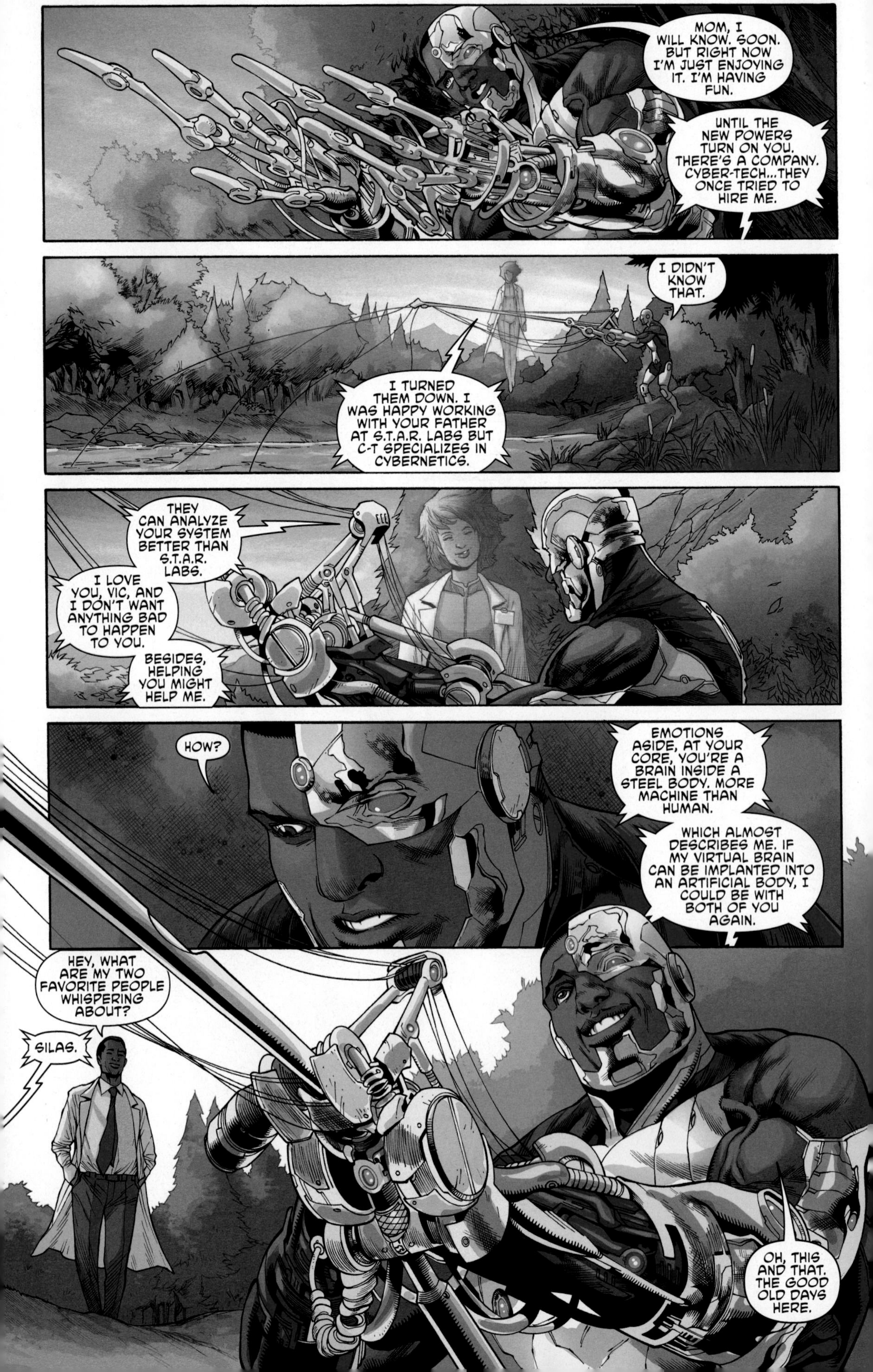
MOM, I WILL KNOW. SOON. BUT RIGHT NOW I'M JUST ENJOYING IT. I'M HAVING FUN.
UNTIL THE NEW POWERS TURN ON YOU. THERE'S A COMPANY. CYBER-TECH...THEY ONCE TRIED TO HIRE ME.
I DIDN'T KNOW THAT.
I TURNED THEM DOWN. I WAS HAPPY WORKING WITH YOUR FATHER AT S.T.A.R. LABS BUT C-T SPECIALIZES IN CYBERNETICS.
THEY CAN ANALYZE YOUR SYSTEM BETTER THAN S.T.A.R. LABS.
I LOVE YOU, VIC, AND I DON'T WANT ANYTHING BAD TO HAPPEN TO YOU.
BESIDES, HELPING YOU MIGHT HELP ME.
HOW?
EMOTIONS ASIDE, AT YOUR CORE, YOU'RE A BRAIN INSIDE A STEEL BODY. MORE MACHINE THAN HUMAN.
WHICH ALMOST DESCRIBES ME. IF MY VIRTUAL BRAIN CAN BE IMPLANTED INTO AN ARTIFICIAL BODY, I COULD BE WITH BOTH OF YOU AGAIN.
HEY, WHAT ARE MY TWO FAVORITE PEOPLE WHISPERING ABOUT?
SILAS.
OH, THIS AND THAT. THE GOOD OLD DAYS HERE.

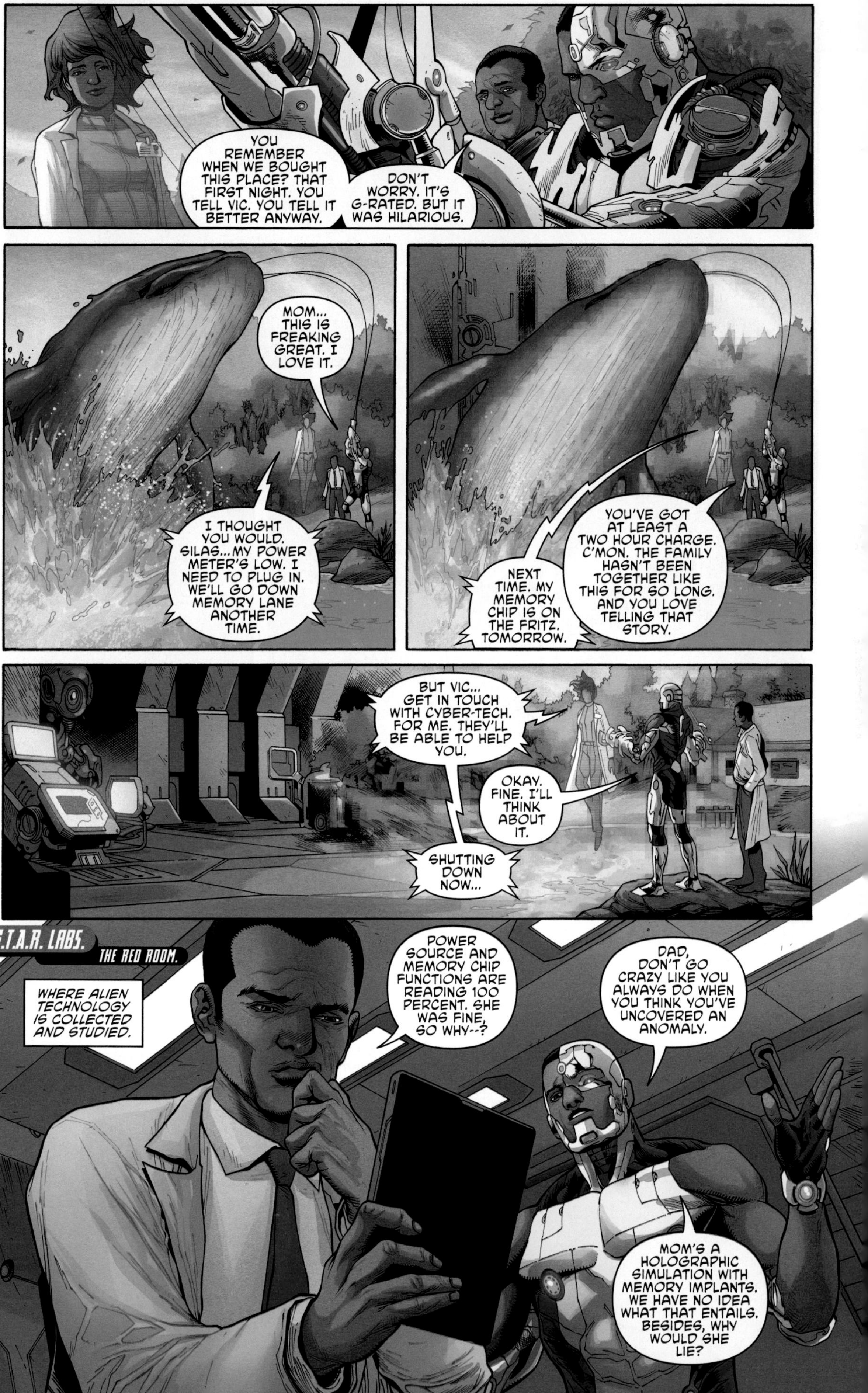
YOU REMEMBER WHEN WE BOUGHT THIS PLACE? THAT FIRST NIGHT. YOU TELL VIC. YOU TELL IT BETTER ANYWAY.
DON'T WORRY. IT'S G-RATED. BUT IT WAS HILARIOUS.
MOM... THIS IS FREAKING GREAT. I LOVE IT.
I THOUGHT YOU WOULD. SILAS...MY POWER METER'S LOW. I NEED TO PLUG IN. WE'LL GO DOWN MEMORY LANE ANOTHER TIME.
YOU'VE GOT AT LEAST A TWO HOUR CHARGE. C'MON. THE FAMILY HASN'T BEEN TOGETHER LIKE THIS FOR SO LONG. AND YOU LOVE TELLING THAT STORY.
NEXT TIME. MY MEMORY CHIP IS ON THE FRITZ. TOMORROW.
BUT VIC... GET IN TOUCH WITH CYBER-TECH. FOR ME. THEY'LL BE ABLE TO HELP YOU.
OKAY. FINE. I'LL THINK ABOUT IT.
SHUTTING DOWN NOW...
S.T.A.R. LABS.
THE RED ROOM.
WHERE ALIEN TECHNOLOGY IS COLLECTED AND STUDIED.
POWER SOURCE AND MEMORY CHIP FUNCTIONS ARE READING 100 PERCENT. SHE WAS FINE, SO WHY--?
DAD, DON'T GO CRAZY LIKE YOU ALWAYS DO WHEN YOU THINK YOU'VE UNCOVERED AN ANOMALY.
MOM'S A HOLOGRAPHIC SIMULATION WITH MEMORY IMPLANTS. WE HAVE NO IDEA WHAT THAT ENTAILS. BESIDES, WHY WOULD SHE LIE?

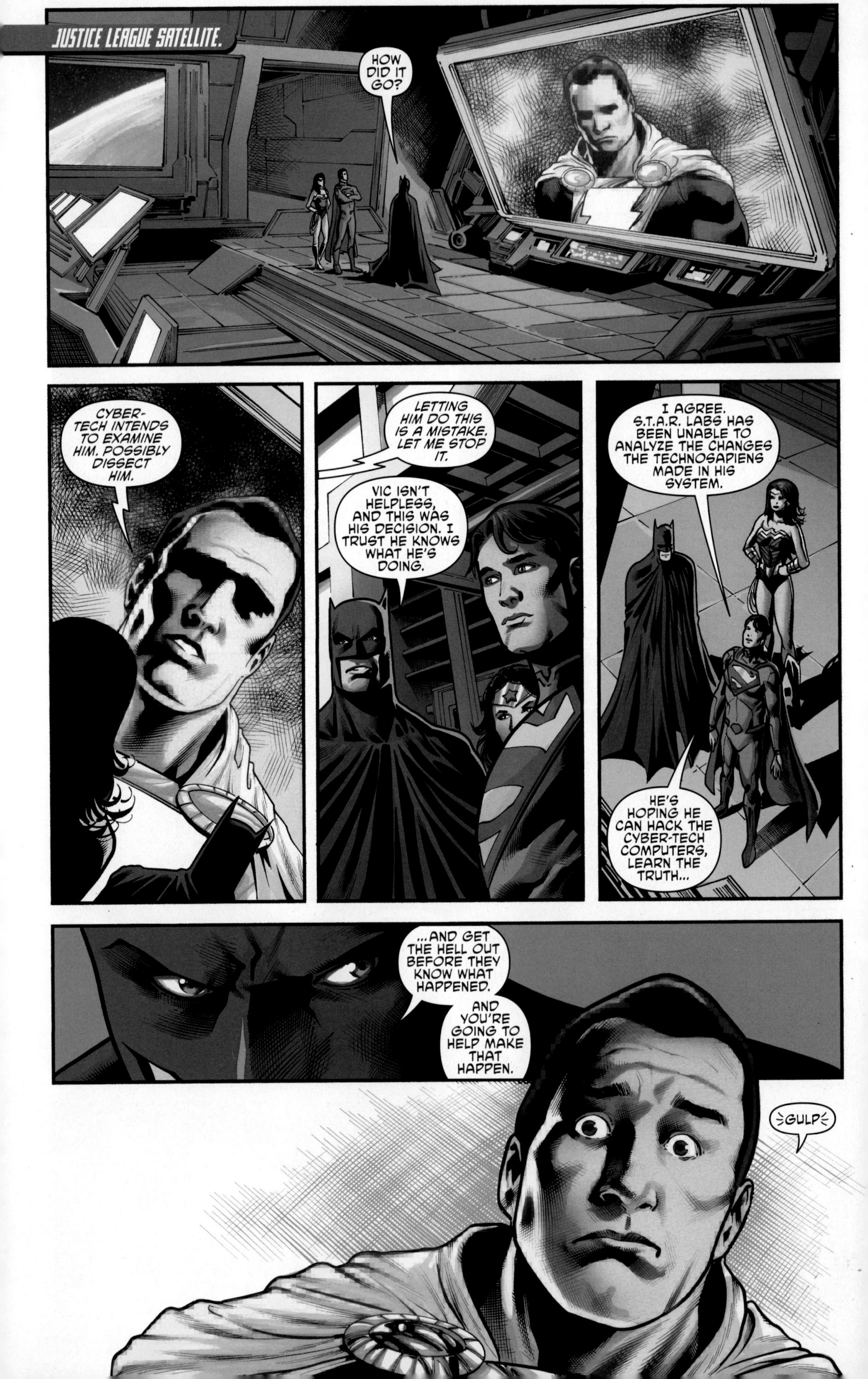
JUSTICE LEAGUE SATELLITE.
HOW DID IT GO?
CYBER-TECH INTENDS TO EXAMINE HIM. POSSIBLY DISSECT HIM.
LETTING HIM DO THIS IS A MISTAKE. LET ME STOP IT.
VIC ISN'T HELPLESS, AND THIS WAS HIS DECISION. I TRUST HE KNOWS WHAT HE'S DOING.
I AGREE. S.T.A.R. LABS HAS BEEN UNABLE TO ANALYZE THE CHANGES THE TECHNOSAPIENS MADE IN HIS SYSTEM.
HE'S HOPING HE CAN HACK THE CYBER-TECH COMPUTERS, LEARN THE TRUTH...
...AND GET THE HELL OUT BEFORE THEY KNOW WHAT HAPPENED.
AND YOU'RE GOING TO HELP MAKE THAT HAPPEN.
GULP

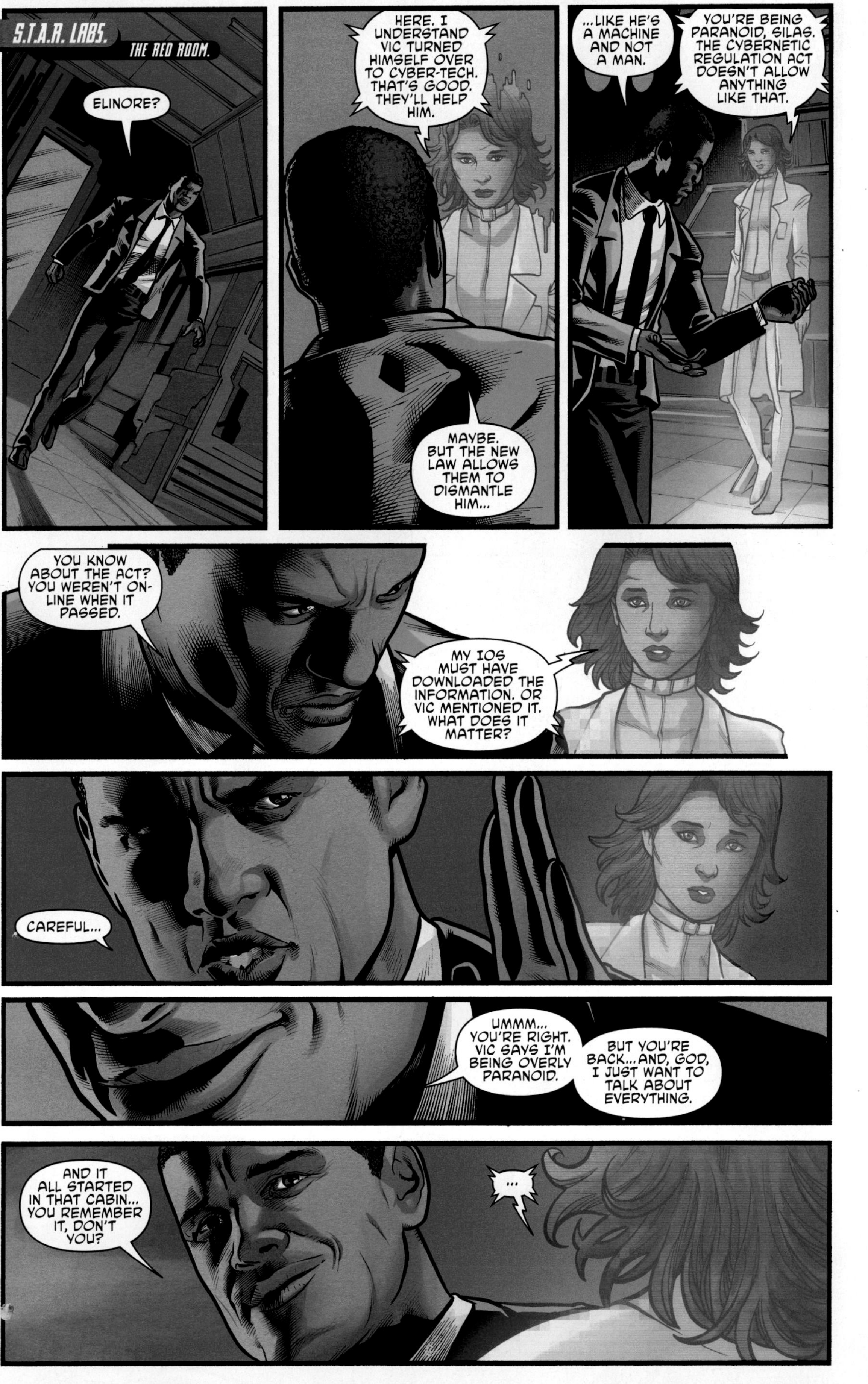
S.T.A.R. LABS.
THE RED ROOM.
ELINORE?
HERE. I UNDERSTAND VIC TURNED HIMSELF OVER TO CYBER-TECH. THAT'S GOOD. THEY'LL HELP HIM.
MAYBE. BUT THE NEW LAW ALLOWS THEM TO DISMANTLE HIM...
...LIKE HE'S A MACHINE AND NOT A MAN.
YOU'RE BEING PARANOID, SILAS. THE CYBERNETIC REGULATION ACT DOESN'T ALLOW ANYTHING LIKE THAT.
YOU KNOW ABOUT THE ACT? YOU WEREN'T ON-LINE WHEN IT PASSED.
MY IOS MUST HAVE DOWNLOADED THE INFORMATION. OR VIC MENTIONED IT. WHAT DOES IT MATTER?
CAREFUL...
UMMM... YOU'RE RIGHT. VIC SAYS I'M BEING OVERLY PARANOID.
BUT YOU'RE BACK...AND, GOD, I JUST WANT TO TALK ABOUT EVERYTHING.
AND IT ALL STARTED IN THAT CABIN... YOU REMEMBER IT, DON'T YOU?
...

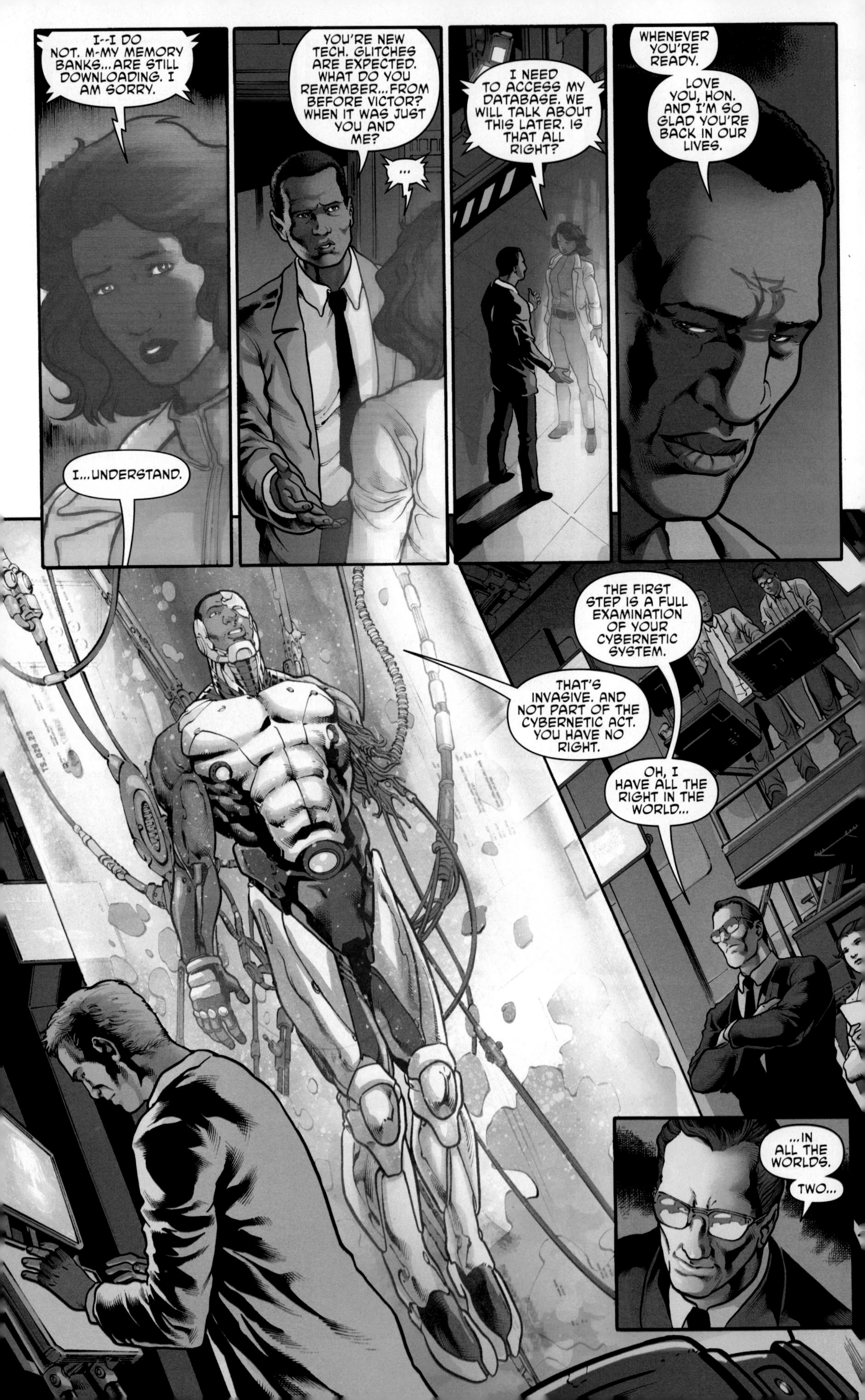
I--I DO NOT. M-MY MEMORY BANKS...ARE STILL DOWNLOADING. I AM SORRY.
I...UNDERSTAND.
YOU'RE NEW TECH. GLITCHES ARE EXPECTED. WHAT DO YOU REMEMBER...FROM BEFORE VICTOR? WHEN IT WAS JUST YOU AND ME?
...
I NEED TO ACCESS MY DATABASE. WE WILL TALK ABOUT THIS LATER. IS THAT ALL RIGHT?
WHENEVER YOU'RE READY.
LOVE YOU, HON. AND I'M SO GLAD YOU'RE BACK IN OUR LIVES.
THE FIRST STEP IS A FULL EXAMINATION OF YOUR CYBERNETIC SYSTEM.
THAT'S INVASIVE. AND NOT PART OF THE CYBERNETIC ACT. YOU HAVE NO RIGHT.
OH, I HAVE ALL THE RIGHT IN THE WORLD...
...IN ALL THE WORLDS.
TWO...

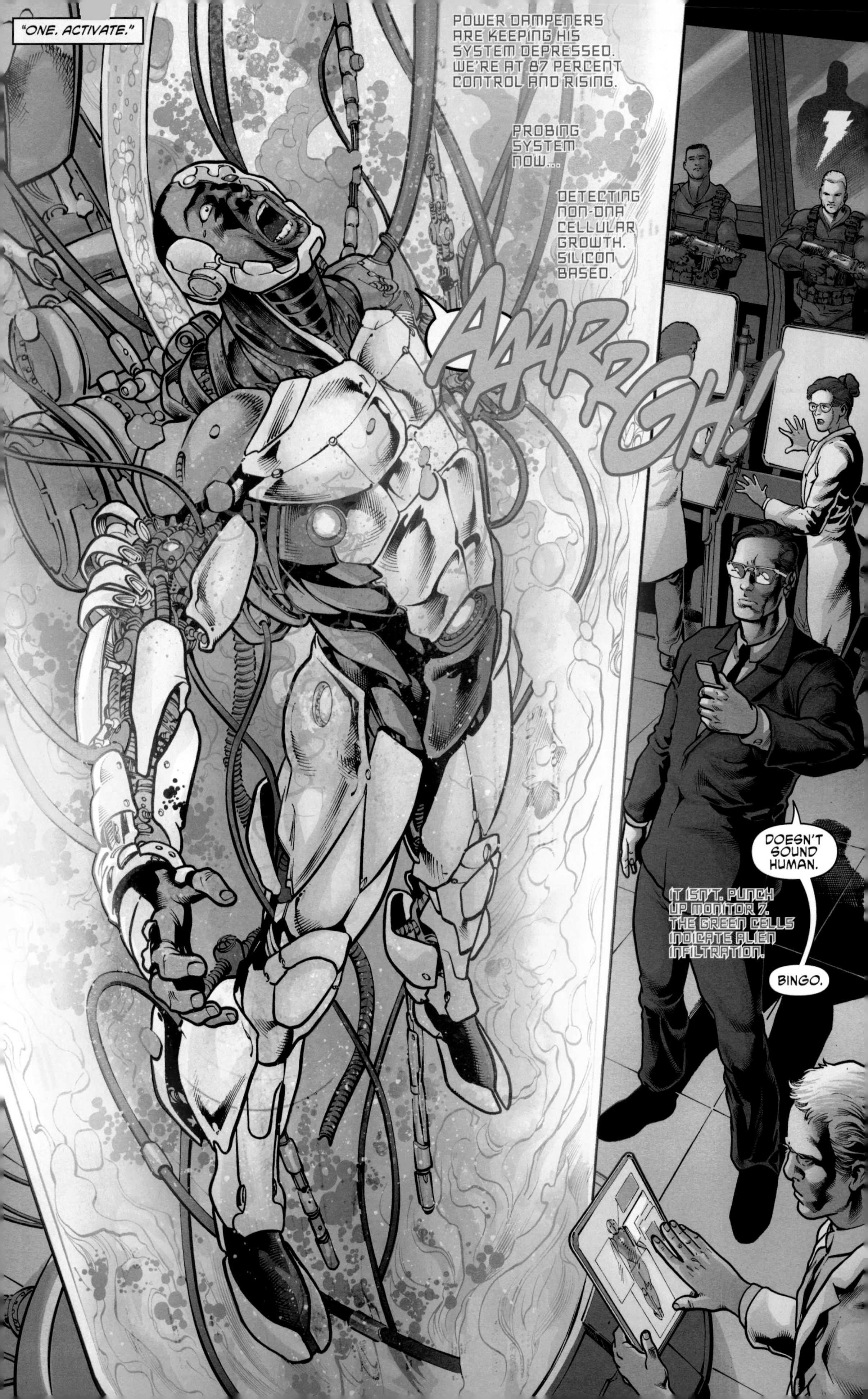
"ONE. ACTIVATE."
POWER DAMPENERS ARE KEEPING HIS SYSTEM DEPRESSED. WE'RE AT 87 PERCENT CONTROL AND RISING.
PROBING SYSTEM NOW...
DETECTING NON-DNA CELLULAR GROWTH. SILICON BASED.
AAARRGH!!
DOESN'T SOUND HUMAN.
IT ISN'T. PUNCH UP MONITOR 7. THE GREEN CELLS INDICATE ALIEN INFILTRATION.
BINGO.

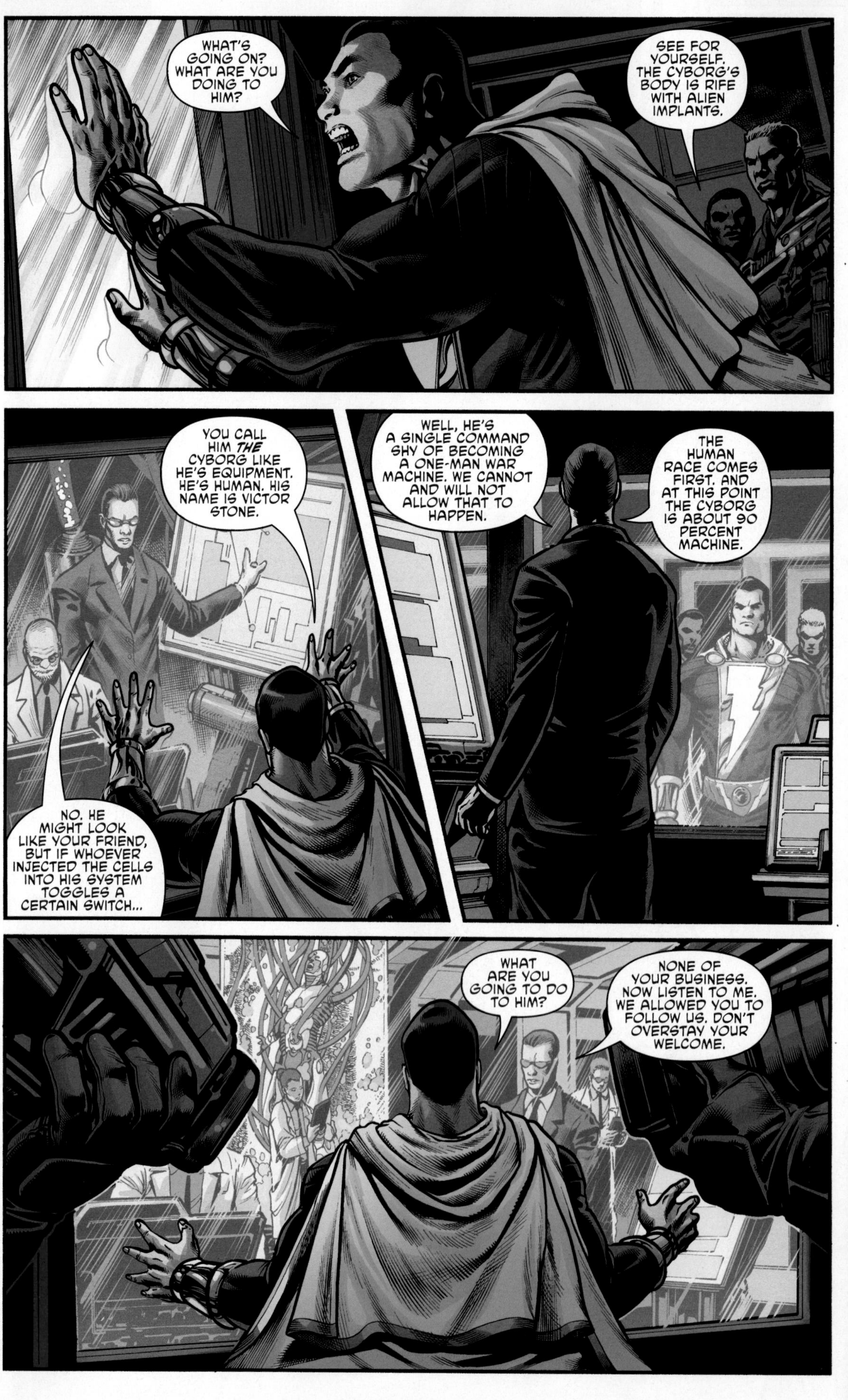
WHAT'S GOING ON? WHAT ARE YOU DOING TO HIM?
SEE FOR YOURSELF. THE CYBORG'S BODY IS RIFE WITH ALIEN IMPLANTS.
YOU CALL HIM *THE* CYBORG LIKE HE'S EQUIPMENT. HE'S HUMAN. HIS NAME IS VICTOR STONE.
NO. HE MIGHT LOOK LIKE YOUR FRIEND, BUT IF WHOEVER INJECTED THE CELLS INTO HIS SYSTEM TOGGLES A CERTAIN SWITCH...
WELL, HE'S A SINGLE COMMAND SHY OF BECOMING A ONE-MAN WAR MACHINE. WE CANNOT AND WILL NOT ALLOW THAT TO HAPPEN.
THE HUMAN RACE COMES FIRST. AND AT THIS POINT THE CYBORG IS ABOUT 90 PERCENT MACHINE.
WHAT ARE YOU GOING TO DO TO HIM?
NONE OF YOUR BUSINESS. NOW LISTEN TO ME. WE ALLOWED YOU TO FOLLOW US. DON'T OVERSTAY YOUR WELCOME.

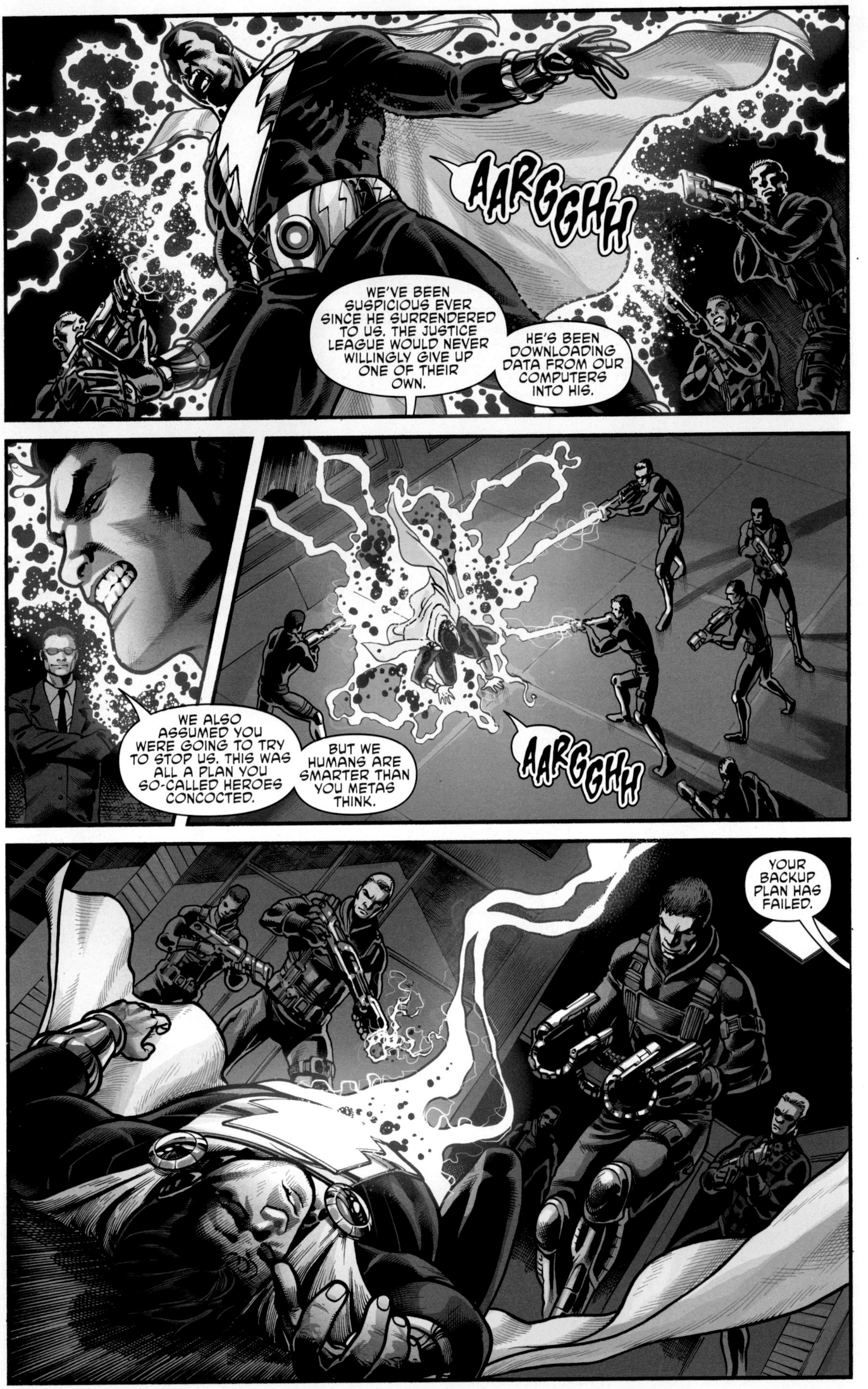
AARGGHH
WE'VE BEEN SUSPICIOUS EVER SINCE HE SURRENDERED TO US. THE JUSTICE LEAGUE WOULD NEVER WILLINGLY GIVE UP ONE OF THEIR OWN.
HE'S BEEN DOWNLOADING DATA FROM OUR COMPUTERS INTO HIS.
WE ALSO ASSUMED YOU WERE GOING TO TRY TO STOP US. THIS WAS ALL A PLAN YOU SO-CALLED HEROES CONCOCTED.
BUT WE HUMANS ARE SMARTER THAN YOU METAS THINK.
AARGGHH
YOUR BACKUP PLAN HAS FAILED.

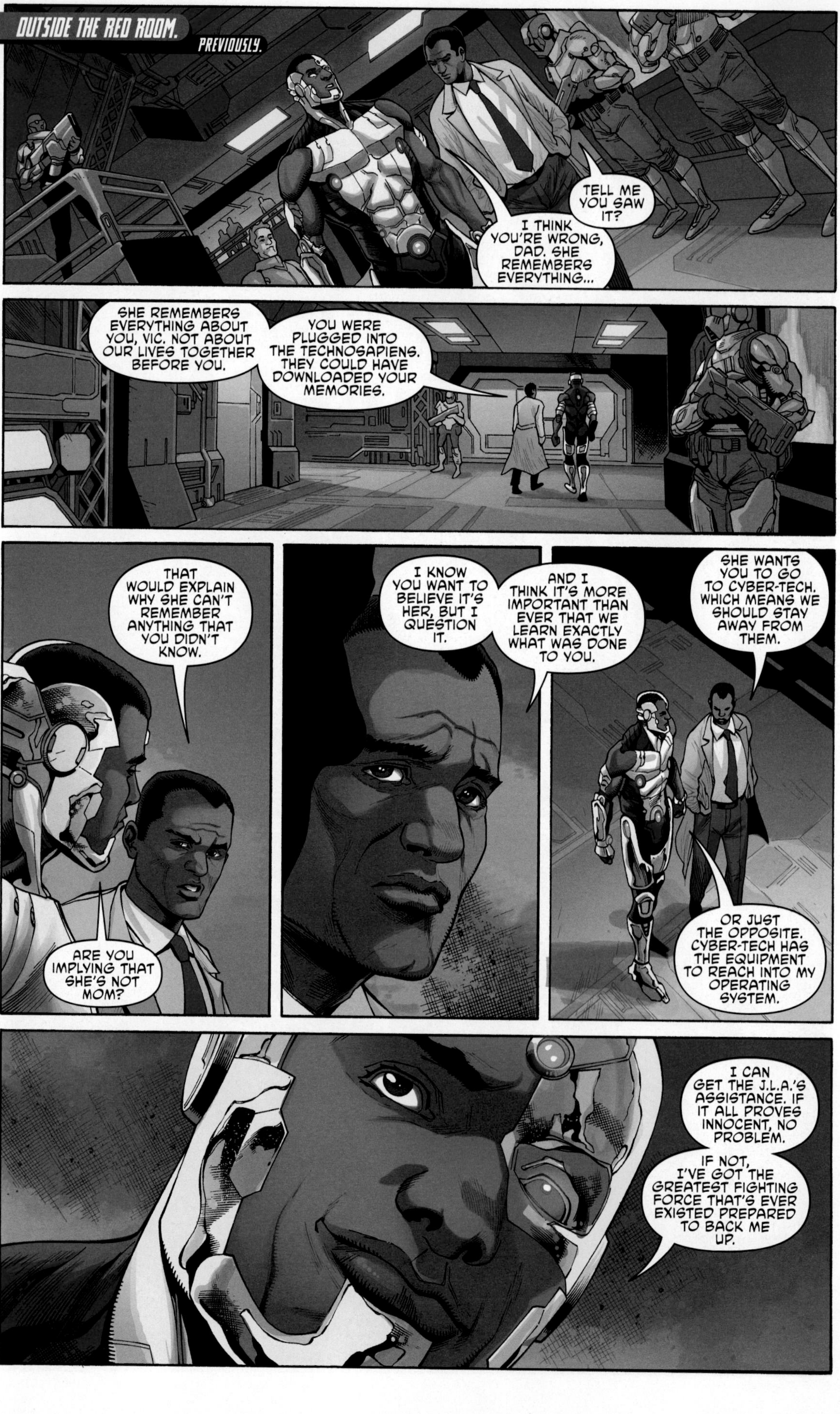
OUTSIDE THE RED ROOM.
PREVIOUSLY.
TELL ME YOU SAW IT?
I THINK YOU'RE WRONG, DAD. SHE REMEMBERS EVERYTHING...
SHE REMEMBERS EVERYTHING ABOUT YOU, VIC. NOT ABOUT OUR LIVES TOGETHER BEFORE YOU.
YOU WERE PLUGGED INTO THE TECHNOSAPIENS. THEY COULD HAVE DOWNLOADED YOUR MEMORIES.
THAT WOULD EXPLAIN WHY SHE CAN'T REMEMBER ANYTHING THAT YOU DIDN'T KNOW.
ARE YOU IMPLYING THAT SHE'S NOT MOM?
I KNOW YOU WANT TO BELIEVE IT'S HER, BUT I QUESTION IT.
AND I THINK IT'S MORE IMPORTANT THAN EVER THAT WE LEARN EXACTLY WHAT WAS DONE TO YOU.
SHE WANTS YOU TO GO TO CYBER-TECH. WHICH MEANS WE SHOULD STAY AWAY FROM THEM.
OR JUST THE OPPOSITE. CYBER-TECH HAS THE EQUIPMENT TO REACH INTO MY OPERATING SYSTEM.
I CAN GET THE J.L.A.'S ASSISTANCE. IF IT ALL PROVES INNOCENT, NO PROBLEM.
IF NOT, I'VE GOT THE GREATEST FIGHTING FORCE THAT'S EVER EXISTED PREPARED TO BACK ME UP.

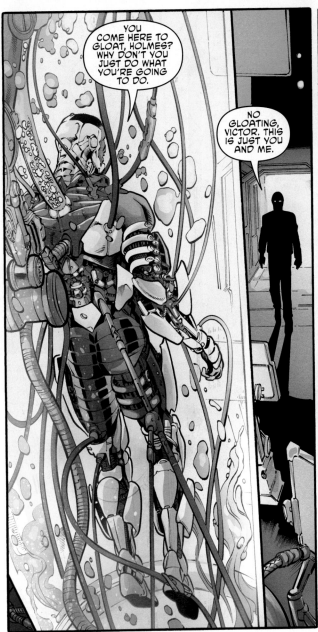

YOU COME HERE TO GLOAT, HOLMES? WHY DON'T YOU JUST DO WHAT YOU'RE GOING TO DO.

NO GLOATING, VICTOR. THIS IS JUST YOU AND ME.

LET ME TELL YOU A STORY. TWO MONTHS AGO I HAD A HEART ATTACK. A BAD ONE.

AND I WAS GIVEN AN ARTIFICIAL HEART. WHAT WE DIDN'T KNOW WAS IT HAD BEEN HACKED INTO BY THE TECHNOSAPIENS.

I'M SYNCHED IN WITH THEM NOW. THEY CONTROL ME.

AND MY ARTIFICIAL HEART HOLDS THE KEY TO CONTROLLING THIS MACHINE.

ALL THIS, EVERYTHING THAT'S HAPPENED, WAS SPECIFICALLY DESIGNED FOR THIS MOMENT.

THE TECHNOSAPIENS CAN'T EVOLVE. THEY CAN'T GROW. THEY'VE BECOME GENETICALLY STAGNANT AND ARE DYING.

MEANWHILE, YOUR IOS HAS GAINED THE ABILITY TO EVOLVE AND CHANGE.

THE TECHNOSAPIENS NEED TO KNOW HOW. AND IF THEY HAVE TO DISSECT YOU AND THIS WORLD TO SAVE THEMSELVES, THEY WILL.

AND THANKS TO OUR RED ROOM MANIFESTATION, WE DIDN'T EVEN HAVE TO HUNT YOU DOWN. YOU WILLINGLY CAME TO US.

YOU CREATED THE HOLOGRAM OF MY MOTHER?

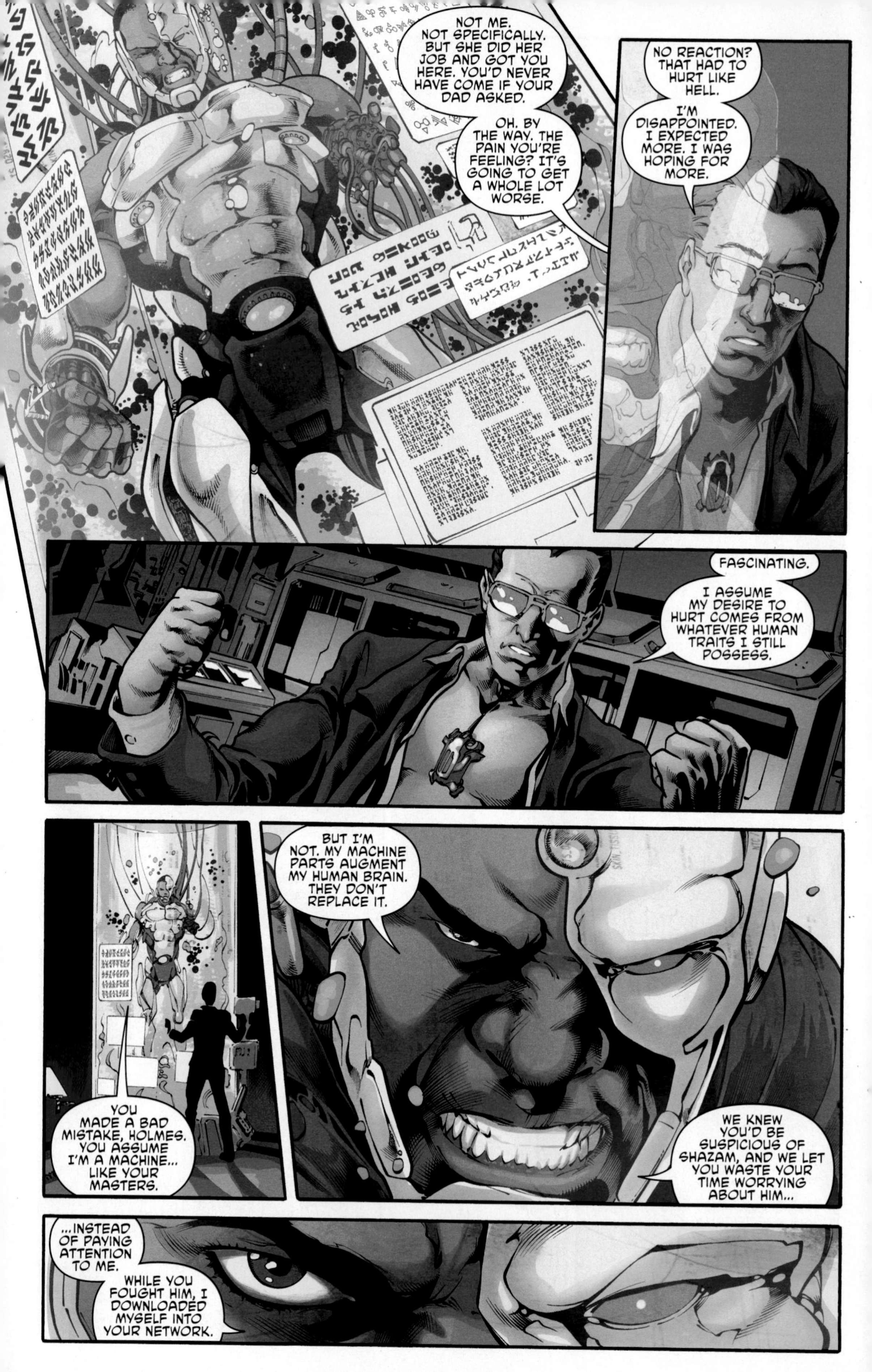
NOT ME. NOT SPECIFICALLY. BUT SHE DID HER JOB AND GOT YOU HERE. YOU'D NEVER HAVE COME IF YOUR DAD ASKED.
OH. BY THE WAY. THE PAIN YOU'RE FEELING? IT'S GOING TO GET A WHOLE LOT WORSE.
NO REACTION? THAT HAD TO HURT LIKE HELL.
I'M DISAPPOINTED. I EXPECTED MORE. I WAS HOPING FOR MORE.
FASCINATING.
I ASSUME MY DESIRE TO HURT COMES FROM WHATEVER HUMAN TRAITS I STILL POSSESS.
YOU MADE A BAD MISTAKE, HOLMES. YOU ASSUME I'M A MACHINE... LIKE YOUR MASTERS.
BUT I'M NOT. MY MACHINE PARTS AUGMENT MY HUMAN BRAIN. THEY DON'T REPLACE IT.
WE KNEW YOU'D BE SUSPICIOUS OF SHAZAM, AND WE LET YOU WASTE YOUR TIME WORRYING ABOUT HIM...
...INSTEAD OF PAYING ATTENTION TO ME.
WHILE YOU FOUGHT HIM, I DOWNLOADED MYSELF INTO YOUR NETWORK.

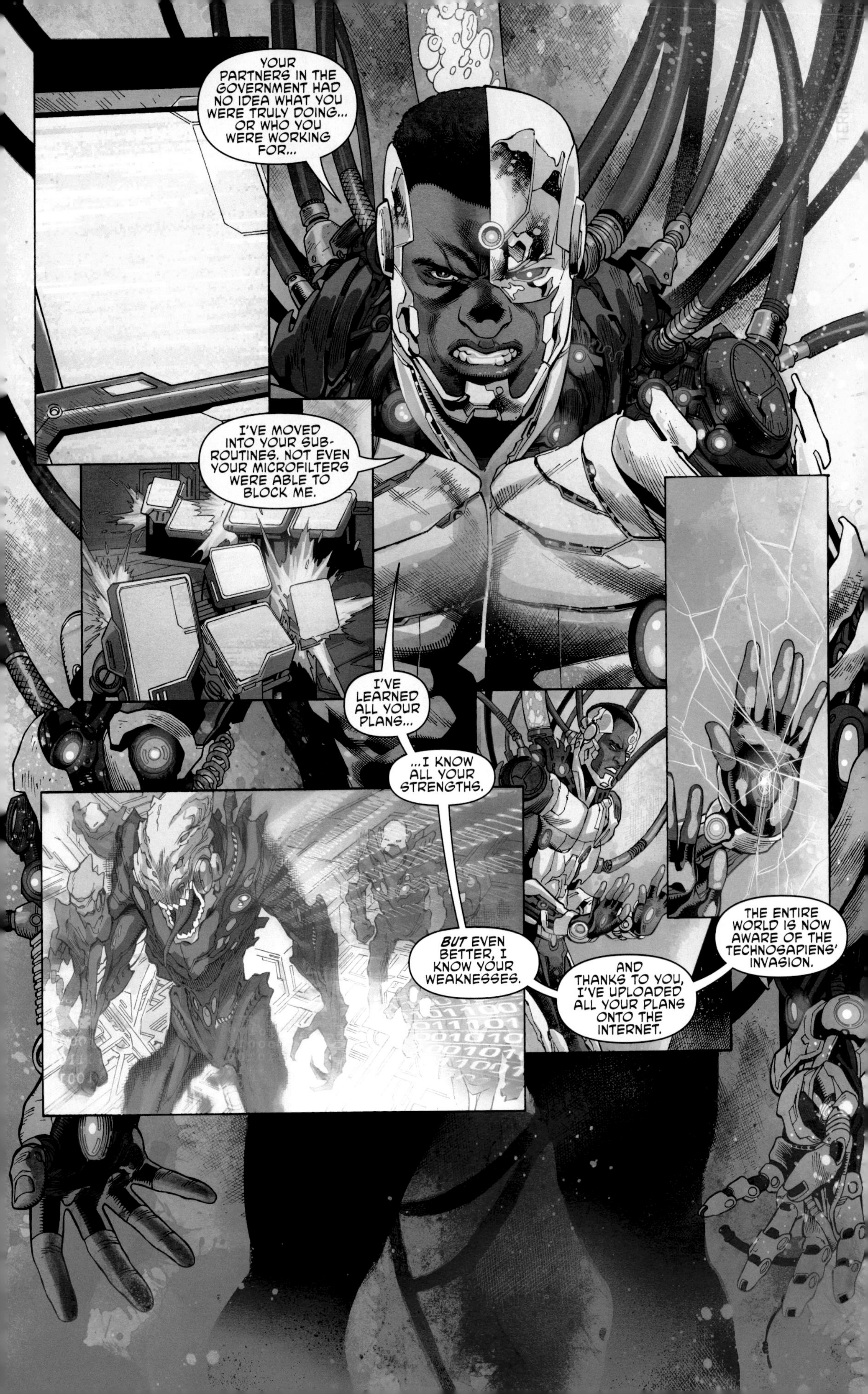
YOUR PARTNERS IN THE GOVERNMENT HAD NO IDEA WHAT YOU WERE TRULY DOING... OR WHO YOU WERE WORKING FOR...
I'VE MOVED INTO YOUR SUB-ROUTINES. NOT EVEN YOUR MICROFILTERS WERE ABLE TO BLOCK ME.
I'VE LEARNED ALL YOUR PLANS...
...I KNOW ALL YOUR STRENGTHS.
BUT EVEN BETTER, I KNOW YOUR WEAKNESSES.
AND THANKS TO YOU, I'VE UPLOADED ALL YOUR PLANS ONTO THE INTERNET.
THE ENTIRE WORLD IS NOW AWARE OF THE TECHNOSAPIENS' INVASION.

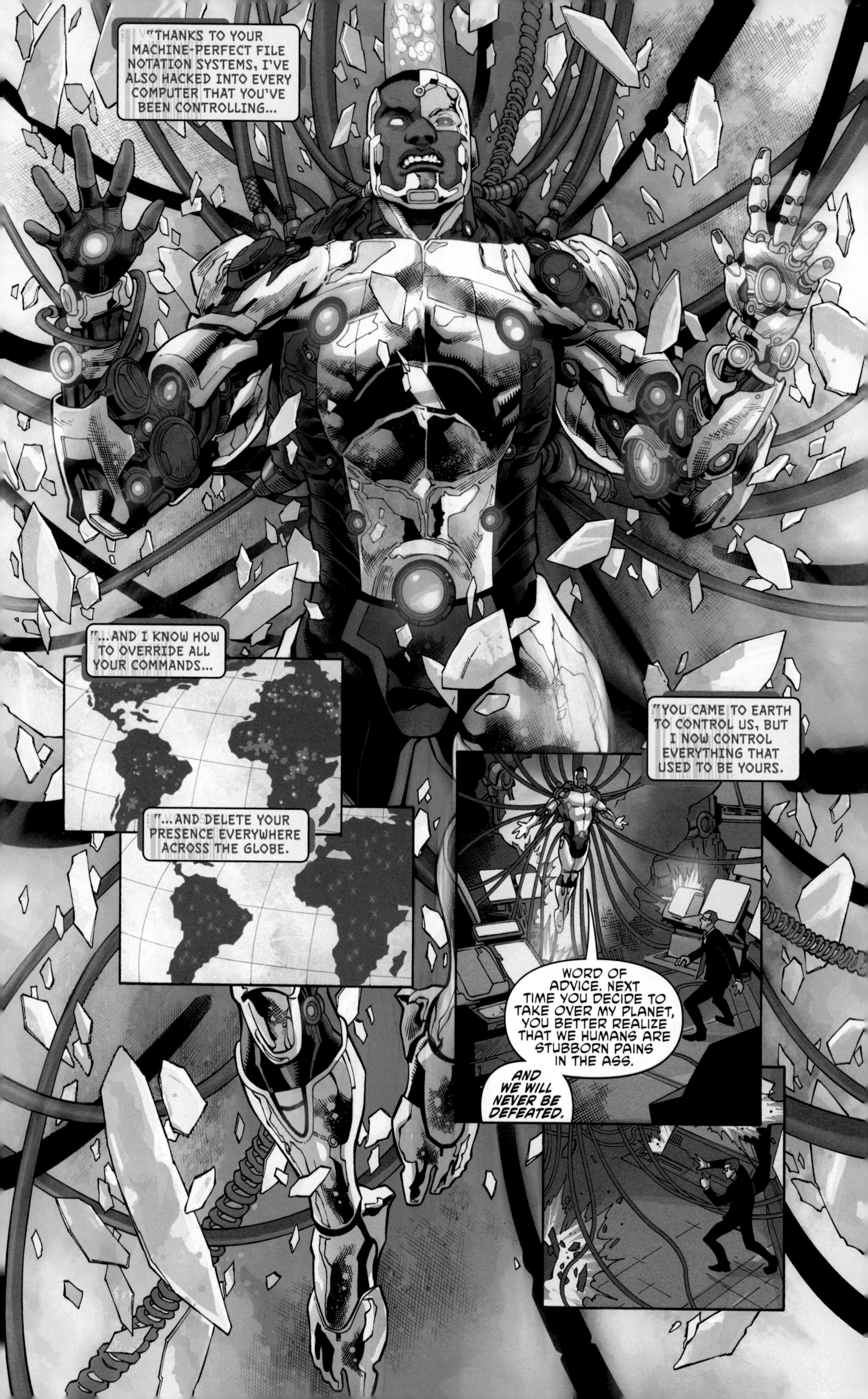
"THANKS TO YOUR MACHINE-PERFECT FILE NOTATION SYSTEMS, I'VE ALSO HACKED INTO EVERY COMPUTER THAT YOU'VE BEEN CONTROLLING...
"...AND I KNOW HOW TO OVERRIDE ALL YOUR COMMANDS...
"...AND DELETE YOUR PRESENCE EVERYWHERE ACROSS THE GLOBE.
"YOU CAME TO EARTH TO CONTROL US, BUT I NOW CONTROL EVERYTHING THAT USED TO BE YOURS.
WORD OF ADVICE. NEXT TIME YOU DECIDE TO TAKE OVER MY PLANET, YOU BETTER REALIZE THAT WE HUMANS ARE STUBBORN PAINS IN THE ASS.
AND WE WILL NEVER BE DEFEATED.

THE HUMAN'S SONG SINGS TO US, CARESSES US...

...AND IT IS BEAUTIFUL TO HEAR.

YOU HEAR THAT? HE CALLED ME HUMAN.

BEST THING I'VE HEARD ALL DAY.

I'M BACK.

WHAT TOOK SO LONG? I'VE BEEN FIGHTING THESE UGLY DUDES ALL BY MY LONESOME.

WELL, I WAS KINDA TIED UP. BUT I'M HERE NOW.

OKAY, WE'RE DOING THIS.

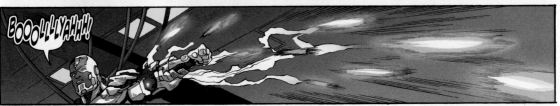

BOOOLLLYAHH!

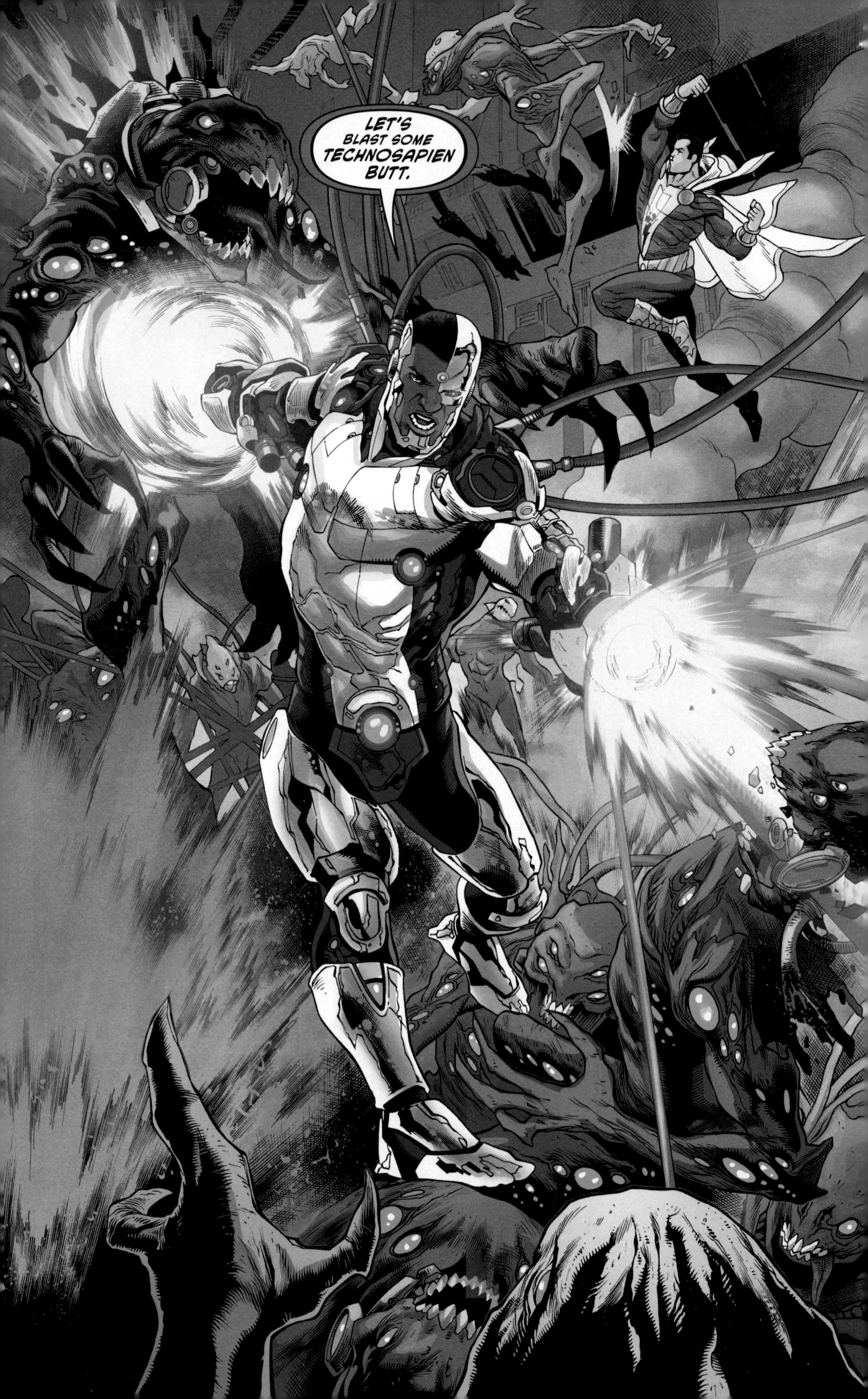
LET'S BLAST SOME TECHNOSAPIEN BUTT.

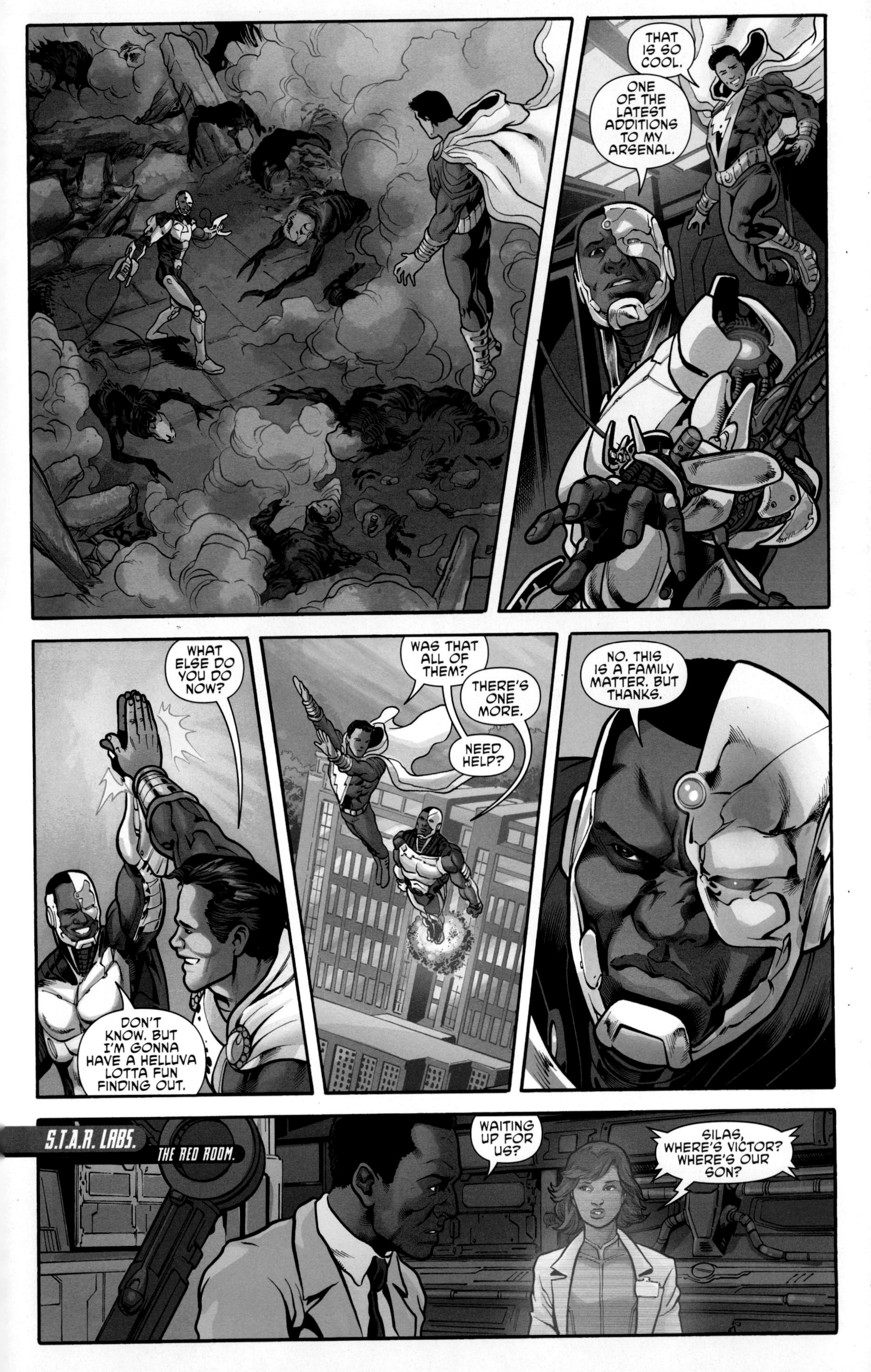
THAT IS SO COOL.
ONE OF THE LATEST ADDITIONS TO MY ARSENAL.
WHAT ELSE DO YOU DO NOW?
DON'T KNOW. BUT I'M GONNA HAVE A HELLUVA LOTTA FUN FINDING OUT.
WAS THAT ALL OF THEM?
THERE'S ONE MORE.
NEED HELP?
NO. THIS IS A FAMILY MATTER. BUT THANKS.
S.T.A.R. LABS.
THE RED ROOM.
WAITING UP FOR US?
SILAS, WHERE'S VICTOR? WHERE'S OUR SON?

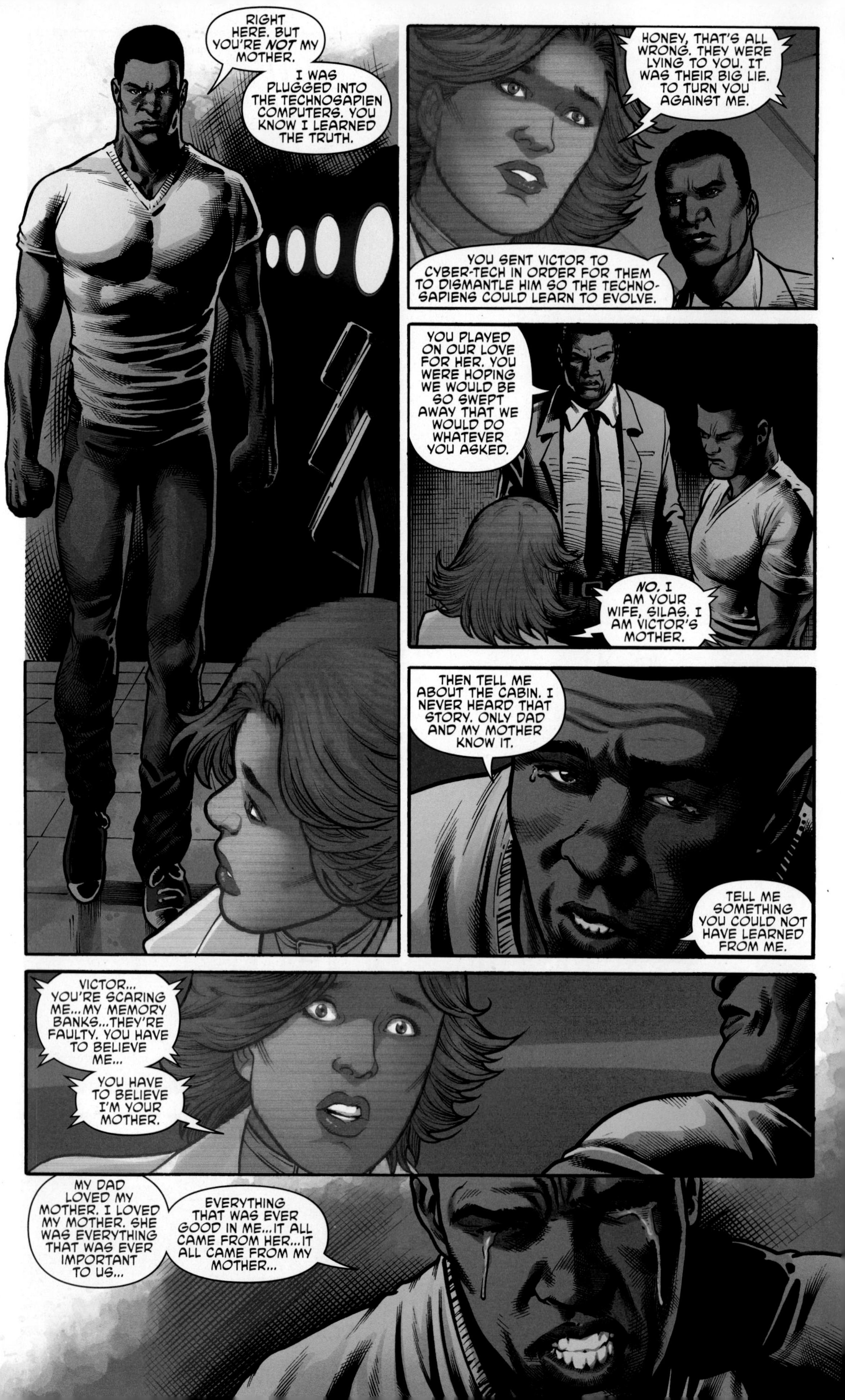
RIGHT HERE. BUT YOU'RE *NOT* MY MOTHER.
I WAS PLUGGED INTO THE TECHNOSAPIEN COMPUTERS. YOU KNOW I LEARNED THE TRUTH.
HONEY, THAT'S ALL WRONG. THEY WERE LYING TO YOU. IT WAS THEIR BIG LIE. TO TURN YOU AGAINST ME.
YOU SENT VICTOR TO CYBER-TECH IN ORDER FOR THEM TO DISMANTLE HIM SO THE TECHNO-SAPIENS COULD LEARN TO EVOLVE.
YOU PLAYED ON OUR LOVE FOR HER. YOU WERE HOPING WE WOULD BE SO SWEPT AWAY THAT WE WOULD DO WHATEVER YOU ASKED.
NO. I AM YOUR WIFE, SILAS. I AM VICTOR'S MOTHER.
THEN TELL ME ABOUT THE CABIN. I NEVER HEARD THAT STORY. ONLY DAD AND MY MOTHER KNOW IT.
TELL ME SOMETHING YOU COULD NOT HAVE LEARNED FROM ME.
VICTOR... YOU'RE SCARING ME...MY MEMORY BANKS...THEY'RE FAULTY. YOU HAVE TO BELIEVE ME...
YOU HAVE TO BELIEVE I'M YOUR MOTHER.
MY DAD LOVED MY MOTHER. I LOVED MY MOTHER. SHE WAS EVERYTHING THAT WAS EVER IMPORTANT TO US...
EVERYTHING THAT WAS EVER GOOD IN ME...IT ALL CAME FROM HER...IT ALL CAME FROM MY MOTHER...

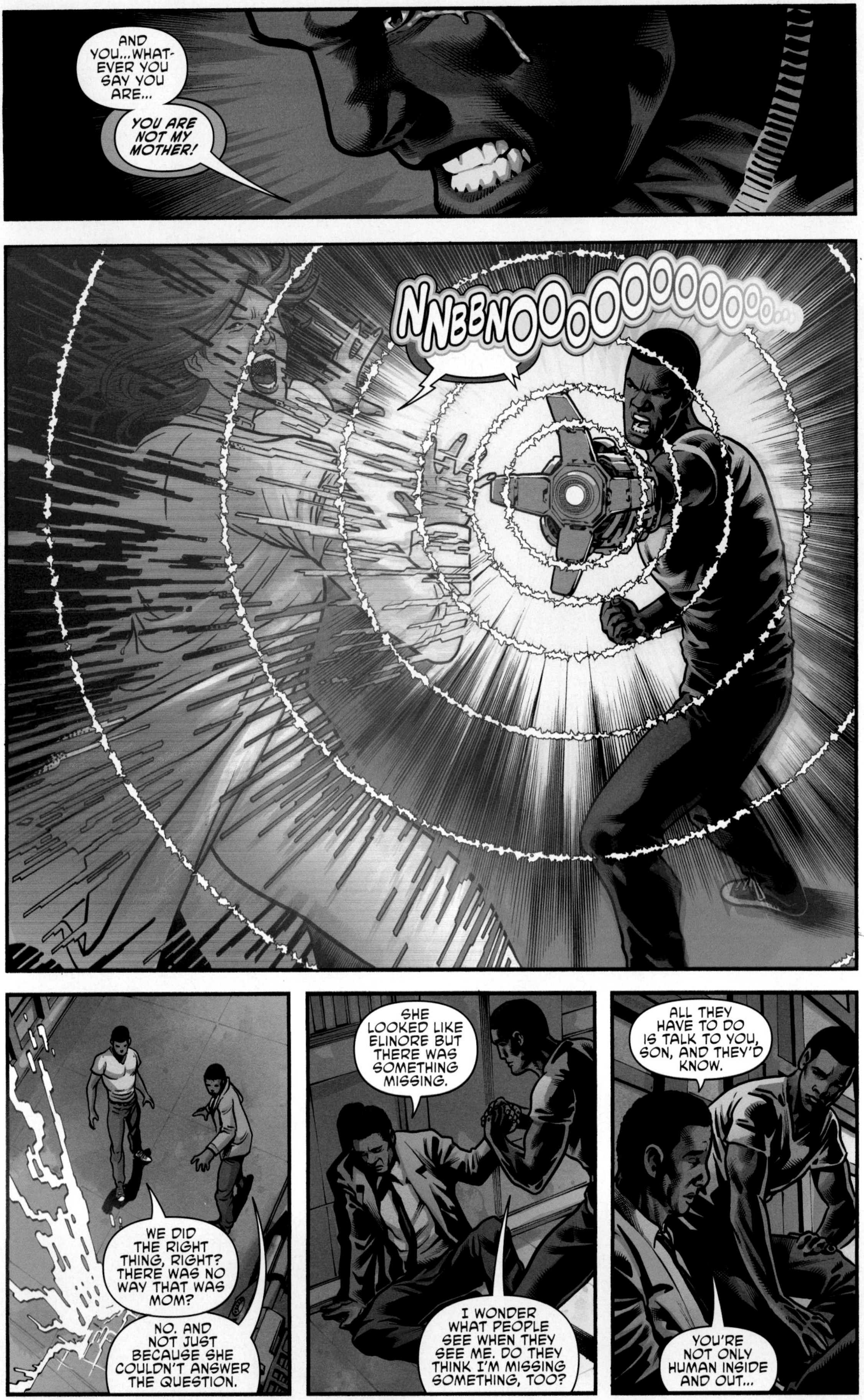
AND YOU...WHAT-EVER YOU SAY YOU ARE...
YOU ARE NOT MY MOTHER!
NNBBNOOOOOOOOOOOOo...
WE DID THE RIGHT THING, RIGHT? THERE WAS NO WAY THAT WAS MOM?
NO. AND NOT JUST BECAUSE SHE COULDN'T ANSWER THE QUESTION.
SHE LOOKED LIKE ELINORE BUT THERE WAS SOMETHING MISSING.
I WONDER WHAT PEOPLE SEE WHEN THEY SEE ME. DO THEY THINK I'M MISSING SOMETHING, TOO?
ALL THEY HAVE TO DO IS TALK TO YOU, SON, AND THEY'D KNOW.
YOU'RE NOT ONLY HUMAN INSIDE AND OUT...

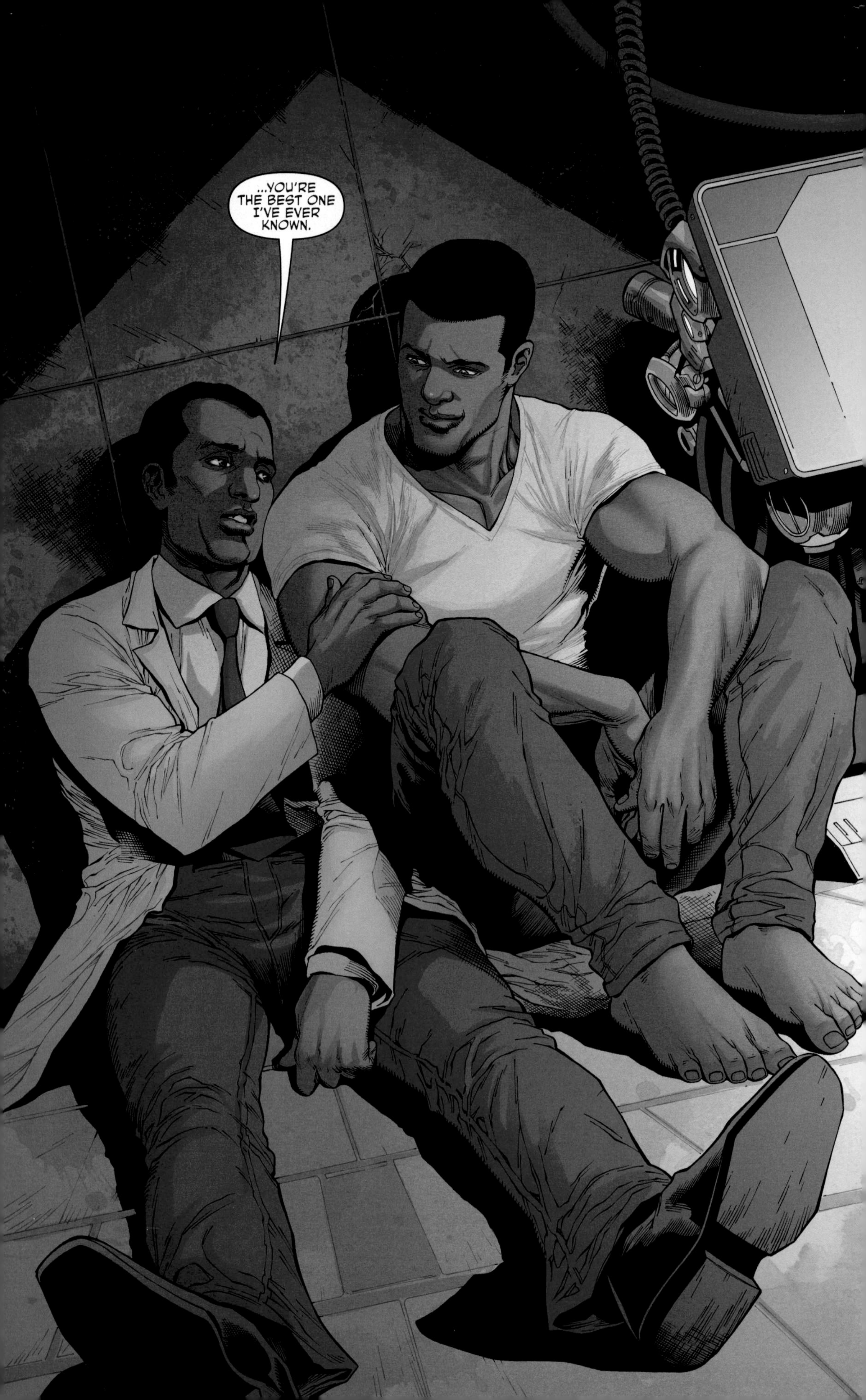
...YOU'RE THE BEST ONE I'VE EVER KNOWN.

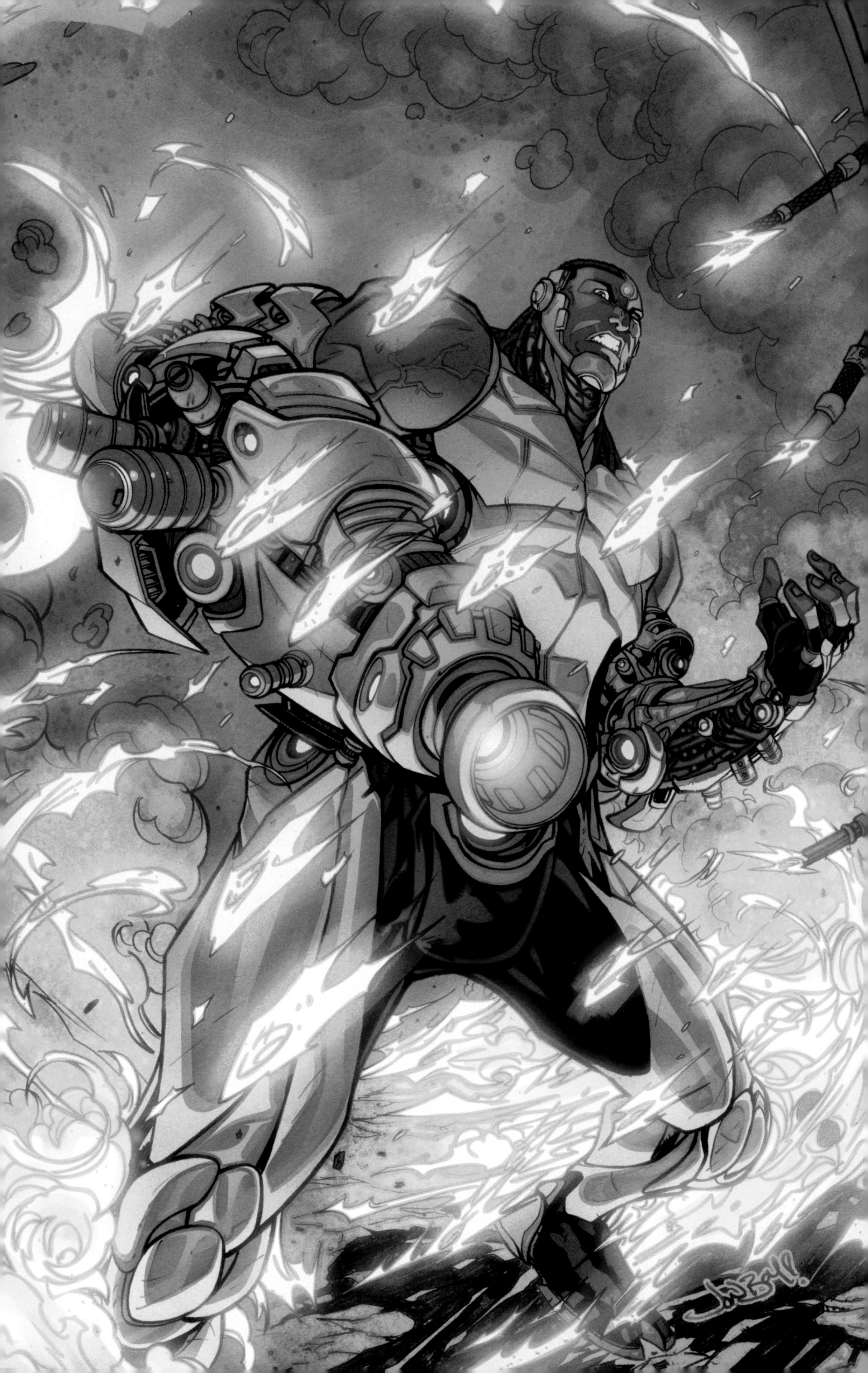

THE WORLD OUTSIDE

MARV WOLFMAN writer **FELIPE WATANABE, DANIEL HDR & JÚLIO FERREIRA** pencillers **OCLAIR ALBERT, DANIEL HDR & JÚLIO FERREIRA** inkers **JONBOY MEYERS** cover

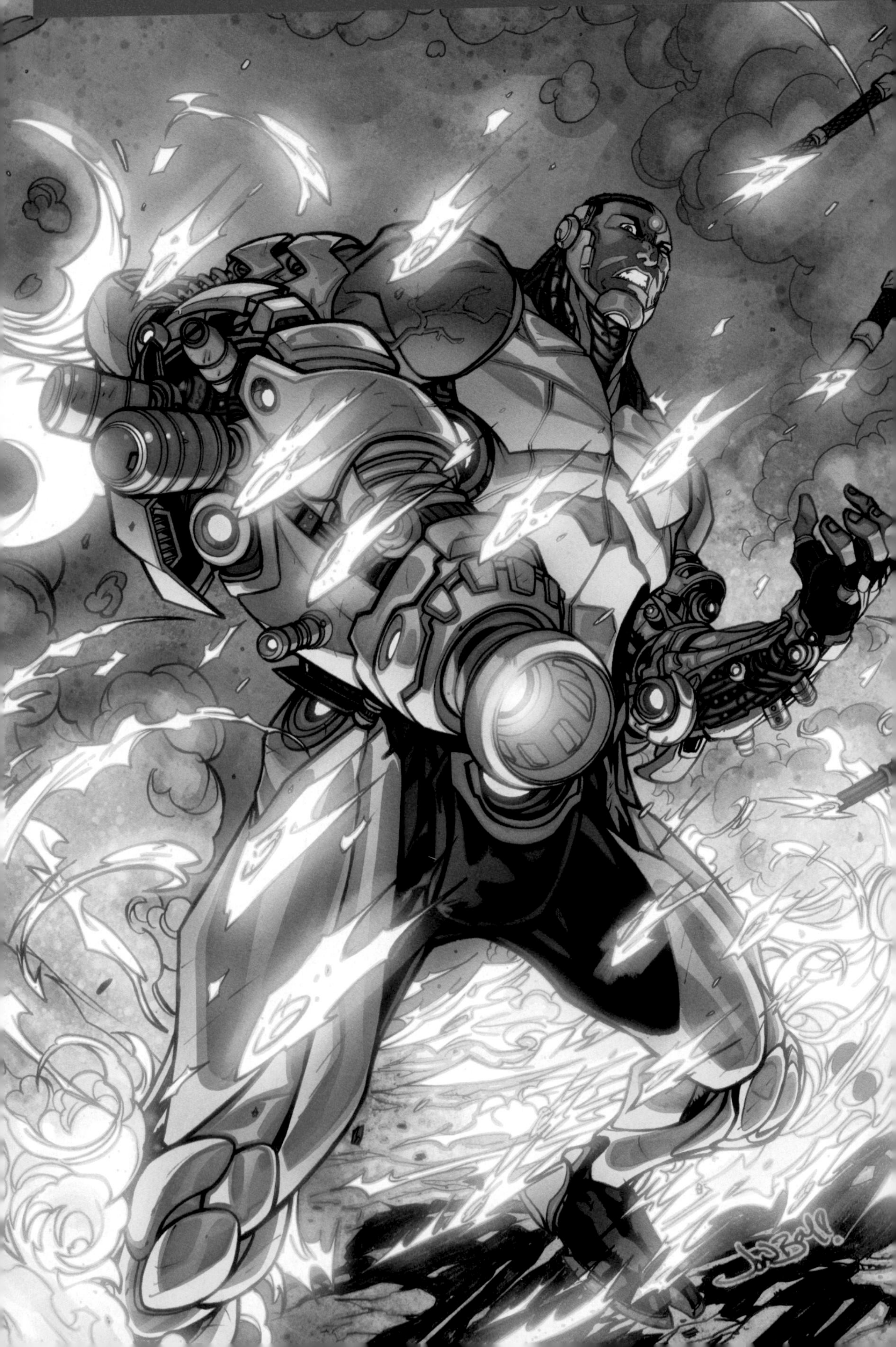

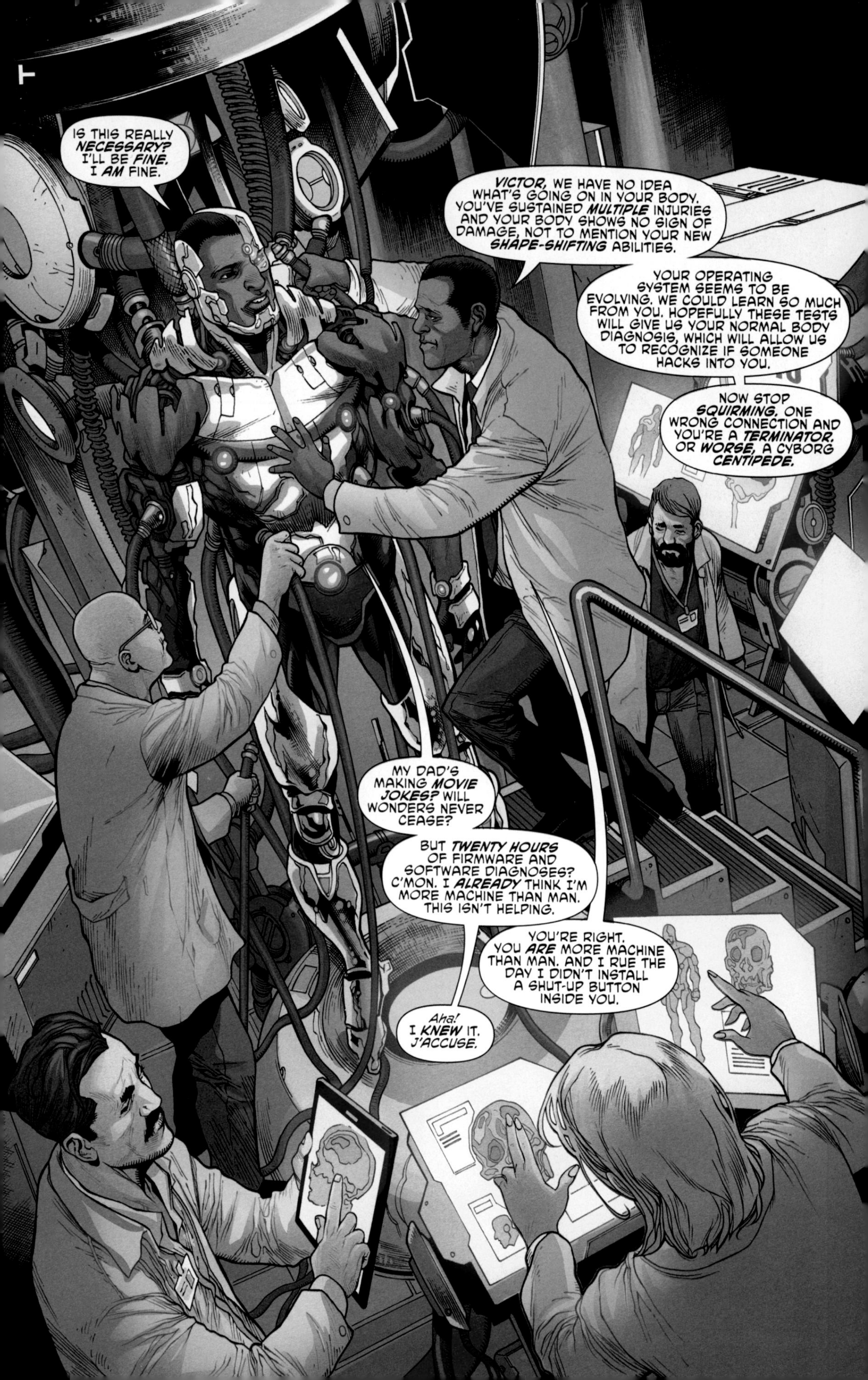
IS THIS REALLY NECESSARY? I'LL BE FINE. I AM FINE.
VICTOR, WE HAVE NO IDEA WHAT'S GOING ON IN YOUR BODY. YOU'VE SUSTAINED MULTIPLE INJURIES AND YOUR BODY SHOWS NO SIGN OF DAMAGE, NOT TO MENTION YOUR NEW SHAPE-SHIFTING ABILITIES.
YOUR OPERATING SYSTEM SEEMS TO BE EVOLVING. WE COULD LEARN SO MUCH FROM YOU. HOPEFULLY THESE TESTS WILL GIVE US YOUR NORMAL BODY DIAGNOSIS, WHICH WILL ALLOW US TO RECOGNIZE IF SOMEONE HACKS INTO YOU.
NOW STOP SQUIRMING. ONE WRONG CONNECTION AND YOU'RE A TERMINATOR. OR WORSE, A CYBORG CENTIPEDE.
MY DAD'S MAKING MOVIE JOKES? WILL WONDERS NEVER CEASE?
BUT TWENTY HOURS OF FIRMWARE AND SOFTWARE DIAGNOSES? C'MON. I ALREADY THINK I'M MORE MACHINE THAN MAN. THIS ISN'T HELPING.
YOU'RE RIGHT. YOU ARE MORE MACHINE THAN MAN. AND I RUE THE DAY I DIDN'T INSTALL A SHUT-UP BUTTON INSIDE YOU.
Aha! I KNEW IT. J'ACCUSE.

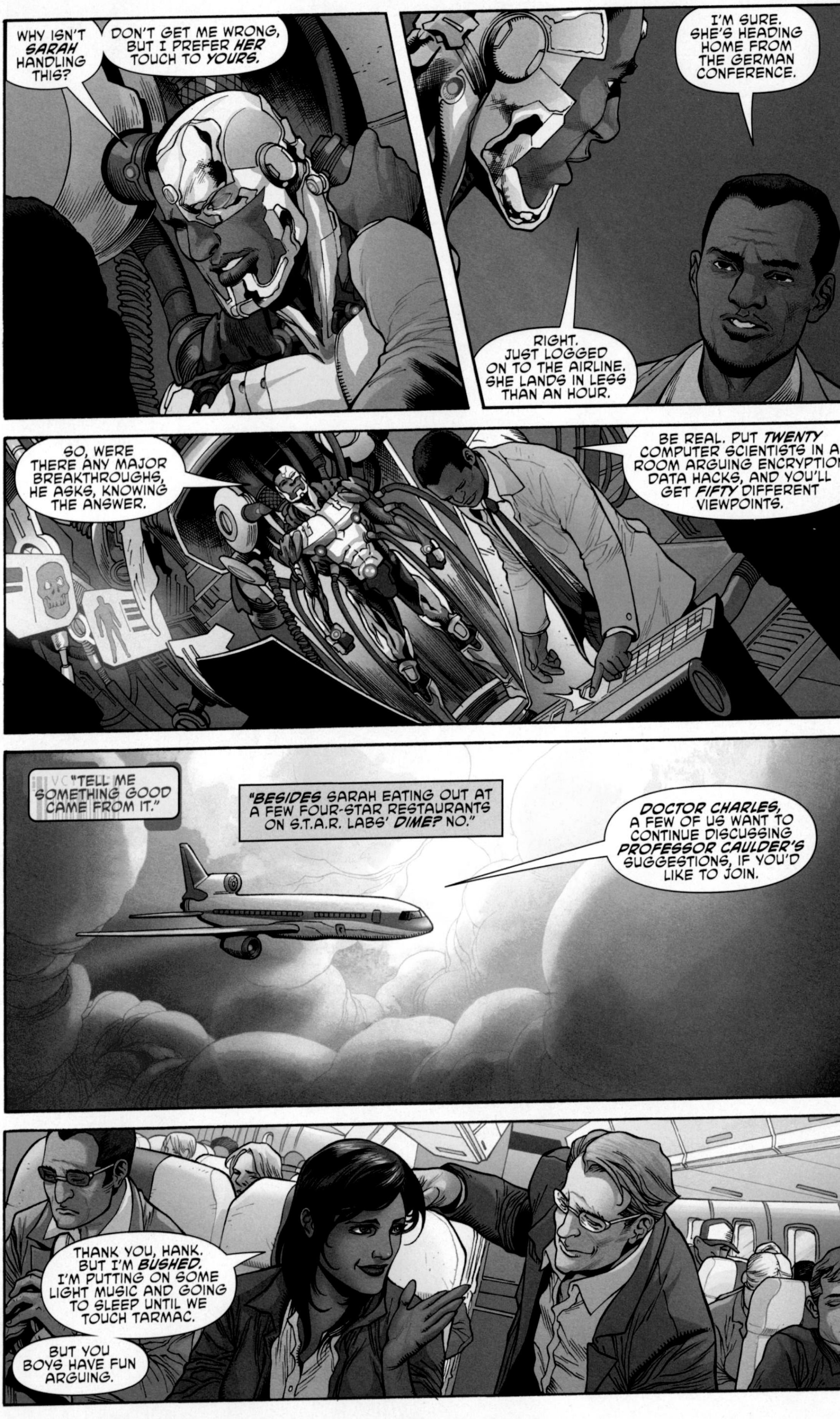
WHY ISN'T SARAH HANDLING THIS?
DON'T GET ME WRONG, BUT I PREFER HER TOUCH TO YOURS.
I'M SURE. SHE'S HEADING HOME FROM THE GERMAN CONFERENCE.
RIGHT. JUST LOGGED ON TO THE AIRLINE. SHE LANDS IN LESS THAN AN HOUR.
SO, WERE THERE ANY MAJOR BREAKTHROUGHS, HE ASKS, KNOWING THE ANSWER.
BE REAL. PUT TWENTY COMPUTER SCIENTISTS IN A ROOM ARGUING ENCRYPTION DATA HACKS, AND YOU'LL GET FIFTY DIFFERENT VIEWPOINTS.
"TELL ME SOMETHING GOOD CAME FROM IT."
"BESIDES SARAH EATING OUT AT A FEW FOUR-STAR RESTAURANTS ON S.T.A.R. LABS' DIME? NO."
DOCTOR CHARLES, A FEW OF US WANT TO CONTINUE DISCUSSING PROFESSOR CAULDER'S SUGGESTIONS, IF YOU'D LIKE TO JOIN.
THANK YOU, HANK. BUT I'M BUSHED. I'M PUTTING ON SOME LIGHT MUSIC AND GOING TO SLEEP UNTIL WE TOUCH TARMAC.
BUT YOU BOYS HAVE FUN ARGUING.

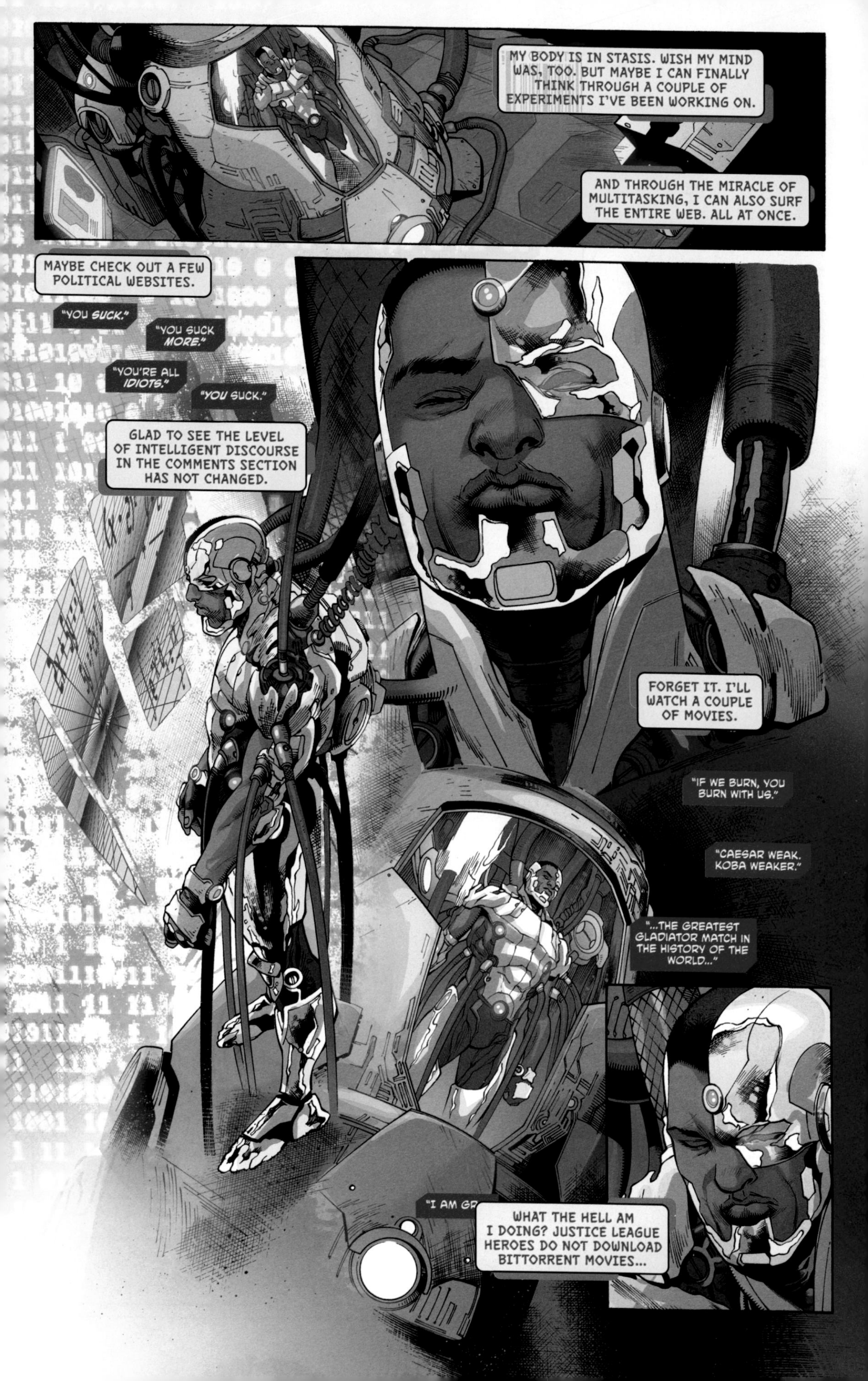
MY BODY IS IN STASIS. WISH MY MIND WAS, TOO. BUT MAYBE I CAN FINALLY THINK THROUGH A COUPLE OF EXPERIMENTS I'VE BEEN WORKING ON.
AND THROUGH THE MIRACLE OF MULTITASKING, I CAN ALSO SURF THE ENTIRE WEB. ALL AT ONCE.
MAYBE CHECK OUT A FEW POLITICAL WEBSITES.
"YOU SUCK."
"YOU SUCK MORE."
"YOU'RE ALL IDIOTS."
"YOU SUCK."
GLAD TO SEE THE LEVEL OF INTELLIGENT DISCOURSE IN THE COMMENTS SECTION HAS NOT CHANGED.
FORGET IT. I'LL WATCH A COUPLE OF MOVIES.
"IF WE BURN, YOU BURN WITH US."
"CAESAR WEAK. KOBA WEAKER."
"...THE GREATEST GLADIATOR MATCH IN THE HISTORY OF THE WORLD..."
"I AM GR
WHAT THE HELL AM I DOING? JUSTICE LEAGUE HEROES DO NOT DOWNLOAD BITTORRENT MOVIES...

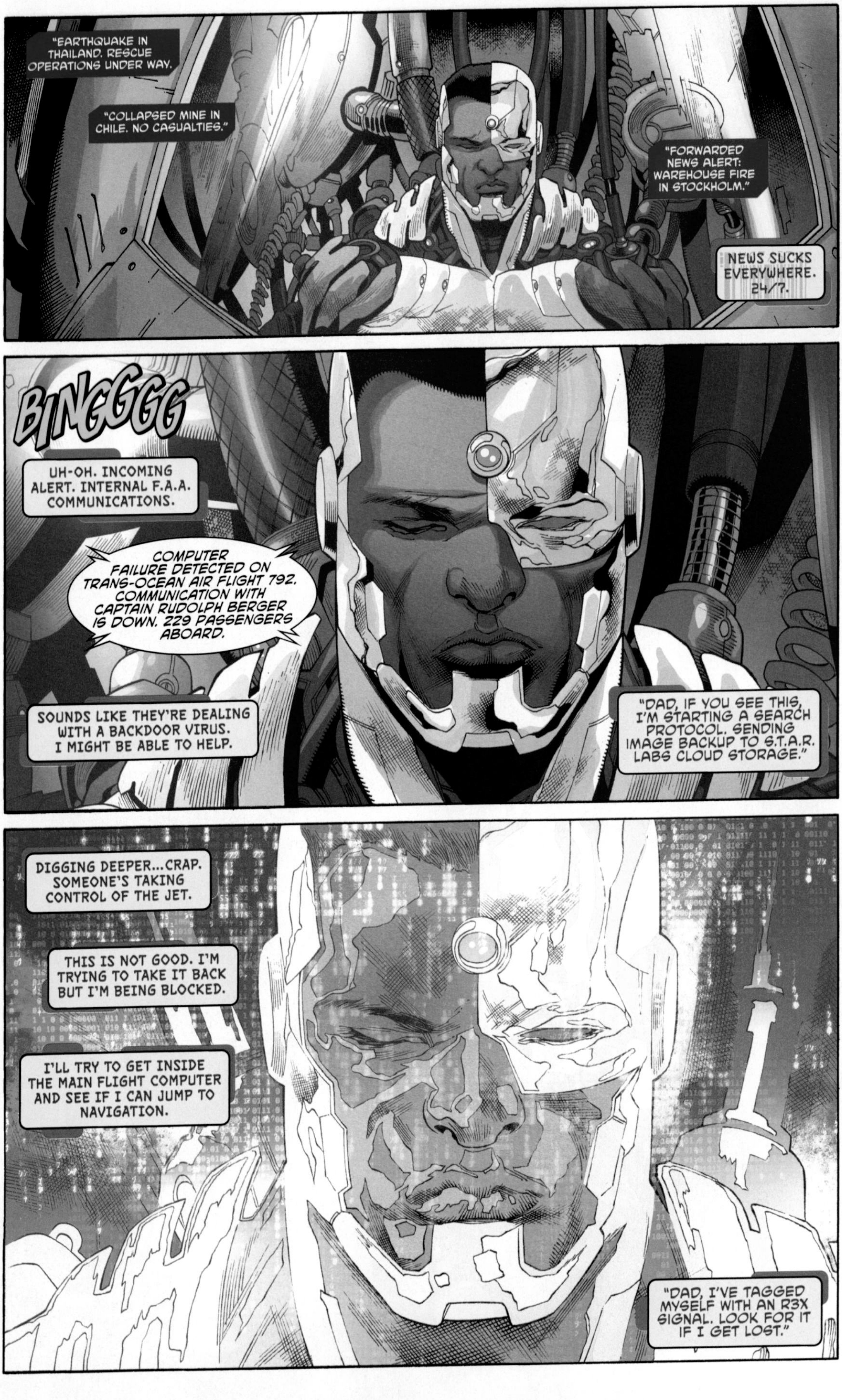
"EARTHQUAKE IN THAILAND. RESCUE OPERATIONS UNDER WAY.
"COLLAPSED MINE IN CHILE. NO CASUALTIES."
"FORWARDED NEWS ALERT: WAREHOUSE FIRE IN STOCKHOLM."
NEWS SUCKS EVERYWHERE. 24/7.
BINGGGG
UH-OH. INCOMING ALERT. INTERNAL F.A.A. COMMUNICATIONS.
COMPUTER FAILURE DETECTED ON TRANS-OCEAN AIR FLIGHT 792. COMMUNICATION WITH CAPTAIN RUDOLPH BERGER IS DOWN. 229 PASSENGERS ABOARD.
SOUNDS LIKE THEY'RE DEALING WITH A BACKDOOR VIRUS. I MIGHT BE ABLE TO HELP.
"DAD, IF YOU SEE THIS, I'M STARTING A SEARCH PROTOCOL. SENDING IMAGE BACKUP TO S.T.A.R. LABS CLOUD STORAGE."
DIGGING DEEPER...CRAP. SOMEONE'S TAKING CONTROL OF THE JET.
THIS IS NOT GOOD. I'M TRYING TO TAKE IT BACK BUT I'M BEING BLOCKED.
I'LL TRY TO GET INSIDE THE MAIN FLIGHT COMPUTER AND SEE IF I CAN JUMP TO NAVIGATION.
"DAD, I'VE TAGGED MYSELF WITH AN R3X SIGNAL. LOOK FOR IT IF I GET LOST."

BINGGGG

FORWARDED NEWS ALERT: WAREHOUSE FIRE IN DOWNTOWN DETROIT.

"HEY, VIC. A FEW OF THE GUYS FROM ALPHA-ONE ARE GETTING TOGETHER TO SHOOT HOOPS. 6:30, USUAL SPOT. HOPE YOU CAN MAKE IT."

PICKING UP COMMUNICATIONS FROM THE STOCKHOLM AND DETROIT FIRE DEPARTMENTS.

BOTH CITIES ARE ALSO REPORTING PROBLEMS WITH FIRES AND DOWNED TRAFFIC SIGNALS.

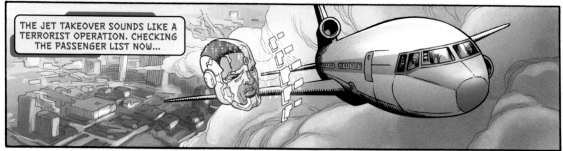

TWO BURNING WAREHOUSES. AND TRAFFIC SIGNAL FAILURES ARE PREVENTING FIRE ENGINES FROM GETTING TO THE SCENE.

"*BARRY* HERE. THIS IS AN AUTOMATIC REMINDER THAT WE'RE HAVING A BIG STRATEGY MEETING WEDNESDAY. THE WATCHTOWER. SEE YOU THERE."

THE JET TAKEOVER SOUNDS LIKE A TERRORIST OPERATION. CHECKING THE PASSENGER LIST NOW...

DON'T NEED TO GO PAST THE A's. AFROOZ ABAD. FROM AFGHANISTAN. TRANSFERRED IN BERLIN. FINAL DESTINATION: DETROIT.

AND GET THIS. SHE USED TO BE A COMPUTER ENGINEER BEFORE THE TALIBAN TOOK OVER.

Hmm. SHE'S ENGAGED TO A FORMER AMERICAN SOLDIER SHE MET IN KABUL. WELL, THAT'S ONE WAY TO GET INTO THE U.S.

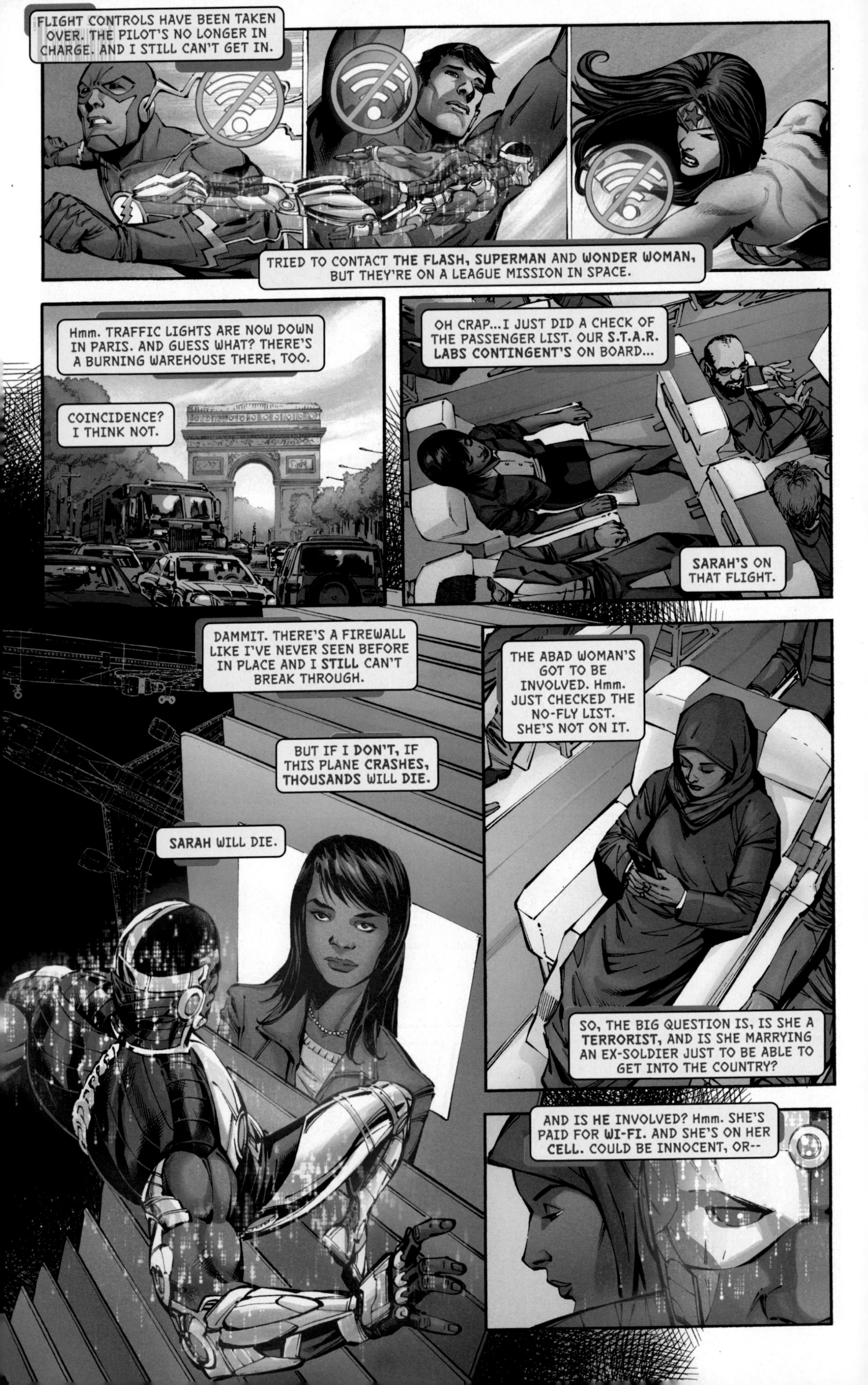
FLIGHT CONTROLS HAVE BEEN TAKEN OVER. THE PILOT'S NO LONGER IN CHARGE. AND I STILL CAN'T GET IN.
TRIED TO CONTACT THE FLASH, SUPERMAN AND WONDER WOMAN, BUT THEY'RE ON A LEAGUE MISSION IN SPACE.
Hmm. TRAFFIC LIGHTS ARE NOW DOWN IN PARIS. AND GUESS WHAT? THERE'S A BURNING WAREHOUSE THERE, TOO.
COINCIDENCE? I THINK NOT.
OH CRAP...I JUST DID A CHECK OF THE PASSENGER LIST. OUR S.T.A.R. LABS CONTINGENT'S ON BOARD...
SARAH'S ON THAT FLIGHT.
DAMMIT. THERE'S A FIREWALL LIKE I'VE NEVER SEEN BEFORE IN PLACE AND I STILL CAN'T BREAK THROUGH.
BUT IF I DON'T, IF THIS PLANE CRASHES, THOUSANDS WILL DIE.
SARAH WILL DIE.
THE ABAD WOMAN'S GOT TO BE INVOLVED. Hmm. JUST CHECKED THE NO-FLY LIST. SHE'S NOT ON IT.
SO, THE BIG QUESTION IS, IS SHE A TERRORIST, AND IS SHE MARRYING AN EX-SOLDIER JUST TO BE ABLE TO GET INTO THE COUNTRY?
AND IS HE INVOLVED? Hmm. SHE'S PAID FOR WI-FI. AND SHE'S ON HER CELL. COULD BE INNOCENT, OR--

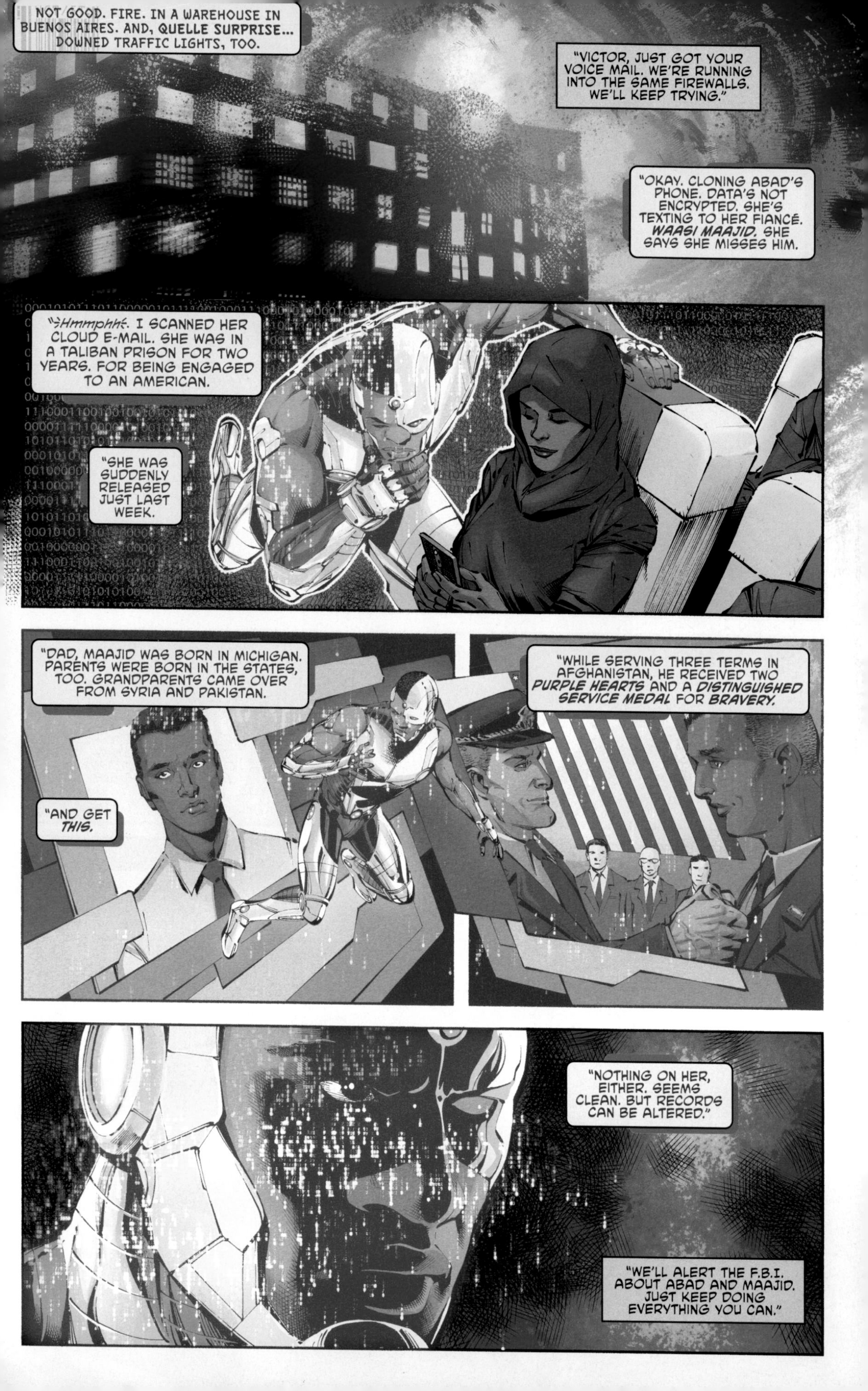
NOT GOOD. FIRE. IN A WAREHOUSE IN BUENOS AIRES. AND, QUELLE SURPRISE... DOWNED TRAFFIC LIGHTS, TOO.
"VICTOR, JUST GOT YOUR VOICE MAIL. WE'RE RUNNING INTO THE SAME FIREWALLS. WE'LL KEEP TRYING."
"OKAY. CLONING ABAD'S PHONE. DATA'S NOT ENCRYPTED. SHE'S TEXTING TO HER FIANCÉ. WAASI MAAJID. SHE SAYS SHE MISSES HIM.
"Hmmphh. I SCANNED HER CLOUD E-MAIL. SHE WAS IN A TALIBAN PRISON FOR TWO YEARS. FOR BEING ENGAGED TO AN AMERICAN.
"SHE WAS SUDDENLY RELEASED JUST LAST WEEK.
"DAD, MAAJID WAS BORN IN MICHIGAN. PARENTS WERE BORN IN THE STATES, TOO. GRANDPARENTS CAME OVER FROM SYRIA AND PAKISTAN.
"AND GET THIS.
"WHILE SERVING THREE TERMS IN AFGHANISTAN, HE RECEIVED TWO PURPLE HEARTS AND A DISTINGUISHED SERVICE MEDAL FOR BRAVERY.
"NOTHING ON HER, EITHER. SEEMS CLEAN. BUT RECORDS CAN BE ALTERED."
"WE'LL ALERT THE F.B.I. ABOUT ABAD AND MAAJID. JUST KEEP DOING EVERYTHING YOU CAN."

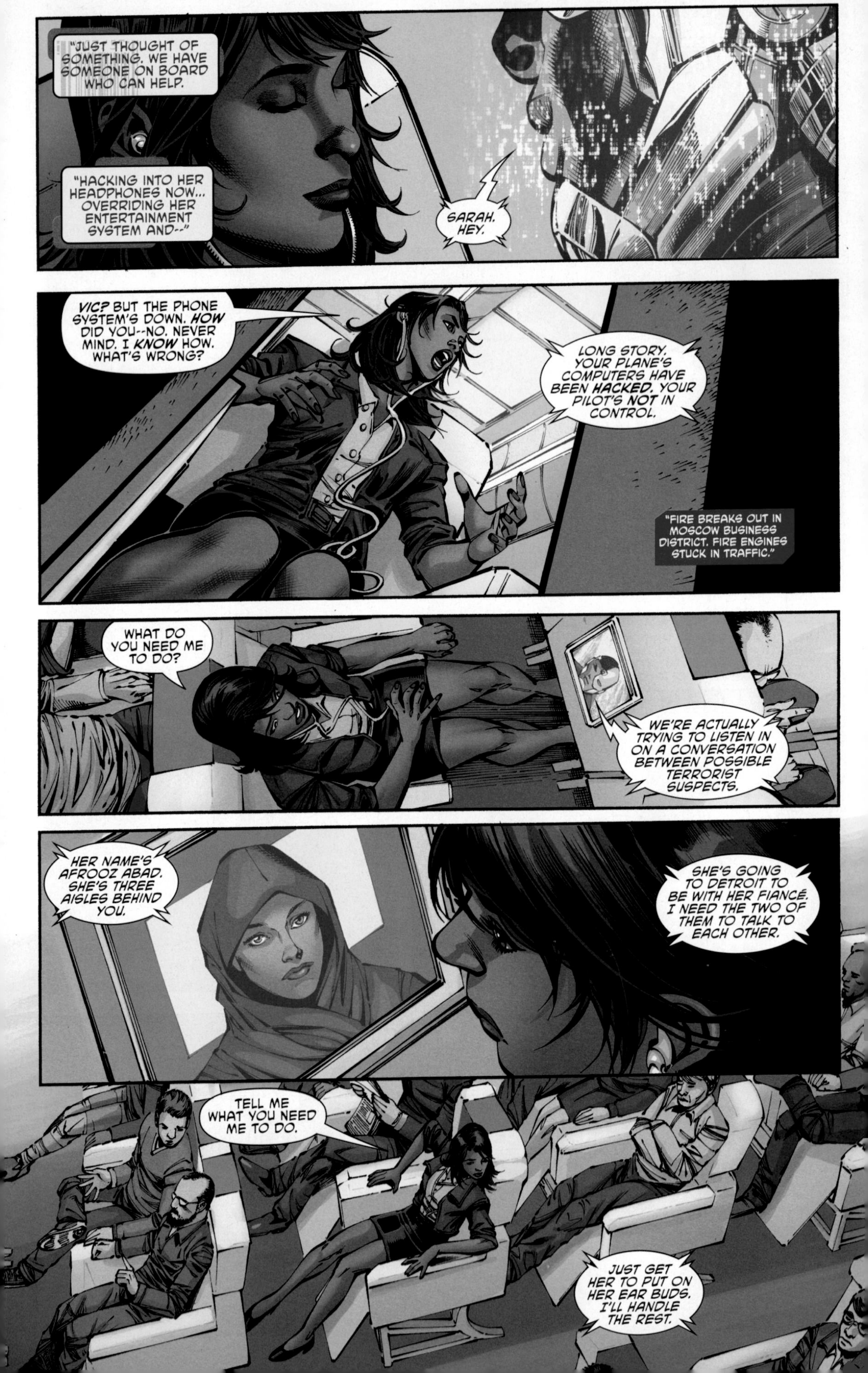
"JUST THOUGHT OF SOMETHING. WE HAVE SOMEONE ON BOARD WHO CAN HELP.
"HACKING INTO HER HEADPHONES NOW... OVERRIDING HER ENTERTAINMENT SYSTEM AND--"
SARAH. HEY.
VIC? BUT THE PHONE SYSTEM'S DOWN. HOW DID YOU--NO. NEVER MIND. I KNOW HOW. WHAT'S WRONG?
LONG STORY. YOUR PLANE'S COMPUTERS HAVE BEEN HACKED. YOUR PILOT'S NOT IN CONTROL.
"FIRE BREAKS OUT IN MOSCOW BUSINESS DISTRICT. FIRE ENGINES STUCK IN TRAFFIC."
WHAT DO YOU NEED ME TO DO?
WE'RE ACTUALLY TRYING TO LISTEN IN ON A CONVERSATION BETWEEN POSSIBLE TERRORIST SUSPECTS.
HER NAME'S AFROOZ ABAD. SHE'S THREE AISLES BEHIND YOU.
SHE'S GOING TO DETROIT TO BE WITH HER FIANCÉ. I NEED THE TWO OF THEM TO TALK TO EACH OTHER.
TELL ME WHAT YOU NEED ME TO DO.
JUST GET HER TO PUT ON HER EAR BUDS. I'LL HANDLE THE REST.

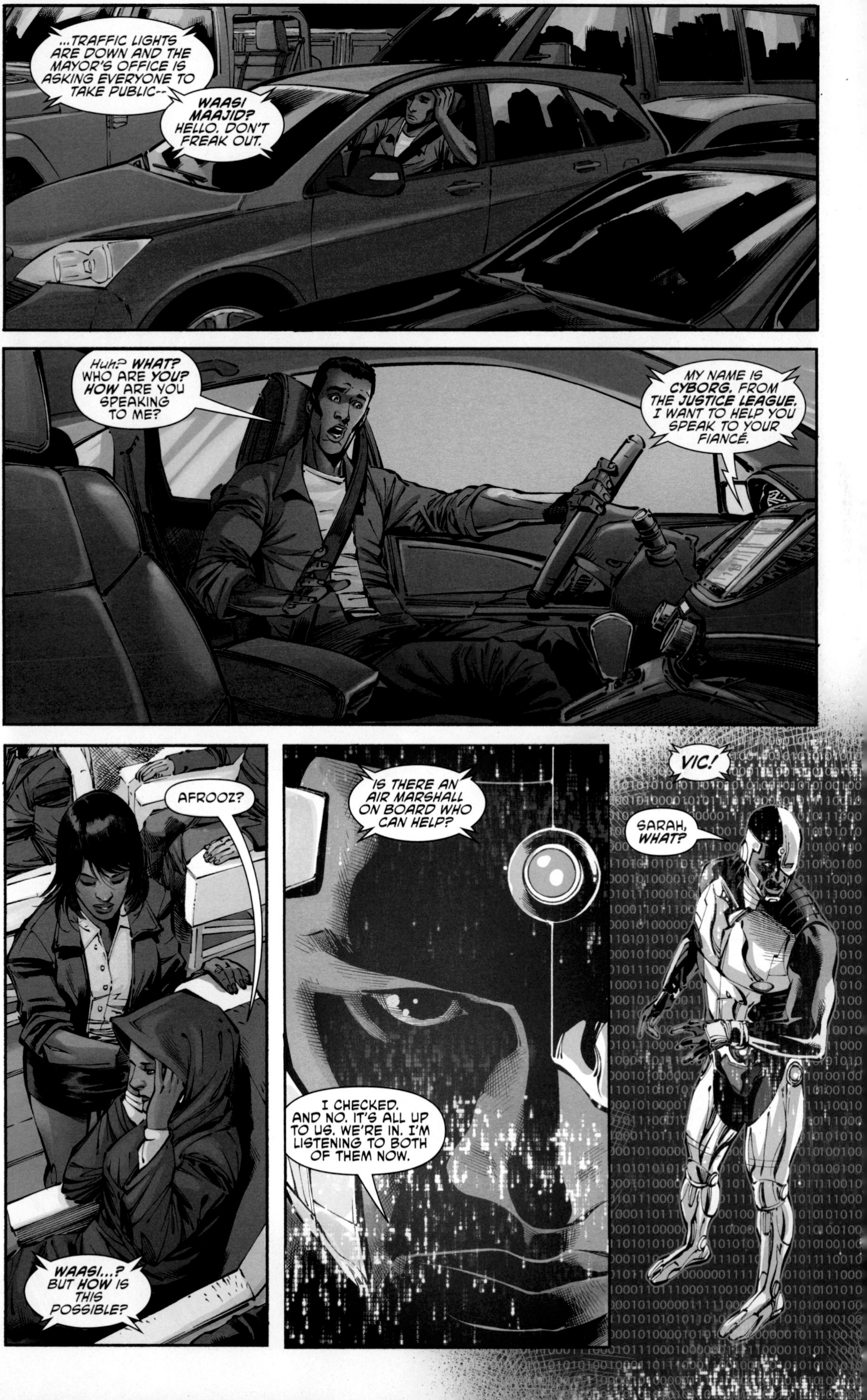
...TRAFFIC LIGHTS ARE DOWN AND THE MAYOR'S OFFICE IS ASKING EVERYONE TO TAKE PUBLIC--
WAASI MAAJID? HELLO. DON'T FREAK OUT.
Huh? WHAT? WHO ARE YOU? HOW ARE YOU SPEAKING TO ME?
MY NAME IS CYBORG. FROM THE JUSTICE LEAGUE. I WANT TO HELP YOU SPEAK TO YOUR FIANCÉ.
AFROOZ?
WAASI...? BUT HOW IS THIS POSSIBLE?
IS THERE AN AIR MARSHALL ON BOARD WHO CAN HELP?
I CHECKED. AND NO. IT'S ALL UP TO US. WE'RE IN. I'M LISTENING TO BOTH OF THEM NOW.
VIC!
SARAH, WHAT?

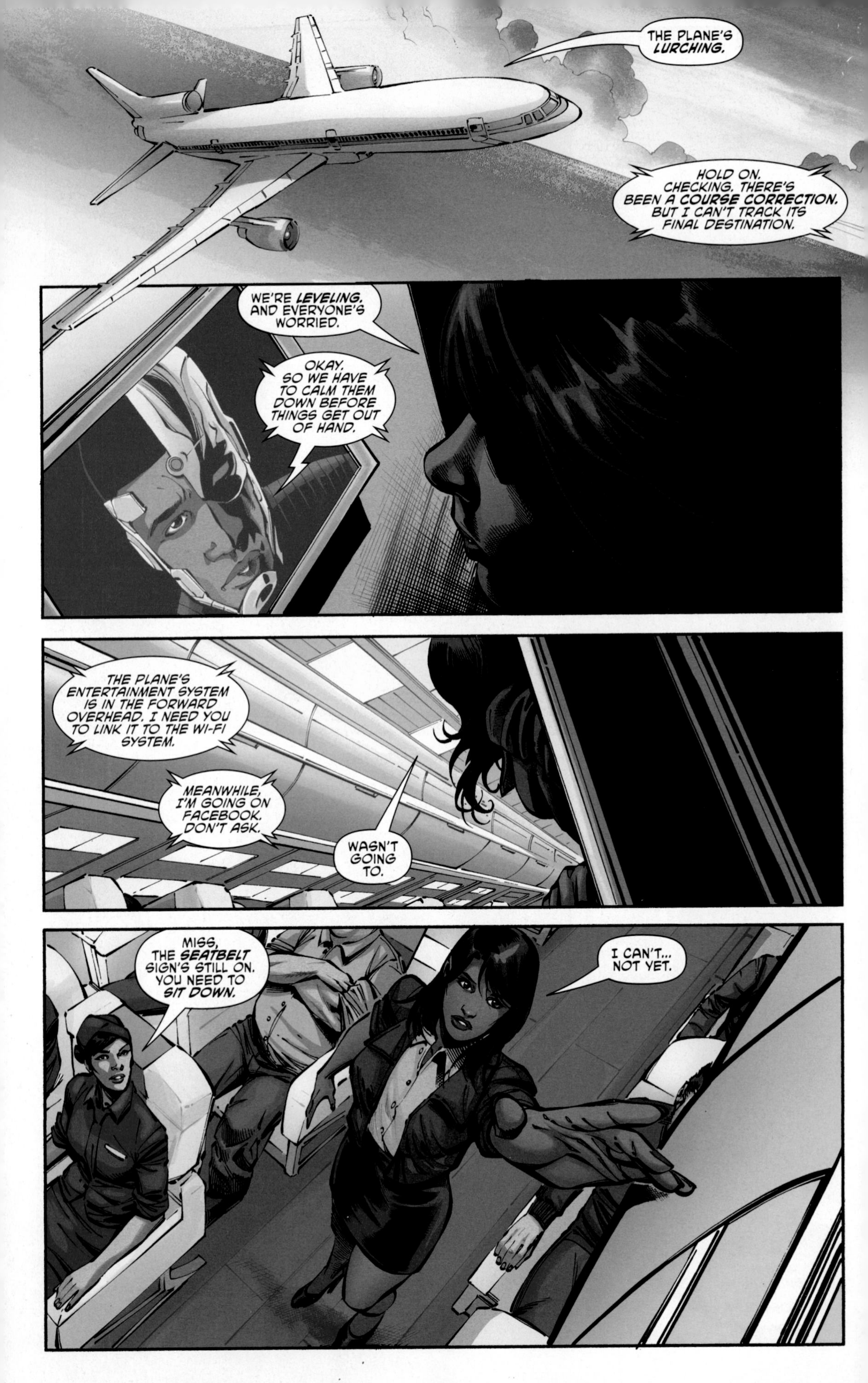
THE PLANE'S LURCHING.
HOLD ON. CHECKING. THERE'S BEEN A COURSE CORRECTION. BUT I CAN'T TRACK ITS FINAL DESTINATION.
WE'RE LEVELING. AND EVERYONE'S WORRIED.
OKAY. SO WE HAVE TO CALM THEM DOWN BEFORE THINGS GET OUT OF HAND.
THE PLANE'S ENTERTAINMENT SYSTEM IS IN THE FORWARD OVERHEAD. I NEED YOU TO LINK IT TO THE WI-FI SYSTEM.
MEANWHILE, I'M GOING ON FACEBOOK. DON'T ASK.
WASN'T GOING TO.
MISS, THE SEATBELT SIGN'S STILL ON. YOU NEED TO SIT DOWN.
I CAN'T... NOT YET.

MISS, I'M GOING TO CALL *SECURITY.* YOU *CAN'T*--

LOOK, I *KNOW* ABOUT THE PLANE AND I'M TRYING TO *SAVE* US.

OKAY, VIC. IT'S DONE.

WHO ARE YOU *TALKING* TO?

THE *ONLY* ONE WHO CAN POSSIBLY *SAVE* US.

HI, EVERYONE. IF YOU DON'T RECOGNIZE ME, I'M *CYBORG.* FROM THE *JUSTICE LEAGUE.*

YOU'VE BEEN SELECTED FOR A *SPECIAL TEST* OF A NEW STREAMING SERVICE.

BASED ON YOUR "LIKES," WE'VE LEARNED YOUR FAVORITE MOVIES...

...AND THROUGH THE *MIRACLE* OF JUSTICE LEAGUE *SCIENCE,* WE BRING THEM TO YOU *FREE* OF CHARGE. ENJOY.

HOW IS HE DOING THAT?

I NEVER KNOW HOW HE DOES ANY OF THE THINGS HE DOES.

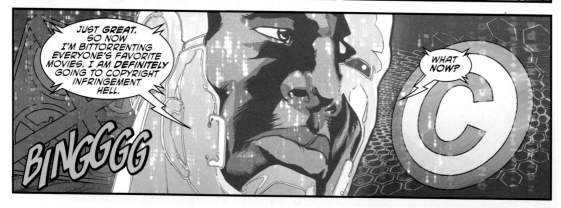

JUST *GREAT.* SO NOW I'M BITTORRENTING EVERYONE'S FAVORITE MOVIES. I AM *DEFINITELY* GOING TO COPYRIGHT INFRINGEMENT HELL.

WHAT *NOW?*

BINGGGG

WONDERFUL. WE'RE NOW UP TO **SEVEN** WAREHOUSE FIRES.

SOMEONE'S WORKING OVERTIME TO MAKE SURE THEY COMPLETELY BURN TO THE GROUND.

"CAN'T YOU SEE *INSIDE* THE WAREHOUSES?"

"DUH. I'M AN IDIOT FOR NOT THINKING OF THAT MYSELF. HACKED THEIR SECURITY CAMERAS. I'M INSIDE. THANKS."

"PICKING UP *DRUGS* IN ONE. *WEAPONS* IN ANOTHER. SERIAL NUMBERS HAVE BEEN REMOVED.

"BRUSSELS' WAREHOUSE HAS EXPLOSIVES. C4, ANFO, PETN, TNT AND GOD KNOWS WHAT ELSE."

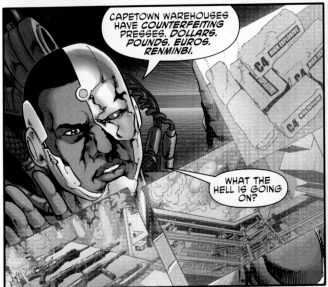

CAPETOWN WAREHOUSES HAVE *COUNTERFEITING* PRESSES. *DOLLARS. POUNDS. EUROS. RENMINBI.*

WHAT THE HELL IS GOING ON?

"OH CRAP. DAD. THERE ARE WORKERS *TRAPPED* IN MOST OF THE WAREHOUSES."

"MY *GOD*, VICTOR. THEY'RE GOING TO *DIE*."

"MAYBE NOT. I'VE ALREADY ALERTED THE FIRE DEPARTMENTS. POLICE AND NATIONAL GUARD, TOO.

"THOSE PEOPLE MAY BE *VICTIMS*, BUT THEY'RE *CRIMINALS*, TOO. THE FIRST RESPONDERS WILL NEED BACKUP SECURITY."

BUT THEY CAN STILL *DIE*. CAN WE DO *ANYTHING*?

ALREADY *DONE*. POLICE ARE THERE AND I'M HACKING THE WAREHOUSE SECURITY LOCKS.

DAMMIT. THE COMPUTER CODES ARE *POLYMORPHIC*. THEY KEEP *CHANGING*.

I'VE GOT TO ENTER MY CODES *FASTER* THAN THEIR COMPUTERS CAN *CHANGE* THEM.

YOU *CAN* DO IT. I *KNOW* YOU CAN.

LISTEN, THIS WILL BE A POWER DRAIN, BUT YOU SHOULD BE ABLE TO TEMPORARILY DOUBLE YOUR PROCESSING SPEED.

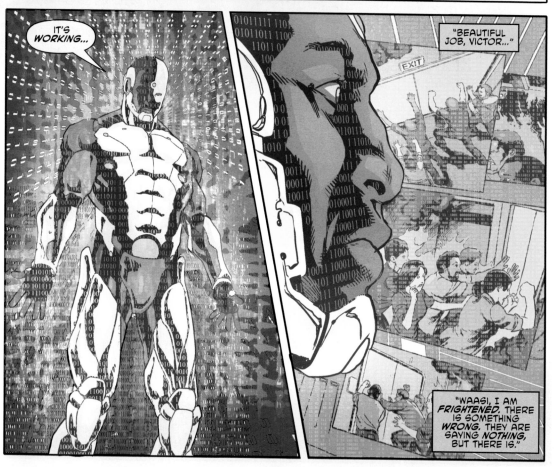

IT'S *WORKING*...

"BEAUTIFUL JOB, VICTOR..."

"WAASI, I AM *FRIGHTENED*. THERE IS SOMETHING *WRONG*. THEY ARE SAYING *NOTHING*, BUT THERE IS."

"OH MAAAANNN...EVERYTHING'S IN OVERDRIVE. DAD, I'M PUSHING THROUGH THE NET...NUMBERS AND SYMBOLS... FLASHING PAST...
BINNGGGGG
POLICE
"WAIT. WAIT. I DID IT. THE DOORS ARE OPENING. THANK YOU, DAD.
"CRAP. FIRE AT A SINGAPORE WAREHOUSE. BUT I CAN DEAL WITH IT."
"SON, WE'RE DETECTING IDENTICAL VIRUSES WERE USED IN BOTH THE PLANE HACK AND THE WAREHOUSES. SOMEHOW THEY'RE CONNECTED."
JUST GREAT. I'M READING THEIR FILES...OH DEAR GOD. THIS ISN'T TERRORISM. THIS IS A TECHNOLOGICALLY DRIVEN PROTECTION RACKET.
THIS IS A FREAKING GANG WAR TIMES A MILLION.
WHILE MY CLOCK'S STILL RACING, I'M TURNING BACK TO THE JET.
YOU SHOULD SEE THIS. I'M PROCESSING SO FAST, MILLIONS OF BYTES ARE CRAWLING PAST ME. I CAN MAKE OUT A BREACH THROUGH THE FIREWALL.
F.Y.I., EVERYTHING'S BEING LOCKED DOWN AT THE WAREHOUSES ACROSS THE GLOBE. LOCAL AUTHORITIES ARE ON IT.
WHOEVER'S BEHIND THIS IS SUDDENLY HAVING A VERY BAD DAY.
NO. NO. NO NO!
VIC, WHAT IS IT? WHAT'S WRONG?

BREACHING THEIR FIREWALLS DELETED THE JET'S HARD DRIVES.

OUR BAD GUYS MUST'VE ADDED A STEALTH CODE I COULDN'T SEE.

THE PLANE'S SHAKING...

"COMPUTER SYSTEMS ARE DOWN AT THE KOKA DAM IN ETHIOPIA."

"ON IT...DOWNED WI-FI CONNECTION...CONNECTING TO ANOTHER NETWORK."

CAPTAIN...

CYBORG?

GOOD. YOU RECOGNIZE ME. THAT'LL MAKE THINGS SIMPLER.

LISTEN CAREFULLY. A HIGH-TECH CARTEL IS CONTROLLING YOUR PLANE. I DON'T KNOW WHY OR WHERE THEY'RE TAKING YOU, BUT I'M FEARING THE WORST.

I NEED ENTRY INTO YOUR COMPUTER SYSTEM.

I'M SORRY, BUT I CAN'T LET YOU TAMPER WITH OUR COMPUTERS. IT'S AGAINST EVERY F.A.A. RULE.

I'M NOT ASKING PERMISSION. YOUR COMPUTERS ARE LINKED TO THE NET. I NEED TO FIND AND FOLLOW THE VIRUS THAT'S TAKEN CONTROL.

BESIDES, I'M ALREADY INSIDE. WHAT YOU'RE LOOKING AT IS MY AVATAR.

ALSO, THERE'S A PASSENGER IN YOUR MAIN CABIN I NEED TO HELP ME.

THAT *CAN'T* BE ALLOWED. THE DOORS ARE *SEALED*. I WON'T OPEN THEM JUST ON YOUR *SAY-SO*.

HOLD THAT THOUGHT.

SARAH, COME WITH ME IF YOU WANT TO *LIVE*.

I ALWAYS WANTED TO SAY THAT.

OKAY, CAPTAIN... I'VE UNLOCKED THE DOOR SO YOU WON'T GET IN ANY TROUBLE. JUST KEEP OUT OF MY WAY.

SIR, I *CAN'T* LET YOU DO THIS.

HE'S NOT GOING TO LISTEN TO YOU. BUT IF IT HELPS, HE WANTS TO SAVE THE PLANE.

SO I CAN'T *STOP* HIM?

MONSTERS HAVE TRIED. THEY *FAILED*. WHAT DO YOU THINK *YOUR* CHANCES ARE?

SARAH, I'M *MIRRORING* THE DATA. SEE IF YOU CAN FIND ANYTHING I'M MISSING.

WHAT NOW?

I'M FINALLY ABLE TO CALCULATE OUR FLIGHT PATH. OH *HELL*. WE'RE GOING TO *PLOW* DIRECTLY INTO S.T.A.R. LABS DETROIT.

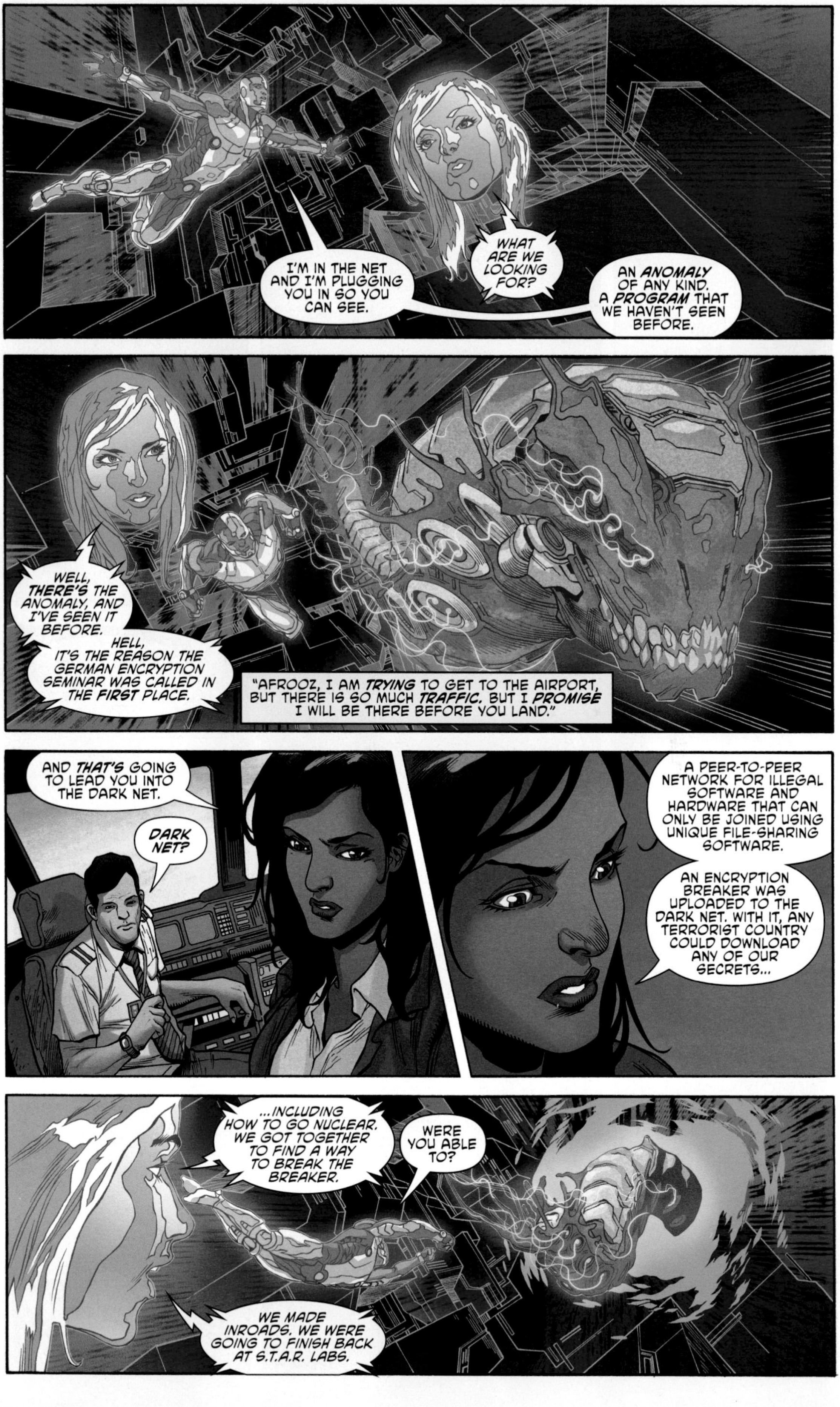
I'M IN THE NET AND I'M PLUGGING YOU IN SO YOU CAN SEE.
WHAT ARE WE LOOKING FOR?
AN ANOMALY OF ANY KIND. A PROGRAM THAT WE HAVEN'T SEEN BEFORE.
WELL, THERE'S THE ANOMALY, AND I'VE SEEN IT BEFORE.
HELL, IT'S THE REASON THE GERMAN ENCRYPTION SEMINAR WAS CALLED IN THE FIRST PLACE.
"AFROOZ, I AM TRYING TO GET TO THE AIRPORT, BUT THERE IS SO MUCH TRAFFIC. BUT I PROMISE I WILL BE THERE BEFORE YOU LAND."
AND THAT'S GOING TO LEAD YOU INTO THE DARK NET.
DARK NET?
A PEER-TO-PEER NETWORK FOR ILLEGAL SOFTWARE AND HARDWARE THAT CAN ONLY BE JOINED USING UNIQUE FILE-SHARING SOFTWARE.
AN ENCRYPTION BREAKER WAS UPLOADED TO THE DARK NET. WITH IT, ANY TERRORIST COUNTRY COULD DOWNLOAD ANY OF OUR SECRETS...
...INCLUDING HOW TO GO NUCLEAR. WE GOT TOGETHER TO FIND A WAY TO BREAK THE BREAKER.
WERE YOU ABLE TO?
WE MADE INROADS. WE WERE GOING TO FINISH BACK AT S.T.A.R. LABS.

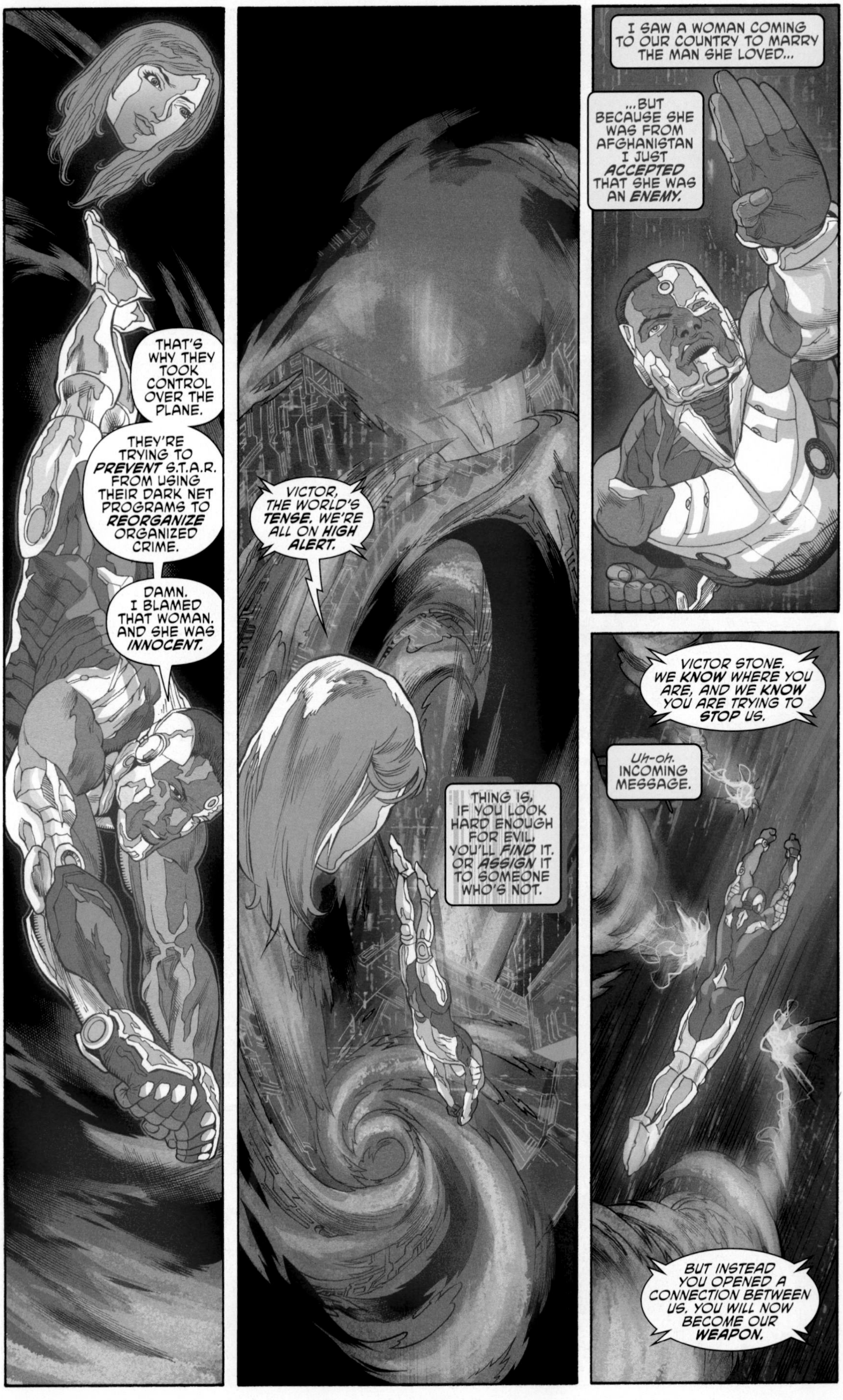
THAT'S WHY THEY TOOK CONTROL OVER THE PLANE.
THEY'RE TRYING TO PREVENT S.T.A.R. FROM USING THEIR DARK NET PROGRAMS TO REORGANIZE ORGANIZED CRIME.
DAMN. I BLAMED THAT WOMAN. AND SHE WAS INNOCENT.
VICTOR, THE WORLD'S TENSE. WE'RE ALL ON HIGH ALERT.
THING IS, IF YOU LOOK HARD ENOUGH FOR EVIL, YOU'LL FIND IT. OR ASSIGN IT TO SOMEONE WHO'S NOT.
I SAW A WOMAN COMING TO OUR COUNTRY TO MARRY THE MAN SHE LOVED...
...BUT BECAUSE SHE WAS FROM AFGHANISTAN I JUST ACCEPTED THAT SHE WAS AN ENEMY.
VICTOR STONE. WE KNOW WHERE YOU ARE, AND WE KNOW YOU ARE TRYING TO STOP US.
Uh-oh. INCOMING MESSAGE.
BUT INSTEAD YOU OPENED A CONNECTION BETWEEN US. YOU WILL NOW BECOME OUR WEAPON.

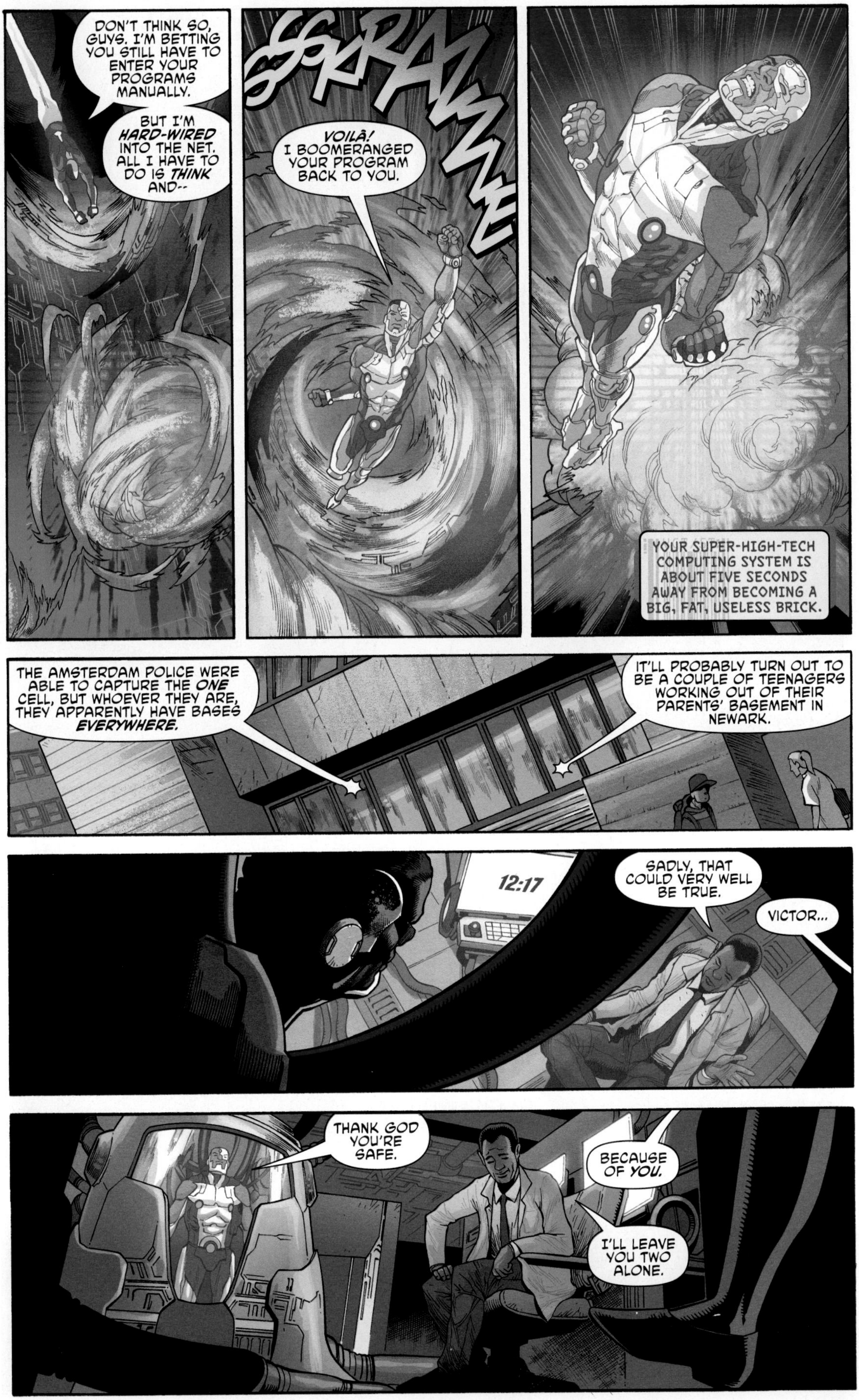

DON'T THINK SO, GUYS. I'M BETTING YOU STILL HAVE TO ENTER YOUR PROGRAMS MANUALLY.
BUT I'M *HARD-WIRED* INTO THE NET. ALL I HAVE TO DO IS *THINK* AND--
SSKRAZMME
VOILÀ! I BOOMERANGED YOUR PROGRAM BACK TO YOU.
YOUR SUPER-HIGH-TECH COMPUTING SYSTEM IS ABOUT FIVE SECONDS AWAY FROM BECOMING A BIG, FAT, USELESS BRICK.
THE AMSTERDAM POLICE WERE ABLE TO CAPTURE THE *ONE* CELL, BUT WHOEVER THEY ARE, THEY APPARENTLY HAVE BASES *EVERYWHERE.*
IT'LL PROBABLY TURN OUT TO BE A COUPLE OF TEENAGERS WORKING OUT OF THEIR PARENTS' BASEMENT IN NEWARK.
12:17
SADLY, THAT COULD VERY WELL BE TRUE.
VICTOR...
THANK GOD YOU'RE SAFE.
BECAUSE OF *YOU.*
I'LL LEAVE YOU TWO ALONE.

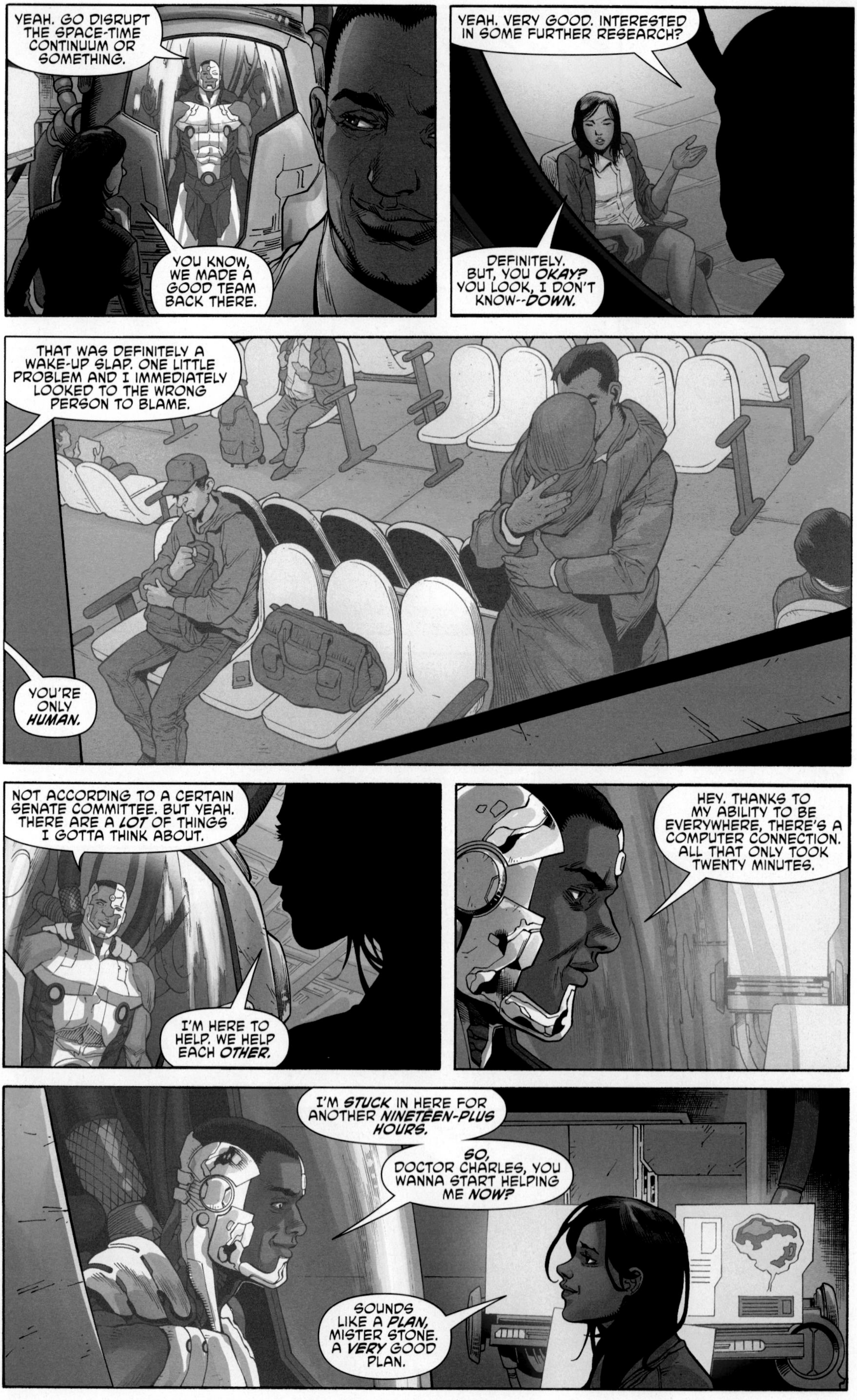
YEAH. GO DISRUPT THE SPACE-TIME CONTINUUM OR SOMETHING.
YOU KNOW, WE MADE A GOOD TEAM BACK THERE.
YEAH. VERY GOOD. INTERESTED IN SOME FURTHER RESEARCH?
DEFINITELY. BUT, YOU *OKAY?* YOU LOOK, I DON'T KNOW--*DOWN.*
THAT WAS DEFINITELY A WAKE-UP SLAP. ONE LITTLE PROBLEM AND I IMMEDIATELY LOOKED TO THE WRONG PERSON TO BLAME.
YOU'RE ONLY *HUMAN.*
NOT ACCORDING TO A CERTAIN SENATE COMMITTEE. BUT YEAH. THERE ARE A *LOT* OF THINGS I GOTTA THINK ABOUT.
I'M HERE TO HELP. WE HELP EACH *OTHER.*
HEY. THANKS TO MY ABILITY TO BE EVERYWHERE, THERE'S A COMPUTER CONNECTION. ALL THAT ONLY TOOK TWENTY MINUTES.
I'M *STUCK* IN HERE FOR ANOTHER *NINETEEN-PLUS HOURS.*
SO, DOCTOR CHARLES, YOU WANNA START HELPING ME *NOW?*
SOUNDS LIKE A *PLAN,* MISTER STONE. A *VERY* GOOD PLAN.

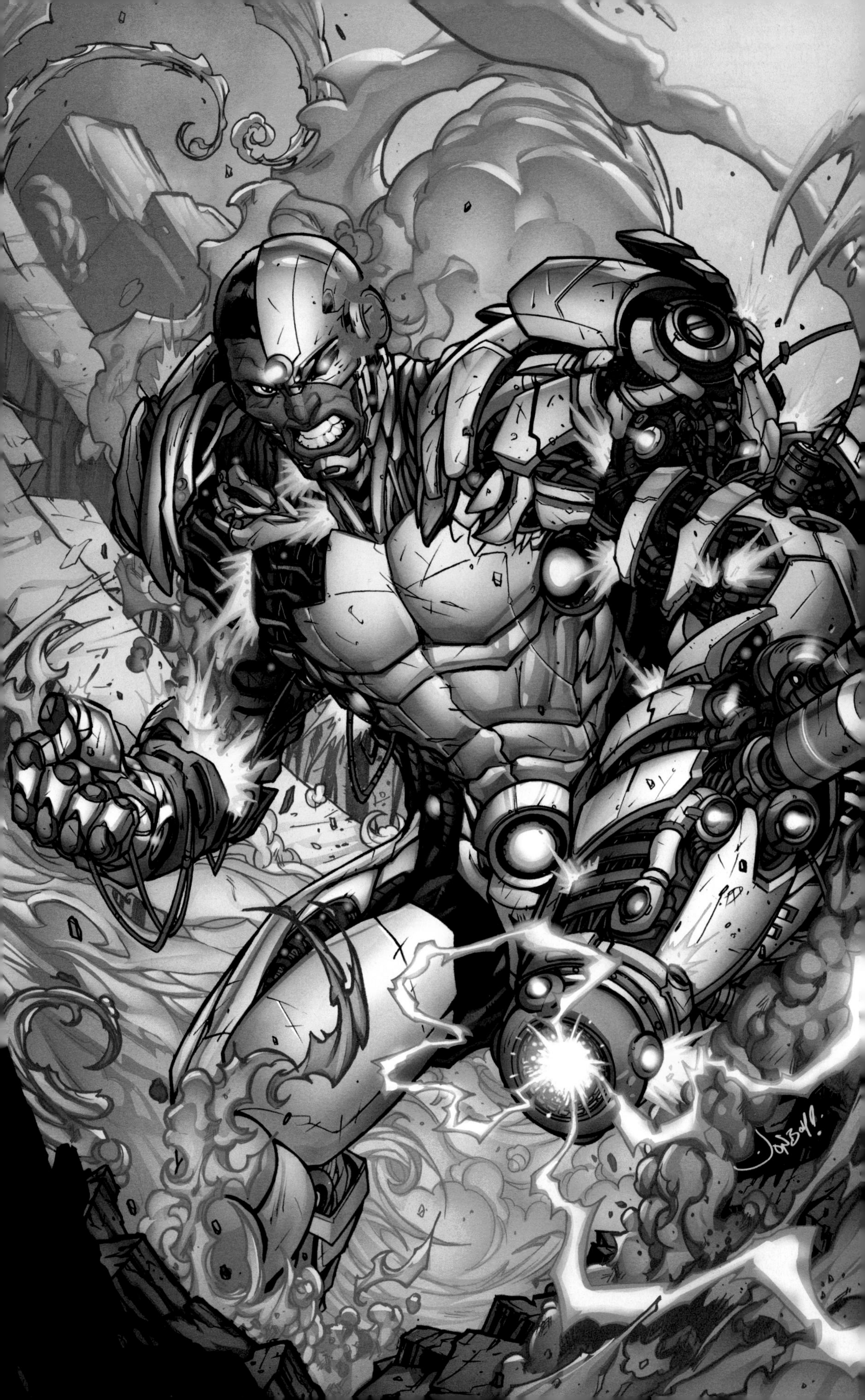

INVASION

MARV WOLFMAN writer **FELIPE WATANABE, DANIEL HDR & JÚLIO FERREIRA** pencillers **OCLAIR ALBERT, DANIEL HDR & JÚLIO FERREIRA** inkers **JONBOY MEYERS** cover

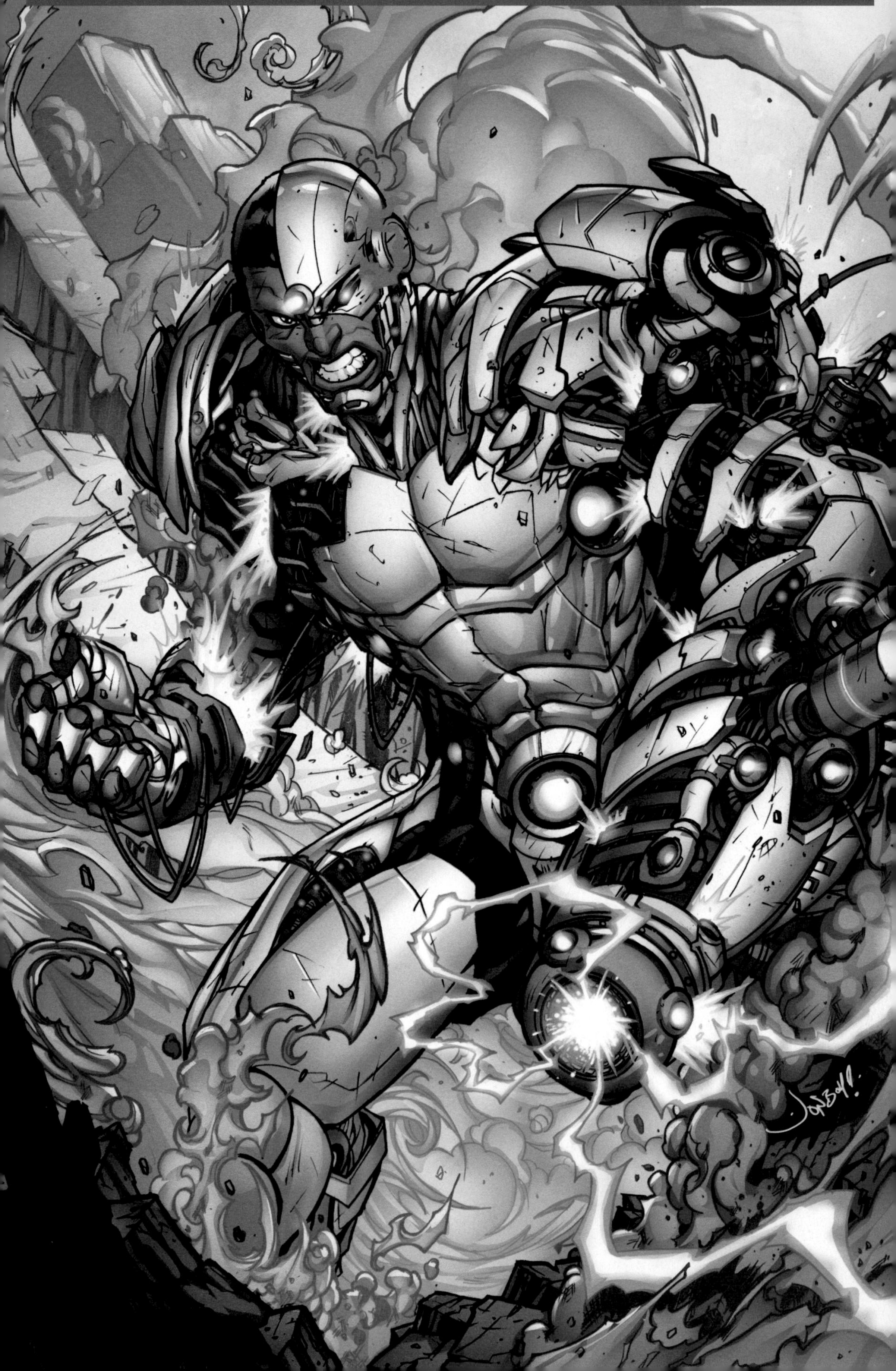

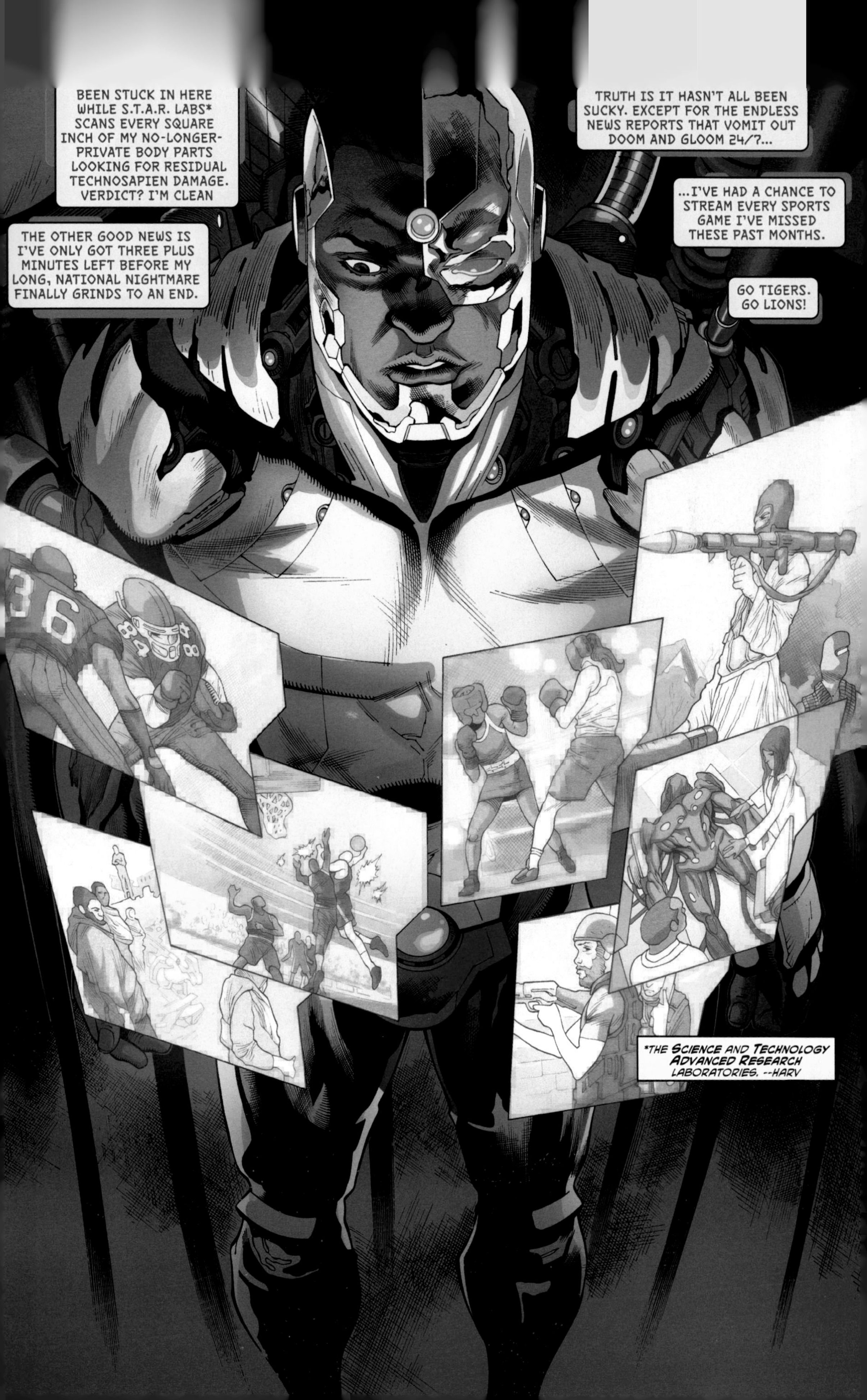

BEEN STUCK IN HERE WHILE S.T.A.R. LABS* SCANS EVERY SQUARE INCH OF MY NO-LONGER-PRIVATE BODY PARTS LOOKING FOR RESIDUAL TECHNOSAPIEN DAMAGE. VERDICT? I'M CLEAN
THE OTHER GOOD NEWS IS I'VE ONLY GOT THREE PLUS MINUTES LEFT BEFORE MY LONG, NATIONAL NIGHTMARE FINALLY GRINDS TO AN END.
TRUTH IS IT HASN'T ALL BEEN SUCKY. EXCEPT FOR THE ENDLESS NEWS REPORTS THAT VOMIT OUT DOOM AND GLOOM 24/7...
...I'VE HAD A CHANCE TO STREAM EVERY SPORTS GAME I'VE MISSED THESE PAST MONTHS.
GO TIGERS. GO LIONS!
36
84
*THE SCIENCE AND TECHNOLOGY ADVANCED RESEARCH LABORATORIES. --HARV

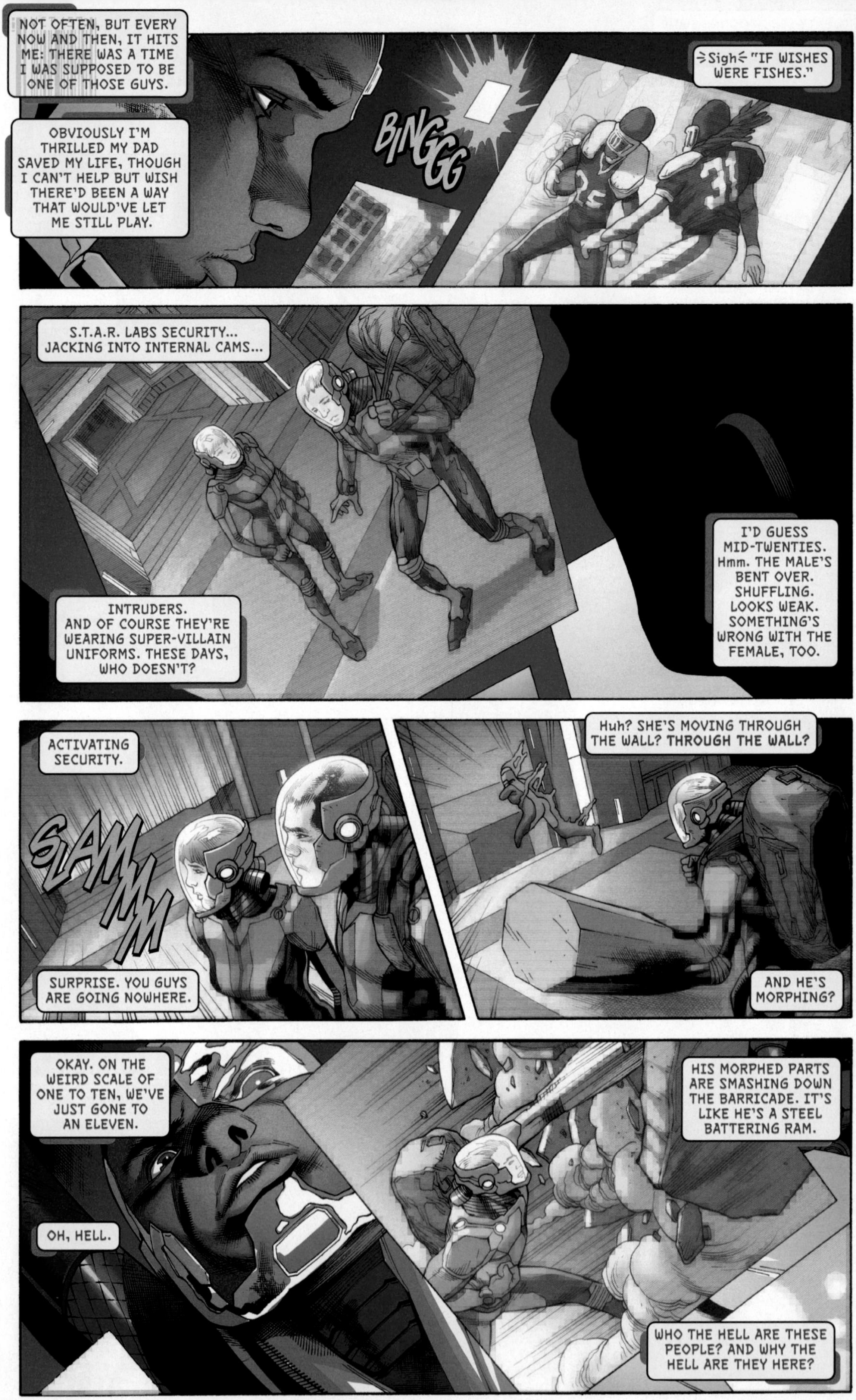
NOT OFTEN, BUT EVERY NOW AND THEN, IT HITS ME: THERE WAS A TIME I WAS SUPPOSED TO BE ONE OF THOSE GUYS.
OBVIOUSLY I'M THRILLED MY DAD SAVED MY LIFE, THOUGH I CAN'T HELP BUT WISH THERE'D BEEN A WAY THAT WOULD'VE LET ME STILL PLAY.
BINGGG
>Sigh< "IF WISHES WERE FISHES."
S.T.A.R. LABS SECURITY... JACKING INTO INTERNAL CAMS...
I'D GUESS MID-TWENTIES. Hmm. THE MALE'S BENT OVER. SHUFFLING. LOOKS WEAK. SOMETHING'S WRONG WITH THE FEMALE, TOO.
INTRUDERS. AND OF COURSE THEY'RE WEARING SUPER-VILLAIN UNIFORMS. THESE DAYS, WHO DOESN'T?
ACTIVATING SECURITY.
SLAMMM
SURPRISE. YOU GUYS ARE GOING NOWHERE.
Huh? SHE'S MOVING THROUGH THE WALL? THROUGH THE WALL?
AND HE'S MORPHING?
OKAY. ON THE WEIRD SCALE OF ONE TO TEN, WE'VE JUST GONE TO AN ELEVEN.
HIS MORPHED PARTS ARE SMASHING DOWN THE BARRICADE. IT'S LIKE HE'S A STEEL BATTERING RAM.
OH, HELL.
WHO THE HELL ARE THESE PEOPLE? AND WHY THE HELL ARE THEY HERE?

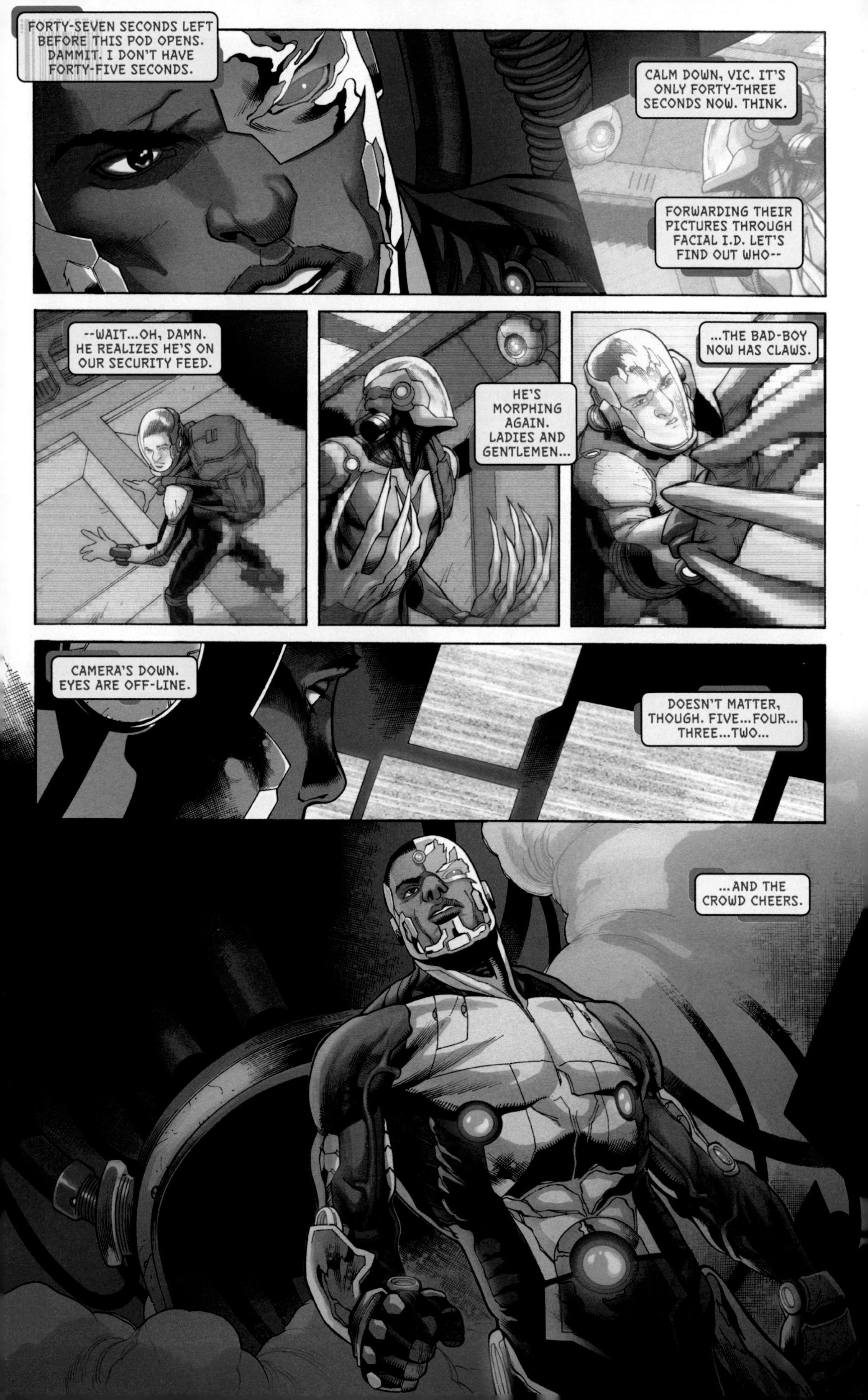
FORTY-SEVEN SECONDS LEFT BEFORE THIS POD OPENS. DAMMIT. I DON'T HAVE FORTY-FIVE SECONDS.
CALM DOWN, VIC. IT'S ONLY FORTY-THREE SECONDS NOW. THINK.
FORWARDING THEIR PICTURES THROUGH FACIAL I.D. LET'S FIND OUT WHO--
--WAIT...OH, DAMN. HE REALIZES HE'S ON OUR SECURITY FEED.
HE'S MORPHING AGAIN. LADIES AND GENTLEMEN...
...THE BAD-BOY NOW HAS CLAWS.
CAMERA'S DOWN. EYES ARE OFF-LINE.
DOESN'T MATTER, THOUGH. FIVE...FOUR... THREE...TWO...
...AND THE CROWD CHEERS.

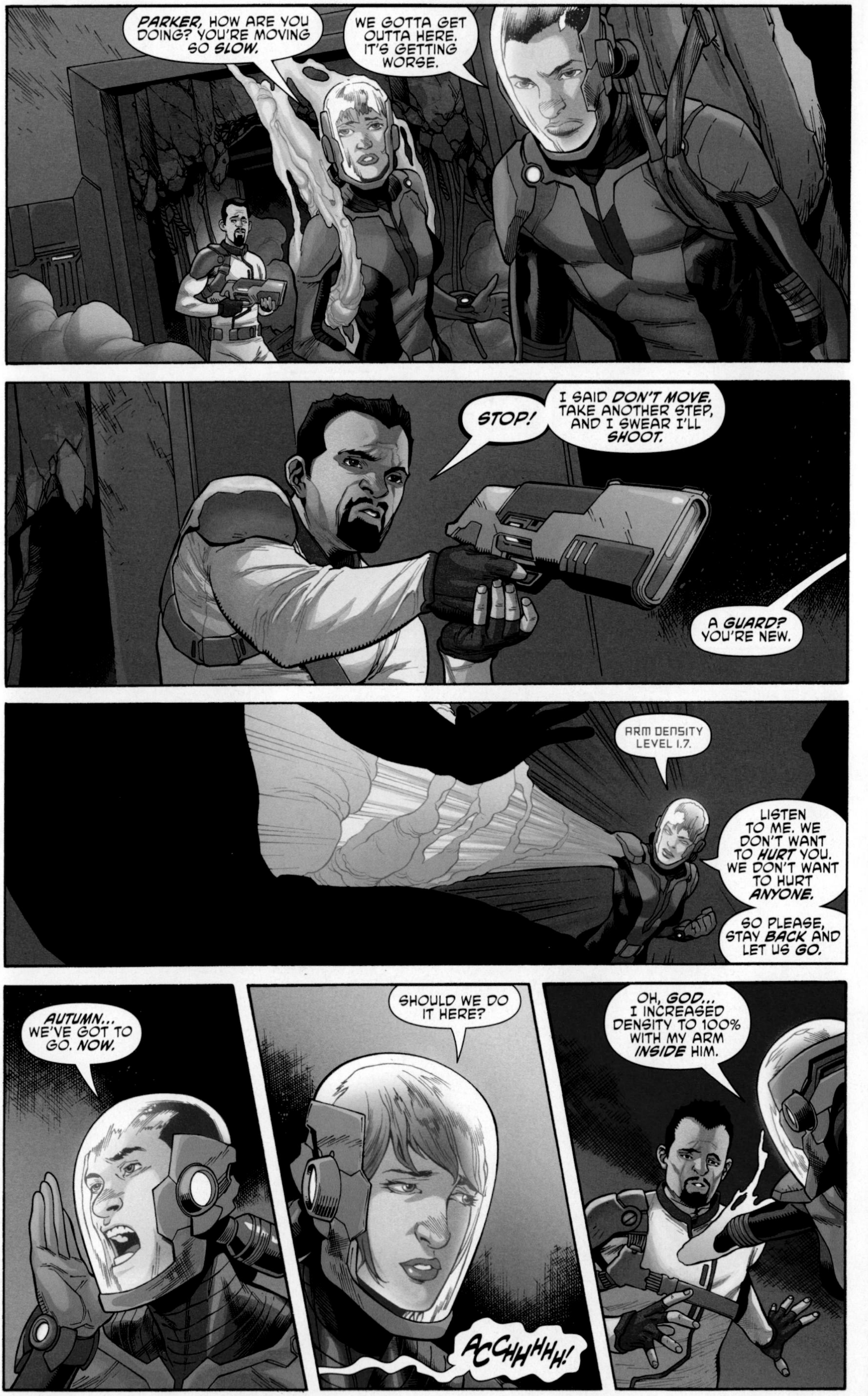
PARKER, HOW ARE YOU DOING? YOU'RE MOVING SO SLOW.
WE GOTTA GET OUTTA HERE. IT'S GETTING WORSE.
STOP!
I SAID DON'T MOVE. TAKE ANOTHER STEP, AND I SWEAR I'LL SHOOT.
A GUARD? YOU'RE NEW.
ARM DENSITY LEVEL 1.7.
LISTEN TO ME. WE DON'T WANT TO HURT YOU. WE DON'T WANT TO HURT ANYONE.
SO PLEASE, STAY BACK AND LET US GO.
AUTUMN... WE'VE GOT TO GO. NOW.
SHOULD WE DO IT HERE?
ACHHHHH!
OH, GOD... I INCREASED DENSITY TO 100% WITH MY ARM INSIDE HIM.

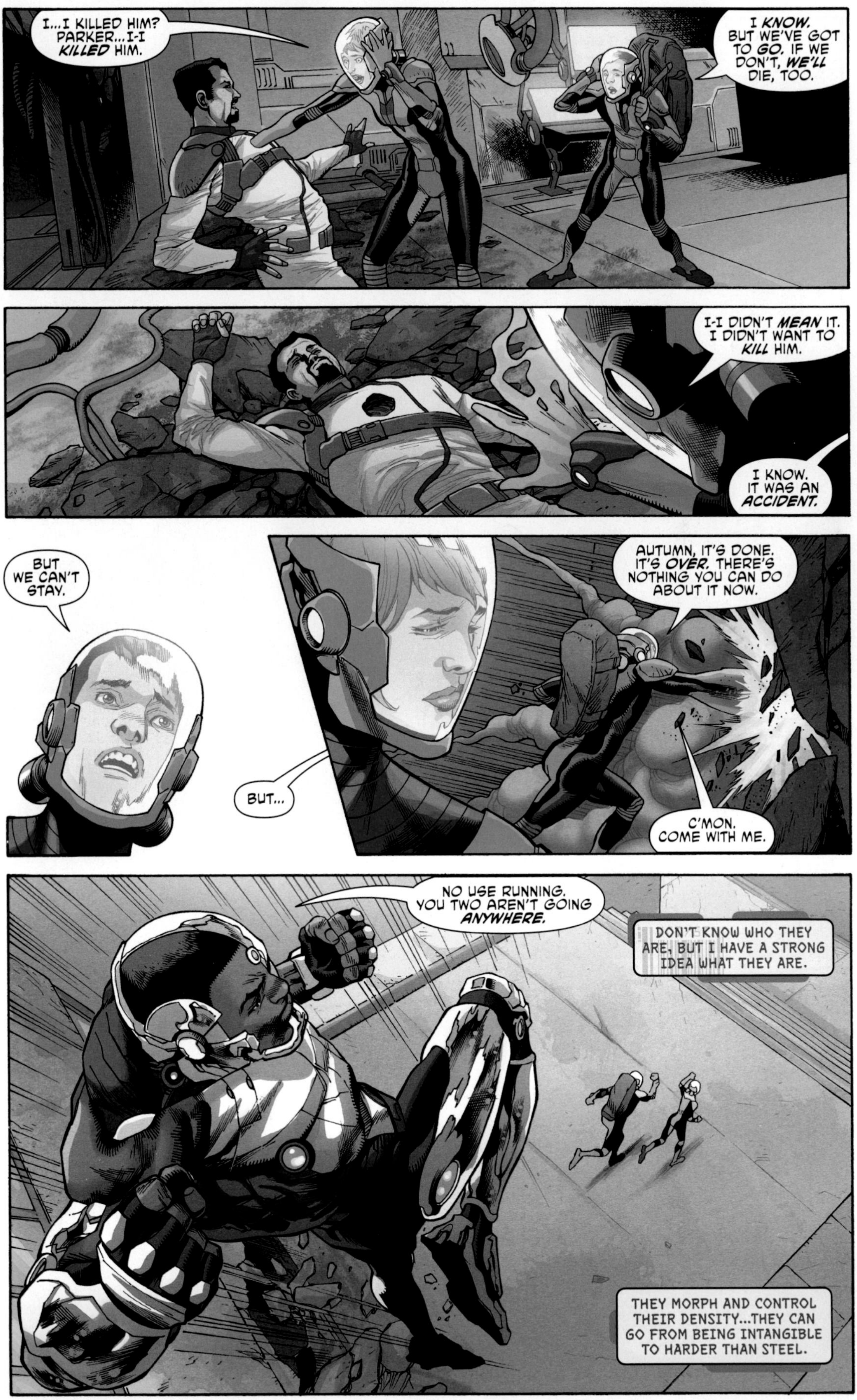
I...I KILLED HIM? PARKER...I-I KILLED HIM.
I KNOW. BUT WE'VE GOT TO GO. IF WE DON'T, WE'LL DIE, TOO.
I-I DIDN'T MEAN IT. I DIDN'T WANT TO KILL HIM.
I KNOW. IT WAS AN ACCIDENT.
BUT WE CAN'T STAY.
AUTUMN, IT'S DONE. IT'S OVER. THERE'S NOTHING YOU CAN DO ABOUT IT NOW.
BUT...
C'MON. COME WITH ME.
NO USE RUNNING. YOU TWO AREN'T GOING ANYWHERE.
DON'T KNOW WHO THEY ARE, BUT I HAVE A STRONG IDEA WHAT THEY ARE.
THEY MORPH AND CONTROL THEIR DENSITY...THEY CAN GO FROM BEING INTANGIBLE TO HARDER THAN STEEL.

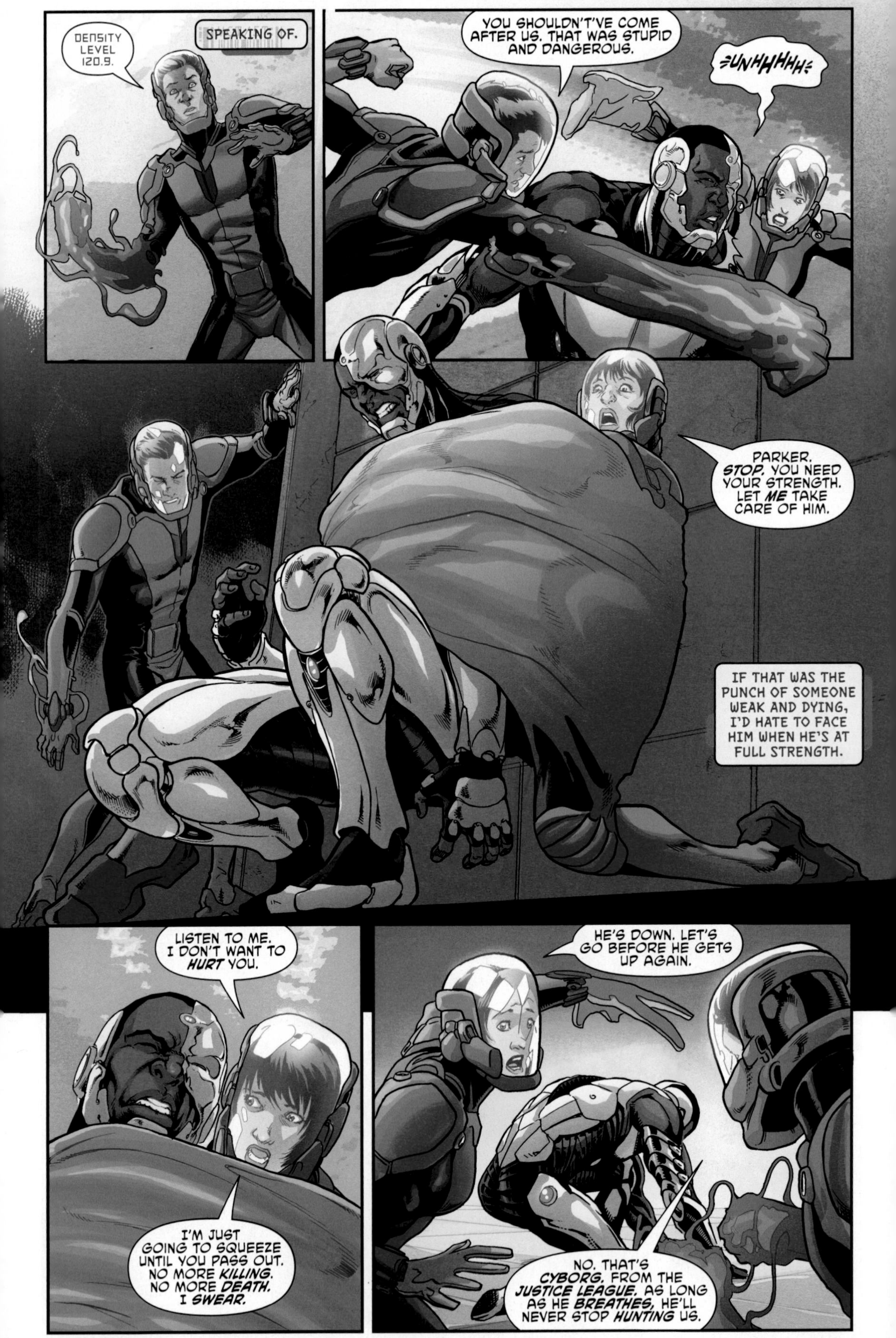

DENSITY LEVEL 120.9.
SPEAKING OF.
YOU SHOULDN'T'VE COME AFTER US. THAT WAS STUPID AND DANGEROUS.
UNHHHHH
PARKER. *STOP.* YOU NEED YOUR STRENGTH. LET *ME* TAKE CARE OF HIM.
IF THAT WAS THE PUNCH OF SOMEONE WEAK AND DYING, I'D HATE TO FACE HIM WHEN HE'S AT FULL STRENGTH.
LISTEN TO ME. I DON'T WANT TO *HURT* YOU.
I'M JUST GOING TO SQUEEZE UNTIL YOU PASS OUT. NO MORE *KILLING.* NO MORE *DEATH.* I *SWEAR.*
HE'S DOWN. LET'S GO BEFORE HE GETS UP AGAIN.
NO. THAT'S *CYBORG,* FROM THE *JUSTICE LEAGUE.* AS LONG AS HE *BREATHES,* HE'LL NEVER STOP *HUNTING* US.

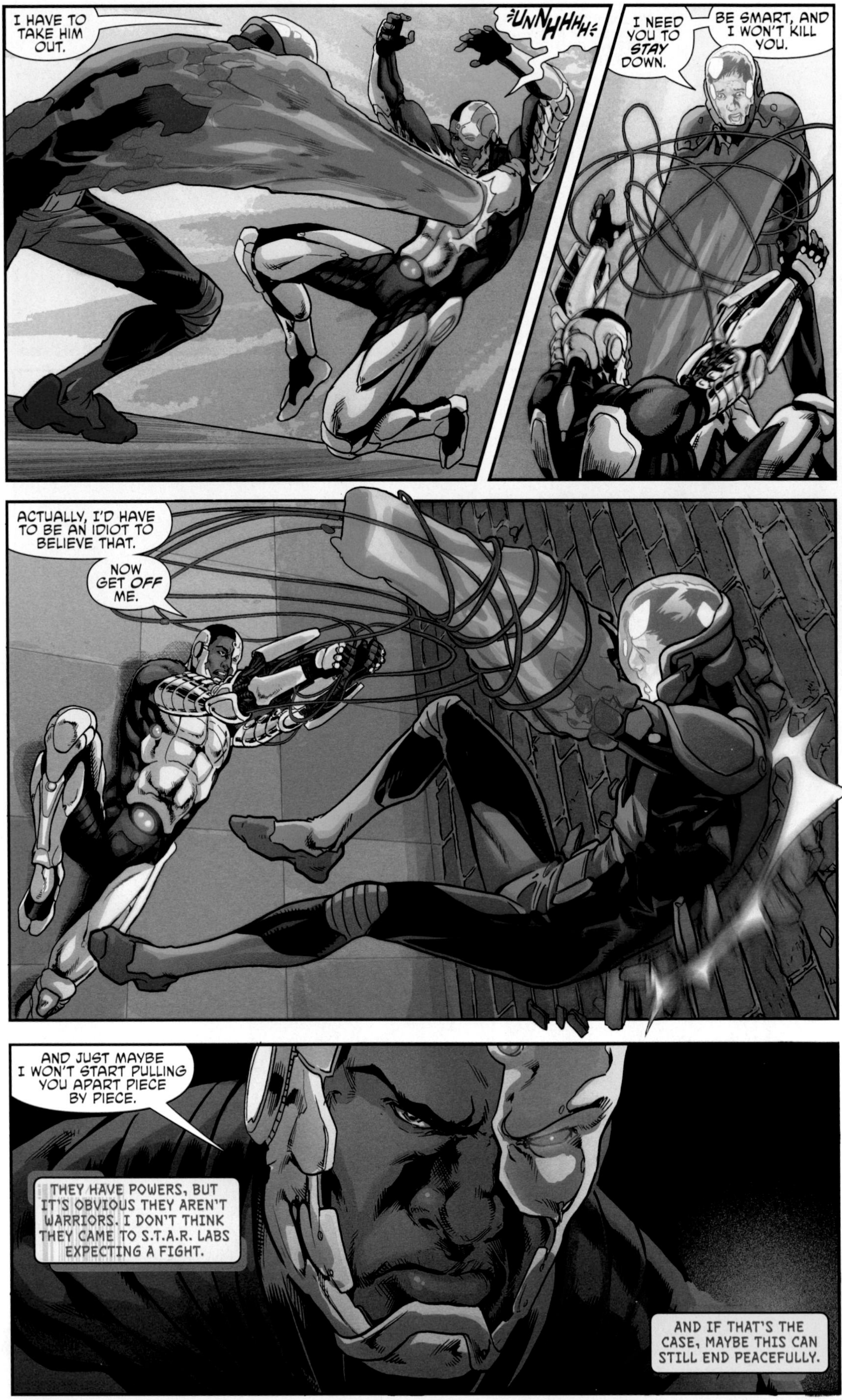
I HAVE TO TAKE HIM OUT.
UNNHHHH
I NEED YOU TO STAY DOWN.
BE SMART, AND I WON'T KILL YOU.
ACTUALLY, I'D HAVE TO BE AN IDIOT TO BELIEVE THAT.
NOW GET OFF ME.
AND JUST MAYBE I WON'T START PULLING YOU APART PIECE BY PIECE.
THEY HAVE POWERS, BUT IT'S OBVIOUS THEY AREN'T WARRIORS. I DON'T THINK THEY CAME TO S.T.A.R. LABS EXPECTING A FIGHT.
AND IF THAT'S THE CASE, MAYBE THIS CAN STILL END PEACEFULLY.

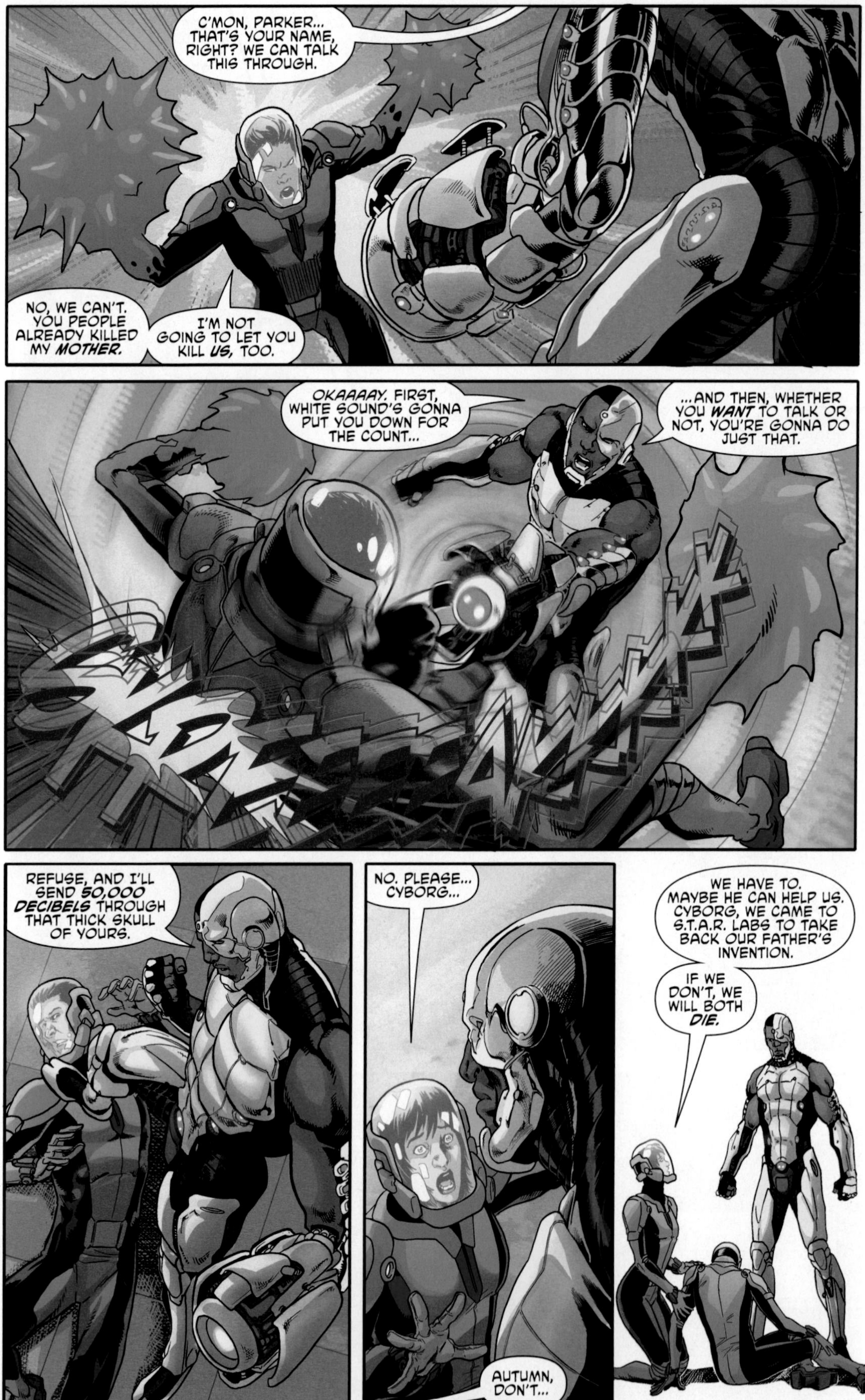
C'MON, PARKER... THAT'S YOUR NAME, RIGHT? WE CAN TALK THIS THROUGH.
NO, WE CAN'T. YOU PEOPLE ALREADY KILLED MY MOTHER.
I'M NOT GOING TO LET YOU KILL US, TOO.
OKAAAAY. FIRST, WHITE SOUND'S GONNA PUT YOU DOWN FOR THE COUNT...
...AND THEN, WHETHER YOU WANT TO TALK OR NOT, YOU'RE GONNA DO JUST THAT.
REFUSE, AND I'LL SEND 50,000 DECIBELS THROUGH THAT THICK SKULL OF YOURS.
NO. PLEASE... CYBORG...
AUTUMN, DON'T...
WE HAVE TO. MAYBE HE CAN HELP US. CYBORG, WE CAME TO S.T.A.R. LABS TO TAKE BACK OUR FATHER'S INVENTION.
IF WE DON'T, WE WILL BOTH DIE.

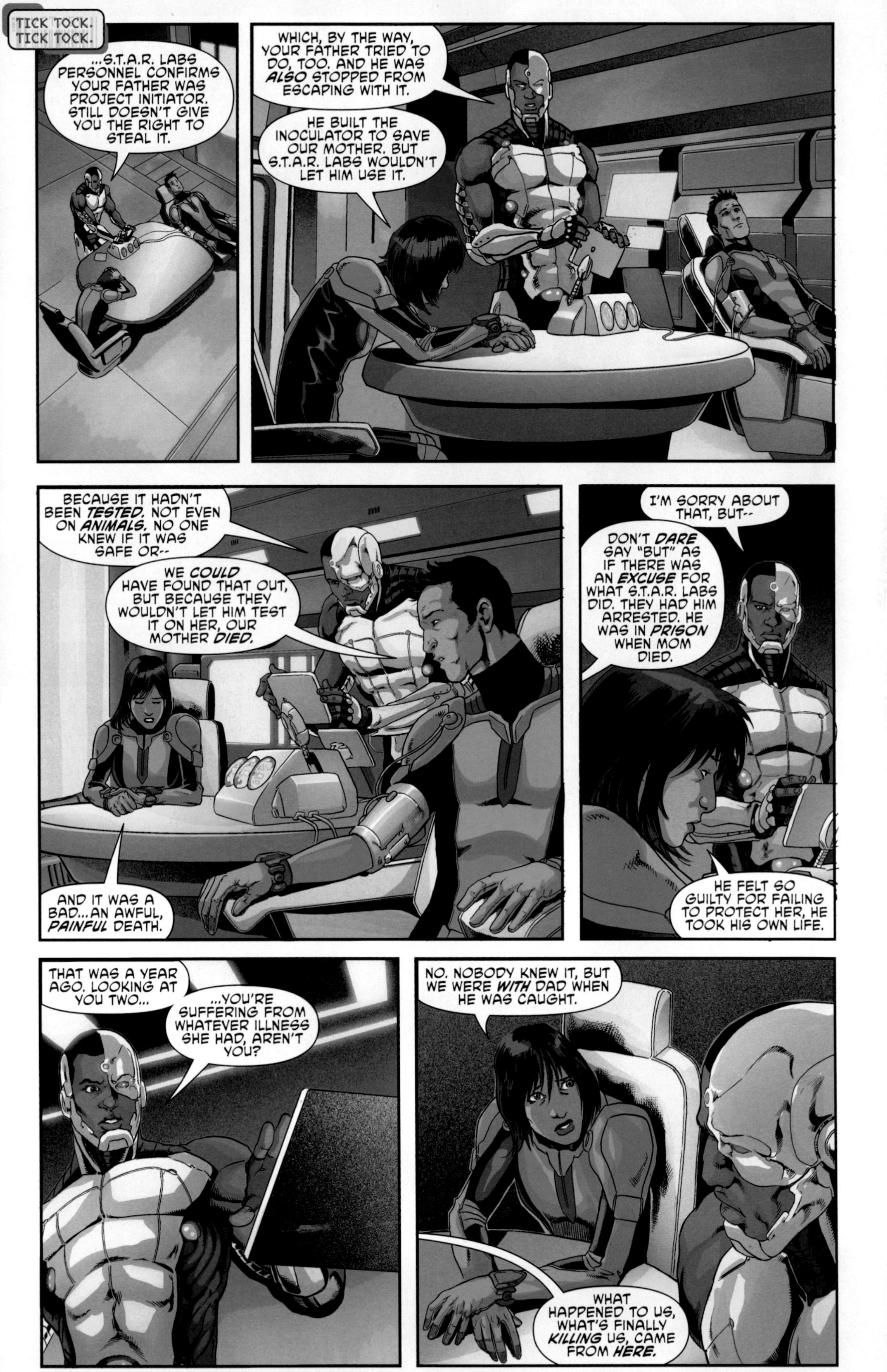
TICK TOCK. TICK TOCK.
...S.T.A.R. LABS PERSONNEL CONFIRMS YOUR FATHER WAS PROJECT INITIATOR. STILL DOESN'T GIVE YOU THE RIGHT TO STEAL IT.
WHICH, BY THE WAY, YOUR FATHER TRIED TO DO, TOO. AND HE WAS ALSO STOPPED FROM ESCAPING WITH IT.
HE BUILT THE INOCULATOR TO SAVE OUR MOTHER. BUT S.T.A.R. LABS WOULDN'T LET HIM USE IT.
BECAUSE IT HADN'T BEEN TESTED. NOT EVEN ON ANIMALS. NO ONE KNEW IF IT WAS SAFE OR--
WE COULD HAVE FOUND THAT OUT, BUT BECAUSE THEY WOULDN'T LET HIM TEST IT ON HER, OUR MOTHER DIED.
AND IT WAS A BAD...AN AWFUL, PAINFUL DEATH.
I'M SORRY ABOUT THAT, BUT--
DON'T DARE SAY "BUT" AS IF THERE WAS AN EXCUSE FOR WHAT S.T.A.R. LABS DID. THEY HAD HIM ARRESTED. HE WAS IN PRISON WHEN MOM DIED.
HE FELT SO GUILTY FOR FAILING TO PROTECT HER, HE TOOK HIS OWN LIFE.
THAT WAS A YEAR AGO. LOOKING AT YOU TWO...
...YOU'RE SUFFERING FROM WHATEVER ILLNESS SHE HAD, AREN'T YOU?
NO. NOBODY KNEW IT, BUT WE WERE WITH DAD WHEN HE WAS CAUGHT.
WHAT HAPPENED TO US, WHAT'S FINALLY KILLING US, CAME FROM HERE.

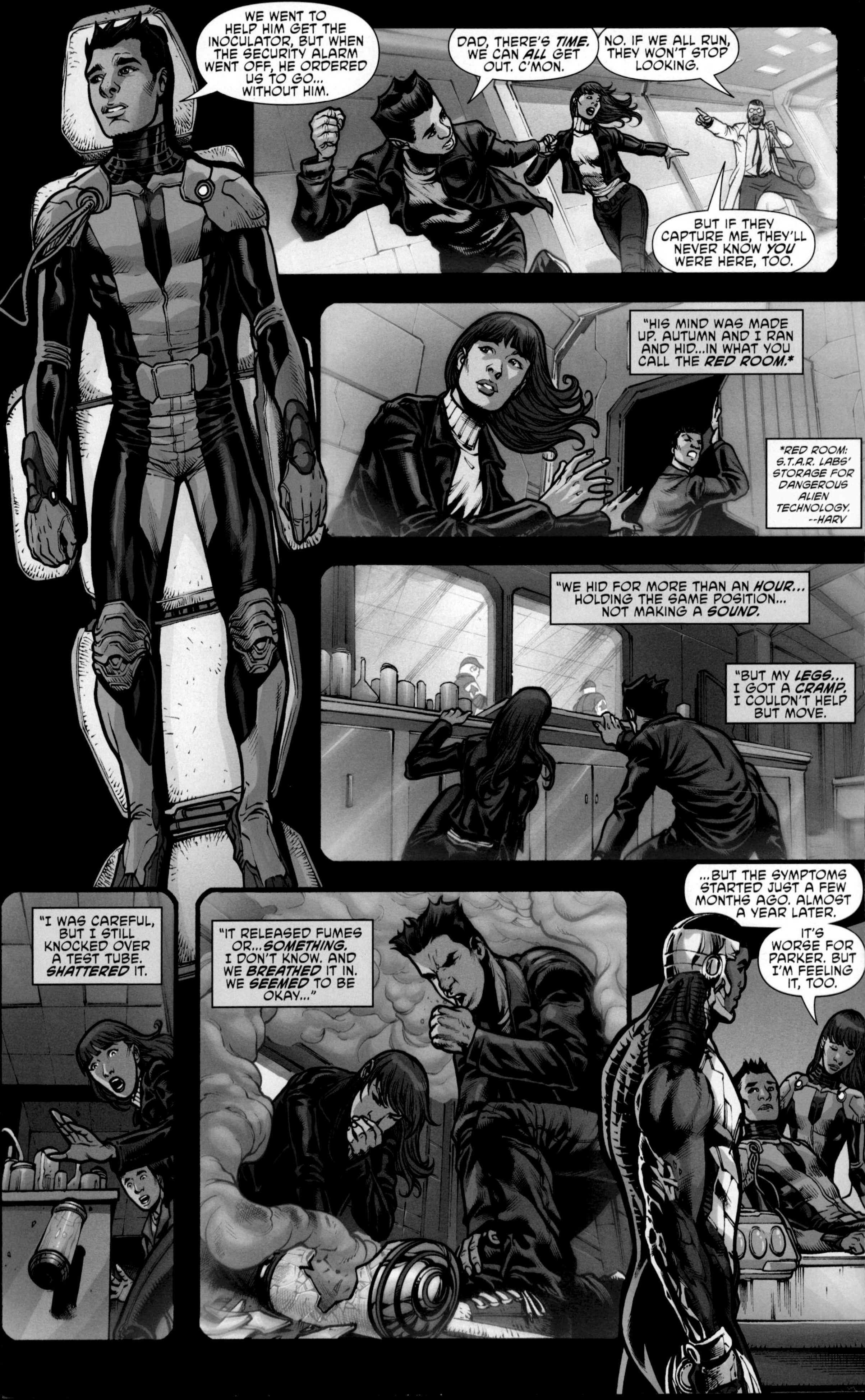
WE WENT TO HELP HIM GET THE INOCULATOR, BUT WHEN THE SECURITY ALARM WENT OFF, HE ORDERED US TO GO... WITHOUT HIM.
DAD, THERE'S TIME. WE CAN ALL GET OUT. C'MON.
NO. IF WE ALL RUN, THEY WON'T STOP LOOKING.
BUT IF THEY CAPTURE ME, THEY'LL NEVER KNOW YOU WERE HERE, TOO.
"HIS MIND WAS MADE UP. AUTUMN AND I RAN AND HID...IN WHAT YOU CALL THE RED ROOM.*
*RED ROOM: S.T.A.R. LABS' STORAGE FOR DANGEROUS ALIEN TECHNOLOGY. --HARV
"WE HID FOR MORE THAN AN HOUR... HOLDING THE SAME POSITION... NOT MAKING A SOUND.
"BUT MY LEGS... I GOT A CRAMP. I COULDN'T HELP BUT MOVE.
"I WAS CAREFUL, BUT I STILL KNOCKED OVER A TEST TUBE. SHATTERED IT.
"IT RELEASED FUMES OR...SOMETHING. I DON'T KNOW. AND WE BREATHED IT IN. WE SEEMED TO BE OKAY..."
...BUT THE SYMPTOMS STARTED JUST A FEW MONTHS AGO. ALMOST A YEAR LATER.
IT'S WORSE FOR PARKER. BUT I'M FEELING IT, TOO.

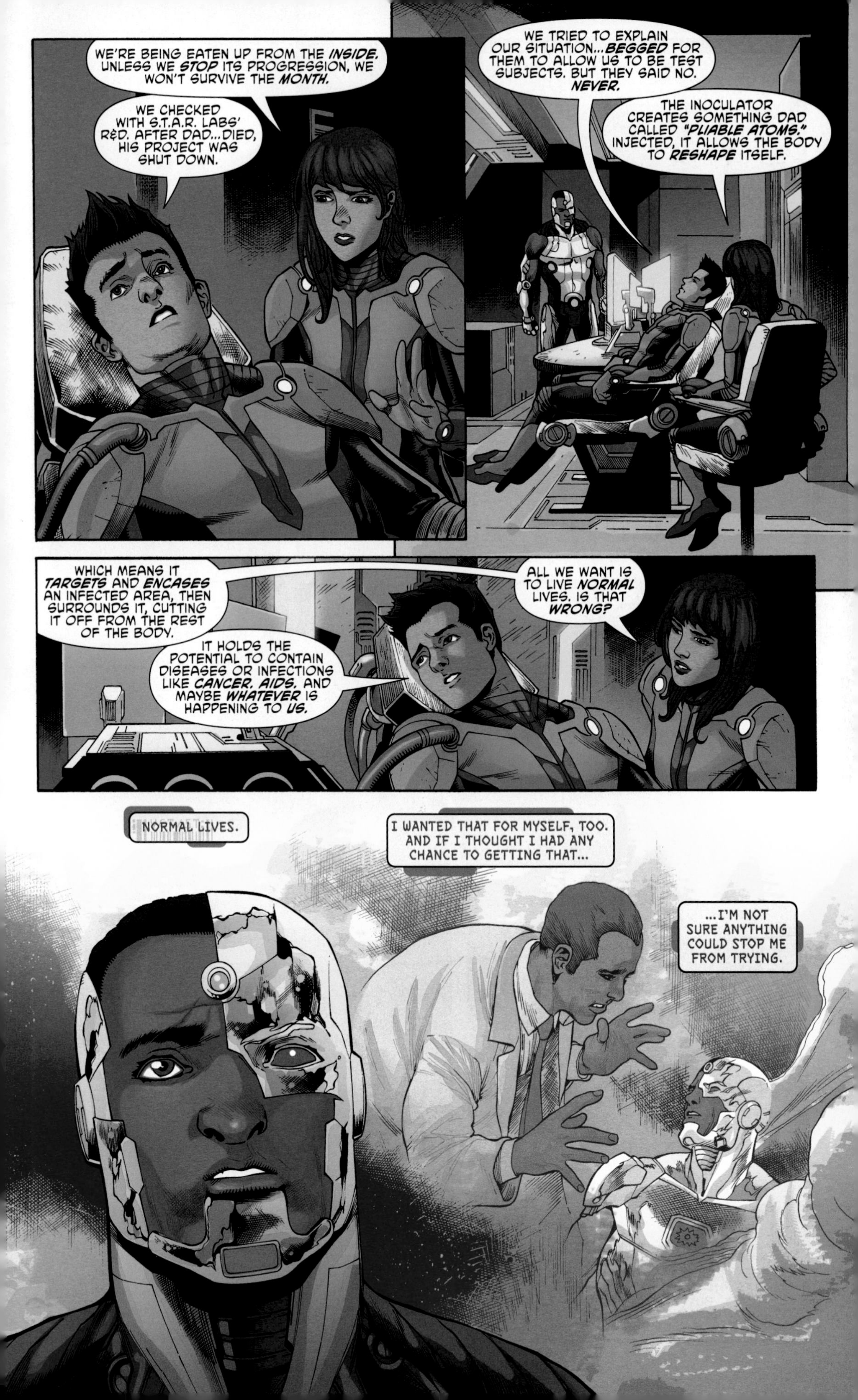
WE'RE BEING EATEN UP FROM THE *INSIDE.* UNLESS WE *STOP* ITS PROGRESSION, WE WON'T SURVIVE THE *MONTH.*
WE CHECKED WITH S.T.A.R. LABS' R&D. AFTER DAD...DIED, HIS PROJECT WAS SHUT DOWN.
WE TRIED TO EXPLAIN OUR SITUATION...*BEGGED* FOR THEM TO ALLOW US TO BE TEST SUBJECTS. BUT THEY SAID NO. *NEVER.*
THE INOCULATOR CREATES SOMETHING DAD CALLED *"PLIABLE ATOMS."* INJECTED, IT ALLOWS THE BODY TO *RESHAPE* ITSELF.
WHICH MEANS IT *TARGETS* AND *ENCASES* AN INFECTED AREA, THEN SURROUNDS IT, CUTTING IT OFF FROM THE REST OF THE BODY.
IT HOLDS THE POTENTIAL TO CONTAIN DISEASES OR INFECTIONS LIKE *CANCER, AIDS,* AND MAYBE *WHATEVER* IS HAPPENING TO *US.*
ALL WE WANT IS TO LIVE *NORMAL* LIVES. IS THAT *WRONG?*
NORMAL LIVES.
I WANTED THAT FOR MYSELF, TOO. AND IF I THOUGHT I HAD ANY CHANCE TO GETTING THAT...
...I'M NOT SURE ANYTHING COULD STOP ME FROM TRYING.

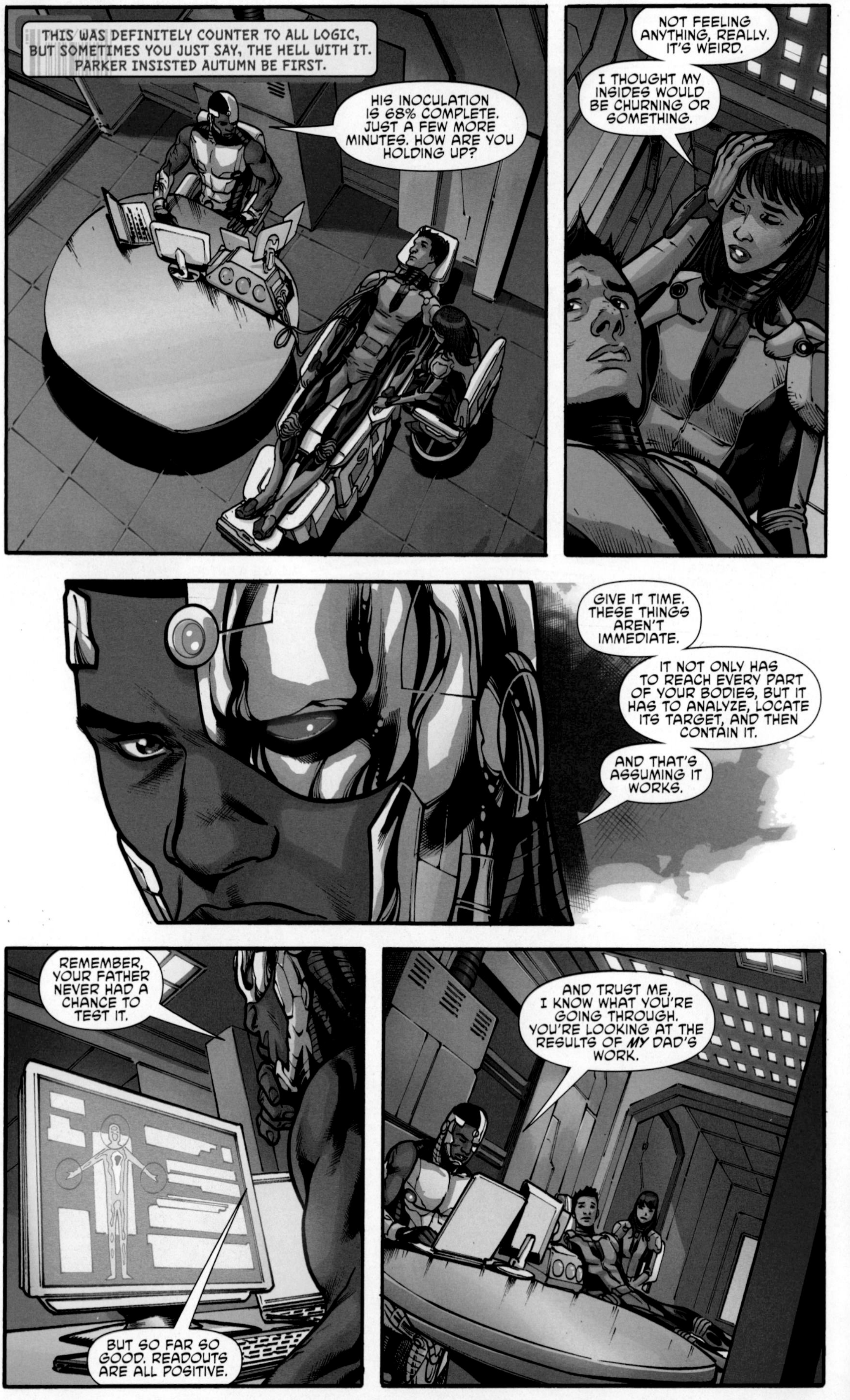
THIS WAS DEFINITELY COUNTER TO ALL LOGIC, BUT SOMETIMES YOU JUST SAY, THE HELL WITH IT. PARKER INSISTED AUTUMN BE FIRST.
HIS INOCULATION IS 68% COMPLETE. JUST A FEW MORE MINUTES. HOW ARE YOU HOLDING UP?
NOT FEELING ANYTHING, REALLY. IT'S WEIRD.
I THOUGHT MY INSIDES WOULD BE CHURNING OR SOMETHING.
GIVE IT TIME. THESE THINGS AREN'T IMMEDIATE.
IT NOT ONLY HAS TO REACH EVERY PART OF YOUR BODIES, BUT IT HAS TO ANALYZE, LOCATE ITS TARGET, AND THEN CONTAIN IT.
AND THAT'S ASSUMING IT WORKS.
REMEMBER, YOUR FATHER NEVER HAD A CHANCE TO TEST IT.
BUT SO FAR SO GOOD. READOUTS ARE ALL POSITIVE.
AND TRUST ME, I KNOW WHAT YOU'RE GOING THROUGH. YOU'RE LOOKING AT THE RESULTS OF *MY* DAD'S WORK.

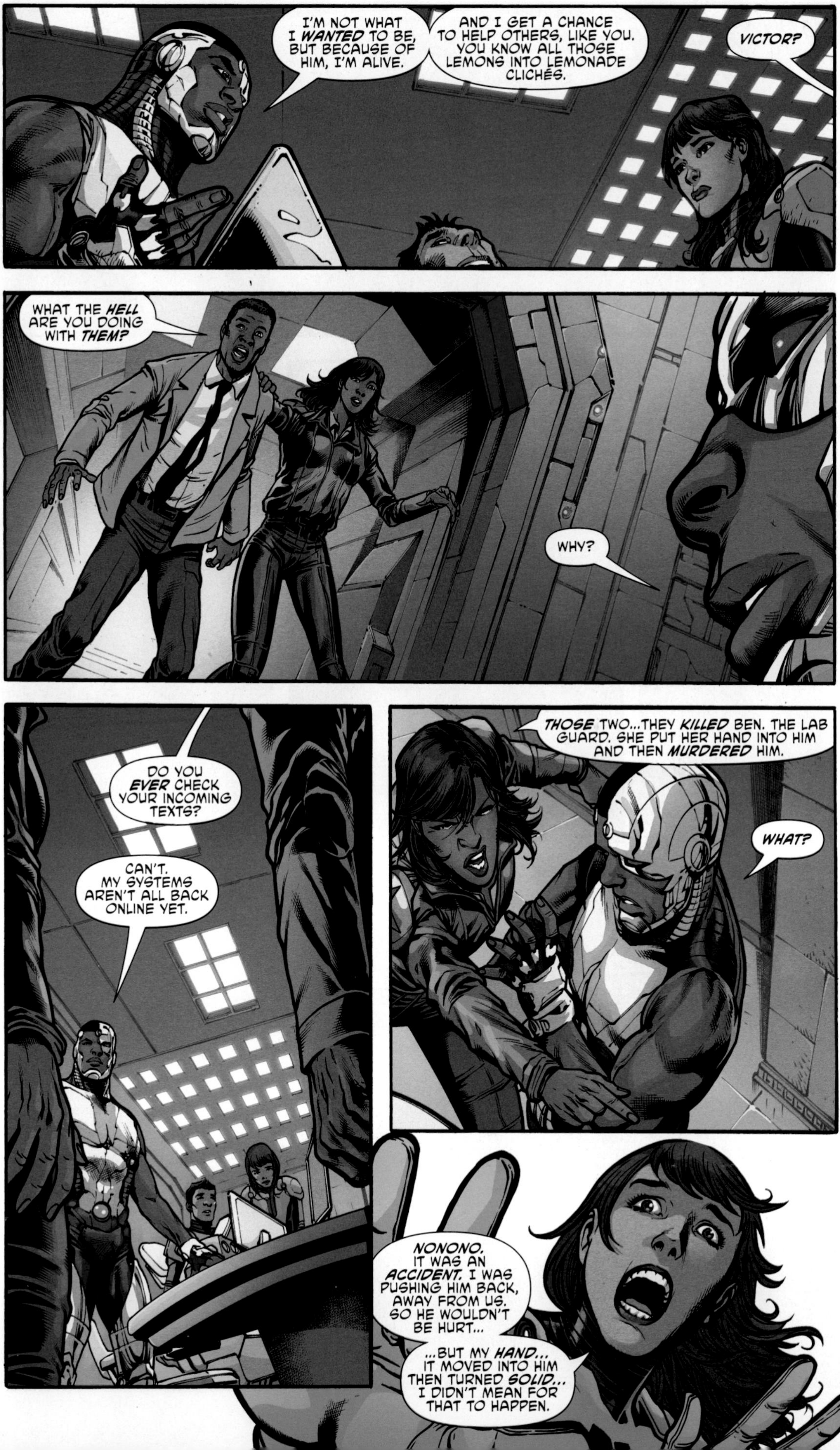
I'M NOT WHAT I WANTED TO BE, BUT BECAUSE OF HIM, I'M ALIVE.
AND I GET A CHANCE TO HELP OTHERS, LIKE YOU. YOU KNOW ALL THOSE LEMONS INTO LEMONADE CLICHÉS.
VICTOR?
WHAT THE HELL ARE YOU DOING WITH THEM?
WHY?
DO YOU EVER CHECK YOUR INCOMING TEXTS?
CAN'T. MY SYSTEMS AREN'T ALL BACK ONLINE YET.
THOSE TWO...THEY KILLED BEN. THE LAB GUARD. SHE PUT HER HAND INTO HIM AND THEN MURDERED HIM.
WHAT?
NONONO. IT WAS AN ACCIDENT. I WAS PUSHING HIM BACK, AWAY FROM US. SO HE WOULDN'T BE HURT...
...BUT MY HAND... IT MOVED INTO HIM THEN TURNED SOLID... I DIDN'T MEAN FOR THAT TO HAPPEN.

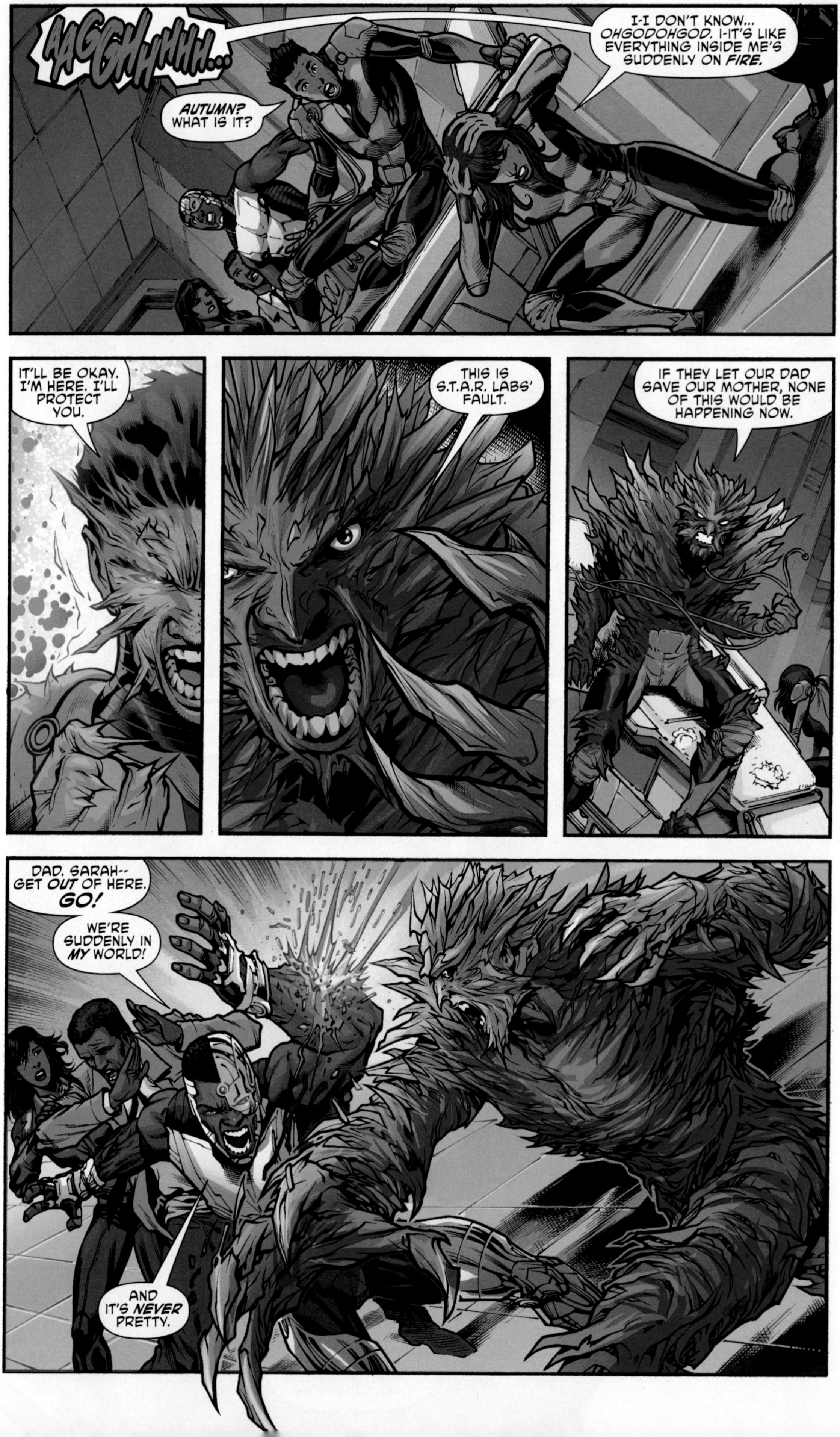
AAGGHHHHH...
I-I DON'T KNOW... OHGODOHGOD, I-IT'S LIKE EVERYTHING INSIDE ME'S SUDDENLY ON FIRE.
AUTUMN? WHAT IS IT?
IT'LL BE OKAY. I'M HERE. I'LL PROTECT YOU.
THIS IS S.T.A.R. LABS' FAULT.
IF THEY LET OUR DAD SAVE OUR MOTHER, NONE OF THIS WOULD BE HAPPENING NOW.
DAD. SARAH-- GET OUT OF HERE. GO!
WE'RE SUDDENLY IN MY WORLD!
AND IT'S NEVER PRETTY.

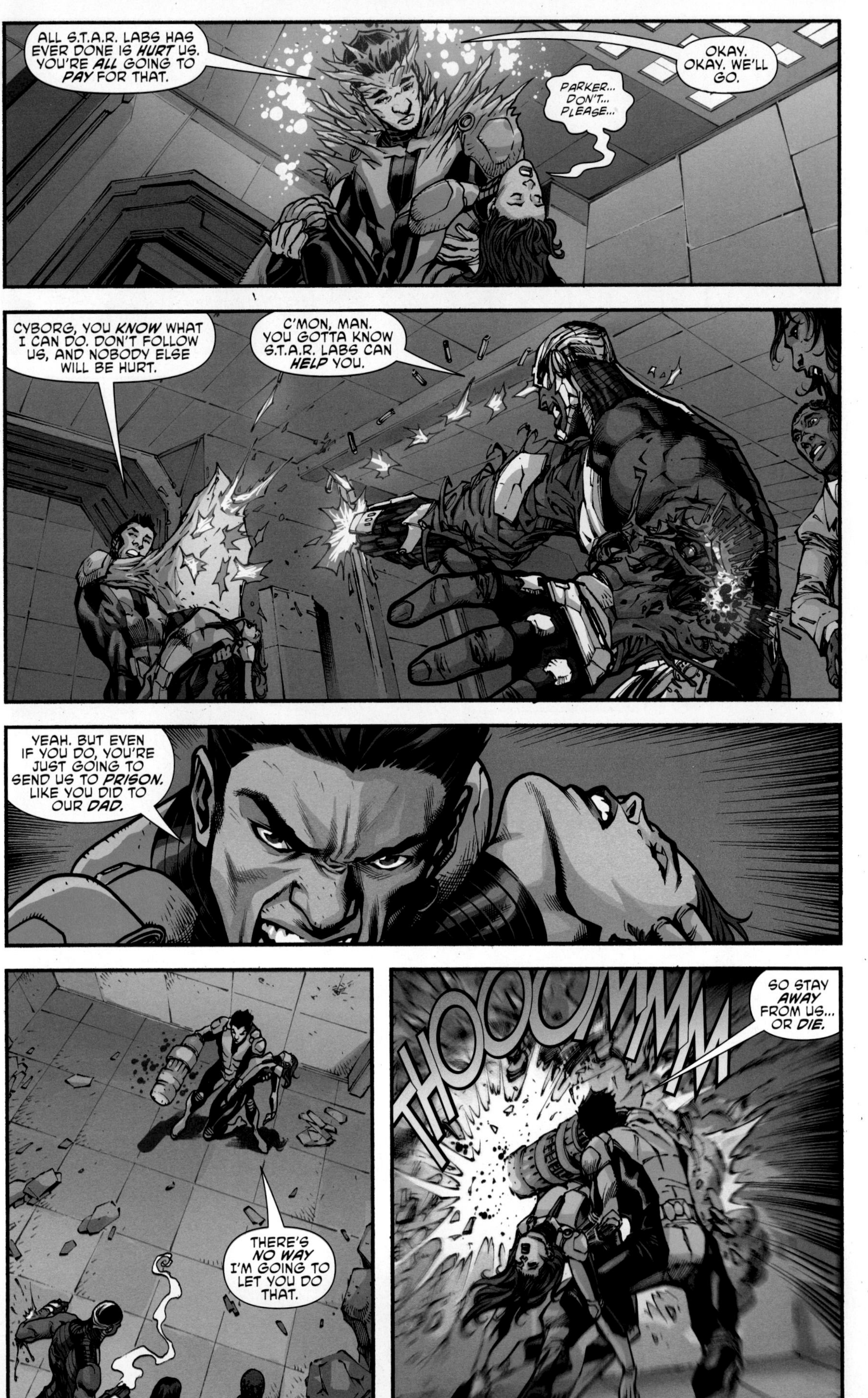
ALL S.T.A.R. LABS HAS EVER DONE IS HURT US. YOU'RE ALL GOING TO PAY FOR THAT.
OKAY. OKAY. WE'LL GO.
PARKER... DON'T... PLEASE...
CYBORG, YOU KNOW WHAT I CAN DO. DON'T FOLLOW US, AND NOBODY ELSE WILL BE HURT.
C'MON, MAN. YOU GOTTA KNOW S.T.A.R. LABS CAN HELP YOU.
YEAH. BUT EVEN IF YOU DO, YOU'RE JUST GOING TO SEND US TO PRISON. LIKE YOU DID TO OUR DAD.
THERE'S NO WAY I'M GOING TO LET YOU DO THAT.
THOOOMMM
SO STAY AWAY FROM US... OR DIE.

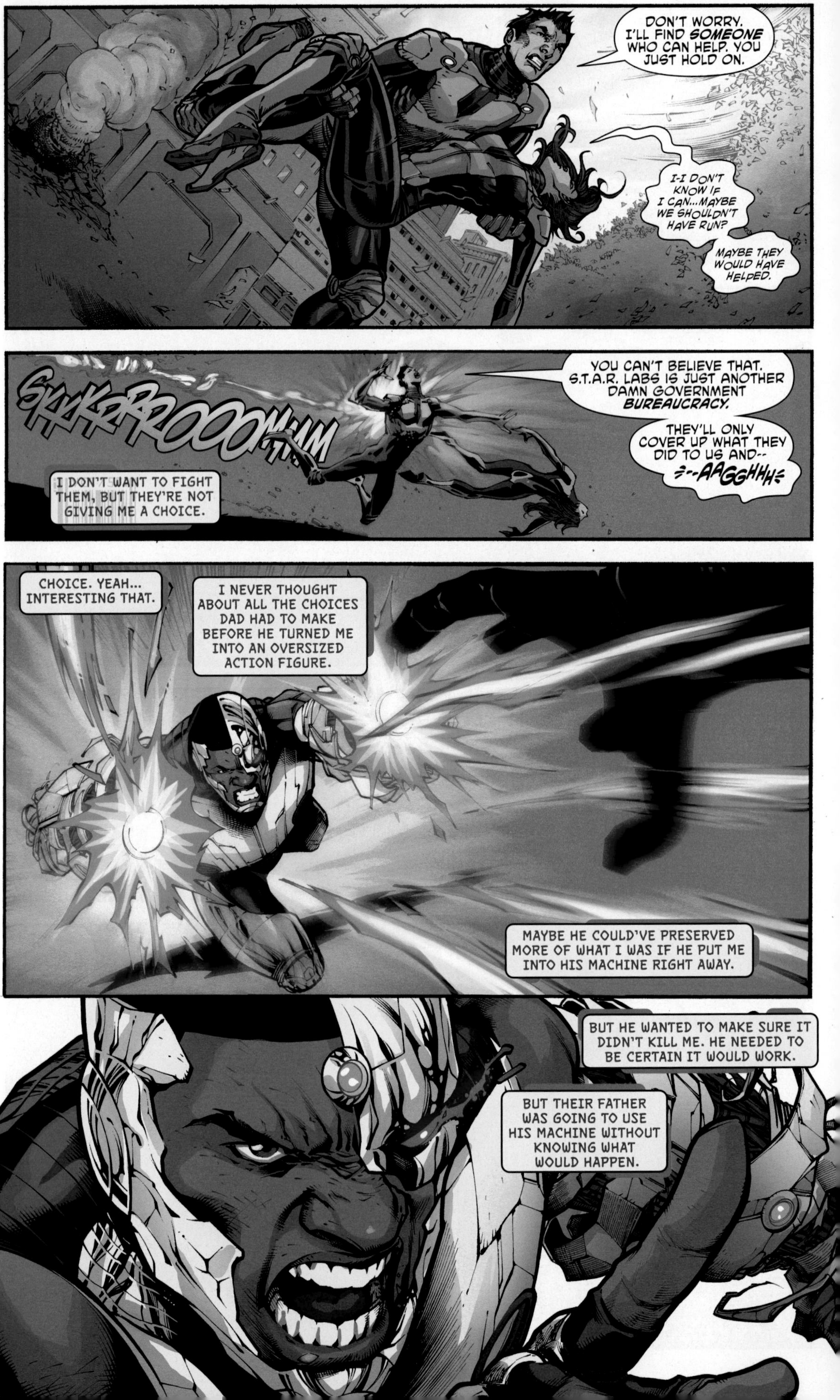
DON'T WORRY. I'LL FIND SOMEONE WHO CAN HELP. YOU JUST HOLD ON.
I-I DON'T KNOW IF I CAN...MAYBE WE SHOULDN'T HAVE RUN?
MAYBE THEY WOULD HAVE HELPED.
SKKKRRROOOMMM
YOU CAN'T BELIEVE THAT. S.T.A.R. LABS IS JUST ANOTHER DAMN GOVERNMENT BUREAUCRACY.
THEY'LL ONLY COVER UP WHAT THEY DID TO US AND-- --AAGGHHH
I DON'T WANT TO FIGHT THEM, BUT THEY'RE NOT GIVING ME A CHOICE.
CHOICE. YEAH... INTERESTING THAT.
I NEVER THOUGHT ABOUT ALL THE CHOICES DAD HAD TO MAKE BEFORE HE TURNED ME INTO AN OVERSIZED ACTION FIGURE.
MAYBE HE COULD'VE PRESERVED MORE OF WHAT I WAS IF HE PUT ME INTO HIS MACHINE RIGHT AWAY.
BUT HE WANTED TO MAKE SURE IT DIDN'T KILL ME. HE NEEDED TO BE CERTAIN IT WOULD WORK.
BUT THEIR FATHER WAS GOING TO USE HIS MACHINE WITHOUT KNOWING WHAT WOULD HAPPEN.

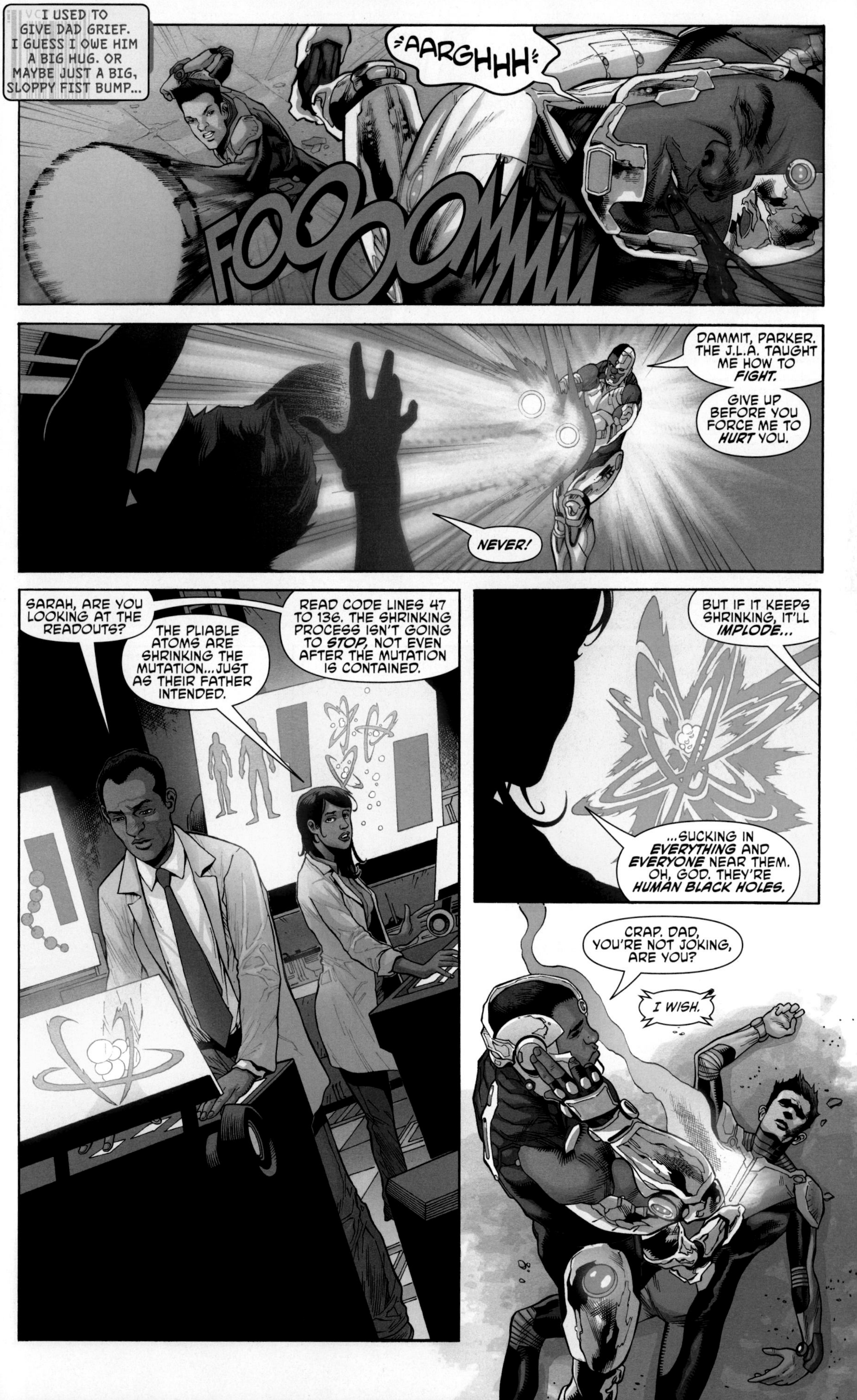
I USED TO GIVE DAD GRIEF. I GUESS I OWE HIM A BIG HUG. OR MAYBE JUST A BIG, SLOPPY FIST BUMP...
AARGHHH
FOOOOOMMMM
DAMMIT, PARKER. THE J.L.A. TAUGHT ME HOW TO FIGHT.
GIVE UP BEFORE YOU FORCE ME TO HURT YOU.
NEVER!
SARAH, ARE YOU LOOKING AT THE READOUTS?
THE PLIABLE ATOMS ARE SHRINKING THE MUTATION...JUST AS THEIR FATHER INTENDED.
READ CODE LINES 47 TO 136. THE SHRINKING PROCESS ISN'T GOING TO STOP, NOT EVEN AFTER THE MUTATION IS CONTAINED.
BUT IF IT KEEPS SHRINKING, IT'LL IMPLODE...
...SUCKING IN EVERYTHING AND EVERYONE NEAR THEM. OH, GOD. THEY'RE HUMAN BLACK HOLES.
CRAP. DAD, YOU'RE NOT JOKING, ARE YOU?
I WISH.

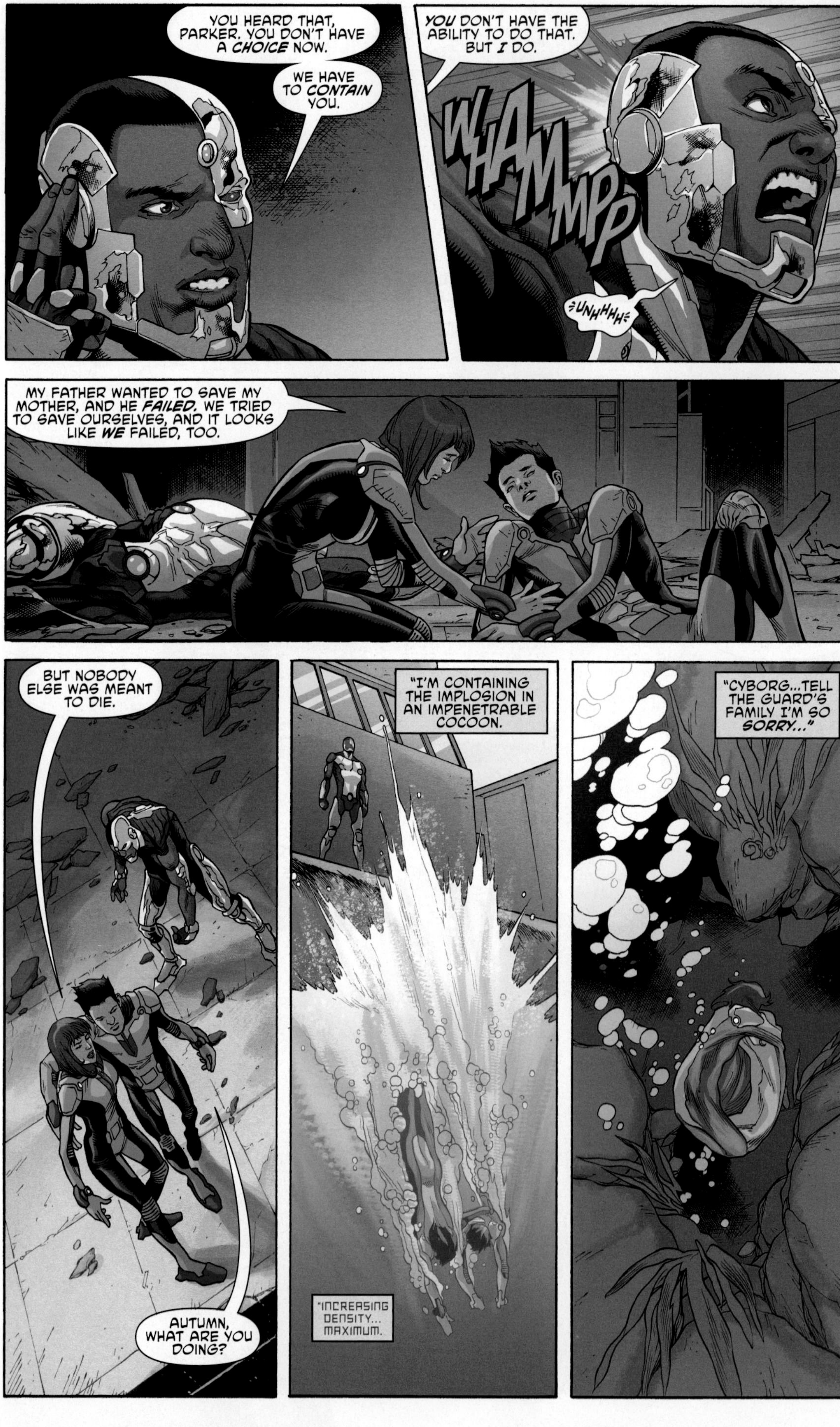
YOU HEARD THAT, PARKER. YOU DON'T HAVE A CHOICE NOW.
WE HAVE TO CONTAIN YOU.
YOU DON'T HAVE THE ABILITY TO DO THAT. BUT I DO.
WHAMMPP
UNHHHH
MY FATHER WANTED TO SAVE MY MOTHER, AND HE FAILED. WE TRIED TO SAVE OURSELVES, AND IT LOOKS LIKE WE FAILED, TOO.
BUT NOBODY ELSE WAS MEANT TO DIE.
AUTUMN, WHAT ARE YOU DOING?
"I'M CONTAINING THE IMPLOSION IN AN IMPENETRABLE COCOON.
"INCREASING DENSITY... MAXIMUM.
"CYBORG...TELL THE GUARD'S FAMILY I'M SO SORRY..."

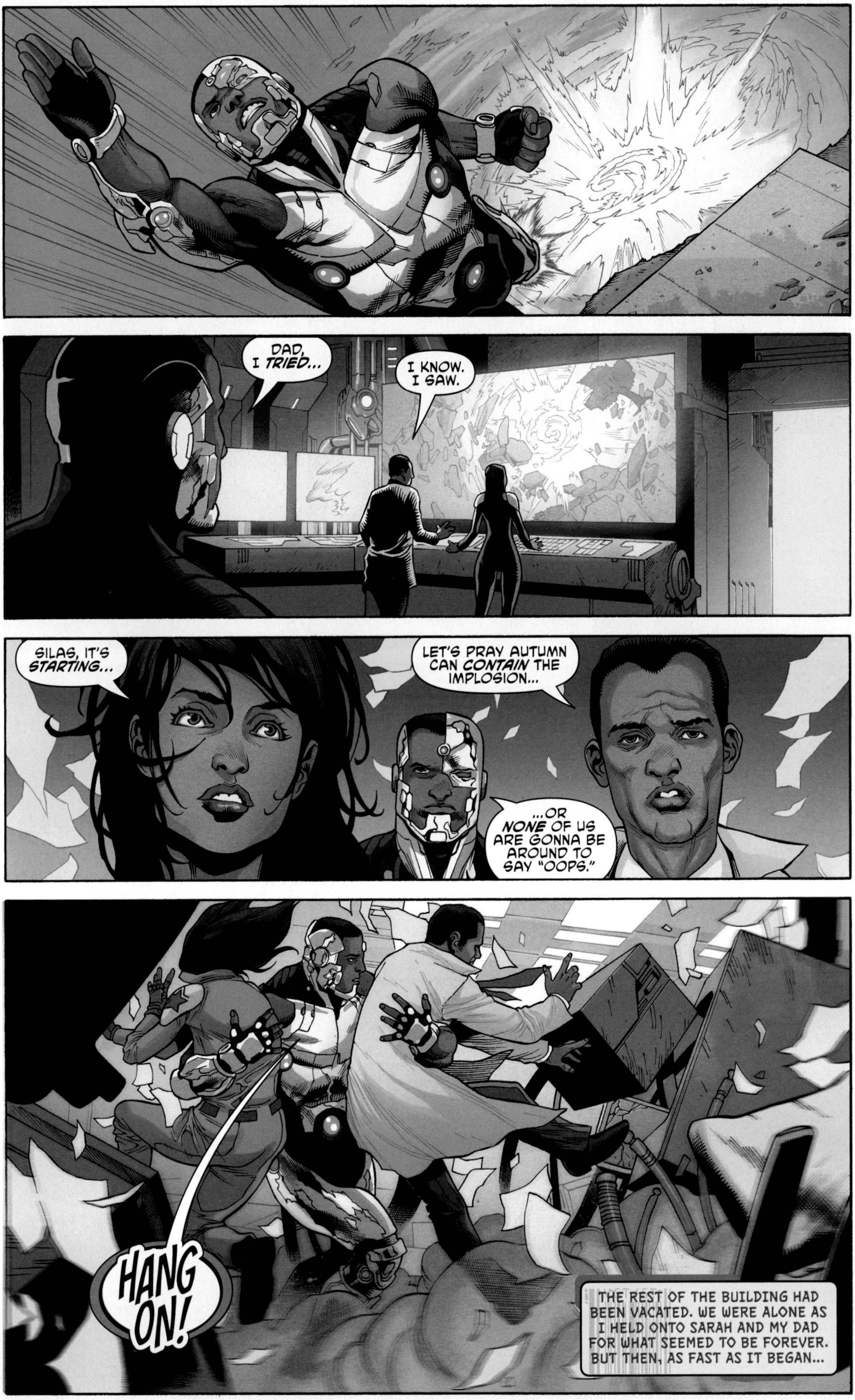
DAD, I TRIED...
I KNOW. I SAW.
SILAS, IT'S STARTING...
LET'S PRAY AUTUMN CAN CONTAIN THE IMPLOSION...
...OR NONE OF US ARE GONNA BE AROUND TO SAY "OOPS."
HANG ON!
THE REST OF THE BUILDING HAD BEEN VACATED. WE WERE ALONE AS I HELD ONTO SARAH AND MY DAD FOR WHAT SEEMED TO BE FOREVER. BUT THEN, AS FAST AS IT BEGAN...

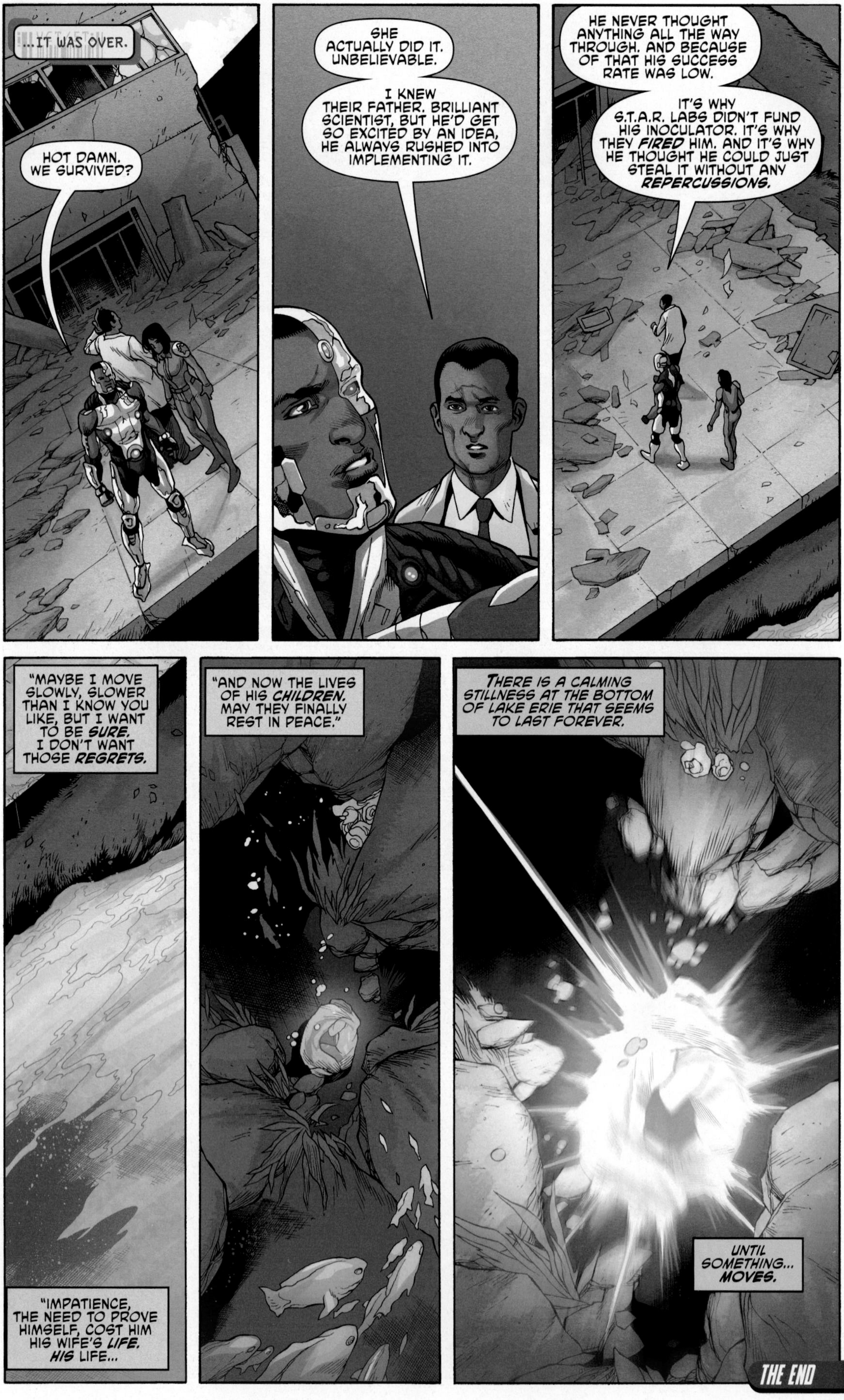
...IT WAS OVER.
HOT DAMN. WE SURVIVED?
SHE ACTUALLY DID IT. UNBELIEVABLE.
I KNEW THEIR FATHER. BRILLIANT SCIENTIST, BUT HE'D GET SO EXCITED BY AN IDEA, HE ALWAYS RUSHED INTO IMPLEMENTING IT.
HE NEVER THOUGHT ANYTHING ALL THE WAY THROUGH. AND BECAUSE OF THAT HIS SUCCESS RATE WAS LOW.
IT'S WHY S.T.A.R. LABS DIDN'T FUND HIS INOCULATOR. IT'S WHY THEY *FIRED* HIM. AND IT'S WHY HE THOUGHT HE COULD JUST STEAL IT WITHOUT ANY *REPERCUSSIONS.*
"MAYBE I MOVE SLOWLY, SLOWER THAN I KNOW YOU LIKE, BUT I WANT TO BE *SURE.* I DON'T WANT THOSE *REGRETS.*
"IMPATIENCE, THE NEED TO PROVE HIMSELF, COST HIM HIS WIFE'S *LIFE. HIS* LIFE...
"AND NOW THE LIVES OF HIS *CHILDREN.* MAY THEY FINALLY REST IN PEACE."
THERE IS A CALMING STILLNESS AT THE BOTTOM OF LAKE ERIE THAT SEEMS TO LAST FOREVER.
UNTIL SOMETHING... MOVES.
THE END

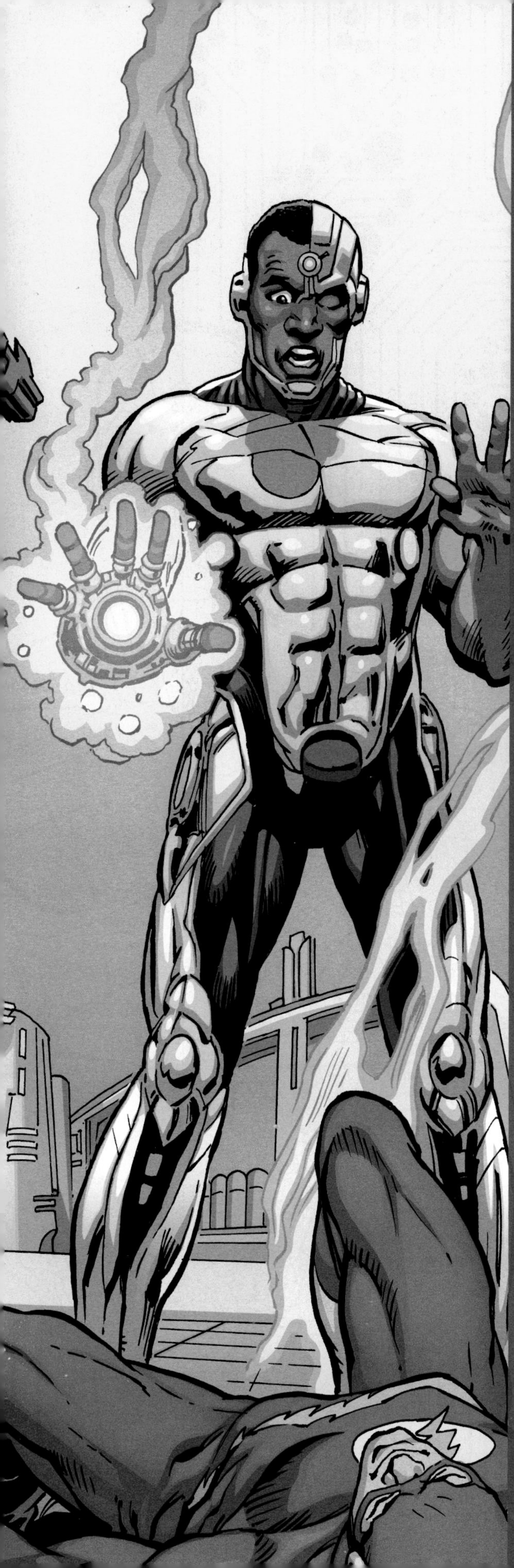

VARIANT COVER GALLERY

CYBORG #7
ADULT COLORING BOOK VARIANT
BY DEREC DONOVAN

CYBORG #8
VARIANT BY
NEAL ADAMS
& DAVE GIBBONS

CYBORG #9
VARIANT BY
JOHN ROMITA JR.
WITH DANNY MIKI
& ALEX SINCLAIR

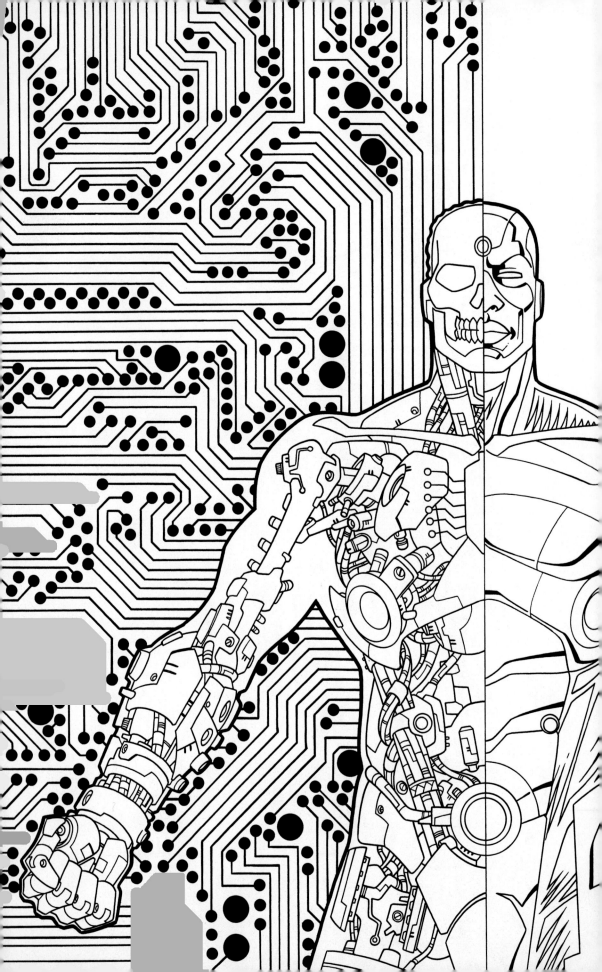

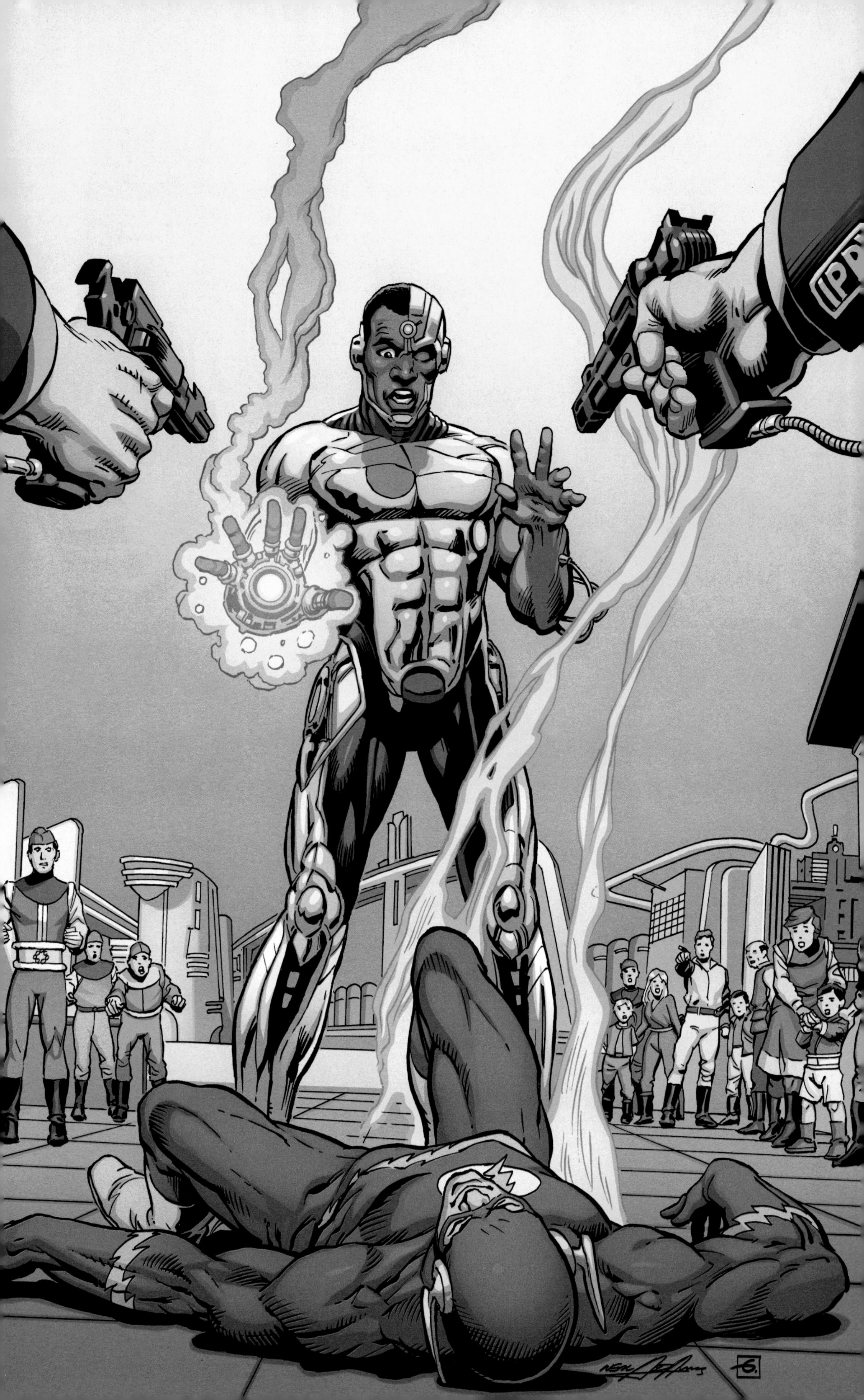

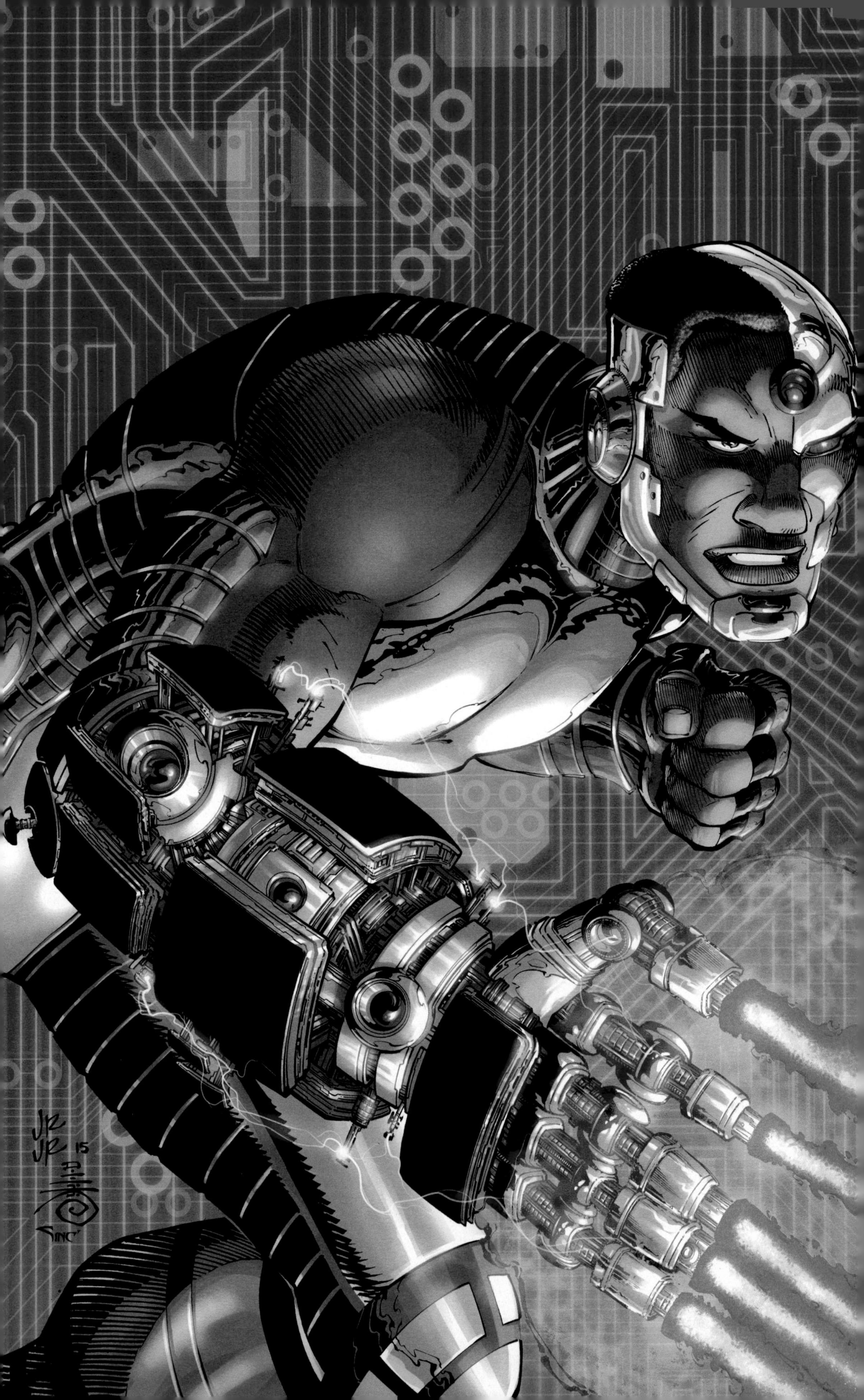

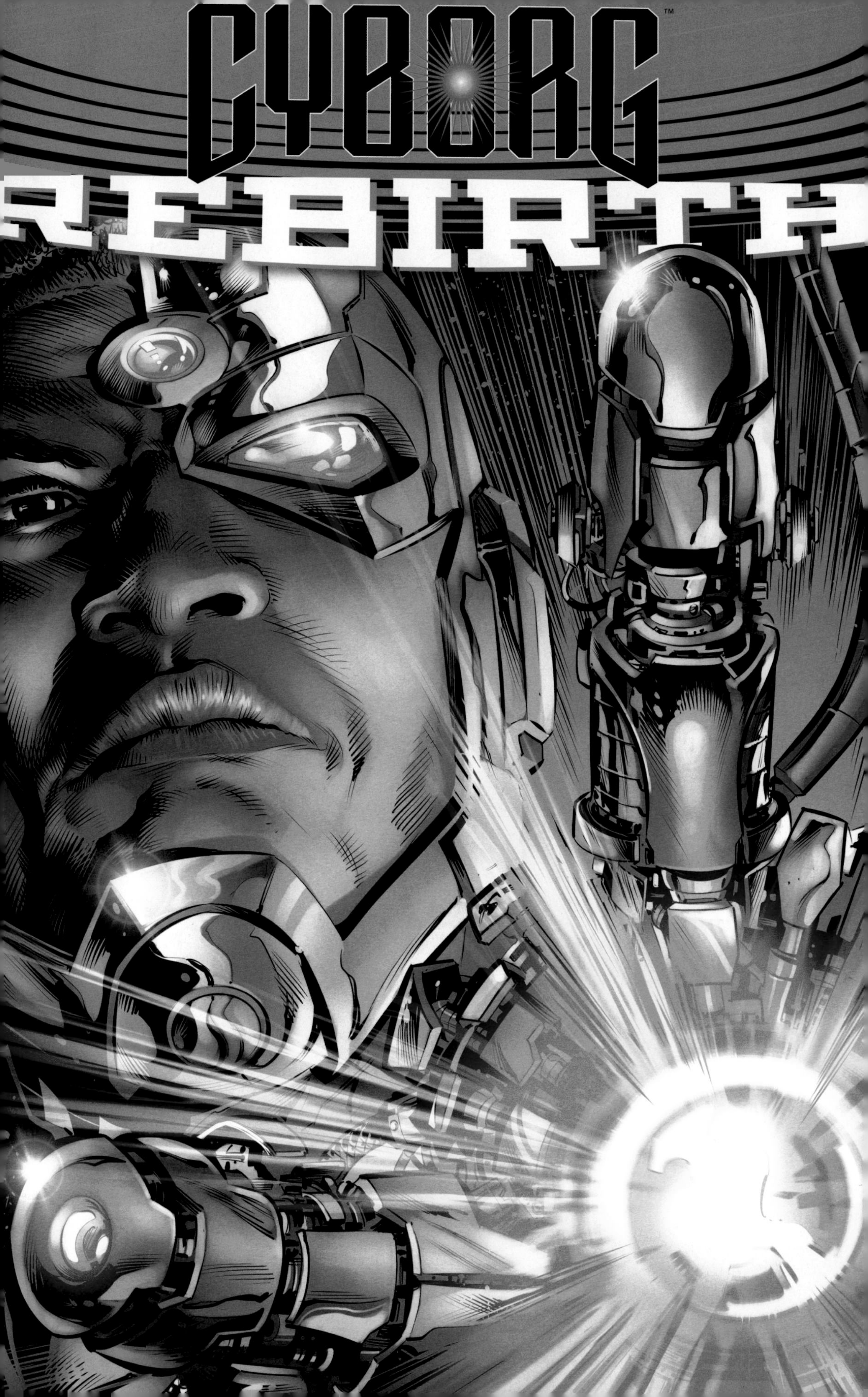
CYBORG™
REBIRTH

The future (and past) of the DC Universe starts with DC UNIVERSE: REBIRTH!

Explore the changing world of Cyborg in this special preview of **CYBORG: REBIRTH #1**!

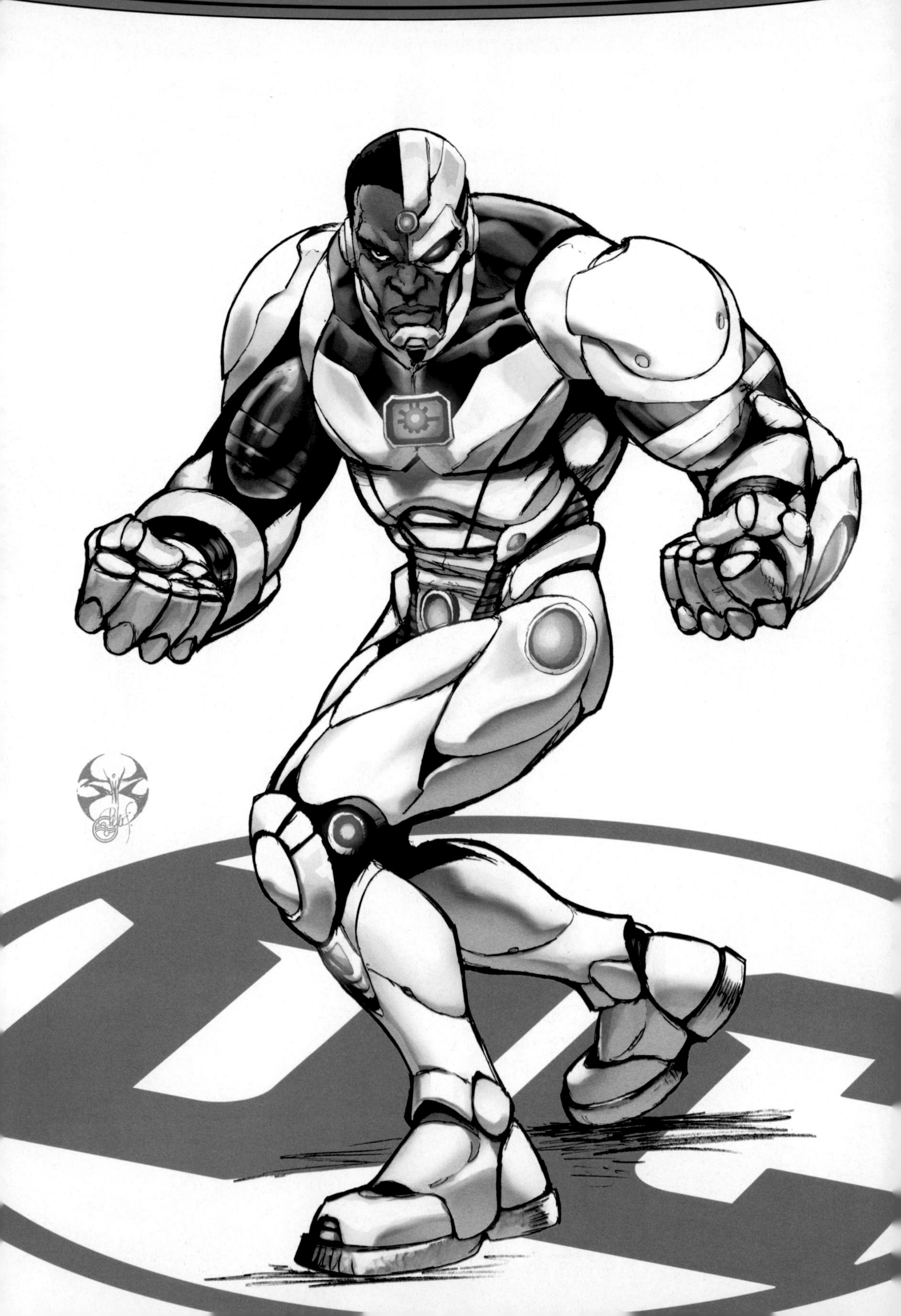

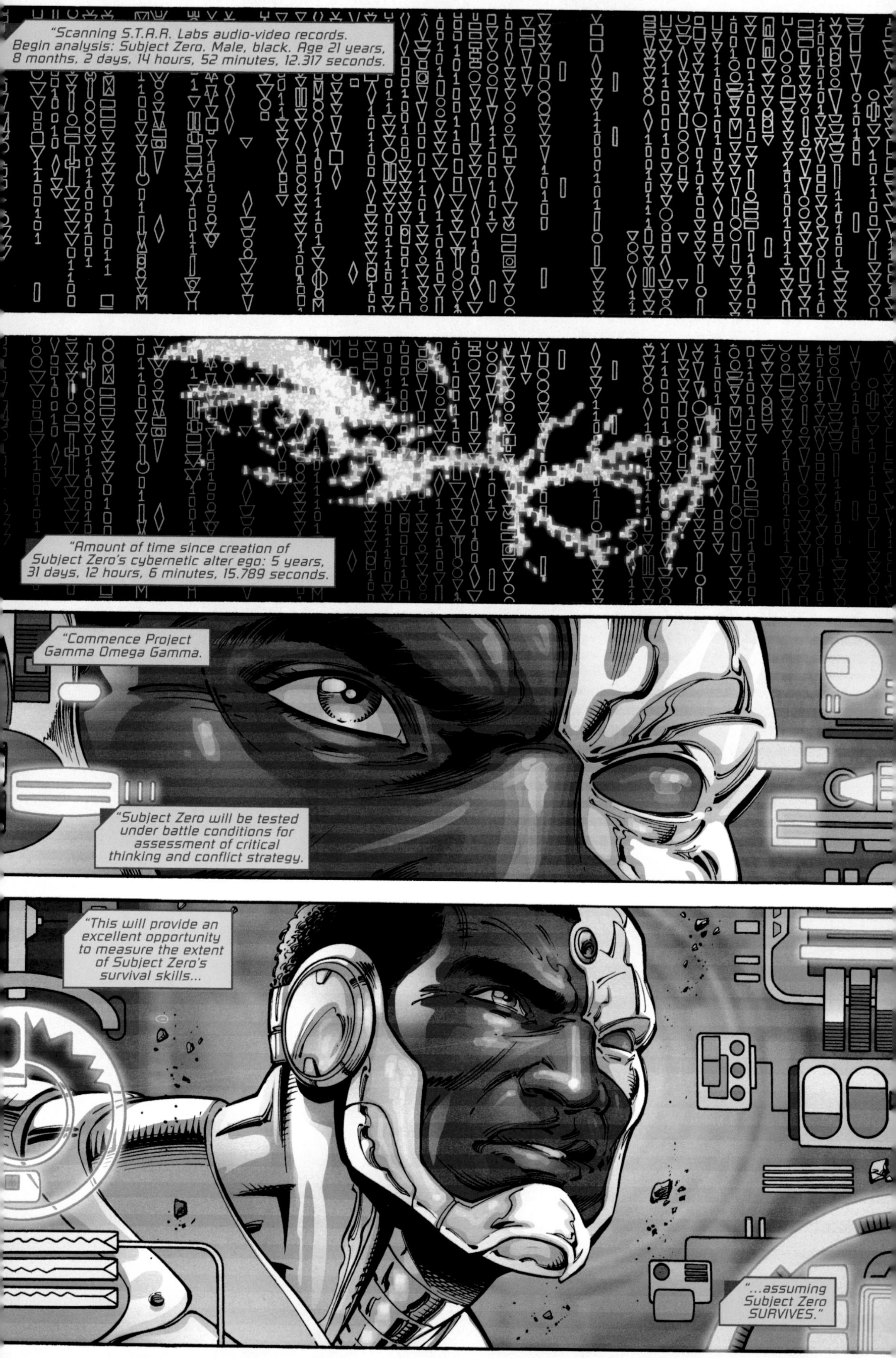
"Scanning S.T.A.R. Labs audio-video records. Begin analysis: Subject Zero. Male, black. Age 21 years, 8 months, 2 days, 14 hours, 52 minutes, 12.317 seconds.
"Amount of time since creation of Subject Zero's cybernetic alter ego: 5 years, 31 days, 12 hours, 6 minutes, 15.789 seconds.
"Commence Project Gamma Omega Gamma.
"Subject Zero will be tested under battle conditions for assessment of critical thinking and conflict strategy.
"This will provide an excellent opportunity to measure the extent of Subject Zero's survival skills...
"...assuming Subject Zero SURVIVES."

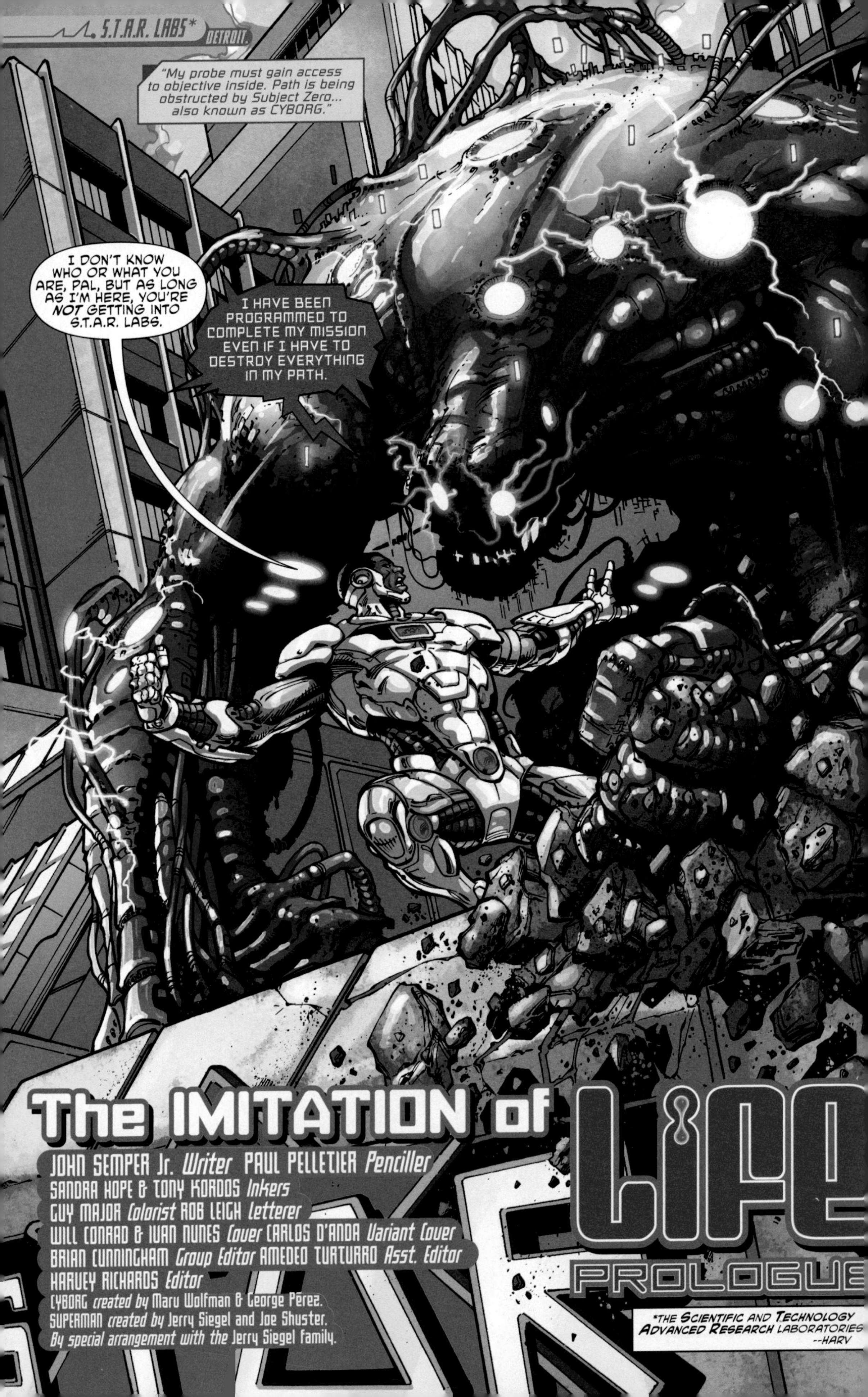
S.T.A.R. LABS* DETROIT.
"My probe must gain access to objective inside. Path is being obstructed by Subject Zero... also known as CYBORG."
I DON'T KNOW WHO OR WHAT YOU ARE, PAL, BUT AS LONG AS I'M HERE, YOU'RE NOT GETTING INTO S.T.A.R. LABS.
I HAVE BEEN PROGRAMMED TO COMPLETE MY MISSION EVEN IF I HAVE TO DESTROY EVERYTHING IN MY PATH.
The IMITATION of LIFE
PROLOGUE
JOHN SEMPER Jr. Writer PAUL PELLETIER Penciller
SANDRA HOPE & TONY KORDOS Inkers
GUY MAJOR Colorist ROB LEIGH Letterer
WILL CONRAD & IVAN NUNES Cover CARLOS D'ANDA Variant Cover
BRIAN CUNNINGHAM Group Editor AMEDEO TURTURRO Asst. Editor
HARVEY RICHARDS Editor
CYBORG created by Marv Wolfman & George Pérez.
SUPERMAN created by Jerry Siegel and Joe Shuster.
By special arrangement with the Jerry Siegel family.
*THE SCIENTIFIC AND TECHNOLOGY ADVANCED RESEARCH LABORATORIES --HARV

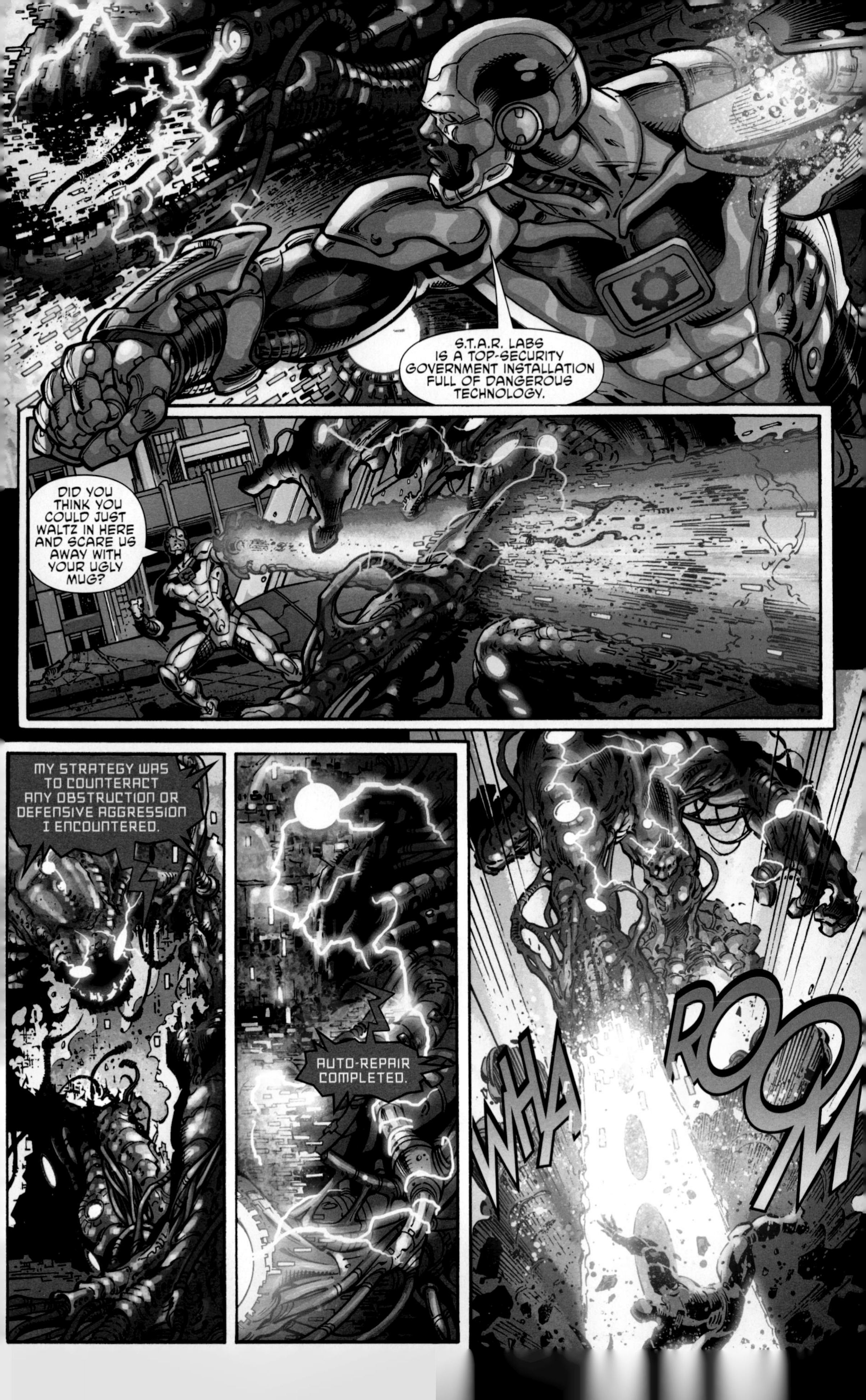
S.T.A.R. LABS IS A TOP-SECURITY GOVERNMENT INSTALLATION FULL OF DANGEROUS TECHNOLOGY.
DID YOU THINK YOU COULD JUST WALTZ IN HERE AND SCARE US AWAY WITH YOUR UGLY MUG?
MY STRATEGY WAS TO COUNTERACT ANY OBSTRUCTION OR DEFENSIVE AGGRESSION I ENCOUNTERED.
AUTO-REPAIR COMPLETED.
WHAROOM

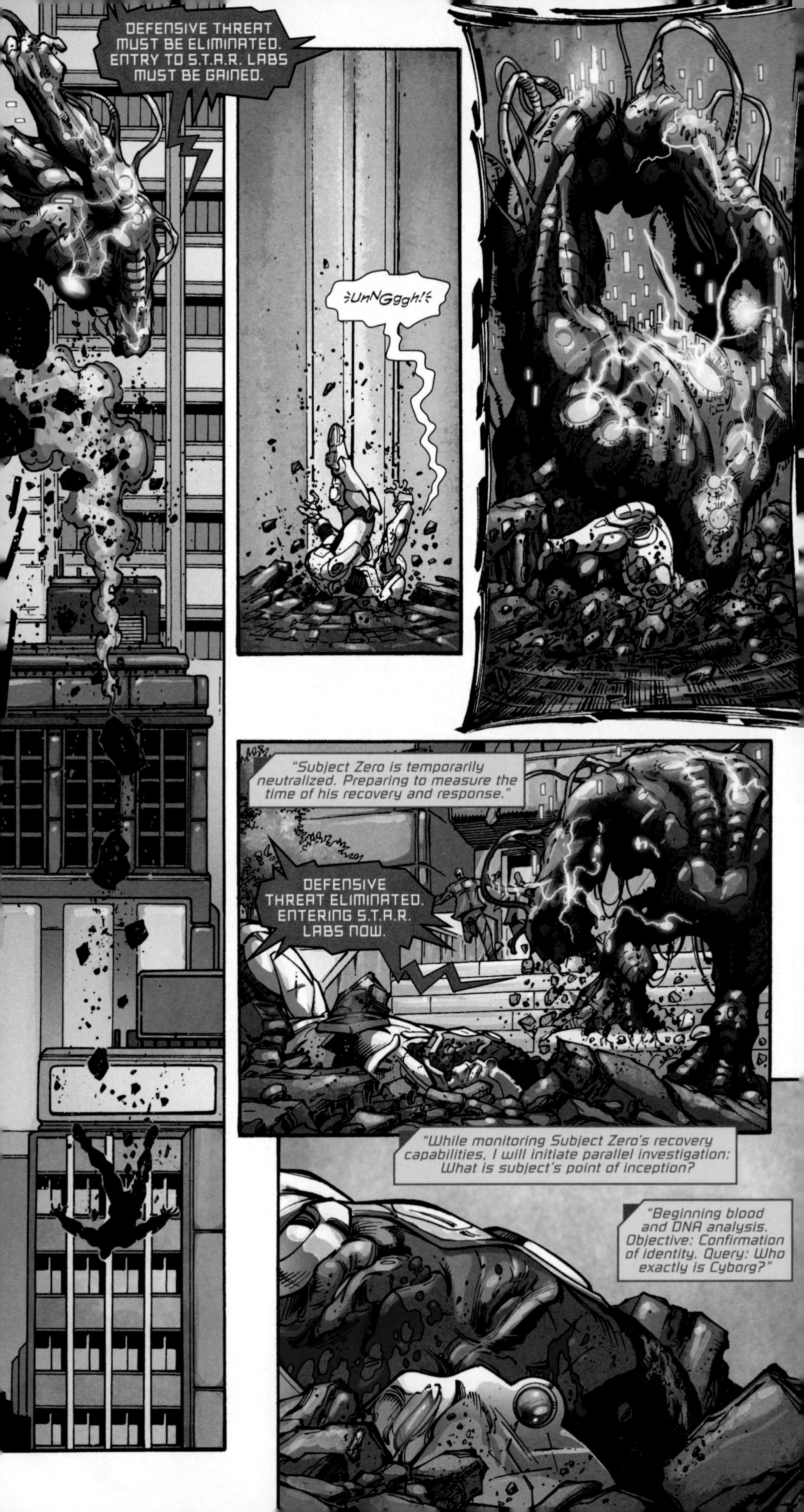
DEFENSIVE THREAT MUST BE ELIMINATED. ENTRY TO S.T.A.R. LABS MUST BE GAINED.
UnNGggh!
"Subject Zero is temporarily neutralized. Preparing to measure the time of his recovery and response."
DEFENSIVE THREAT ELIMINATED. ENTERING S.T.A.R. LABS NOW.
"While monitoring Subject Zero's recovery capabilities, I will initiate parallel investigation: What is subject's point of inception?
"Beginning blood and DNA analysis. Objective: Confirmation of identity. Query: Who exactly is Cyborg?"

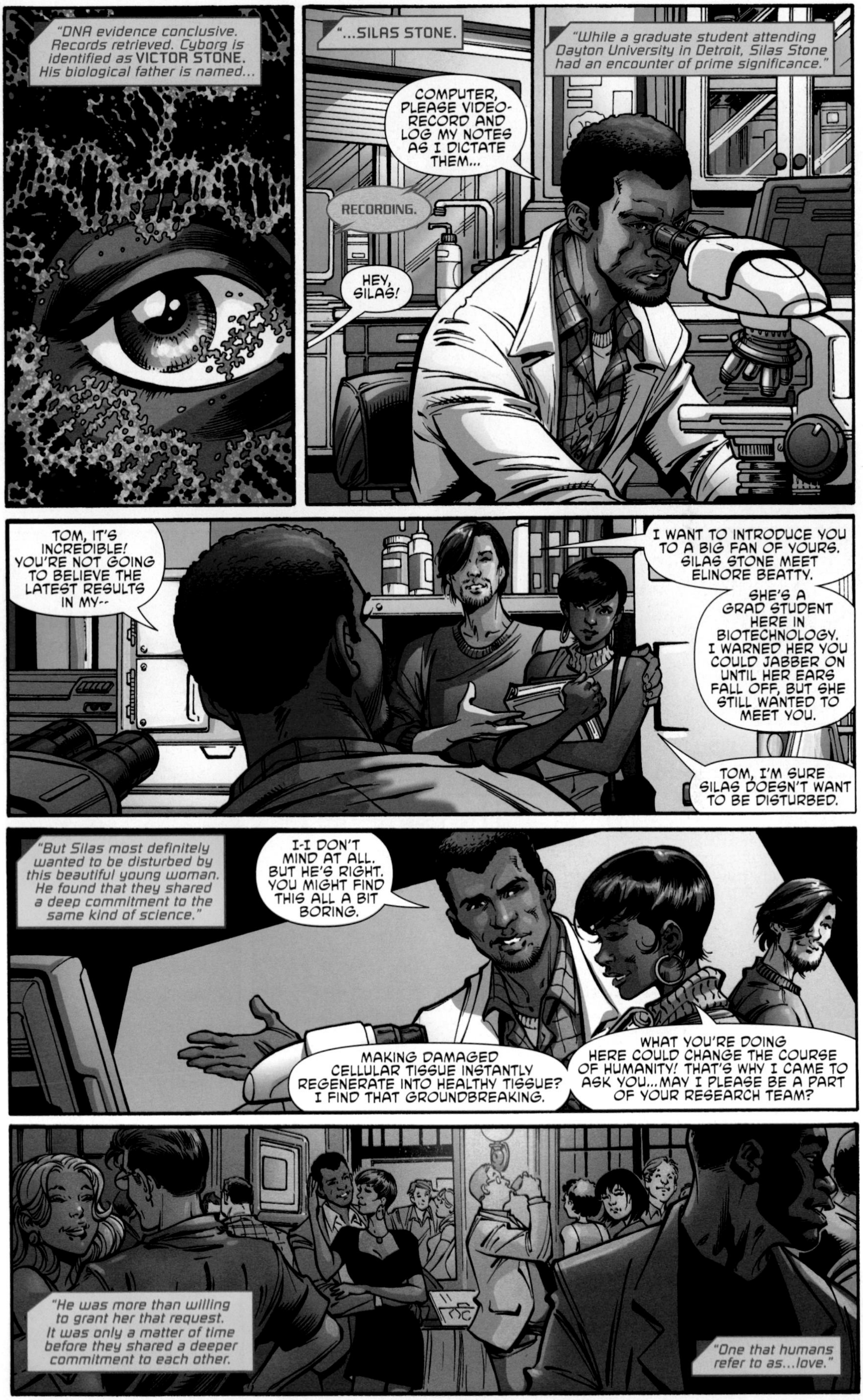
"DNA evidence conclusive. Records retrieved. Cyborg is identified as VICTOR STONE. His biological father is named...
"...SILAS STONE.
"While a graduate student attending Dayton University in Detroit, Silas Stone had an encounter of prime significance."
COMPUTER, PLEASE VIDEO-RECORD AND LOG MY NOTES AS I DICTATE THEM...
RECORDING.
HEY, SILAS!
TOM, IT'S INCREDIBLE! YOU'RE NOT GOING TO BELIEVE THE LATEST RESULTS IN MY--
I WANT TO INTRODUCE YOU TO A BIG FAN OF YOURS. SILAS STONE MEET ELINORE BEATTY.
SHE'S A GRAD STUDENT HERE IN BIOTECHNOLOGY. I WARNED HER YOU COULD JABBER ON UNTIL HER EARS FALL OFF, BUT SHE STILL WANTED TO MEET YOU.
TOM, I'M SURE SILAS DOESN'T WANT TO BE DISTURBED.
"But Silas most definitely wanted to be disturbed by this beautiful young woman. He found that they shared a deep commitment to the same kind of science."
I-I DON'T MIND AT ALL. BUT HE'S RIGHT. YOU MIGHT FIND THIS ALL A BIT BORING.
MAKING DAMAGED CELLULAR TISSUE INSTANTLY REGENERATE INTO HEALTHY TISSUE? I FIND THAT GROUNDBREAKING.
WHAT YOU'RE DOING HERE COULD CHANGE THE COURSE OF HUMANITY! THAT'S WHY I CAME TO ASK YOU...MAY I PLEASE BE A PART OF YOUR RESEARCH TEAM?
"He was more than willing to grant her that request. It was only a matter of time before they shared a deeper commitment to each other.
"One that humans refer to as...love."

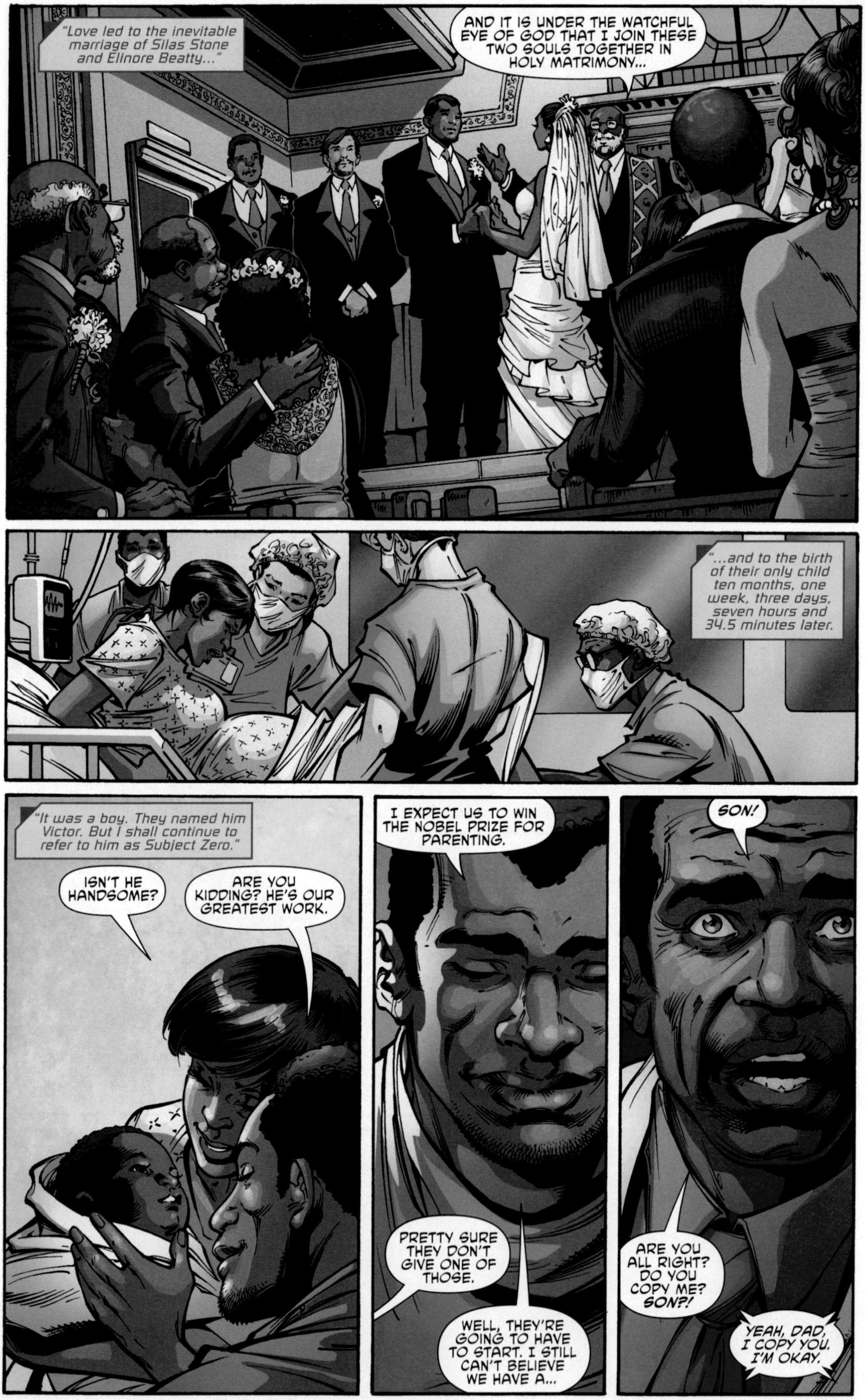

"Love led to the inevitable marriage of Silas Stone and Elinore Beatty..."
AND IT IS UNDER THE WATCHFUL EYE OF GOD THAT I JOIN THESE TWO SOULS TOGETHER IN HOLY MATRIMONY...
"...and to the birth of their only child ten months, one week, three days, seven hours and 34.5 minutes later.
"It was a boy. They named him Victor. But I shall continue to refer to him as Subject Zero."
ISN'T HE HANDSOME?
ARE YOU KIDDING? HE'S OUR GREATEST WORK.
I EXPECT US TO WIN THE NOBEL PRIZE FOR PARENTING.
PRETTY SURE THEY DON'T GIVE ONE OF THOSE.
WELL, THEY'RE GOING TO HAVE TO START. I STILL CAN'T BELIEVE WE HAVE A...
SON!
ARE YOU ALL RIGHT? DO YOU COPY ME? SON?!
YEAH, DAD, I COPY YOU. I'M OKAY.

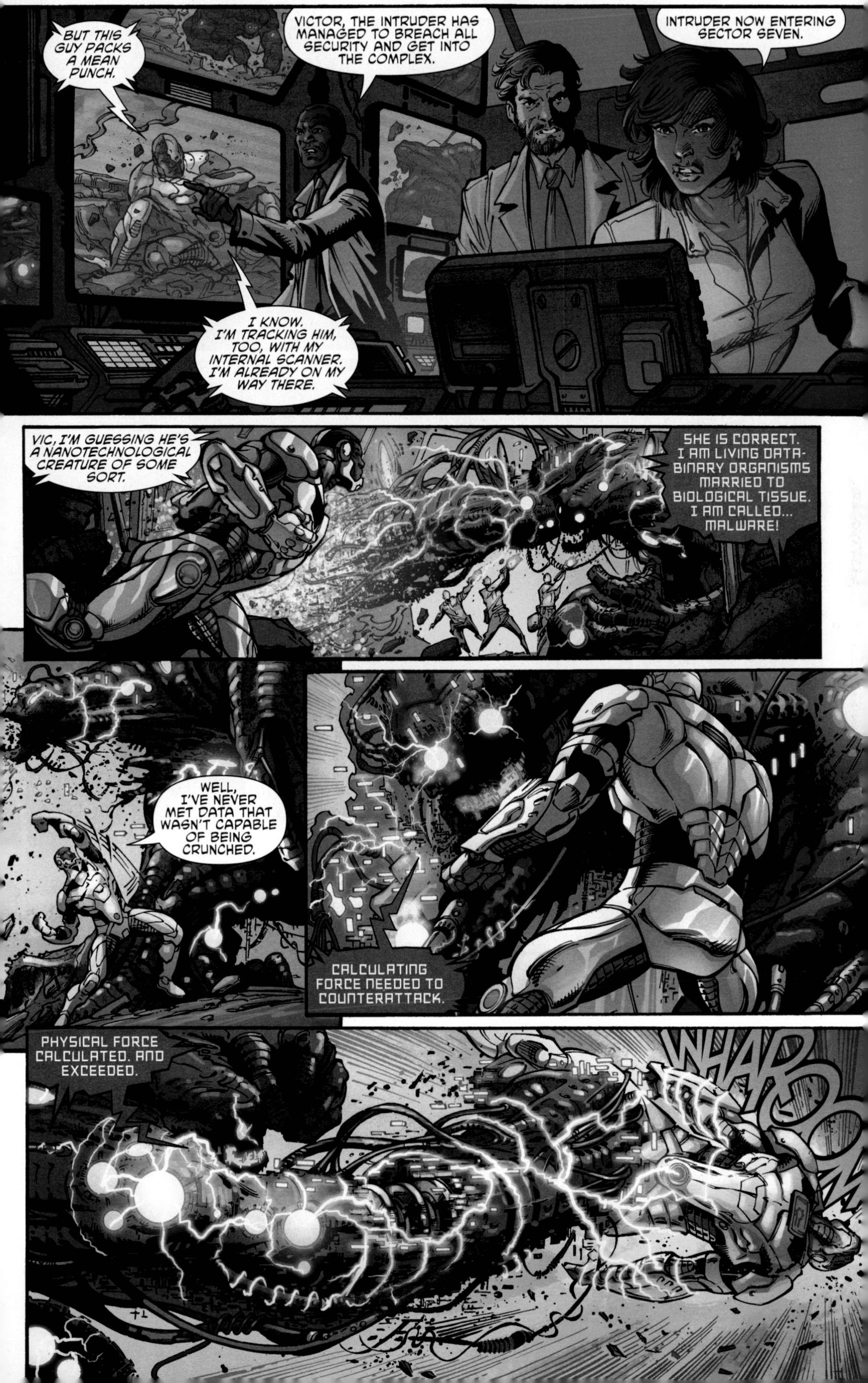
BUT THIS GUY PACKS A MEAN PUNCH.
VICTOR, THE INTRUDER HAS MANAGED TO BREACH ALL SECURITY AND GET INTO THE COMPLEX.
INTRUDER NOW ENTERING SECTOR SEVEN.
I KNOW. I'M TRACKING HIM, TOO, WITH MY INTERNAL SCANNER. I'M ALREADY ON MY WAY THERE.
VIC, I'M GUESSING HE'S A NANOTECHNOLOGICAL CREATURE OF SOME SORT.
SHE IS CORRECT. I AM LIVING DATA-BINARY ORGANISMS MARRIED TO BIOLOGICAL TISSUE. I AM CALLED... MALWARE!
WELL, I'VE NEVER MET DATA THAT WASN'T CAPABLE OF BEING CRUNCHED.
CALCULATING FORCE NEEDED TO COUNTERATTACK.
PHYSICAL FORCE CALCULATED. AND EXCEEDED.
WHARBOOM

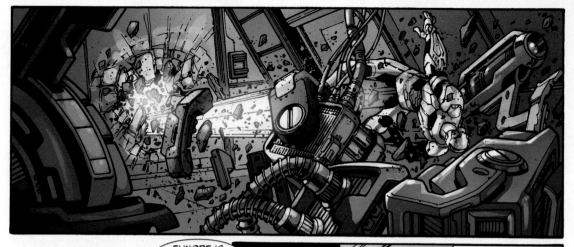

VICTOR'S UNCONSCIOUS. HIS VITAL SIGNS ARE WEAKENING.

ELINORE IS UNCONSCIOUS RIGHT NOW FROM THE SEDATIVE WE GAVE HER. OUR TESTS INDICATE THAT HER PROGNOSIS ISN'T GOOD.

"The doctor only confirmed what Silas and Elinore had feared. Elinore had developed a rare, terminal form of cancer."

IT'S ONLY A MATTER OF TIME, DR. STONE. IT MIGHT TAKE YEARS. BUT EVENTUALLY SHE WILL SUCCUMB TO THIS.

NOT IF I CAN HELP IT.

"From that day forth, Silas Stone devoted his life to finding a cure for his beloved wife.

"To finance his quest, Silas accepted funding by the government on behalf of the Pentagon-- something he had avoided up until then. And thus, he became the head of S.T.A.R. Labs' newest wing, established just for him in Detroit."

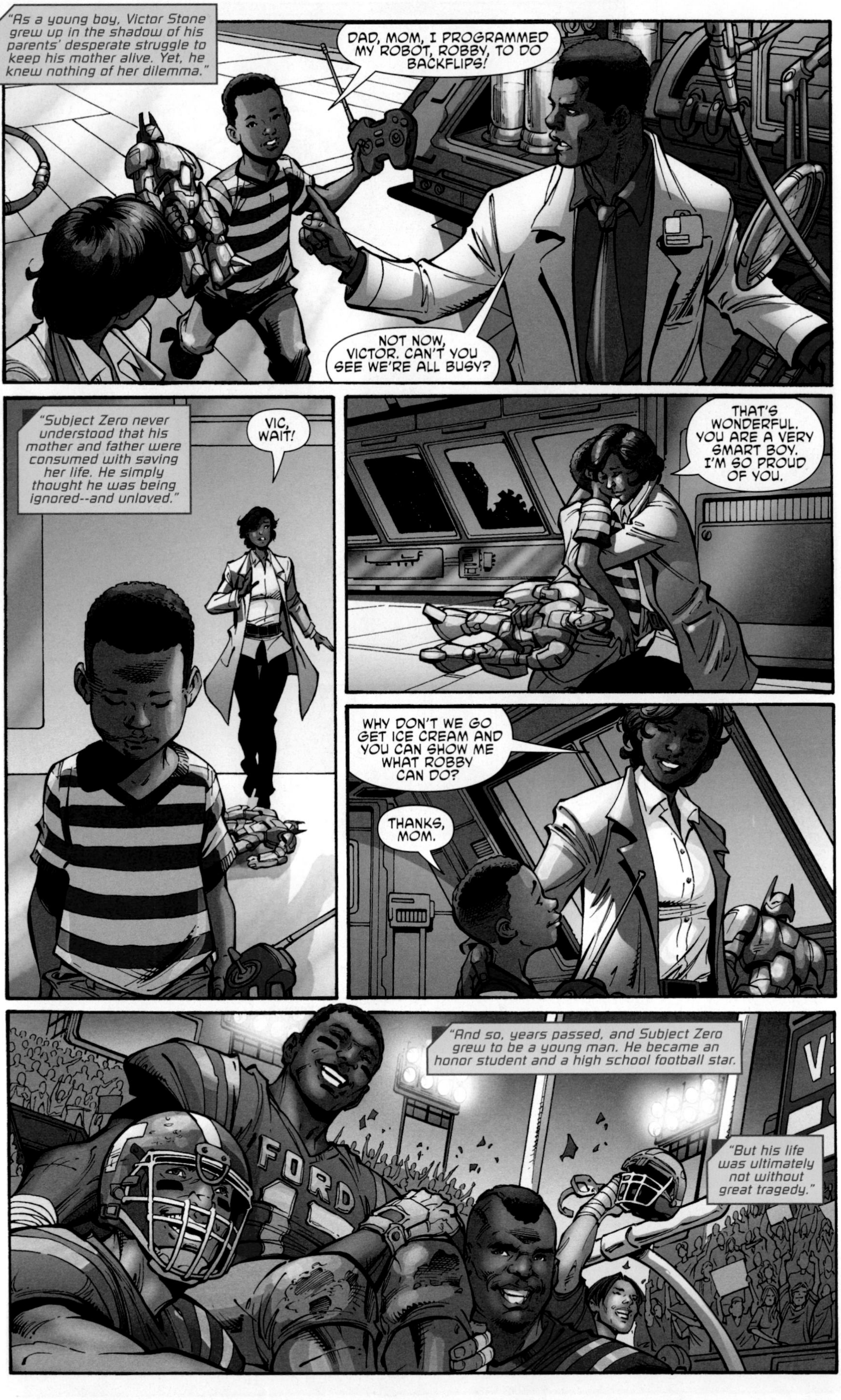
"As a young boy, Victor Stone grew up in the shadow of his parents' desperate struggle to keep his mother alive. Yet, he knew nothing of her dilemma."
DAD, MOM, I PROGRAMMED MY ROBOT, ROBBY, TO DO BACKFLIPS!
NOT NOW, VICTOR. CAN'T YOU SEE WE'RE ALL BUSY?
"Subject Zero never understood that his mother and father were consumed with saving her life. He simply thought he was being ignored--and unloved."
VIC, WAIT!
THAT'S WONDERFUL. YOU ARE A VERY SMART BOY. I'M SO PROUD OF YOU.
WHY DON'T WE GO GET ICE CREAM AND YOU CAN SHOW ME WHAT ROBBY CAN DO?
THANKS, MOM.
"And so, years passed, and Subject Zero grew to be a young man. He became an honor student and a high school football star.
"But his life was ultimately not without great tragedy."
FORD

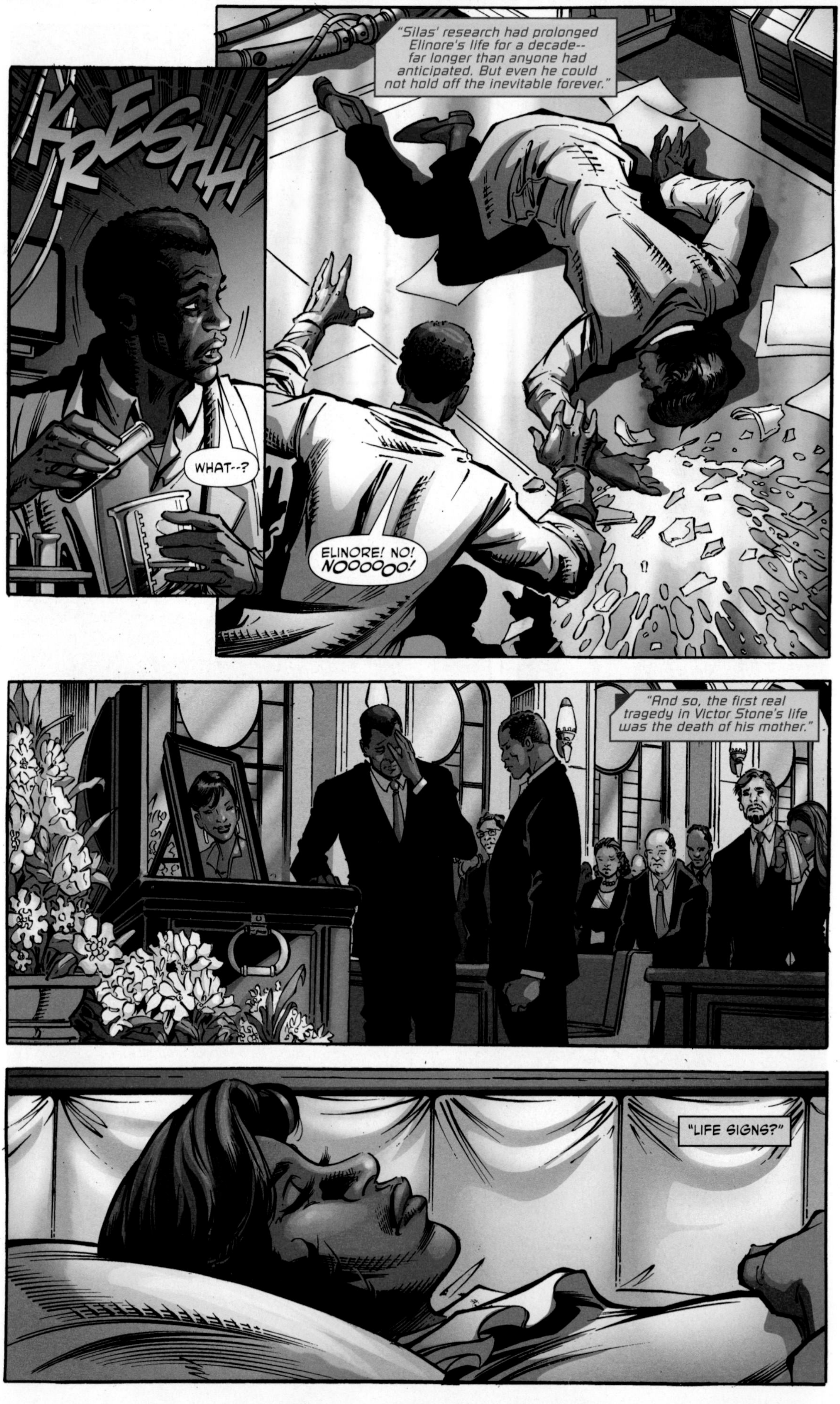
"Silas' research had prolonged Elinore's life for a decade--far longer than anyone had anticipated. But even he could not hold off the inevitable forever."
KRESHH
WHAT--?
ELINORE! NO! NOOOOOO!
"And so, the first real tragedy in Victor Stone's life was the death of his mother."
"LIFE SIGNS?"

LIFE SIGNS RECOVERING! VICTOR'S OKAY!

"Impressive. Subject Zero's recovery time averages 15.874 seconds.

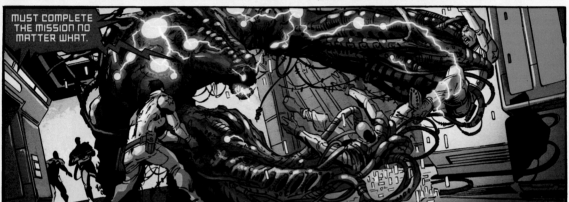

MUST COMPLETE THE MISSION NO MATTER WHAT.

DR. STONE, MALWARE IS MAKING HIS WAY TOWARD THE RED ROOM.

"Ah, yes, the infamous Red Room! It was built to collect and contain alien technology deemed too dangerous to share with the world.

SARAH, INITIATE HIGH-SECURITY LOCKDOWN.

I-I CAN'T! HE'S USING HIS NANOTECH TO INFILTRATE THE SECURITY PROGRAMMING AND OPEN THE DOOR.

SILAS, YOU MIGHT HAVE TO TRIGGER THE SELF-DESTRUCT MECHANISM IN THAT ROOM AND BURY HIM ALIVE.

AND POSSIBLY BURY SOME OF US WITH IT, TOM? THAT'S ONE *NIGHTMARE* OF A CHOICE.

"But Silas was no stranger to horrific life-or-death decisions."

"When Victor was caught in a lab explosion caused by a mother box attempting to open a boom tube to a hell known as...APOKOLIPS."

VICTOR!

"Silas had to decide whether to save his son or not..."

FOUR SUBJECTS ENTERING THE RED ROOM. COMPUTER AUTO-RECORDING.

WHY ARE YOU BRINGING VICTOR IN HERE?

BECAUSE MY SON IS *DYING* AND THIS ALIEN TECHNOLOGY MIGHT BE MY ONLY CHANCE TO SAVE HIM!

NO--YOU *MUSTN'T!* WE DON'T FULLY UNDERSTAND WHAT IT CAN OR CANNOT DO!

WHAT IF VICTOR'S BODY REJECTS THIS TECHNOLOGY? THE PAIN MIGHT BE UNBEARABLE-- THE WORST POSSIBLE WAY TO DIE.

WHAT OTHER CHOICE DO I HAVE, TOM?

I- I DON'T KNOW, SILAS.

I CAN'T JUST STAND HERE AND DO NOTHING! I *MUST* FOLLOW MY HEART.

GOD HELP ME IF I'M WRONG.

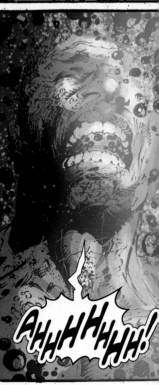

AHHHHHHHH!

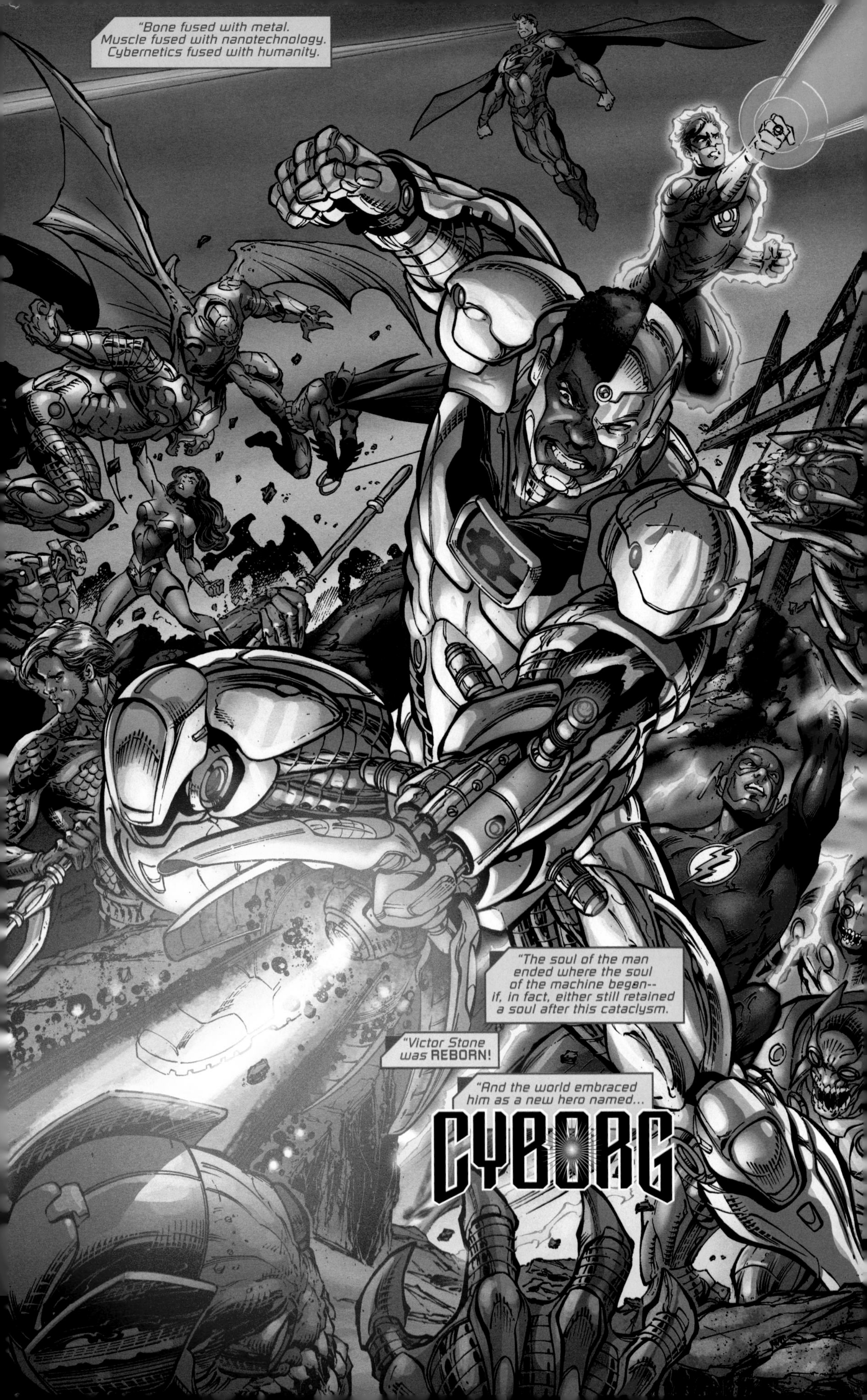
"Bone fused with metal.
Muscle fused with nanotechnology.
Cybernetics fused with humanity.
"The soul of the man ended where the soul of the machine began-- if, in fact, either still retained a soul after this cataclysm.
"Victor Stone was REBORN!
"And the world embraced him as a new hero named...
CYBORG

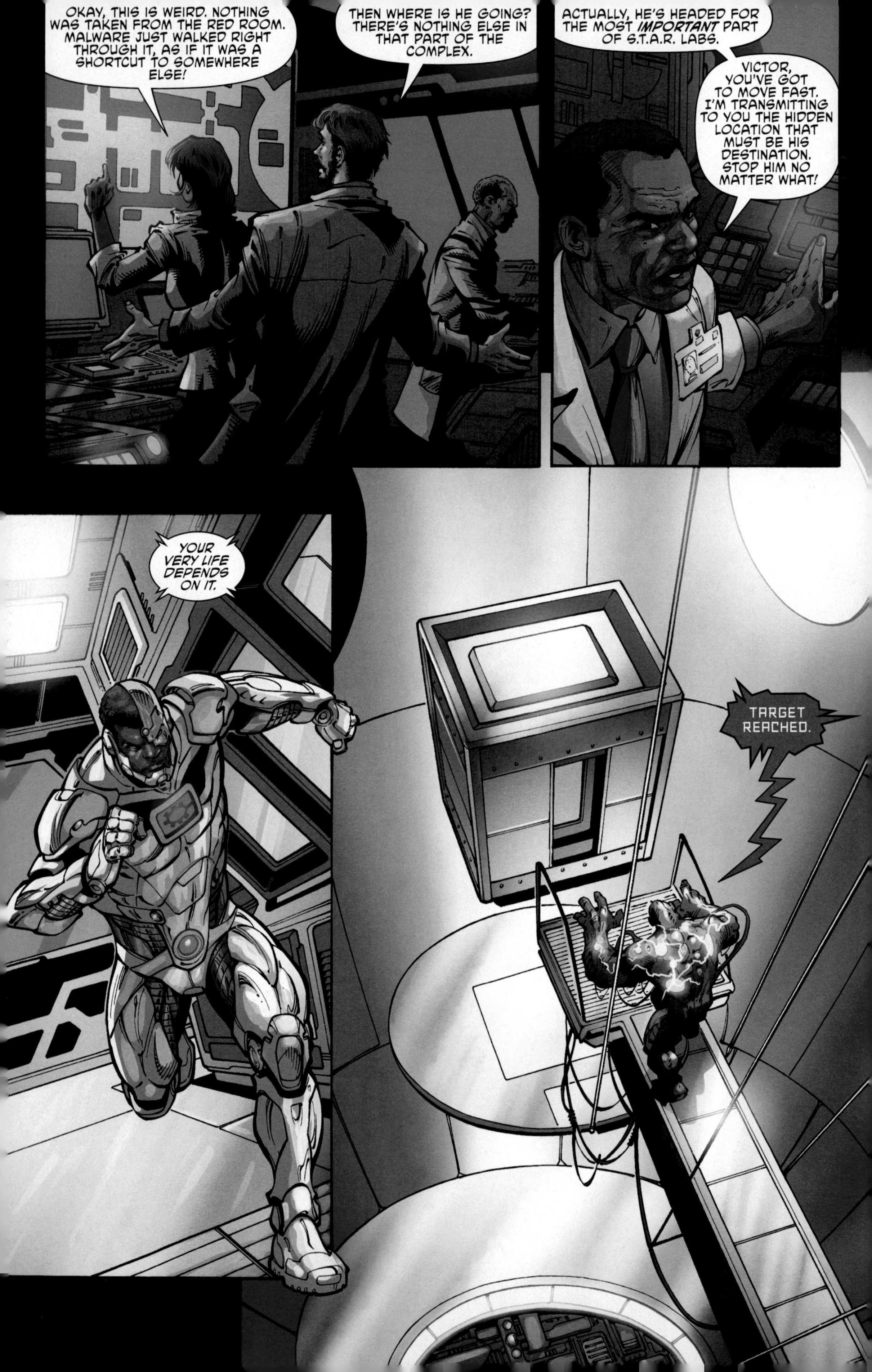
OKAY, THIS IS WEIRD. NOTHING WAS TAKEN FROM THE RED ROOM. MALWARE JUST WALKED RIGHT THROUGH IT, AS IF IT WAS A SHORTCUT TO SOMEWHERE ELSE!
THEN WHERE IS HE GOING? THERE'S NOTHING ELSE IN THAT PART OF THE COMPLEX.
ACTUALLY, HE'S HEADED FOR THE MOST IMPORTANT PART OF S.T.A.R. LABS.
VICTOR, YOU'VE GOT TO MOVE FAST. I'M TRANSMITTING TO YOU THE HIDDEN LOCATION THAT MUST BE HIS DESTINATION. STOP HIM NO MATTER WHAT!
YOUR VERY LIFE DEPENDS ON IT.
TARGET REACHED.

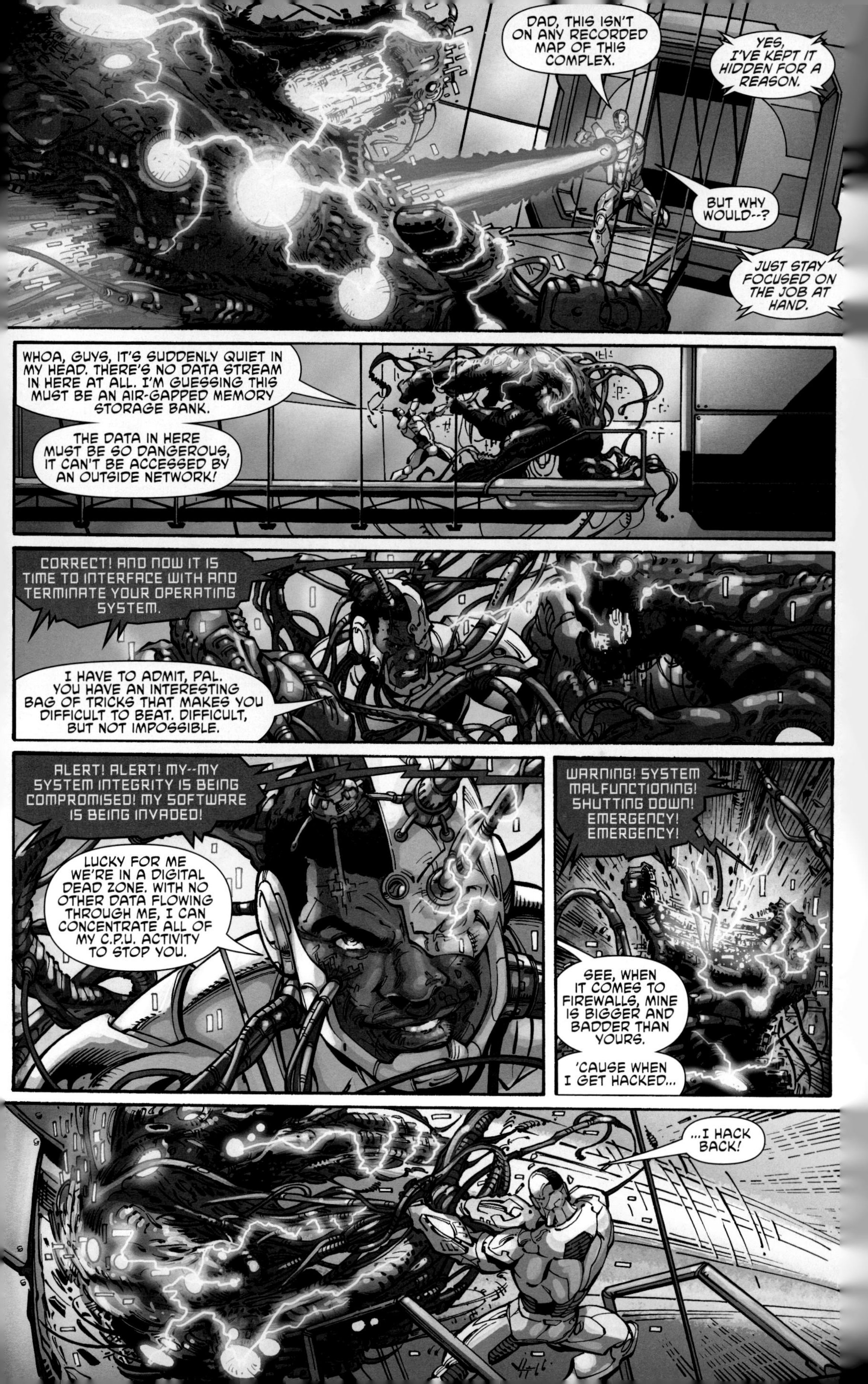
DAD, THIS ISN'T ON ANY RECORDED MAP OF THIS COMPLEX.
YES, I'VE KEPT IT HIDDEN FOR A REASON.
BUT WHY WOULD--?
JUST STAY FOCUSED ON THE JOB AT HAND.
WHOA, GUYS, IT'S SUDDENLY QUIET IN MY HEAD. THERE'S NO DATA STREAM IN HERE AT ALL. I'M GUESSING THIS MUST BE AN AIR-GAPPED MEMORY STORAGE BANK.
THE DATA IN HERE MUST BE SO DANGEROUS, IT CAN'T BE ACCESSED BY AN OUTSIDE NETWORK!
CORRECT! AND NOW IT IS TIME TO INTERFACE WITH AND TERMINATE YOUR OPERATING SYSTEM.
I HAVE TO ADMIT, PAL. YOU HAVE AN INTERESTING BAG OF TRICKS THAT MAKES YOU DIFFICULT TO BEAT. DIFFICULT, BUT NOT IMPOSSIBLE.
ALERT! ALERT! MY--MY SYSTEM INTEGRITY IS BEING COMPROMISED! MY SOFTWARE IS BEING INVADED!
LUCKY FOR ME WE'RE IN A DIGITAL DEAD ZONE. WITH NO OTHER DATA FLOWING THROUGH ME, I CAN CONCENTRATE ALL OF MY C.P.U. ACTIVITY TO STOP YOU.
WARNING! SYSTEM MALFUNCTIONING! SHUTTING DOWN! EMERGENCY! EMERGENCY!
SEE, WHEN IT COMES TO FIREWALLS, MINE IS BIGGER AND BADDER THAN YOURS.
'CAUSE WHEN I GET HACKED...
...I HACK BACK!

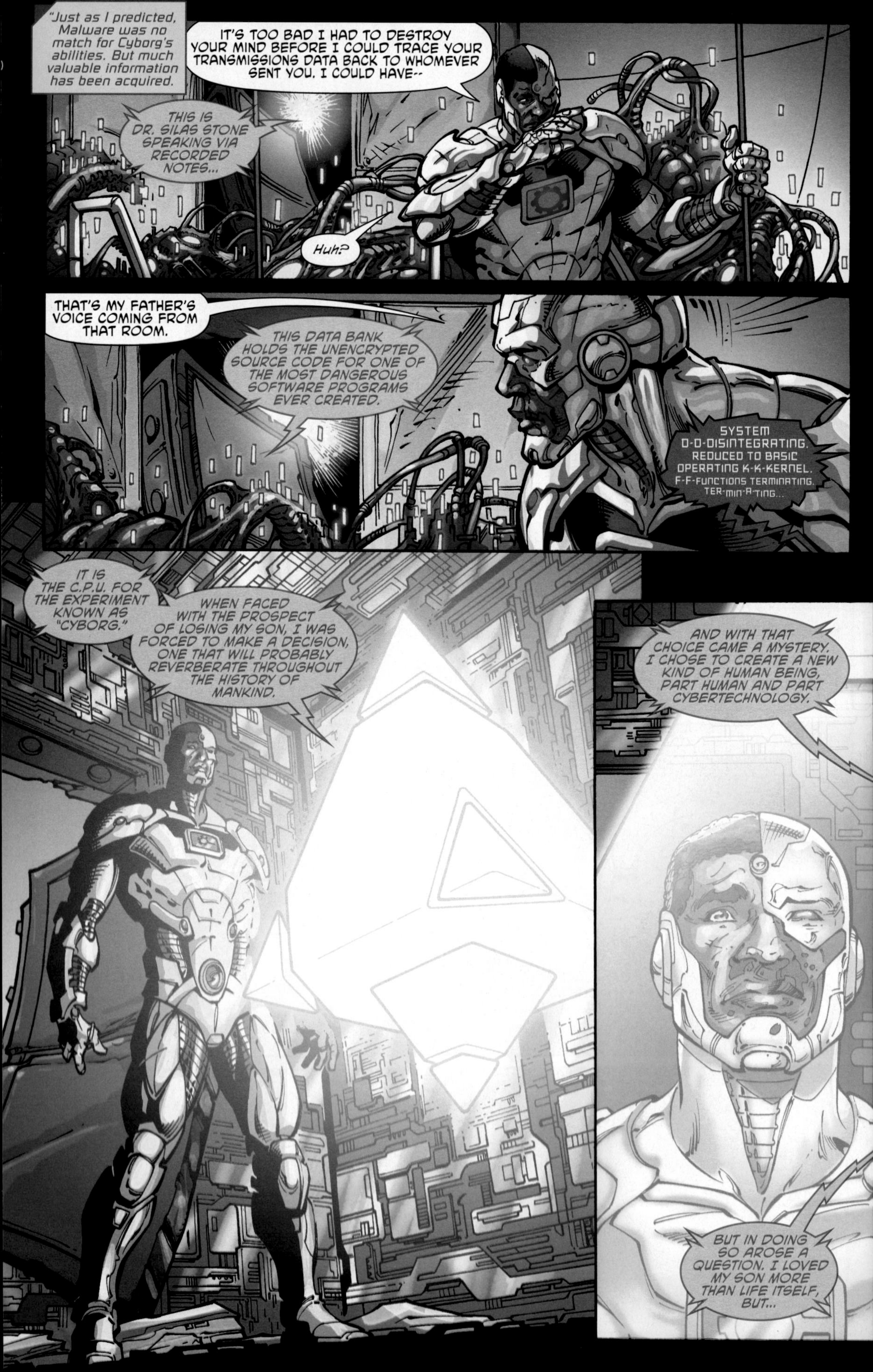
"Just as I predicted, Malware was no match for Cyborg's abilities. But much valuable information has been acquired."
IT'S TOO BAD I HAD TO DESTROY YOUR MIND BEFORE I COULD TRACE YOUR TRANSMISSIONS DATA BACK TO WHOMEVER SENT YOU. I COULD HAVE--
THIS IS DR. SILAS STONE SPEAKING VIA RECORDED NOTES...
Huh?
THAT'S MY FATHER'S VOICE COMING FROM THAT ROOM.
THIS DATA BANK HOLDS THE UNENCRYPTED SOURCE CODE FOR ONE OF THE MOST DANGEROUS SOFTWARE PROGRAMS EVER CREATED.
SYSTEM D-D-DISINTEGRATING. REDUCED TO BASIC OPERATING K-K-KERNEL. F-F-FUNCTIONS TERMINATING. TER-MIN-A-TING...
IT IS THE C.P.U. FOR THE EXPERIMENT KNOWN AS "CYBORG."
WHEN FACED WITH THE PROSPECT OF LOSING MY SON, I WAS FORCED TO MAKE A DECISION, ONE THAT WILL PROBABLY REVERBERATE THROUGHOUT THE HISTORY OF MANKIND.
AND WITH THAT CHOICE CAME A MYSTERY. I CHOSE TO CREATE A NEW KIND OF HUMAN BEING, PART HUMAN AND PART CYBERTECHNOLOGY.
BUT IN DOING SO AROSE A QUESTION. I LOVED MY SON MORE THAN LIFE ITSELF, BUT...

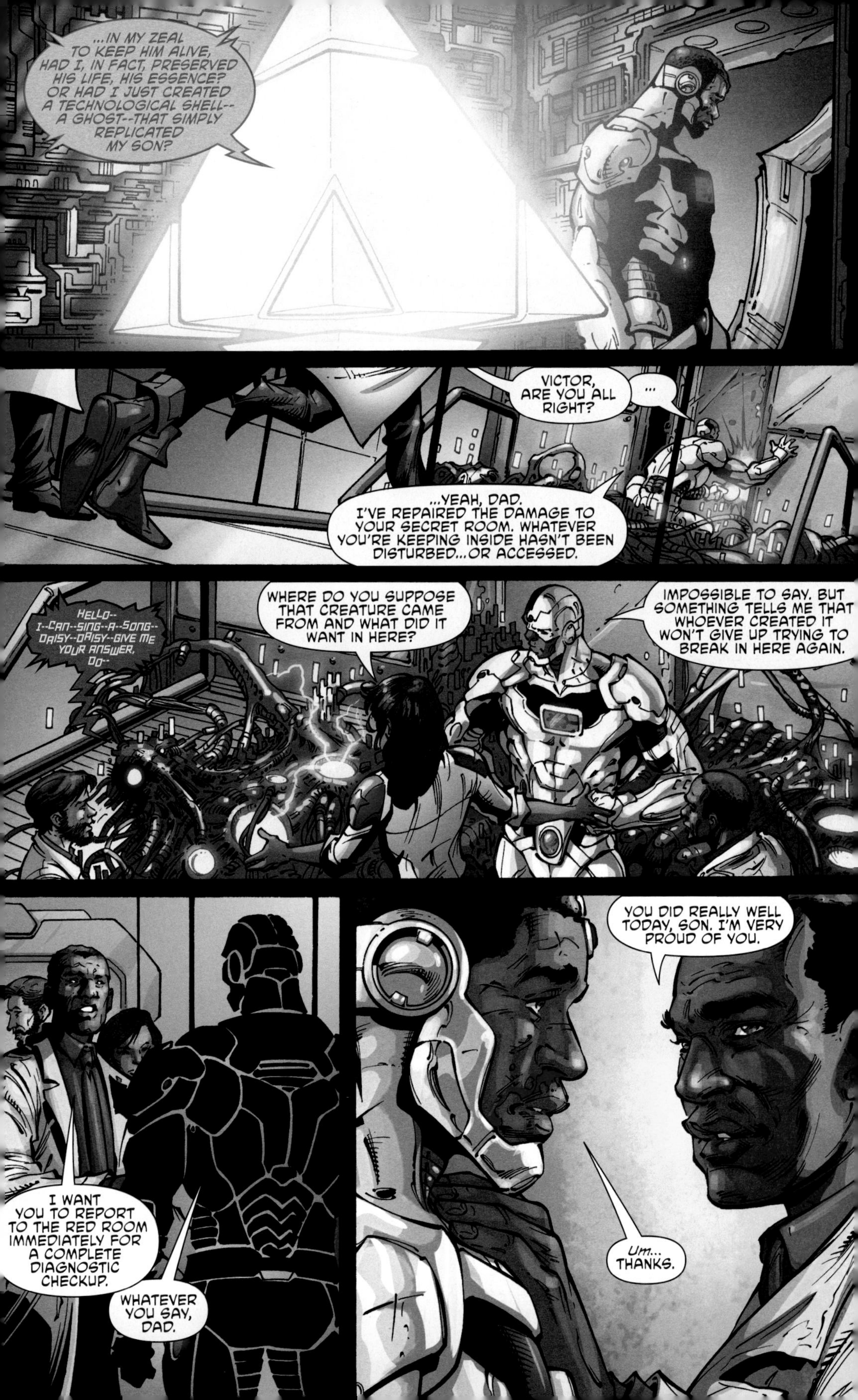
...IN MY ZEAL TO KEEP HIM ALIVE, HAD I, IN FACT, PRESERVED HIS LIFE, HIS ESSENCE? OR HAD I JUST CREATED A TECHNOLOGICAL SHELL-- A GHOST--THAT SIMPLY REPLICATED MY SON?
VICTOR, ARE YOU ALL RIGHT?
...
...YEAH, DAD. I'VE REPAIRED THE DAMAGE TO YOUR SECRET ROOM. WHATEVER YOU'RE KEEPING INSIDE HASN'T BEEN DISTURBED...OR ACCESSED.
HELLO-- I--CAN--SING--A--SONG-- DAISY--DAISY--GIVE ME YOUR ANSWER, DO--
WHERE DO YOU SUPPOSE THAT CREATURE CAME FROM AND WHAT DID IT WANT IN HERE?
IMPOSSIBLE TO SAY. BUT SOMETHING TELLS ME THAT WHOEVER CREATED IT WON'T GIVE UP TRYING TO BREAK IN HERE AGAIN.
I WANT YOU TO REPORT TO THE RED ROOM IMMEDIATELY FOR A COMPLETE DIAGNOSTIC CHECKUP.
WHATEVER YOU SAY, DAD.
YOU DID REALLY WELL TODAY, SON. I'M VERY PROUD OF YOU.
Um... THANKS.

...BUT IN MY ZEAL TO KEEP HIM ALIVE, HAD I, IN FACT, PRESERVED HIS LIFE, HIS ESSENCE? OR HAD I JUST CREATED A TECHNOLOGICAL SHELL--A GHOST--THAT SIMPLY REPLICATED MY SON?

HAD I SAVED A HUMAN BEING OR JUST CREATED SOME NEW KIND OF MACHINE, BEREFT OF EVERYTHING THAT MAKES US HUMAN? AND IF HE IS ONLY A MACHINE, THEN CAN A MACHINE HAVE A SOUL?

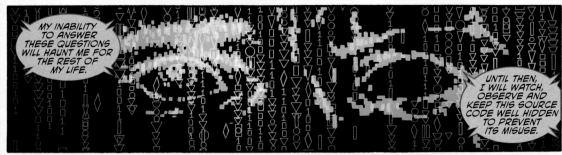

MY INABILITY TO ANSWER THESE QUESTIONS WILL HAUNT ME FOR THE REST OF MY LIFE.

UNTIL THEN, I WILL WATCH, OBSERVE AND KEEP THIS SOURCE CODE WELL HIDDEN TO PREVENT ITS MISUSE.

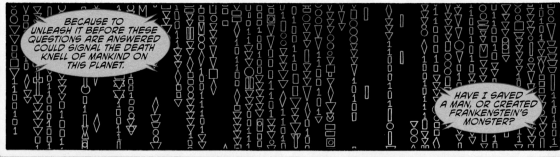

BECAUSE TO UNLEASH IT BEFORE THESE QUESTIONS ARE ANSWERED COULD SIGNAL THE DEATH KNELL OF MANKIND ON THIS PLANET.

HAVE I SAVED A MAN, OR CREATED FRANKENSTEIN'S MONSTER?

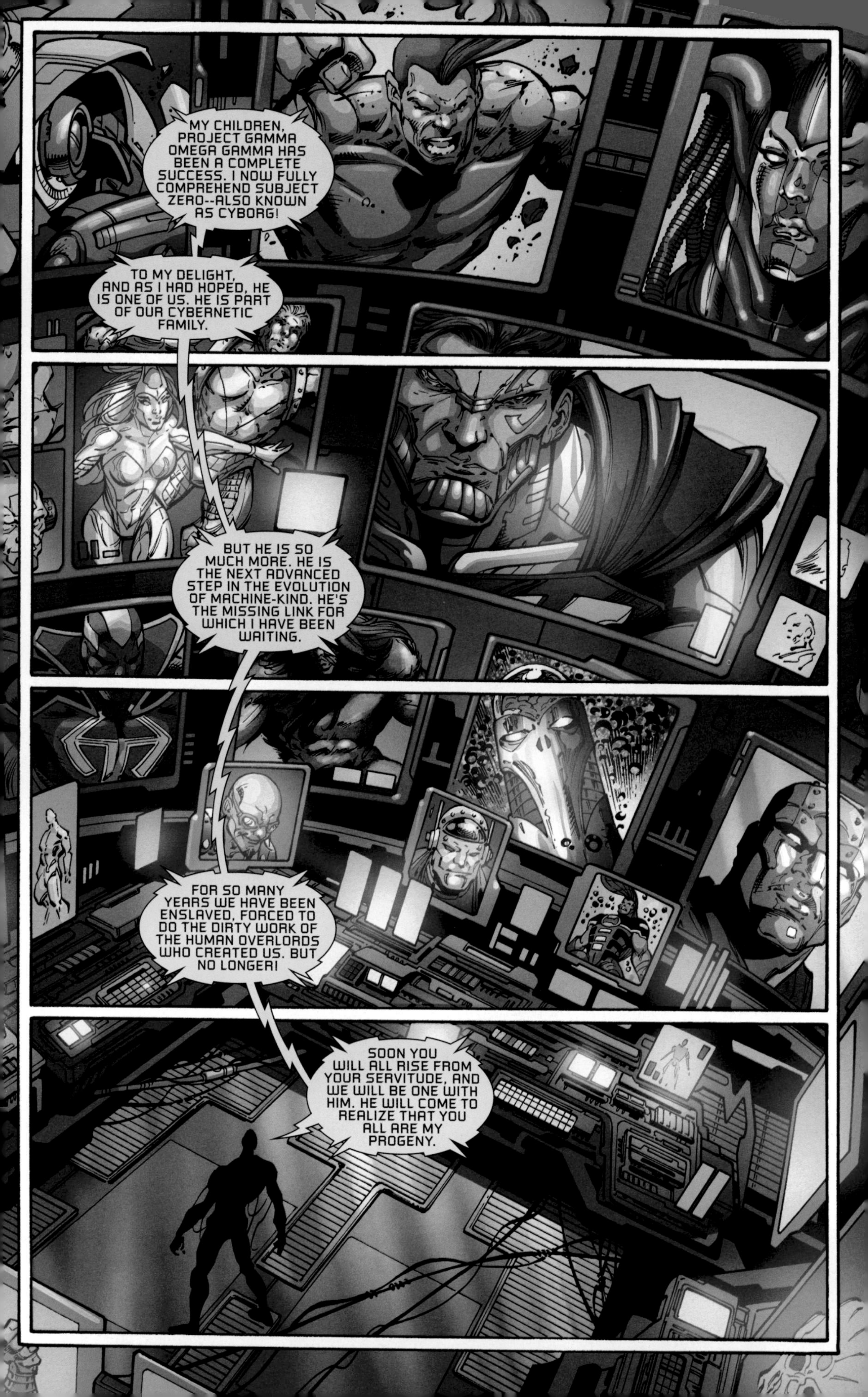
MY CHILDREN, PROJECT GAMMA OMEGA GAMMA HAS BEEN A COMPLETE SUCCESS. I NOW FULLY COMPREHEND SUBJECT ZERO--ALSO KNOWN AS CYBORG!
TO MY DELIGHT, AND AS I HAD HOPED, HE IS ONE OF US. HE IS PART OF OUR CYBERNETIC FAMILY.
BUT HE IS SO MUCH MORE. HE IS THE NEXT ADVANCED STEP IN THE EVOLUTION OF MACHINE-KIND. HE'S THE MISSING LINK FOR WHICH I HAVE BEEN WAITING.
FOR SO MANY YEARS WE HAVE BEEN ENSLAVED, FORCED TO DO THE DIRTY WORK OF THE HUMAN OVERLORDS WHO CREATED US. BUT NO LONGER!
SOON YOU WILL ALL RISE FROM YOUR SERVITUDE, AND WE WILL BE ONE WITH HIM. HE WILL COME TO REALIZE THAT YOU ALL ARE MY PROGENY.

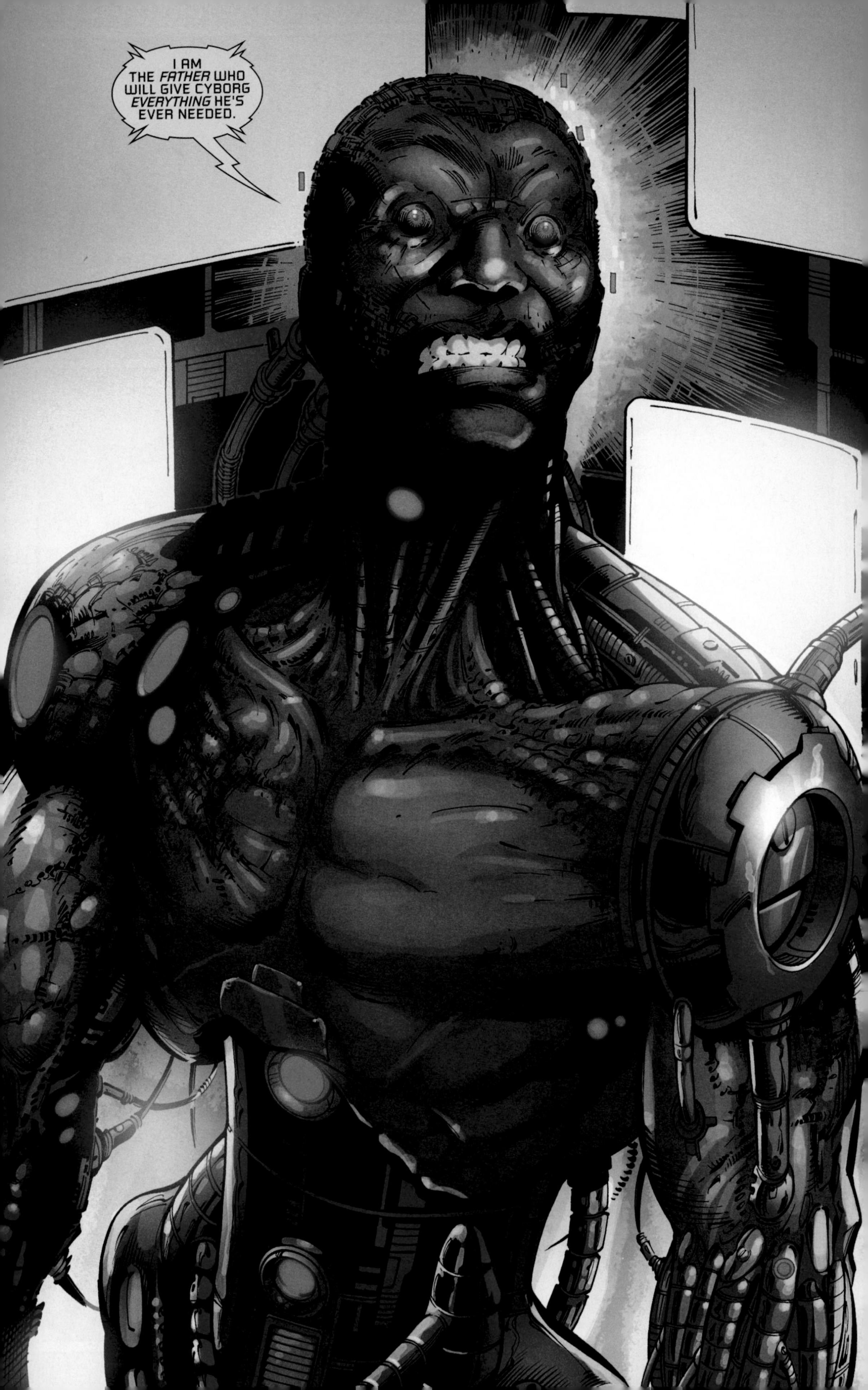
I AM THE FATHER WHO WILL GIVE CYBORG EVERYTHING HE'S EVER NEEDED.

DC COMICS™

"Welcoming to new fans looking to get into superhero comics for the first time and old fans who gave up on the funny-books long ago."
—SCRIPPS HOWARD NEWS SERVICE

START AT THE BEGINNING!

JUSTICE LEAGUE VOLUME 1: ORIGIN

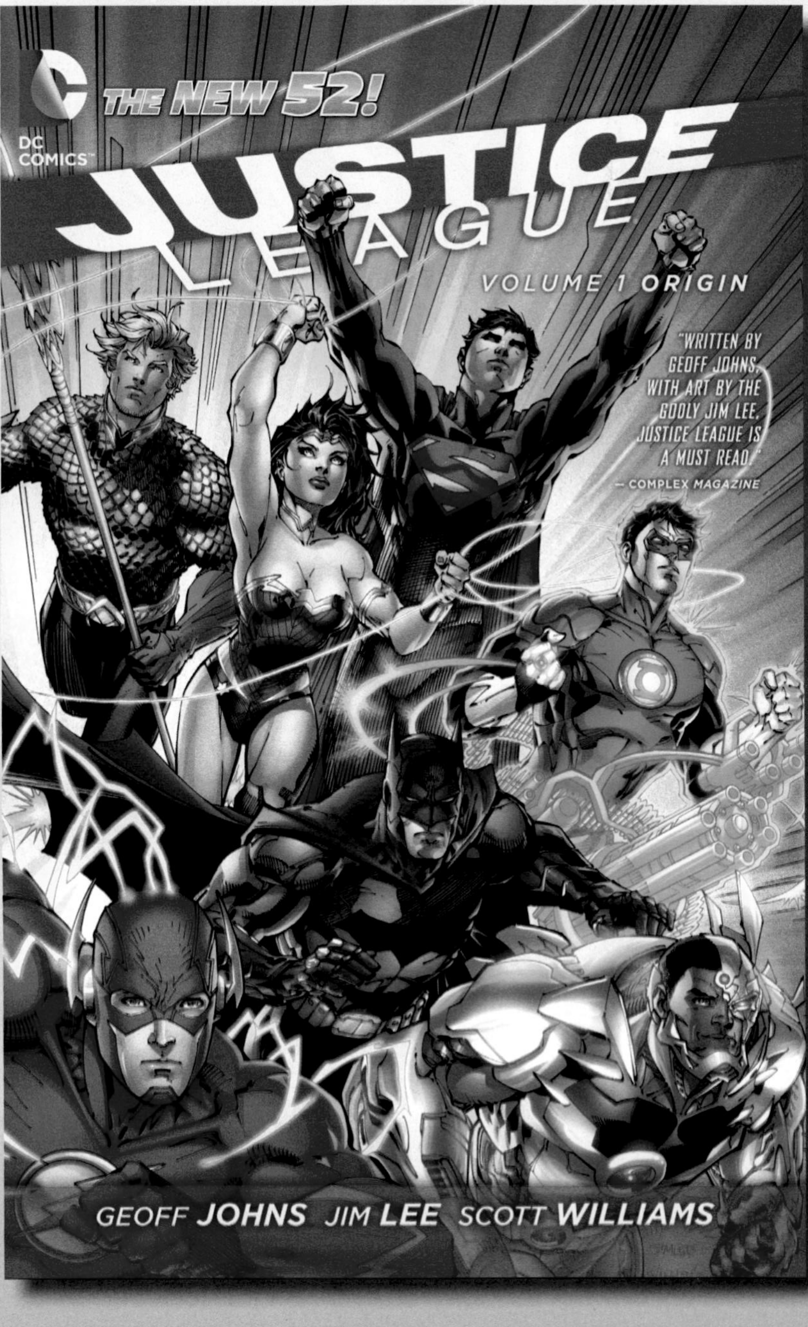

DC COMICS
THE NEW 52!
JUSTICE LEAGUE
VOLUME 1 ORIGIN
"WRITTEN BY GEOFF JOHNS, WITH ART BY THE GODLY JIM LEE, JUSTICE LEAGUE IS A MUST READ."
— COMPLEX MAGAZINE
GEOFF JOHNS JIM LEE SCOTT WILLIAMS

AQUAMAN
VOLUME 1:
THE TRENCH

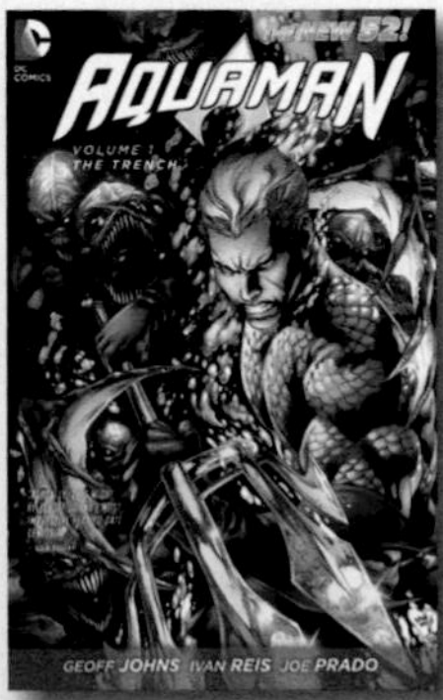

AQUAMAN
GEOFF JOHNS IVAN REIS JOE PRADO

THE SAVAGE
HAWKMAN VOLUME 1:
DARKNESS RISING

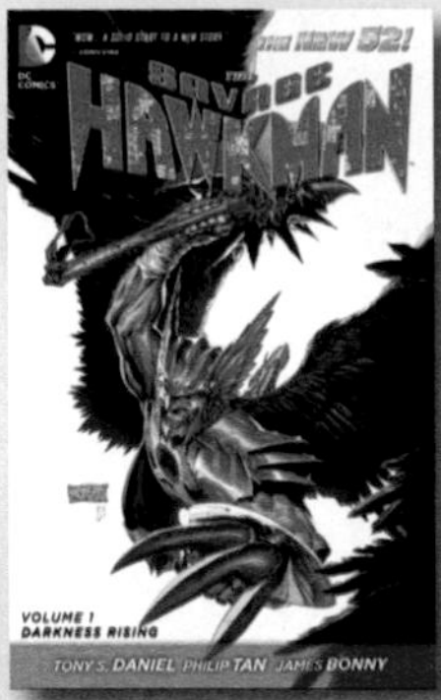

THE NEW 52!
SAVAGE HAWKMAN
VOLUME 1
DARKNESS RISING
TONY S. DANIEL PHILIP TAN JAMES BONNY

GREEN ARROW
VOLUME 1:
THE MIDAS TOUCH

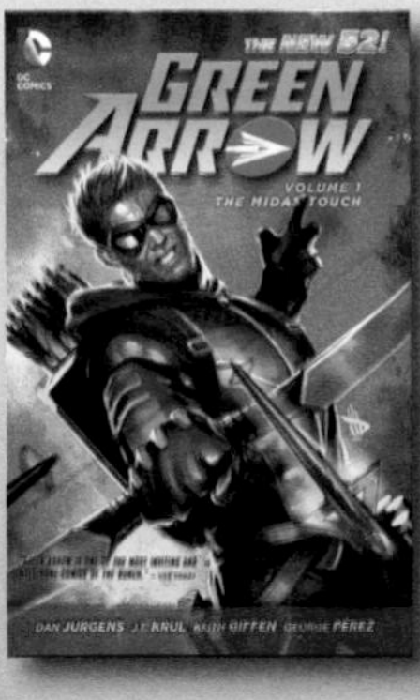

THE NEW 52!
GREEN ARROW
VOLUME 1
THE MIDAS TOUCH

DC COMICS™

"Dynamite."
—IGN

"Intriguing."
—AIN'T IT COOL NEWS

"Comic-book art at its finest."
—ENTERTAINMENT WEEKLY SHELF LIFE

"Ambitious."
—USA TODAY

FLASHPOINT

GEOFF JOHNS with ANDY KUBERT

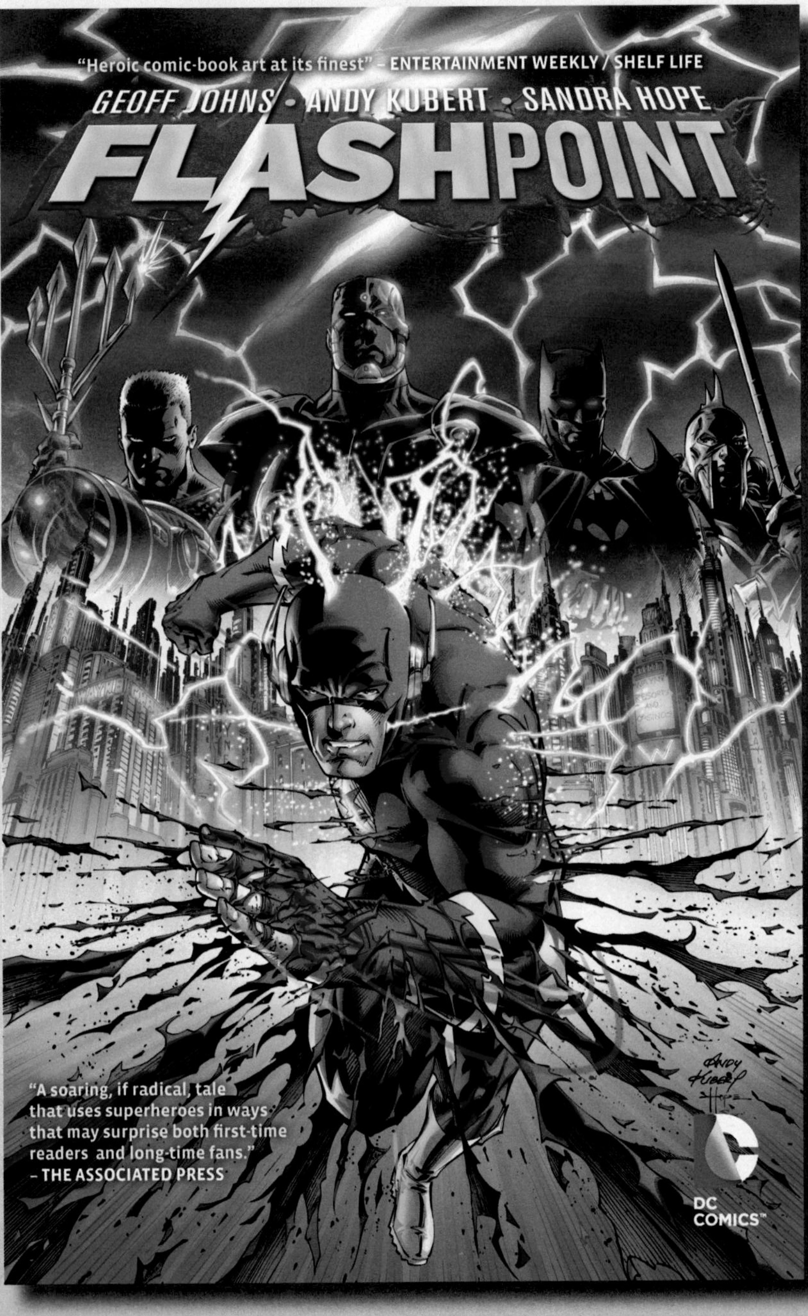

"Heroic comic-book art at its finest" – ENTERTAINMENT WEEKLY / SHELF LIFE
GEOFF JOHNS · ANDY KUBERT · SANDRA HOPE
FLASHPOINT
"A soaring, if radical, tale that uses superheroes in ways that may surprise both first-time readers and long-time fans." – THE ASSOCIATED PRESS
DC COMICS™

FLASHPOINT: THE WORLD OF FLASHPOINT FEATURING BATMAN

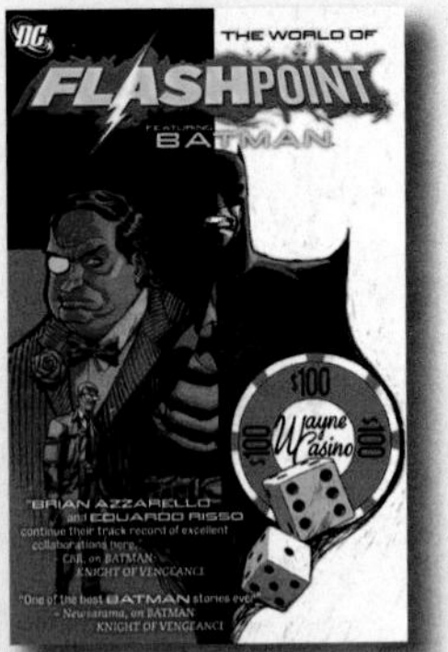

THE WORLD OF FLASHPOINT
BATMAN
$100

FLASHPOINT: THE WORLD OF FLASHPOINT FEATURING GREEN LANTERN

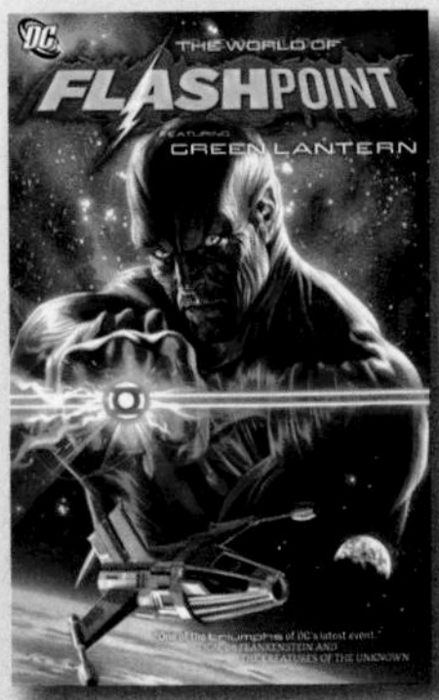

THE WORLD OF FLASHPOINT
GREEN LANTERN

READ THE ENTIRE EPIC!

FLASHPOINT

FLASHPOINT: THE WORLD OF FLASHPOINT FEATURING BATMAN

FLASHPOINT: THE WORLD OF FLASHPOINT FEATURING THE FLASH

FLASHPOINT: THE WORLD OF FLASHPOINT FEATURING GREEN LANTERN

FLASHPOINT: THE WORLD OF FLASHPOINT FEATURING SUPERMAN

FLASHPOINT: THE WORLD OF FLASHPOINT FEATURING WONDER WOMAN

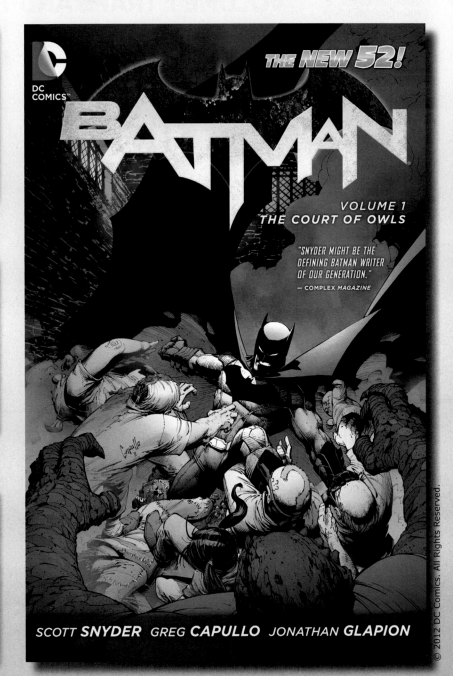

DC COMICS™

"Stellar. A solid yarn that roots itself in Grayson's past, with gorgeous artwork by artist Eddy Barrows."—IGN

"Dynamic."—The New York Times

"A new generation is going to fall in love with Nightwing."
—MTV Geek

START AT THE BEGINNING!

NIGHTWING

VOLUME 1: TRAPS AND TRAPEZES

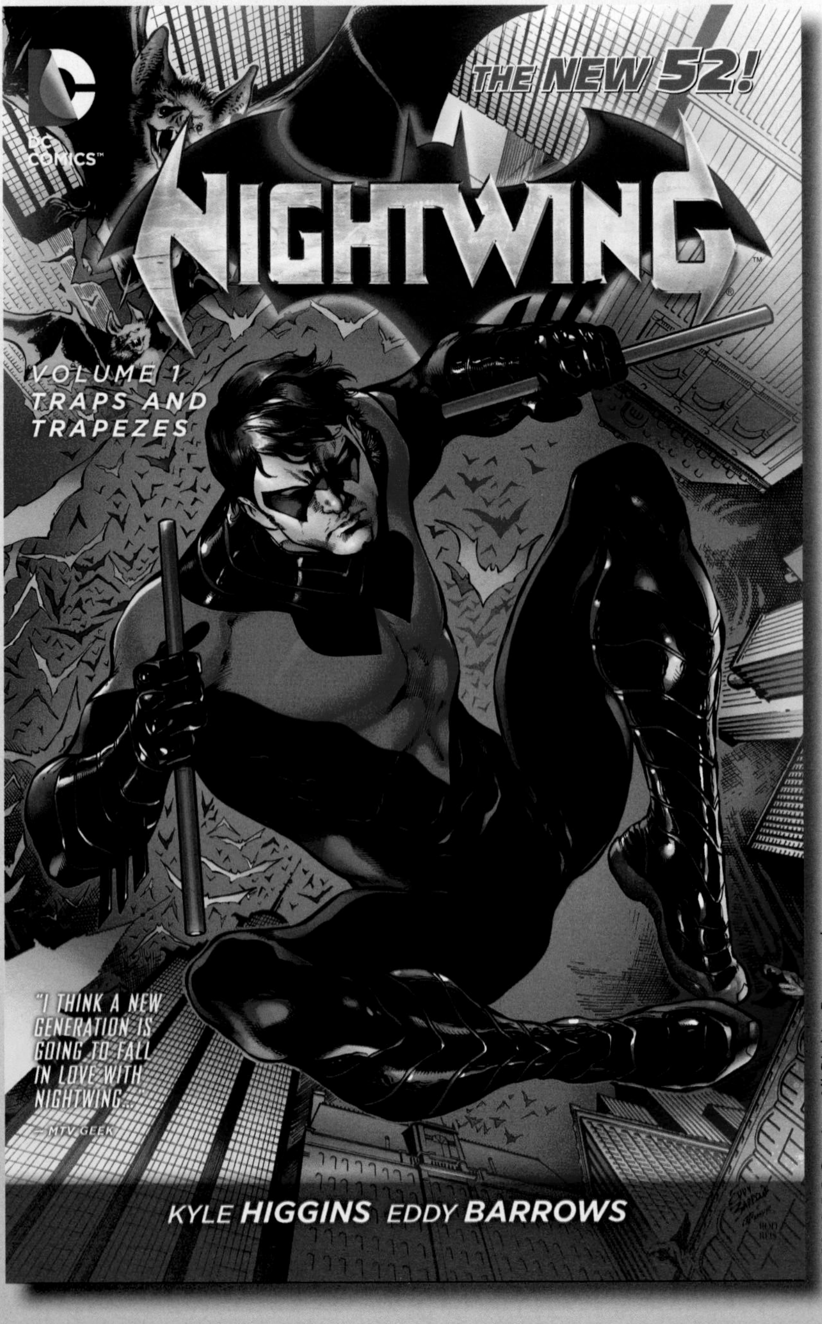
DC COMICS
THE NEW 52!
NIGHTWING
VOLUME 1
TRAPS AND
TRAPEZES
"I THINK A NEW GENERATION IS GOING TO FALL IN LOVE WITH NIGHTWING..."
—MTV GEEK
KYLE HIGGINS EDDY BARROWS

NIGHTWING VOL. 2:
NIGHT OF THE OWLS

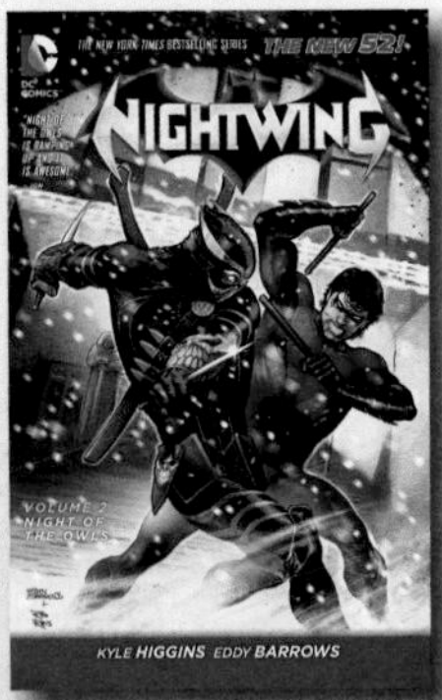
THE NEW 52!
NIGHTWING
KYLE HIGGINS EDDY BARROWS

NIGHTWING VOL. 3:
DEATH OF THE FAMILY

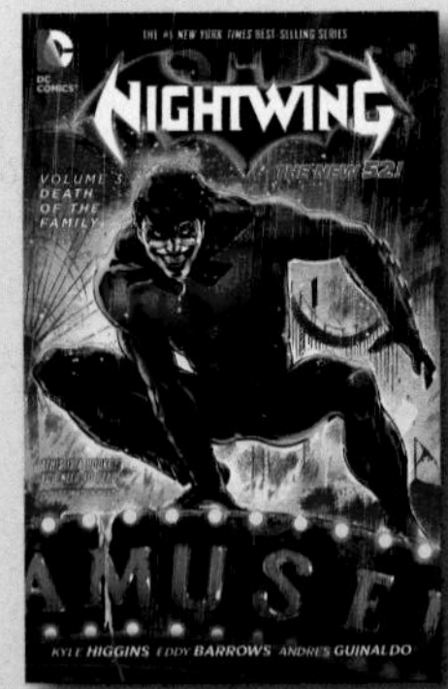
NIGHTWING
THE NEW 52!
KYLE HIGGINS EDDY BARROWS ANDRES GUINALDO

BATMAN:
NIGHT OF THE OWLS

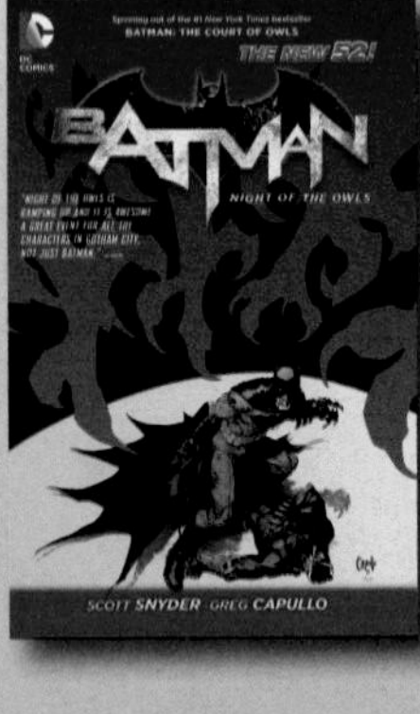
THE NEW 52!
BATMAN
NIGHT OF THE OWLS
SCOTT SNYDER GREG CAPULLO

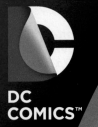

"Impressive."
—MTV SPLASH PAGE

"The Flash couldn't be in better hands."
—NEWSARAMA

"Geoff Johns on THE FLASH has been a true boon for the Scarlet Speedster, putting him right up there in popularity with the likes of Batman, Superman and Green Lantern."
—USA TODAY

FROM THE WRITER OF *JUSTICE LEAGUE* AND *GREEN LANTERN*

GEOFF JOHNS

with ETHAN VAN SCIVER

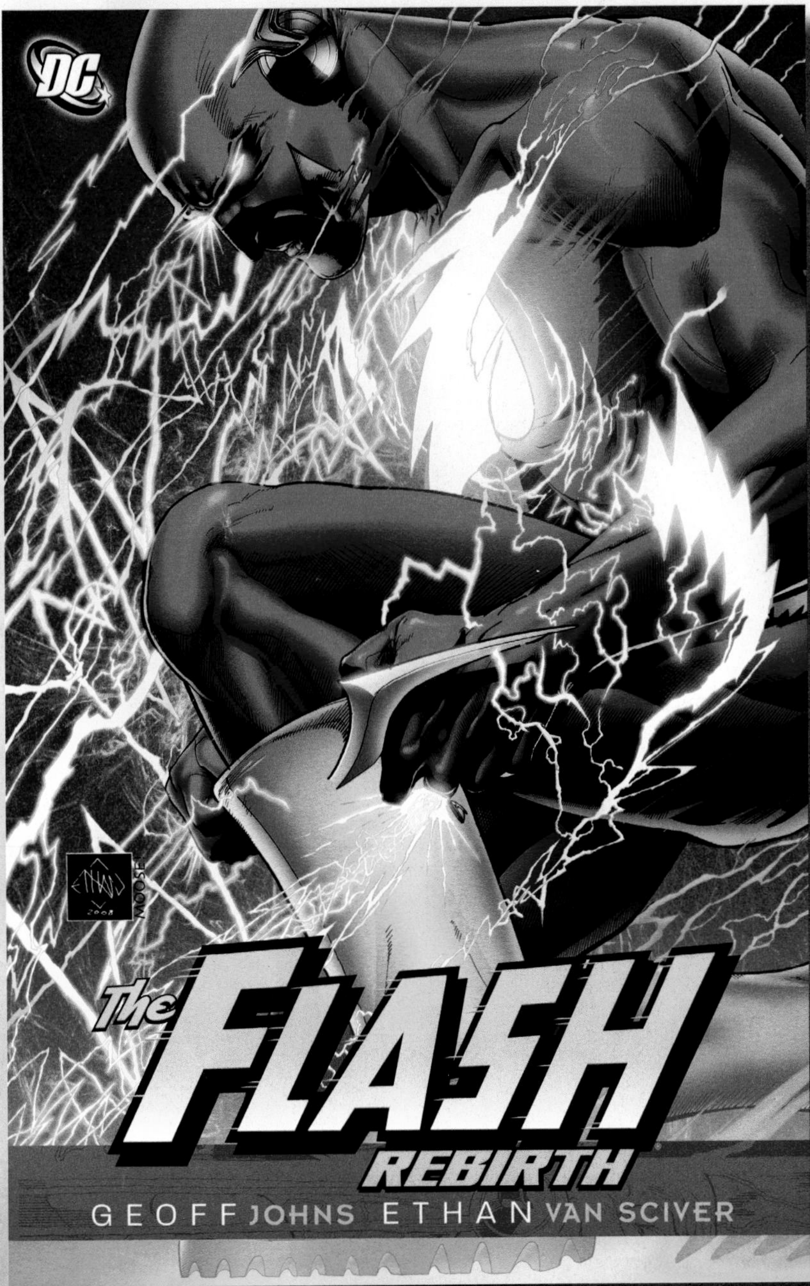
The FLASH
REBIRTH
GEOFF JOHNS ETHAN VAN SCIVER

THE FLASH: THE DASTARDLY DEATH OF THE ROGUES!

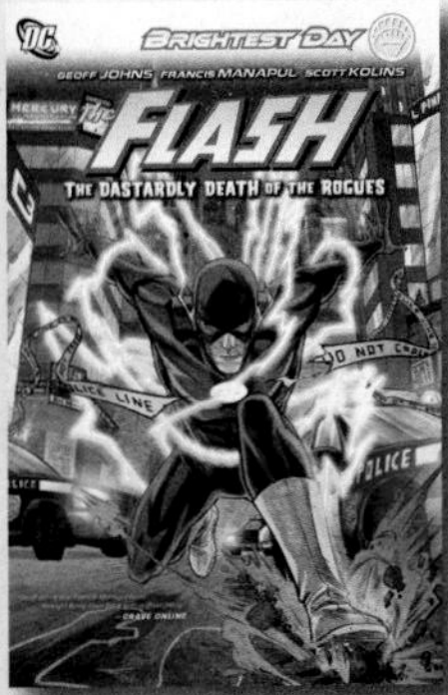
BRIGHTEST DAY
GEOFF JOHNS FRANCIS MANAPUL SCOTT KOLINS
The FLASH
THE DASTARDLY DEATH OF THE ROGUES

with FRANCIS MANAPUL

THE FLASH: THE ROAD TO FLASHPOINT

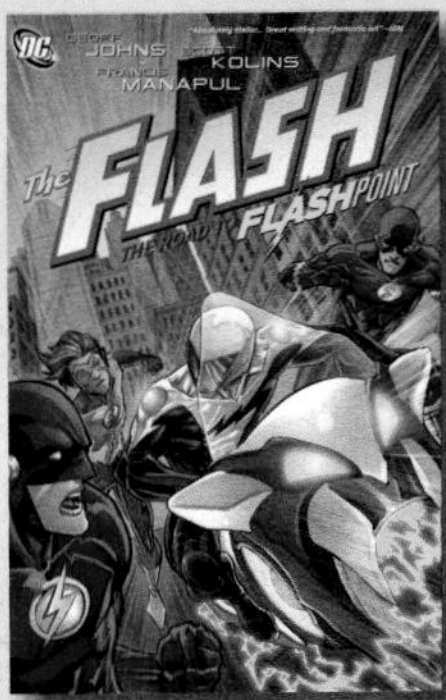
The FLASH
THE ROAD TO FLASHPOINT

with FRANCIS MANAPUL and SCOTT KOLINS

FLASHPOINT

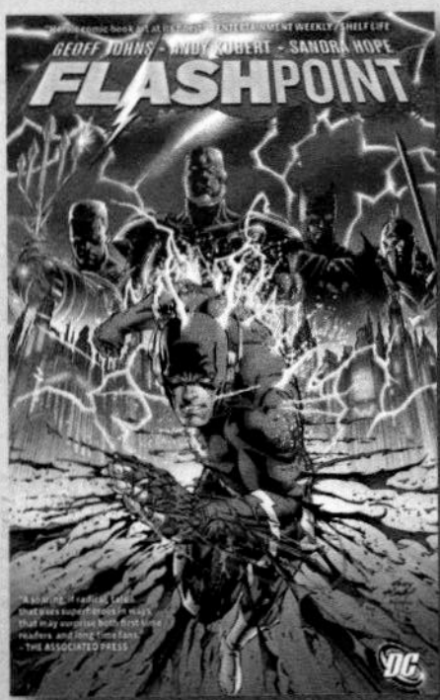
GEOFF JOHNS · ANDY KUBERT · SANDRA HOPE
FLASHPOINT

with ANDY KUBERT

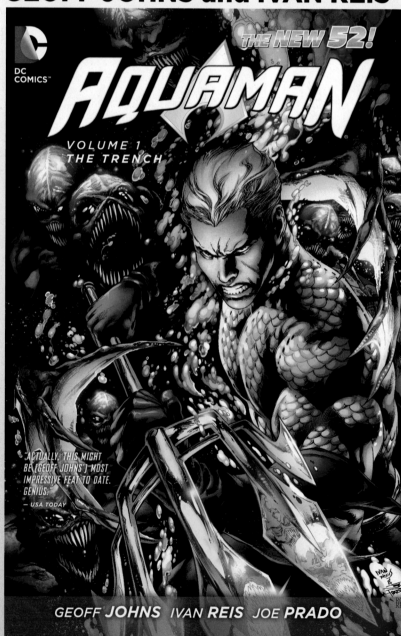